ASSASSINATIONS
—AND—
CONSPIRACIES

ASSASSINATIONS
— AND —
CONSPIRACIES

BY
RODNEY CASTLEDEN

Futura

A Futura Book

First published by Futura in 2007

ISBN-13: 978-1-7088-0782-8
ISBN-10: 1-7088-0782-8

Produced by Omnipress, Eastbourne

Printed in the EU

Futura
An imprint of
Little, Brown Book Group
Brettenham House
Lancaster Place
London WC2E 7EN

Photo credits: Getty Images

for Adrial – a lesson or two in conspiracy

CONTENTS

Introduction 8

Part 1: Assassinations

ASSASSINATIONS IN THE ANCIENT WORLD

ASSASSINATIONS IN THE MEDIEVAL AND RENAISSANCE WORLD

ASSASSINATIONS IN THE 18TH AND 19TH CENTURIES

ASSASSINATIONS OF THE PRESENT DAY

Part 2: Conspiracies – Real and Imagined

RELIGIOUS CONSPIRACIES

POLITICAL CONSPIRACIES

FAILED ASSASSINATIONS

CELEBRITY-STALKERS

MILITARY CONSPIRACIES

INTRODUCTION

THE WORD 'ASSASSIN' originated in the name of an extreme Muslim sect. The Crusader knights came across these original assassins in the eleventh century. The first Grand Master of the sect built the stronghold of Alamut in Iran, and sent out his followers to kill the leaders of the rival Sunni Muslims – or occasionally the Christian interlopers. The word 'assassin' was originally an Arabic word for fundamentalist.

An assassination is no ordinary murder; it always has a distinct political motive. The victim is usually a political leader, or is seen by the killer as politically influential. Throughout history the killing of a ruler, often with careful planning, has been used as a political expediency. In the days of kingship and empire, the palace coup involving the sudden murder of the ruler was a common enough event. Frequently, it was a way of resolving a power struggle or a way for a usurper to clear a path to the top. Shakespeare's *Richard III* is a depiction, if highly coloured and highly fictionalized, of the typically unscrupulous way in which medieval princes advanced themselves. Kings protected themselves and consolidated their power by having powerful subjects and sometimes close relatives assassinated.

In modern times, assassination is more democratic. Instead of princes killing one another to gain or retain power, increasingly ordinary people resort to assassination as a means of removing a political hate figure. The target may be an oppressor, or a figure seen as dangerously liberal. There is an ideological element when extreme religious, social and political affiliations are involved. The murder of the civil rights campaigner Martin Luther King is an example of this type of ideological killing. Sometimes the assassin is a fanatic who has a completely insane view of the victim. It is sobering to think that Queen Victoria, a constitutional monarch who had virtually no power at all, was the target of several unsuccessful assassination attempts.

But there is also a wild card. Throughout history there have been people who will destroy for the sake of being the centre of attention. Long ago in Ephesus, a man called Herostratus set fire to the great Temple of Diana, one of the most celebrated wonders of the ancient world. Why did he destroy a building that was universally admired as a magnificent piece of architecture? Simply in order to be remembered, to become part of history. And it works. John Wilkes Booth, Charles Guiteau, Lee Harvey Oswald, Sirhan Sirhan all killed high-profile American politicians in order to give their own lives some meaning, to become significant historical figures in their own right. To an extent writing about them reinforces this kind of behaviour, which makes me feel slightly uncomfortable about producing this book; it gives these psychologically damaged and dangerously inadequate people their reason to kill. On the other hand, it is impossible to describe the death of Abraham Lincoln without mentioning Booth, and impossible to understand why Lincoln died without exploring aspects of Booth's life. These assassins have elbowed their way into the spotlight of history whether we like it or not.

Because of the epoch-making assassinations of Abraham Lincoln and John F. Kennedy, and the killings of Martin Luther King and Bobby Kennedy, assassination has been seen by some people as an American fixation. But it is by no means exclusive to the United States of America; assassination was, as we shall see, an extremely popular political tool in ancient Rome. It is daunting to see how few Roman emperors died of natural causes.

It almost goes without saying that assassination is still just as prevalent as it always was. Sometimes modern organization and technology have made it possible for the assassins, or at least their masters, to escape detection. We know, for instance, the name of the man who shot Pope John Paul II in 1980; but do we know who his masters were, who ultimately commissioned him to do the shooting? It is hard to be sure. This, of course, is part of the fascination of assassination. There is often an intriguing plot behind an assassination, and sometimes a hint of a deeper and more elusive conspiracy behind that. This has given rise to an entire way of looking at events that has been called 'conspiracy theory'. Seen through the eyes of conspiracy theorists, the world is a shifting kaleidoscope of secretly planned events, hired hit men, middlemen and paymasters, a prismatic world where we can have no confidence of any ultimate reality. Conspiracy theory has become almost an art form, like science fiction. How many people shot JFK? A simple enough question, but millions of words in books and newspaper articles have been expended in trying to answer it. Was Princess Diana's death an accident? It seems unlikely that we shall ever know for sure.

The American secret intelligence service, the CIA, has routinely used assassination as a political tool. The CIA characteristically avoids using the word assassination for these acts, preferring the euphemism 'pre-emptive man-hunting'. But the effect on the victim is the same.

This book examines the circumstances surrounding assassinations. Some assassinations are spontaneous and relatively unplanned events, but because the target is by definition a person of high political profile, often surrounded by bodyguards and other security measures, a substantial amount of pre-planning and plotting is usually essential. The conspiracy behind an assassination is itself a source of endless fascination; the idea of a secret plot unfolding behind the mundane events of our everyday lives, unknown and unsuspected by both the victim and the general public, is both alarming and exciting. This book does not merely focus on the murders, but the reasons and motives of the killers, as far as we can find them out. It also explores the results, the effects of the assassination on subsequent events, which were often far from what the assassins expected – and far from what they desired.

There is an important practical and moral lesson to be learnt here. Would-be assassins should understand from studying the assassinations of the past that they are usually totally unproductive, and often counter-productive. To put it at its simplest, if you want to achieve something, history tells you that you should not go about it by killing someone. Assassination does not work.

A recent book about assassinations asked the question 'Is assassination an effective political tool?' Given the emotional impact and the media impact of an assassination, the answer is surprising. The conclusion is that in nearly every case assassination is either ineffective or counter-productive. The clear lesson of history is that assassination is a very bad idea, not merely on ethical grounds but for the purely practical reason that it does not work. Yet still it goes on. The reason may be the powerful symbolic value that assassination can have. A people or a pressure group that feels, rightly or wrongly, that it can make no headway with its government by legitimate means, may kill the head of state as a way of expressing itself, as a way of shaking the ruling elite into a realization – 'Look, this is what we think of you!' – a forceful way of rejecting the way in which it is being treated.

The high symbolic value of assassination makes it rather surprising that Al-Qaeda has not used it. The organization clearly has no scruples about killing people; indeed, it seems to go out of its way to kill innocent people indiscriminately in large numbers. It seems odd that work has not gone into planning a high-profile assassination. Maybe that will be the next stage in the terror war. The IRA certainly saw the symbolic value of assassination, murdering Lord Mountbatten in Ireland and attempting to murder Lady Thatcher and her cabinet at the Grand Hotel in Brighton.

If assassinations are practically ineffective, why do people resort to assassination as a solution? Sometimes it is attention-seeking on the part of the killer, and here we can see an affinity with celebrity-stalker killings. Sometimes it is an act of exasperation. Powerful political leaders can sometimes appear to be impervious to argument, persuasion or pressure, impossible to remove from power in any way; the only way is to kill them. Yet it may be better to let even the monsters and tyrants live. Towards the end of the Second World War British intelligence organized a plot to assassinate Hitler at his mountain retreat near Berchtesgarten in Bavaria. In the end it was decided that, even though it appeared to be perfectly possible for a sniper hiding behind a tree to kill Hitler during his solitary afternoon walk down to a café for tea, it was better to let him live. By that stage he was making serious strategic mistakes in his foreign policy; it was more likely that the war would end sooner with him staying alive and in power. So, hated though he was, Hitler was allowed to go on living so that he could continue to lead Germany rapidly to ruin. All too often the heart rules the head and killing is seen as the solution. As we shall see, it very rarely is.

Assassination is essentially a political act. The victim has to be a political leader or a person of significant political influence and the motive of the killer has also to be political. The murder of John Lennon was therefore not an assassination. Whether the murder of Jill Dando was an assassination depends on who committed the murder and why – and that is still not beyond question. If she was killed by a stalker, she was not assassinated. The killing of soldiers during warfare, whether they are on-duty or off-duty when they are killed, cannot really be called assassination. The death of Michael Collins, the commander-in-chief of the Irish Republican Army, in an ambush in 1922, was not an assassination.

Assassinations are sometimes the work of one person working alone; often they are the result of long and careful planning by several people – in other words conspiracy. The long-running debate about the JFK assassination is fundamentally about whether a team of conspirators was involved, or just a lone gunman. Not all conspiracies to assassinate come to fruition, of course, and the most famous unsuccessful assassination conspiracy was the Gunpowder Plot of 1605.

And many more conspiracies are about matters other than murder. The final part of this book deals with a selection of these conspiracies. The bombing of the Grand Hotel in Brighton in 1984 killed several people, but it failed to kill Mrs Thatcher, the British prime minister of the day, and her cabinet. It was nevertheless a very effective conspiracy in that it showed that the IRA *could* wipe out the British cabinet. Other conspiracies are less obvious. There is the curious ancient conspiracy to airbrush an important female disciple from the biography of Jesus, apparently simply because she was a woman. There is the much more dangerous modern-day conspiracy to make us all believe that man-made carbon dioxide is causing global warming. These conspiracies are fascinating not only because of the way in which they operate, but because of the mindset of the people who think it is somehow all right to be selective with the truth in order to make other people change their lives. Conspiracies are very much part of the world as it has always been, and an integral part of the world as it is today. We need to understand how they work, how to recognize them – and, if possible, how to defeat them.

PART ONE

ASSASSINATIONS

ASSASSINATIONS
IN THE
ANCIENT WORLD

AGAMEMNON

1250 BC

IN THE NINETEENTH century, before Troy was discovered on the coast of north-west Turkey and before Mycenae in Greece was excavated, people thought of Agamemnon as a fictional character invented by Homer. Today it looks increasingly likely that Agamemnon was a historical figure; certainly the Trojan War was a genuine historical episode. In legendary history – and it is very hard to differentiate between history and legend in ancient Greece – Agamemnon was the son of King Atreus and the brother of Menelaus. Like his father he was the king of the city-state of Mycenae (according to Homer) and the king of neighbouring Argos (according to later accounts). This discrepancy or geographical shift tells us a lot about the way the classical Greeks reshaped their ancestral past to suit their contemporary political needs. When Homer wrote the *Iliad* in the eighth century BC, Mycenae could still be remembered as a city with a great past. By the time Aeschylus wrote his drama *Agamemnon* 300 years later, in the fifth century BC, the old city of Mycenae was in ruins, and had been supplanted by the city of Argos, 12km away. Both Mycenae and Argos have been supplanted in modern times by the town of Nauplion. Homer's Agamemnon is likely to be closer to the Bronze Age reality, not just because the text was written down first (750 BC compared with 458 BC) but because we know from the archaeology of Mycenae and Argos that Mycenae was the greater city in the thirteenth century BC.

Agamemnon was king of Mycenae, 20km north of modern Nauplion, and also commander-in-chief of the Greek forces in the Trojan War. He married Clytemnestra and had several children including Iphigenia, Orestes and Electra. The Trojan War was (according to Homer's version) a war of honour. Paris, a prince of Troy in the north-west of what is today Turkey, visited the palace of Menelaus in Sparta and abused his host's hospitality by abducting Menelaus's queen, Helen. It was natural for Agamemnon as the brother of Menelaus, to organize and lead the expedition to get her back.

. When the Greeks assembled at Aulis, in the channel between the Greek mainland and the island of Euboea, their fleet was bottled up there by contrary winds. The seer Calchas revealed that this misfortune was due to Agamemnon's foolish boast that he was a better hunter than the goddess Artemis. To remove Artemis' curse on the expedition, Agamemnon would have to sacrifice his daughter Iphigenia. He was reluctant, but agreed to it.

The name of Agamemnon is well known to us from Homer's *Iliad*, where we hear of his exploits commanding the Greek coalition in the Trojan War. Everyone knows that Homer also wrote a sequel, the *Odyssey*, dealing with the protracted voyage home of Odysseus, one of the Greek heroes of the war. What most people don't realise is that behind both of those texts lies a much larger and more ambitious sequence of poems, the Epic Cycle, which have not survived to modern times, but which were well known in antiquity. Homer drew on these early sagas for the *Iliad* and the Odyssey in the eighth century BC; other poets in the next two or three centuries drew on other sagas. The *Iliad*, or its precursor, was followed by no less than three more epic poems telling the rest of the story of the Trojan War. They were followed by the Nostoi, which described the voyages home of several of the Greek heroes, including Agamemnon, and ended with a description of Agamemnon's assassination when he arrived back in Greece.

The Nostoi has not survived, but poetry and dramas based on the poem have. When Agamemnon's fleet sailed into the Bay of Argos, signals were passed back from the coastal city of Tiryns to Argos and from there to Mycenae. In the palace at Mycenae, Agamemnon's wife Clytemnestra waited for him with her lover Aegisthus, who was ruling Mycenae in Agamemnon's place. Perhaps on arrival Agamemnon thought little of this, as someone had to act as regent in his absence.

Agamemnon did not suspect his wife at all, but she was angry with Agamemnon for agreeing to sacrifice their daughter Iphigenia for the sake of the Trojan expedition. She wanted revenge for her daughter's murder. After Agamemnon had bathed in the palace after his journey, Clytemnestra handed him a shirt or tunic, the neck of which had been cunningly sewn up. While Agamemnon was momentarily trapped inside the tunic, Clytemnestra and Aegisthus stabbed him to death. To secure their position, they then had to massacre all of Agamemnon's entourage as well. It is thought that the dead king was buried in a great beehive tomb right outside the Lion Gate, the one that has ironically been mis-named 'The Tomb of Clytemnestra'. It was the last in the series of beehive tombs to be built at Mycenae, and would have been incredibly conspicuous, as if guarding the entrance to the citadel, and dazzling in the sunshine in its coating of white plaster.

Eventually, eight years later, Orestes returned to Mycenae to avenge his father's murder, killing both Aegisthus and his faithless, murderous mother.

There was a tendency up until the nineteenth century to regard this marvellous story and all the other stories embedded in the Epic Cycle as pure fiction. Now it is clear from archaeology that Troy existed, that the Mycenaean Greeks really did go on forays across to attack Troy and other Anatolian cities, that they really did capture and abduct women in the thirteenth century BC. There is no reason to doubt that Agamemnon existed and that the events that were dramatized by Aeschylus in his play *Agamemnon* really happened. The Hittite great king wrote letters to Agamemnon, but frustratingly did not name him; instead he addressed him as 'King of Ahhiya' or Achaea. The reason for writing was the Hittite king's irritation with what seems to be the large-scale destabilization of the whole of the west coast of Anatolia, the fringe of his empire. There are references to the fact that Greeks and Hittites have already fought over 'Wilusa', which was the ancient name of Troy. In the circumstances, the correspondence is amazingly polite.

PHILIP II OF MACEDON

336 BC

PHILIP II BECAME king of Macedon in 359 BC and was the father of Alexander the Great (Alexander III) and Philip III. Born in Pella in 382 BC, Philip was the youngest son of King Amyntas III and Queen Eurydice. For over three years in his youth Philip was held hostage first in Illyria then in Thebes, which was the leading city of Greece at that time. While he was held at Thebes, Epaminondas supervised his training in diplomacy and warfare. Eventually he was allowed to return to Macedonia. Philip had two older brothers, Alexander II and Perdiccas III. Their violent deaths led to Philip's accession to the throne of Macedonia in 359 BC. He initially occupied the throne by proxy, acting as regent for Amyntas IV, his baby nephew, but clearly the kingdom needed a man, and a warrior-king at that, and it was not difficult for Philip to assume the throne for himself.

Philip used his great skill at warfare to make a reality of his ambitious dream of a greater Macedonia. He subdued the hill tribes in 358 BC – and in a single battle. The following year he seized Amphipolis, a gold-rich town that had been colonized by Athens. It was in 357 BC that Philip married Olympias, a Molossian princess. In 355 BC, foreshadowing the megalomania of his son Alexander, he took the town of Crenides and named it after himself – Philippi. Apparently unstoppable, the Macedon king went on to attack Abdera and Maronea on the coast of Thrace. He also took Methone, which had been colonized by the Athenians; it was during the siege there that Philip lost an eye. Only when he reached Thermopylae in 352 BC did he meet determined opposition, and the Athenian resistance there made Philip think twice about trying to attack central Greece.

At the Battle of Crocus Field in 352 BC, Philip decisively defeated the Phocian army and made himself ruler of Thessaly. The presence of Macedonians on the island of Euboea not far to the north of Athens was felt as a distinct threat by the Athenians. Philip was occupied for several years in subduing the hill-country in north-west Greece and in securing control of the coastal cities. He laid siege to the main coastal city, Olynthus, in 349 BC. It first allied itself with Philip, but later shifted its allegiance to Athens. The Athenians left Olynthus to its fate and Philip finally took the city in 348 BC, and destroyed it.

Philip had by this time created something like a small empire with Macedonia at its core, but he was still not satisfied. The expansion would continue. The Athenians decided to make peace with Philip. Then in 342 BC, Philip launched a major onslaught on the Scythians and three years later he laid siege, unsuccessfully, to the city of Byzantium.

In the landmark Battle of Chaeronea in 338 BC, Philip defeated a combined force of Theban and Athenian warriors. As a tribute to the bravery of the Sacred Band of Thebes, Philip set up a monument in the form of a marble lion. It still stands. Philip then in the following year founded the League of Corinth. This was a strong defensive and offensive alliance in which members agreed that they would never fight one another. Philip was naturally to head the League. It was also natural that he should be elected as commander-in-chief of the alliance's projected invasion of the Persian empire.

Then, in 336 BC, at this crucial moment when the great invasion of Persia was about to be launched, Philip was murdered. Some aspects of Philip's assassination are well-known, such as the name of his assassin, Pausanias, who was a member of the king's bodyguard, but the extent of the conspiracy surrounding the event is a matter of continuing debate. Aristotle and Diodorus Siculus both say that Pausanias was a young lover of Philip's who had been replaced by another, younger, man. In other words, the jilted lover killed the king out of jealousy. Pausanias is said to have bided his time until the wedding of Cleopatra, Philip's daughter by Olympias (Philip had eight wives) and Alexander's full sister. As Philip walked un-guarded into the theatre at Aegae in Macedonia for the wedding ceremony, Pausanias stabbed him to death out of revenge.

But there may be more to the assassination than that. Philip of Macedon was a very ambitious man; his son and successor Alexander was even more ambitious and the assassination cleared the path for Alexander's accession to the throne. Alexander was 20 years old and already an accomplished military commander. He was probably impatient to have his turn at expanding the Macedonian empire, and so may have been the instigator of the assassination conspiracy. Aristotle was Alexander's tutor, and therefore may have closed his eyes to the possibility that Alexander had plotted to have his father killed. The lurid story of sexual jealousy told by both Aristotle and Diodorus may be true, but it may not be the whole story. In court circles

Pausanias was probably known to harbour a grudge against Philip and may have been selected as someone who could be 'turned' into an assassin by a certain amount of provocation, perhaps combined with promises of reward. His rejection by Philip made him a pliable tool for others.

It must also be significant that suspicion fell on Alexander and his mother Olympias immediately after the murder took place. The ancient historian Plutarch adds detail to the story, turning the murder into a larger conspiracy. He has Pausanias complaining to Olympias, and portrays Olympias as the instigator of the assassination; she was the one who incited him to kill Philip. He confirms that some suspicion fell upon Alexander because, when Pausanias complained to him, he cryptically quoted from Euripides – *'The giver of the bride, the bridegroom, and the bride'* – apparently implying that his father was not going to be the sole victim. After gaining the throne, Alexander had Attalus, his father's general, killed. Olympias had Cleopatra, her latest rival in the dead king's bed and not to be confused with her own daughter of the same name, killed with or without Alexander's blessing. She killed Cleopatra with her baby son, who was a potential future rival to her own son. It was safer to have them both out of the way. Another ancient commentator, Justin, thought that Olympias was very heavily involved in the conspiracy, saying that she provided getaway horses for Pausanias, crowned his body after his summary execution, and built him a lavish tomb.

At this distance and with insufficient evidence to go on, it is impossible to say whether Alexander or his mother were really party to the assassination. If Pausanias did complain to them about his treatment they might well have sympathized, but felt they could do nothing to help; it is also possible that Pausanias might have taken their sympathy for encouragement to murder Philip, which they by no means intended themselves. Some historians have suspected Alexander's involvement because three of his friends caught and killed Pausanias before he could talk, in other words before he could incriminate Alexander. On the other hand it is just as easy to explain that they were armed and on duty, and had just watched Pausanias murder their king, and slaughtering him out of hand was in the context an understandable reaction. Pausanias tripped on a root while running to the horses, and was easily overpowered and killed as he lay on the ground.

The speed with which Alexander took the throne has also been seen as a sign of guilt by some. On the other hand, from the number of supposed rivals he had to execute at the start of his reign, any delay on Alexander's part could have resulted in his own death. His speed and ruthlessness are not sufficient proof of guilt. The motives for the murder, and the question whether Alexander was involved in a conspiracy to kill his father, have been debated throughout history, and will continue to be debated.

On November 8, 1977, it seemed as if we might at last get to the truth of the matter. The Greek archaeologist Manolis Andronikos announced that he had found the unopened tomb of Philip II at Vergina. The discovery was of great archeological importance. After the initial excitement, some doubts were expressed as to whether this was really Philip's tomb, but recent forensic examination of the skeleton show the same fearsome wound in the right eye that Philip is known to have suffered 18 years before his death. Philip was very sensitive about any reference to his eye, however indirect and became angry if anyone mentioned the Cyclops – which some people may have called him behind his back. There was no trace of the stab wound that killed him, but as an experienced bodyguard Pausanias would almost certainly have delivered an upward thrust between Philip's ribs, an injury that would leave the skeleton unmarked, yet launch the reign of Alexander the Great.

POMPEY

48 BC

GNAEUS POMPEIUS MAGNUS, usually referred to as Pompey or Pompey the Great, was a Roman general, born in 106 BC. Pompey had a long military career, beginning when he was 17. When Marcus Aemilius Lepidus tried to march on Rome, it was Pompey who defeated him and drove him out of Italy in 77 BC. After fighting in Spain from 76 to 71 BC, he returned successful and by chance encountered a contingent of Spartacus's defeated slave army, which he massacred. On arriving in Rome, Pompey demanded a triumph and permission to stand for consulship.

The senate rather grudgingly allowed Pompey his consulship, and he entered into a political alliance with Crassus; Pompey and Crassus were consuls together in 70 BC. Pompey's popularity grew and he acquired the command of the greater part of the empire, specifically to eradicate piracy in the Mediterranean and so guarantee Rome's corn supply. In this he was completely successful. The price of corn fell immediately and piracy was eradicated within 40 days.

The zenith of Pompey's career was the year 61 BC when he returned to Rome as the conqueror of Spain, Africa and Asia. Up to this point his career had been entirely dependent on military success. From this point on, its decline would be associated with his lack of political skill. The empire did not in any case have room for two such men, and the rise of Julius Caesar inevitably meant the fall of Pompey.

Pompey was Julius Caesar's greatest rival, but he tried to resolve the power struggle through civil war, which was disastrous. Pompey's army was defeated near Pharsalus in Greece by Caesar's army in 48 BC. After that defeat, Pompey was not only ruined as a political force, he was doomed. He became a fugitive. He headed by sea to Egypt, where he hoped to take refuge. He set sail from Cyprus on a Seleucian trireme with his wife, and his followers sailed along with him in a flotilla of warships and merchant vessels, and arrived safely in Egyptian waters. He anchored offshore and sent a messenger to the Egyptian ruler, King Ptolemy XII, to ask for his protection against Caesar. Ptolemy and his advisers wanted to avoid any possible repercussions if they took the wrong side in the power struggle. The fate of Pompey the Great was determined by Potheinus the eunuch, Theodotus of Chios (a hired teacher of rhetoric) and Achillas the Egyptian; these were the chief counsellors of the king among the chamberlains. They could not agree; some wanted to let Pompey land, others wanted to send him away. Making full use of his powerful rhetoric, Theodotus argued that they could not safely do either. If they received Pompey, they would have Caesar for an enemy and Pompey for a master; if they rejected him, Pompey would blame them for casting him off, and Caesar for making him continue his pursuit. The only remaining course of action was to send for the man and put him to death. This would please Caesar and they would have nothing more to fear from Pompey. 'A dead man does not bite.'

Ptolemy decided that Theodotus was right: it seemed that the only course of action open to him was to have Pompey killed. With Pompey dead, Caesar would be appeased and Pompey himself could no longer be a threat.

Pompey's assassination was accomplished very simply. Ptolemy entrusted the execution of it to an Egyptian called Achillas. He took two Roman soldiers with him: Septimius, who had at one time served under Pompey, and a centurion. They were commissioned to bring Pompey ashore in a small boat. Pompey's fellow travellers had come aboard his ship to see what was going on and were uneasy to see a reception that looked neither royal nor welcoming. They advised Pompey to have his ship rowed back out to sea for safety. But Septimius stood up in the fishing boat, flatteringly addressing Pompey in Latin as 'Imperator', and Achillas invited him to come aboard because the sea was too shallow to land a trireme. As soldiers lined the shore, Pompey's wife Cornelia realised that he was in a fatal trap and gave him a farewell embrace before he stepped into the boat with two of his centurions and two servants, Philip and Scythes. Achillas held out his hand to help him onto the boat and Pompey turned to his wife and son and, reciting a verse of Sophocles, boarded the boat. It was a long way from the trireme to the land, and his companions in the boat were unnervingly silent. He looked at Septimius and said: 'Surely I am not mistaken: you are an old comrade of mine!' But Septimius only nodded and there was profound silence again, so Pompey took out his notes for the speech he had prepared to greet Ptolemy, and read them. As the boat neared the shore, Cornelia and the others watching from the trireme began to take heart as they saw many people gathering at the landing place as if preparing to give Pompey a dignified welcome.

But as Pompey took Philip's hand to help him stand up in the boat, Septimius ran him through with his sword from behind. Then Salvius and Achillas drew their daggers and stabbed him. Pompey made no effort to defend himself. He covered his face with his toga, groaned and fell dead. He was 59 years old. Pompey's family and friends watched in horror, letting out a collective involuntary wailing cry that could be heard on the beach; they weighed anchor and rowed away from the scene as fast as they could. They were given extra speed by a following wind, so that the Egyptians could not catch up with them. As soon as the murder was done, the assassins cut off their victim's head as a trophy and took it to prove to Caesar that he was dead. It was an ignominious end to a dazzling career.

Philip stayed with the headless body, washed it with sea-water, and used the remains of an old fishing boat on the beach to raise a funeral pyre. An old Roman who had served with Pompey when young walked up and insisted on helping with the makeshift funeral. He wanted to share in the honour, which he said would make up for the many unhappinesses and hardships he had suffered in Egypt. He would at least have tended the funeral pyre of the greatest commander. Not long after, Caesar arrived in Egypt. He turned away with loathing from the man who showed him Pompey's severed head and burst into tears; he had Achillas and Potheinus killed. Ptolemy himself was defeated in battle and disappeared. Theodotus escaped Caesar's anger, fleeing from Egypt, but he was eventually caught after Caesar's own assassination – and then put to death.

There was to be a poignant and ironic postscript to Pompey's fall. When, only four years later, Julius Caesar himself was assassinated, in a manner that was much more public and spectacular, he was destined to die at Pompey's feet, under the memorial statue erected in Pompey's Hall.

JULIUS CAESAR

44 BC

IN 45 BC, Julius Caesar was at the peak of his success, easily the most powerful figure in the Roman world. In every age there are some people who shower celebrities with excessive honours, and this is what happened to Caesar. Others looked on in mounting alarm as they saw Caesar emerging as a dictator. In February 44 BC, he declared himself dictator for life. It was this act that turned many Senators against him. It is still not known whether Caesar really wanted these personal honours. He certainly claimed that he did not and said that he should have honours taken away rather than piled upon him. The rumour went round Rome that Julius Caesar aspired to be king. It was naturally assumed that men who reached a certain level in the race for honours would want to climb to the next rung, and that Caesar would want the crown.

He said he did not want honours, yet went on accepting them, so as not to appear ungrateful. He was appointed 'perpetual dictator' and he started wearing the red boots of the kings of Alba Longa. His friend and supporter Mark Antony offered him the diadem, a white linen band which was the Greek symbol of monarchy. Caesar refused the offered diadem, but it is not clear whether this was genuine modesty or a gesture calculated to please the crowd. He was a very difficult man to read.

The plot to assassinate Caesar before he could be offered the diadem a second time, when he might accept, seems to have originated with Cassius. Cassius was aggrieved because he felt he had been slighted by not being chosen for a command in the forthcoming war against Parthia. Cassius persuaded his brother-in-law Brutus to join the plot. Brutus was fanatical and merciless. He had fought on Pompey's side at Pharsalia, like Cassius, and Caesar had generously pardoned both of them. He had in effect been more than generous to both men and they owed him a large debt of gratitude. Perhaps that was one of the reasons why they hated him – the humiliating sense of obligation. Neither Cassius nor Brutus had any real reason to assassinate Julius Caesar, but Cassius's minor feeling of slight combined with Brutus's tendency to fanaticism were enough to do it. It became an obsession. Sixty members of the senate were persuaded that the only resolution to the problem was assassination.

Recent historical research suggests that Caesar was not ambitious for himself, that he represented genuine popular democratic tendencies among the Roman people. His enemies and assassins did not really stand for liberty, but for the interests of a small elite within the ruling class using the power of the Roman state for personal enrichment and the exploitation of the masses. There was a class struggle in Rome between the *optimates* (the best) who represented the wealthy landowners and the *popularis* (friends of the people) who tried to improve the living standards of ordinary citizens of the republic. Julius Caesar introduced laws to improve conditions for the poor, and this revealed him as an opponent of the *optimates*. It may, ironically, be this that cost him his life on 15 March, 44 BC.

Whatever their real motives, the conspirators met in secret, assembling a few at a time in each other's homes, to discuss exactly where and how to assassinate Caesar. One proposal was to attack him on the Sacred Way, which was one of his favourite walks. Another was to attack him as he crossed a bridge on his way to appoint magistrates in the Field of Mars; one group of conspirators would push him off the bridge, then others waiting below would kill him. A third proposal was to attack at a coming gladiatorial show. The advantage of that would be that, because of the occasion, no suspicion would be aroused by the sight of swords or daggers. But the plan that won approval was to kill him while he sat at a senate meeting that was about to be called in the Hall of Pompey, partly because he would be isolated (only senators could be present), and the conspirators would be wearing togas in which daggers could easily be concealed.

Careful though the conspirators were, it was inevitable that rumours of the assassination plan leaked out. Caesar's friends tried to warn him, to stop him going to the senate house. There were rumours; there were also bad omens. A few months before, settlers at Capua were demolishing some tombs of great antiquity, to build country houses. They found ancient vases in a tomb, which was said to be that of Capys, the founder of Capua, together with a bronze tablet, inscribed: 'When the bones of Capys shall be discovered, a descendant of his shall be murdered by his kinsmen, and then avenged at heavy cost to Italy.' Superstition played a major role in Roman life. When Caesar was offering sacrifice, the soothsayer Spurinna gave him his most famous warning: to beware of great danger which would come not later than 'the ides of March' – perhaps the most famous prophecy in history. On the day before the ides of that month it was said that a little bird called the king-bird flew into the Hall of Pompey with a sprig of laurel, pursued by others of various kinds from the grove hard by, which tore it to pieces in the hall.

Caesar's doctors tried to make him stay at home because he was suffering from one of his regular vertigo attacks, but his wife, Calpurnia, was frightened by a dream in which she saw him lying dead. She tried hard to make him stay at home that day. Indeed that same night Caesar himself had dreamt that he was flying above the clouds, clasping the hand of Jupiter. But Brutus, whom Caesar trusted as a friend, persuaded him that it was stupid to pay attention to a woman's dreams and idle gossip, and also that it would be insulting to the senate to stay at home. Caesar was persuaded by Brutus's arguments and he set off for the senate. A note telling him details of the plot was pressed into his hand on the way, but unfortunately he did not read it immediately; he put it with other notes that he intended to read later.

Before entering the Hall of Pompey, Caesar made sacrifice, but the priests interpreted the sacrifice unfavourably. The omens were against Caesar. The priests went on making sacrifices in the hope of producing a favourable result. Caesar was annoyed and called off any further divination till sunset. Because of the bad omens Caesar's friends asked him to put off the meeting of the senate for that day, and he agreed to do this. But messengers arrived to tell him that the senate was full. It was Brutus again who persuaded him to ignore the babblings of the priests, and led him by the hand into the senate which was close at hand. He met Spurinna, laughed at his prediction and called him a false prophet; the ides of March were come without bringing him harm. Spurinna replied that they had come but not gone.

The Senators stood up as a mark of respect as he entered. The conspirators gathered round Caesar as he sat on his chair under the statue of Pompey. Next to him stood Tillius Cimber, whose brother had been exiled by Caesar. Cimber grasped the mantle of Caesar's toga and pulled it off his shoulders, apparently to constrain his arms and expose his throat. Caesar tried to rise but was held down by Cimber and became exceedingly annoyed. Then the conspirators lunged at Caesar with their daggers. Servilius Casca was the first to strike, but nerves affected his aim and he only wounded Caesar slightly in the throat. Caesar rose to defend himself, caught Casca's arm and ran it through with his stylus, but as he tried to leap to his feet he was stopped by another wound, as Casca's brother drove his sword into his ribs. Caesar groaned, but after that made no sound. He saw drawn daggers on every side and knew that it was all over. In an extraordinary gesture, Caesar drew his robe up to cover his face, so that no-one should see his face as he died; he also held the lower part of his toga down so that as he fell the lower part of his body too would remain covered. It was an act of remarkable fastidiousness in the midst of an horrific onslaught of slashing, stabbing steel blades. Even at this moment he tried to maintain his decency and dignity. Cassius struck him once, then tried to strike again, but in the mayhem wounded Brutus in the hand.

Caesar fell at the foot of Pompey's statue. Now that the conspiracy had succeeded, all the conspirators wanted to appear to have had some part in the murder and stabbed him as he lay on the marble pavement. Bleeding from many wounds – some sources said 23, some said 35 – Caesar was still alive. In the opinion of the physician Antistius, none of them would have been fatal except the second one. Finally Brutus stepped forward to give him the death stroke. According to one source Caesar said in Greek (not Latin), 'You too, my son?', and died, but this may not be true. If Caesar had covered his face he would not have been able to tell who gave him which wound.

The chamber quickly emptied. The conspirators ran for safety, and the non-conspirators likewise. Caesar's body was left there, lifeless and alone for some time, until three slaves came to put it on a litter and carry it home, with one arm hanging limply down. Caesar's body was carried to his house on a litter, through weeping crowds of people. The assassins had misjudged the situation badly. Instead of being seen as liberators, they were reviled as murderers. Caesar's close friend Mark Antony was able to take control of Rome.

The immediate aftermath of the murder was a paralysed shock. The sheer pointlessness of the assassination was underlined by the assassins' failure to create an alternative government in the days and weeks that followed. Caesar had not nominated a political heir, but he had left a huge amount of money to one man. He had left three-quarters of his estate to the eighteen year old Gaius Octavius, the son of his niece Atia. Octavius had been sent to Greece to serve with the legions in the preparations for the war with Parthia. Now, of course, he returned to Rome at the head of Caesar's legions to claim his inheritance. With that huge fortune, and with Caesar's evident blessing behind him, he was bound to wield enormous power. After a period of chaos and civil war the assassination of Julius Caesar led to the reign of Augustus, and therefore, ironically, to a long line not of kings but of emperors.

Several historians have noticed the striking parallels between the fate of Julius Caesar and that of Jesus. It may be that the early cult of Christianity evolved out of a Jewish branch of the *divus iulius*, the cult of the deified Caesar. Jesus's baptism at a significant crossing-place in the Jordan was paralleled by Caesar's crossing of the Rubicon. Caesar, like Jesus, was both a king and a friend of the poor. Caesar, like Jesus, was cruelly betrayed by someone he thought was a friend and supporter. But perhaps the parallels are coincidental.

CALIGULA

AD 41

THE ROMAN EMPEROR Gaius Julius Caesar Augustus Germanicus is always known by his childhood nickname, Caligula. He was born into the Julio-Claudian dynasty in AD 12 and became the third Roman emperor, ruling from AD 37–41. He is remembered for his extravagance, unpredictability, quirkiness, immorality, despotism and cruelty, and for his assassination in AD 41 by his own guards.

Caligula's reign is the least documented of his dynasty and the descriptions of his four years are meagre, unsatisfactory and unrelentingly hostile. The Roman historian Suetonius referred to Caligula as a monster. The events of his reign are unclear, and Caligula himself emerges as a caricature of a crazed megalomaniac. One popular anecdote tells how Caligula appointed his horse, Incitatus, to a seat on the senate. But the story is based on a single misunderstood near-contemporary reference, in which Suetonius repeats an unattributed rumour that Caligula was *thinking* about doing it; he evidently thought his horse was at least as clever as the senators.

Caligula is often presented as having incestuous relationships with his sisters, especially his younger sister Drusilla, but there is no evidence to support this story either. His reign was too short, and the surviving accounts too sensationalized, for any policies to be discerned. There were two episodes that gained attention: Caligula's military activities on the northern frontier, and his demand for divine honours. His military activities are portrayed as ludicrous, with Gauls dressed up as Germans at his triumph and Roman troops ordered to collect seashells on the beaches of Gaul as 'spoils of the sea'. Caligula set his sights on military glory. He had never been involved in military achievement of any kind, and knew that a conquest would deeply impress the people of Rome. Following in the steps of his father, Germanicus, Caligula launched a strange campaign into Germania. However, this campaign seems to have been interrupted by a conspiracy against him. It is difficult to be sure what happened, but a legate of the Germania Legions, Gnaeus Lentulus Gaetulicus, and Caligula's brother-in-law, Marcus Aemilius Lepidus, were executed.

It was when nothing came of the Germania expedition that Caligula shifted his attention to Britain. Again, there was no tangible result. According to Suetonius, rather than cross to Britain to achieve his goals of conquest he simply marched the legions to the Channel shore in a show of strength.

Finally, as if intending to bring the war to an end, he drew up a line of battle on the sea shore, arranging his ballistas and other artillery; and when no one knew or could imagine what he was going to do, he suddenly ordered them to gather shells and fill their helmets and the folds of their gowns, calling them 'spoils from the Ocean'.

Caligula demanded a triumph from the senate for his victory over Neptune, which of course was awarded.

Included in the triumph were Gauls dressed as Germans and the spoils taken from the beach.

The religious policy Caligula pursued was very different from his predecessors. In the time of Augustus the Cult of the Deified Emperor was to the fore, though Augustus protested that he was not himself divine; he cleverly directed the focus of the cult onto the collective spirit of his family. Tiberius, who followed Augustus, was not interested in the cult. Caligula on the other hand developed it on a grand scale. The temple of Castor and Pollux in the Forum had a direct link with the Imperial palace and Caligula had it re-dedicated to himself; he used to appear in his temple, attired in the costume of a god. He went so far as insisting that those in his presence must recognize him as a god. It was unheard-of, and Augustus would have been shocked. Direct worship of Caligula himself followed. The heads of the statues of many of the gods in Rome were replaced with the head of Caligula, and Caligula demanded to be worshipped as an epiphany of the gods. His plan to erect a statue of himself as Zeus in the Jewish Temple in Jerusalem was blocked by Herod Agrippa and others to avert open rebellion in Judaea.

Many wild anecdotes were told about the archetypal mad bad emperor, to show his heedlessness for human dignity and life, his waywardness and his sexual exploits. The anecdotes show him as conceited, overbearing, self-centred, savagely funny – and of course above all else mad. Suetonius wrote that Caligula often said, 'Let them hate, so long as they fear,' but Suetonius attributes the same saying to Tiberius, which reduces its credibility. Whatever else may be said, Caligula's reign was turbulent and short. When he died, there were few who were sorry.

A conspiracy to assassinate Caligula formed among a small group of officers of the Praetorian Guard, apparently acted out of personal motives. Already under suspicion by Caligula, the Praetorian Prefects really had little choice but to authorize the deed or face certain execution themselves. It is likely that the officers had the support of some senators, many of whom must also have wanted to see Caligula's reign come to an end. As with conspiracies in general, the plot may have been more extensive than the contemporary sources indicate. It is even possible that Claudius, Caligula's uncle and successor, may have known of the plot and even condoned it, but there is little actual evidence either way.

On 24 January AD 41, during games held in honour of the Divine Augustus, three officers of the Praetorian Guard, the tribune Cassius Chaerea and two other guards, attacked the 28-year-old Caligula in a secluded corridor of the imperial palace as he went to address a troupe of young male actors. They attacked him and stabbed him to death. Cassius, who had an unblemished military record, seems to have been the leader, the prime mover in the plot. He had known Caligula all his life. Suetonius offers a possible motive, though we have to remind ourselves that, vivid though his writing is, Suetonius is not always reliable. He says that Cassius had had to endure years of verbal abuse from Caligula regarding his alleged effeminacy, and that the taunts possibly had their origin in an abnormality in Cassius's genitals; Suetonius tells us that Caligula often gave watchwords such as 'Priapus' or 'Venus' when Cassius was on duty. On this final occasion, Cassius asked the emperor for the watchword and, when the emperor gave it, he struck the first blow with his sword. The other conspirators joined him in running Caligula through with their swords, just a short distance away from the rest of the emperor's entourage. Caligula's German guards were furious at this attack, but their response was too late: their emperor already lay dead on the ground. Cassius struck his final blow into Caligula's genitals. Cassius and Cornelius Sabinus, another tribune, found Caligula's wife Caesonia and their infant daughter – and vengefully killed them too.

The assassination was a significant step in the political development of the Praetorian Guard. They had taken the initiative in a big way – in removing an emperor. In the years to come they were to do so again and again. In the official version of Caligula's assassination, Claudius, the stammering old fool and uncle of the emperor, was found cowering behind some curtains. The Praetorian Guard saw him as a harmless and ineffectual character who could easily be controlled, so they installed him as the new emperor. But there is another way of viewing events. Claudius had been clever enough to survive the terrible reign of his nephew. The exemplary style of government he introduced suggests a more adept political operator. It seems quite possible that he was party to the plot, either to gain the imperial crown for himself or to secure his own safety. As the only obvious legitimate successor to Caligula, Claudius was in continuous danger from him; contemporary descriptions suggest that he was terrified of Caligula. Either way, while the senate may have been hoping for a return to the Republic, Claudius was taken by the Praetorians to the safety of their camp.

Rome had waited in horror at the onset of Caligula's mental illness, praying that he would recover, but the recovery was only partial. Modern historians have suggested that Caligula had encephalitis. Ancient biographers described Caligula having a 'brain fever'. Philo of Alexandria judged that it was a straightforward nervous breakdown, as Caligula was not used to the pressures of constant public attention after being out of the public eye for most of his life. One visitor to his court saw the emperor as no more than a vicious practical joker. Modern psychologists would probably see Caligula as delusional, and suffering from antisocial personality disorder. Given Caligula's unpopularity as emperor, it is difficult to separate fact from fiction. Which of the colourful stories told about him are true it is impossible to tell. The abandonment of the campaign to conquer Britain in favour of gathering seashells on the Channel coast as 'spoils' in a battle with Neptune is one of the most remarkable of them. What is clear, though, is that Caligula was totally unsuited to be emperor and psychologically unequal to the challenge of the role.

On the other hand, most of the historical evidence comes from contemporaries who were of Roman senatorial rank. These were people whose power had been severely checked and therefore had axes to grind. The evidence of Suetonius in particular is unreliable; when he criticizes an emperor's administration he also accuses him of indulging in sexual perversion as a way of clinching his argument. It is very unlikely that this association was historically accurate. The surviving records of Caligula were all written by his political opponents, those most damaged and thwarted by his attempt to enforce his absolute authority. Many of the sensational accusations levelled at Caligula could be viewed as politically motivated attacks.

Caligula had a difficult relationship with an unsym-pathetic and unco-operative senate, one that had begun to resume ruling the Empire as it had before Caesar and Augustus. In the year AD 39 there was a political rift between Caligula and his senate. It is from this point forward that Caligula's reign takes on a despotic tone. It may have seemed logical to him to take the role of emperor to its next level – divine monarchy. He might have got Rome to accept this if he had gone about it with more subtlety and diplomacy, with more respect and more humanity, but his approach was too brutal, too grotesque. The complexities and decencies of Roman society demanded that at least a facade of the emperor as 'first-citizen' must be maintained.

Regardless of whether Caligula is viewed as an insane monarch or simply a misguided politician, the conclusion remains the same. History has sensationalized him. But Caligula was an important figure. His reign highlighted an inherent weakness in Augustus's model for the role of the emperor; it exposed it for what it really was – a monarchy in which the only constraint on the emperor's behaviour was his own reserves of self-discipline. There was no regulatory mechanism in the system to ensure that Augustus's idea of a 'first among equals' would be guaranteed. Caligula showed that the only method of retiring an unsatisfactory emperor was assassination. Caligula would be the first of many emperors to be assassinated in the years to come – he became the model.

CLAUDIUS

54

TIBERIUS CLAUDIUS CAESAR Augustus Germanicus was the fourth Roman emperor. He was the son of Drusus and Antonia, and born in Lugdunum (Lyons) in Gaul in 10 BC. Among his grandparents were Mark Antony and the Empress Livia.

Claudius was seen as an unlikely candidate for the imperial throne. It was said he had some physical and mental disability and his family kept him out of the public eye for this reason, until his consulship with his nephew Caligula in 37. Claudius's afflictions were a disappointment to his family, who wanted sons who would become generals, heroes and emperors. His mother dismissed him as a monster, a by-word for stupidity. For several years she handed the useless boy over to his grandmother Livia, who was also irritated by him; she sent him short angry letters of reproof. Both women assumed the problem was laziness and lack of willpower. In his teens, Claudius developed scholarly interests, which the family encouraged, probably so that his disappearance into the background could be rationalized.

Probably his disability saved him from being murdered during the purges in the reigns of Tiberius and Caligula, simply because neither thought of him as a contender or potential successor. His survival led to his being declared emperor after Caligula's assassination; at that time he was the last adult male in the family. He had not been prepared for high office, so it is surprising that he turned out to be an able administrator and a great builder of public works. He also expanded the empire, including the conquest of Britain. He was very actively and personally involved in the running of the legal system, presiding at trials. In spite of these strengths, the Roman aristocracy saw him as vulnerable, perhaps because of his image as a fool. As a result, Claudius was continually obliged to weed out disloyal and subversive senators.

The physical disability gave him weak knees that gave way under him and a shaking head. He also had a stammer and tended to dribble. He was even so not physically deformed in any way, and was an imposing and dignified figure when seated. The physical quirks became far less obvious after he became emperor, and Claudius himself claimed that he had exaggerated his disability to save his life. Some have thought that Claudius was suffering from polio, but this leaves many of the symptoms unexplained, and a more credible theory is that he suffered from cerebral palsy. It is possible that the whole set of symptoms was an elaborate act, acquired in childhood as a defence mechanism, and developed and exaggerated over many years as a life-preserver, to turn himself into a harmless figure of fun. Perhaps, once safe on the imperial throne, he was unable to shed the act. It had become automatic.

Claudius was generous and lowbrow, liked a joke, laughed uncontrollably, and liked to eat with ordinary people – a sort of *Carry On* emperor. He was also said to be excessively trusting, and easily manipulated by his wives and servants. The surviving writings of Claudius show him as intelligent, well-read, conscientious, and with an eye for detail and justice.

The young Claudius's interest in history created new problems. He started work on a history that was either too truthful or too critical of Octavian. The events described were too recent, and the account may have reminded Augustus that Claudius was his rival Antony's grandson. His mother and grandmother put a stop to it, and it may have amounted to the final proof that Claudius was not fit for public office. He was pushed firmly into the background. When Augustus died, his successor Tiberius was also unwilling to let Claudius anywhere near public office. Claudius was the family liability.

In spite of his family's contempt, from very early on the general public respected Claudius. When his house burned down, the senate asked for it to be rebuilt at the public expense. They also requested that Claudius be allowed to debate in the senate. Tiberius denied both requests. After the death of Tiberius' son, Drusus, Claudius was proposed as a potential heir, but this was a highly dangerous proposal for Claudius – the reign of terror of the Praetorian Sejanus was at its peak – and Claudius declined this high-risk promotion. The next emperor, Caligula, relentlessly teased his uncle Claudius, played practical jokes on him and humiliated him in front of the senate. Claudius suffered severe weight loss due to stress during Caligula's reign.

In the turbulent wake of Caligula's assassination, Claudius emerged as the successor. Whether Claudius engineered this, or was simply the victim of circumstances, as contemporary historians describe, is impossible to tell. Josephus, a contemporary historian, claimed that Herod Agrippa, the king of Judaea, advised Claudius through this period. The senate expected to nominate one of themselves as the new emperor, but eventually accepted the Praetorian Guards' choice, Claudius; in return, Claudius pardoned nearly all the assassins. To ensure the continuing support of the Praetorians, he made them gifts of money.

Under Claudius, the empire underwent its first major expansion since the reign of Augustus. The most important conquest was the conquest of Britain. In 43, Claudius sent Aulus Plautius with four legions to Britain after an appeal from an ousted tribal ally. Britain was an attractive target for Rome because of its material wealth – particularly mines and slaves. It was also a safe haven for Gallic rebels. Claudius himself travelled to the island after the initial invasion, bringing reinforcements. The senate granted him a triumph for his efforts. When the British leader, Caratacus, was finally captured in 50, Claudius treated him well, letting him live out his days on land provided by Rome, an unusual end for an enemy commander.

Claudius personally judged many of the legal cases tried during his reign. He settled disputes and embarked on many public works, both in the capital and in the provinces, including roads and canals. The port at Ostia was part of Claudius's solution to the continual winter grain shortages. He set about developing the senate into a more efficient, representative body, urged senators to debate the bills that he introduced. He also created new patrician families.

In spite of this, many senators remained hostile to Claudius and they were behind many of the conspiracies to assassinate him. Appius Silanus was executed early in

Claudius's reign under questionable circumstances. Then a large rebellion supported by several senators was launched by the senator Vinicianus and Scribonianus, the governor of Dalmatia. Many other senators took part in various conspiracies and were condemned. Claudius's son-in-law, Pompeius Magnus, was executed for his part in a conspiracy. In 46, Asinius Gallus was exiled for plotting with several of Claudius's own freedmen. Valerius Asiaticus was executed without public trial for unstated reasons. In a speech over a year later Claudius singled out Asiaticus for special condemnation, suggesting that the charge must have been much more serious. Asiaticus is known to have been a claimant to the throne in the chaos following Caligula's death, so he may well have gone on nursing hopes of becoming emperor.

As many as 35 senators were executed for offences during Claudius' reign. Claudius had to respond decisively to conspiracy against him, but the response must have soured the relationship between senate and emperor. The relationship was further worsened by Claudius's promotion to positions of high office freedmen like Callistus, Narcissus and Polybius. The senate resented the promotion of these low-born men.

Perhaps inevitably, Claudius eventually fell victim to one of the many assassination plots. He died in the early hours of October 13, in 54. He was murdered by poison, possibly contained in mushrooms. According to some accounts, Halotus, his taster, was the poisoner; according to others it was Xenophon, his doctor. Some say he died following a single dose at dinner, and some say he recovered only to be poisoned again. All the accounts agree that his wife

Agrippina was behind the murder, not the senate. Agrippina came into the marriage with Nero, a son from a previous marriage and she wanted him to follow Claudius as emperor. Agrippina persuaded him to adopt her son so that Nero would be in line to become emperor. Although Claudius had a son of his own, Brittanicus, who should have succeeded him as emperor, Claudius at first shielded him from responsibility as heir to the throne, probably with the idea of keeping him safe, and promoted the older Nero as his successor. But Britannicus was approaching the age of majority, and when he reached it there would be no need to have Nero as heir. Claudius had also unwisely begun to talk of divorce. Agrippina most likely acted to ensure the succession of Nero before Claudius could divorce her and disinherit her son.

Claudius's favourite mushroom, considered a delicacy by Roman aristocrats in general, was *Amanita caesarea*. Claudius's trusted servant Locusta laced the dish with the juice of another mushroom, *Amanita phalloides*. *Amanita phalloides* contains chemicals that produce degenerative changes in the liver, kidney and cardiac muscles. The next day Claudius fell seriously ill and called Xenophon, who was his personal physician and seems to have been another conspirator in the crime. Xenophon used a large dose of colocynth, an extract obtained from the bitter apple. This poison was administered as an enema so that Claudius would not detect its bitter taste. The enema and mushroom poisoning, together, ensured the death of Claudius.

That at any rate is one version of how Claudius died. A few modern commentators doubt that Claudius was murdered at all: given his age he could have died of old age or illness. On the other hand, those family members who were allowed to survive seem to have been constitutionally long-lived: Livia died at 85 or 86, Tiberius died at 77, Antonia committed suicide at 72. Claudius was only 64.

Claudius was deified by the senate almost immediately. His will was suppressed and never read. Claudius had changed it shortly before his death to recommend either Nero and Britannicus jointly or just Britannicus, who would be considered a man in a few months.

Agrippina did not trust Claudius's secretary Narcissus and sent him away to Campania, ostensibly to take advantage of the warm baths there to relieve his gout, shortly before Claudius's death. Immediately after the assassination Narcissus returned to Rome, where Agrippina had him imprisoned. Within weeks she had him executed. The last act of Narcissus was to burn all of Claudius's letters, probably to stop them from being used against him in what was going to be a hostile new regime. Most of Claudius's laws were annulled, on the grounds that he was too stupid and senile to have meant them. This view of Claudius, that he was an old idiot, remained the official one for the duration of Nero's reign – and for many centuries to come.

NERO

68

THE DEATH OF Claudius while he was still married to Agrippina cleared the way for her son to become emperor. Nero (Domitius Ahenobarbus, known as Nero Claudius Caesar) was still only 16 years old, but with the help of the prefect of the Praetorian Guard, Sextus Afranius Burrus, Agrippina was able to rule on her son's behalf as regent. She was the sister of Caligula, the wife of Claudius and the mother of Nero: a woman unique in Roman history.

Agrippina's dominance over her son was not to last for long. Nero was keen to rule on his own and he soon pushed her to one side, moving her out of the imperial palace. It seems that she may have anticipated that Nero might let her down, and that for this reason she was holding Claudius's son Britannicus in reserve. When in February 55 Britannicus died suddenly at a dinner party in the palace, Agrippina was alarmed. She must have guessed that Nero had had him poisoned. She should also have begun to fear for her own safety.

Nero was a physically unattractive figure: fair-haired, with weak blue eyes, a fat neck, a pot belly and a body covered with spots. He usually wore a sort of unbelted dressing gown, a scarf and no shoes. His personality was full of contradictions. He was artistic, sporting, brutal, weak, sensual, erratic, extravagant, sadistic and bisexual. As time passed he became deranged, but at first things went well, largely due to the guidance of Burrus and Seneca. The senate was treated with respect. Sensible legislation was introduced to improve public order, and reforms were made to the treasury. Nero himself was ready to consider some radically new and liberal ideas, such as ending the killing of gladiators in public spectacles, which seems extraordinary in view of his heedlessness of other people's lives later on.

It may have been largely due to the influence of his tutor Seneca, but Nero started out as a promisingly humane ruler, potentially the best of emperors. When the city prefect Lucius Pedanius Secundus was murdered by one of his slaves, the law required that all four hundred slaves of Pedanius's household must be put to death; the humane Nero was intensely upset to have to allow these executions.

It was retreat from such terrible decisions which caused him to withdraw more and more, devoting himself to such interests as horse racing, singing, acting, dancing, poetry and sex. Seneca and Burrus tried to restrict his excesses, encouraging him to have an affair with a freed woman named Acte, provided that he understood that marriage to her was impossible. Agrippina was outraged at this. She was jealous of Acte, deplored her son's dabbling in the arts and was foolish enough to tell everyone what she thought. This increased Nero's hostility towards his mother.

Then Nero took as his mistress the beautiful Poppaea Sabina. She was the wife of his partner in many exploits, Marcus Salvius Otho. In 58 Otho was dispatched to be governor of Lusitania, no doubt to get him out of the way. Agrippina wrongly saw the friend's departure as an opportunity to reassert herself, and sided with Nero's wife,

Octavia, who naturally opposed her husband's affair with Poppaea Sabina. Nero's response was to make a series of attempts on Agrippina's life. He tried three times to poison her. Once he tried to kill her by rigging the ceiling over her bed so that it would collapse on her. He supplied her with a sinking boat in an attempt to drown her in the Bay of Naples; the boat duly sank but Agrippina gamely swam ashore. In the end, in 59, he tried a more direct and less artistic method. He sent an assassin who clubbed and stabbed her to death.

Nero admitted his responsibility, reporting to the senate that his mother had plotted to have him killed, forcing him to act first in self-defence. The senate appeared to accept this. There had never been any love lost between the senate and Agrippina. Nero celebrated his mother's murder by staging wild orgies and creating two new festivals of chariot racing and athletics. He staged music festivals, which gave him the opportunity to sing in public while accompanying himself on the lyre. This was a political mistake, as actors and musicians were regarded as socially inferior; the emperor was stooping too low.

In 62 Nero's reign underwent a significant transformation. First Burrus died, of natural causes. He was succeeded by two men who held his office jointly: Faenius Rufus and Gaius Ofonius Tigellinus. The latter was a very bad influence, encouraging Nero's excesses rather than curbing them. Tigellinus also revived the hated treason courts. Seneca found Tigellinus and the new regime too much to bear and resigned. This left Nero without any sensible advisers and his life spiralled out of control. He divorced Octavia, then had her executed on a trumped-up charge of adultery, to make way for Poppaea Sabina whom he married. Poppaea too was later killed; Suetonius says that Nero kicked her to death when she complained at his coming home late.

He then launched into stage appearances in public. His first performance was in Naples. The theatre was shortly afterwards destroyed in an earthquake, which was taken by Romans as a bad omen. A few months later Nero made his second stage appearance, this time in Rome. The senate was appalled. The empire was nevertheless still responsibly governed, so the senate was prepared to tolerate the mad emperor.

Then, in July 64, a great fire ravaged Rome for six days, destroying huge areas of the city. Whatever other faults Nero may have had, whatever other mistakes he may have made, he did not fiddle while Rome burned.

Suetonius describes him singing from a tower, watching as the fire consumed Rome. Tacitus wrote; *'At the very time that Rome burned, he mounted his private stage and, reflecting present disasters in ancient calamities, sang about the destruction of Troy.'* But Tacitus also took care to point out that this story was a rumour. To Nero's credit, it does indeed appear that he had done his best to control the fire. Perhaps he sang out of grief, when he knew that no more could humanly be done.

Nevertheless, it was a grave political error to use a vast area between the Palatine and the Equiline hills, where housing had been utterly destroyed by the fire, to build his Golden Palace and accompanying gardens. The scale of this complex was only possible because of the fire. It was natural that the Romans had their suspicions about who had started it. Nero did rebuild large residential areas of Rome at his own expense but, even so, the dazzling spectacle of the Golden Palace and its parks left a question hanging in the smoky air.

Because a conspiracy was being talked about and he

himself was being accused, Nero looked for others on whom the fire could be blamed. He singled out the Christians and launched a spectacular and brutal persecution, the first of a cycle of persecutions. Many Christians were arrested and thrown to the wild beasts in the circus. Some were crucified. Many were burned to death at night, serving as 'lighting' in Nero's gardens.

Nero's relationship with the senate deteriorated sharply, largely due to the execution of suspects through Tigellinus and his revived treason laws.

Then in 65 there was a major plot against Nero led by Gaius Calpurnius Piso. The plot was uncovered and 19 executions and suicides followed; Piso and Seneca were among those who died. Now there were no trials: people suspected or disliked by Nero were sent notes ordering them to commit suicide.

Nero let the reins of power slip from his hands. He recklessly left Rome to go on tour in Greece. He performed in the Greek theatres. He won the chariot race in the Olympic Games, in spite of falling out of his chariot, and collected works of art; he opened a canal, which was never finished.

Back in Rome the executions continued and many distinguished citizens perished in the terror. Eventually Helius, his regent, fearing catastrophe, travelled to Greece to summon back his master. By January 68 Nero was back in Rome, but it was too late. In March one of the governors of Gaul, Gaius Julius Vindex, withdrew his oath of allegiance to the emperor and encouraged the governor of northern and eastern Spain, Galba, to do the same. Vindex's troops were defeated by the Rhine legions who marched in from Germany, and Vindex committed suicide. But after that the

German troops also refused to recognize Nero's authority any longer. The governor of North Africa also withdrew support for Nero. The elderly Galba informed the senate that he was available to head a government if required, and waited.

In Rome, Nero did nothing in response. Tigellinus was ill and Nero fantasized about the tortures he would inflict on the rebels when he defeated them. Then came the critical decision that spelt the end for Nero. The Praetorian Prefect, Nymphidius Sabinus, persuaded his troops to abandon their allegiance to the emperor. The senate condemned the emperor Nero to be flogged to death. When Nero heard this astonishing sentence he chose to commit suicide instead, which he did on 9 June 68 with the assistance of a secretary. His last words were, 'What an artist the world loses in me.' It was a remarkable end to a remarkable reign. It could be argued that he was not exactly assassinated, because he committed suicide first; and maybe if the senate's order had been carried out it would have been an execution of sorts. Nero's death was somehow all of these, a snuffing-out not by a lone assassin, but by an entire empire.

The empire from the time of Augustus to the time of Nero had been controlled fundamentally through military tyranny. Nero's death, whatever terms we use to describe it, brought with it a great wave of changes. In the space of one remarkable year, 68–69, Rome had *five* emperors, Nero and three who reigned briefly after him: Galba, Otho and Vitellius. The fifth was Vespasian, who restored the peace and brought stability to the empire. He also established the Flavian dynasty as the legitimate succession to the imperial throne of Rome.

DOMITIAN

96

THE EMPEROR DOMITIAN was seen by contemporaries as tall, fairly good-looking and with a tendency to blush. Like his father he became bald and wrote a pamphlet called *The Care of the Hair*, in which he quoted a line from the *Iliad* on the short-lived nature of beauty; Domitian was a realist. The poet Martial referred to Domitian's baldness in a poem and was not punished for it, showing a reasonable level of tolerance. He was rather a prude and he enforced morality laws in much the same spirit as Augustus.

Domitian must have come across the comment of the emperor Tiberius that being in control of the state was like holding a wolf by the ears. He discovered that any relaxation of power brought disaster. Domitian promoted his regime with a display of magnificence that was little different from that of Augustus. In his relations with the senate, Domitian took the office of emperor to its logical progression: autocracy. The powers of the senate had been whittled away, but they jealously guarded their privileges and were horrified at the expectation that they should merely assent to Domitian's policies. It is not surprising that the senate smiled on his murder. Even so, Domitian had his good side. He was large-minded enough to grant honours, even to his bitterest enemies. He had a great sense of duty and skill as an administrator.

Domitian was extremely authoritarian. To him, people were a means to an end; the terrible way he treated his astrologer proves that. He built a facade of grandeur for the office of emperor, and in effect hid behind it; it is difficult to know the man behind the public facade. Domitian said that nobody believes in conspiracies until the emperor is dead. This reveals the boiling paranoia that drove him, particularly after the rebellion of Saturninus, and his drive for greater personal security led to his downfall. As he became more and more suspicious of those nearest to him, he pushed them deeper into a defensive conspiracy. The disempowered senate was powerless to prevent the murder, and many senators were delighted.

The emperor Domitian was murdered as the result of a carefully planned palace conspiracy on 18 September, 96. Unusually, in the murder of an emperor, the conspirators were not rivals from other noble houses who wanted his throne, but members of his own household. The time and place were chosen with deliberation. Suetonius is often an unreliable historian, but in this instance he has given us the most detailed account, which he heard from a boy who was tending the Lares shrine where Domitian was killed and who actually witnessed the murder.

The conspirators were Parthenius, an influential chamberlain, Stephanus – the steward of Domitian's niece Domitilla – Clodianus, Satur, Segeras, Entellus, Maximus and an unnamed gladiator. They had the support of the praetorian prefects Petronius Secundus and Norbanus. It would have been impossible for the conspiracy to succeed if at least one of the prefects had not been involved. The empress Domitia knew about it.

The day of his death approached. The day before, Domitian

said, 'There will be blood on the Moon as she enters Aquarius, and a deed will be done for everyone to talk about throughout the world.' The fateful day arrived at midnight when (in Chaldean astrology) the Moon entered Mars; Domitian sprang from his bed in terror as the dangerous hours of ill omen began. They were to end in the fifth hour, which was predicted to be the hour of his death, so he stayed in the safety of his bedroom throughout that time. This powerful superstition of Domitian's was understood in the household, so when Domitian asked the time of day from a servant, who was also in on the conspiracy, he was given the wrong time; the servant said it was the sixth hour. The cosmic danger had passed.

Relaxing his guard, and believing that he had after all cheated fate, Domitian agreed to see Stephanus in his bedroom when he asked to see the emperor with urgent information regarding a conspiracy. The assassins had, according to Suetonius, deliberately timed their attack to coincide with an astrologically predicted disaster for Domitian; they were agents of his destiny. This may sound like a piece of storytelling, but the Romans were genuinely superstitious, and even Vespasian had his court astrologer; decisions on how or whether to act were taken according to the positions of the celestial bodies. A re-creation of the positions of the planets at the time of Domitian's assassination shows readily identifiable portents as interpreted in ancient times; he was going to have a bad day. It is also interesting to note that when Domitian's natal horoscope, for 24 October, 51, is reconstructed it sheds significant light on his paranoia. His birth at that particular moment made him a marked man in a superstitious society, a man bound to die a violent death by the sword, and Domitian knew all his life that that was to be his fate. All Rome knew that the stars foretold the demise of Domitian. No wonder he was frightened.

Some time before his own death Domitian executed his astrologer, Ascletario-Asclation. This unfortunate courtier became the major focus of Domitian's effort to foil Fate. Domitian asked Ascletario about the astrologer's own death, to which Ascletario replied that he would die soon and that he would be torn apart by dogs. Domitian's intention was to have Ascletario die differently and so change the course of destiny – his own included. Domitian had the astrologer executed immediately and his body quickly cremated. But there was a sudden storm which put out the funeral pyre and roaming feral dogs set to work devouring the unfortunate Ascletario's body. This remarkable incident was witnessed by the comic actor, Latinus, when he was on his way to have dinner with Domitian. No doubt Latinus thought the incident would make an entertaining anecdote over dinner. It is all too easy to imagine Domitian's discomfort as he listened to Latinus's no doubt animated and highly colourful account of the appearance of the *dogs*.

In spite of everything, the emperor could not alter the course of destiny. He must die stabbed by swords as his horoscope foretold . . .

At this unpropitious moment, Stephanus gave Domitian a document to occupy him and as the emperor read it the steward stabbed him in the groin with a dagger. Domitian fought back, disarming Stephanus and injuring him. Domitian called to the boy to give him a dagger kept hidden under a pillow but the weapon had had its blade removed. The other conspirators were close by and, realizing that Stephanus was in difficulties, rushed the emperor and stabbed him repeatedly.

The pretext for the assassination of Domitian was the execution of Flavius Clemens and Domitian's secretary Epaphroditus. Epaphroditus had been Nero's secretary and helped him to commit suicide. Domitian had become increasingly suspicious and this had spread alarm amongst his courtiers, none of whom felt safe any more. Stephanus specifically wanted revenge for the execution of Clemens. It was said by one ancient commentator that Domitian had made a decision to kill the conspirators and written their names on a wooden tablet, that this was discovered and given to Domitia. This sounds very unlikely, but it is easy to imagine the conspirators saying it after the assassination to justify their actions. They evidently felt unsafe, and the death of the astrologer gave them good cause to feel unsafe. They used Domitian's horoscope as a kind of catalyst: by going with destiny they stood the best chance of success. In their assassination of Domitian the conspirators brought off that great rarity – the self-fulfilling prophecy.

There were other reasons for dissatisfaction with Domitian. He had executed senators; he was too rigorous in the enforcement of his financial policy; he had become increasingly arrogant. These reasons might have predisposed senators and prefects to condone the actions of Domitian's servants. The empress Domitia may have accepted that the harsh political realities of the day demanded the death of her husband, but it is intriguing that 25 years later she was still referring to herself with pride as 'Domitian's wife'. Domitia also showed appropriate devotion when she ordered the creation of a statue of her husband.

Nerva was another leading politician of the day who seems to have known about the conspiracy. Several people were approached by the praetorian prefect to be Domitian's successor, all of whom declined. When Nerva was approached he accepted without question, as if he had plenty of time to consider his position – since before the assassination.

Nerva had some slight imperial family connections that seemed to justify his selection, at least in the absence of other more obvious candidates. His uncle had accompanied Tiberius into exile. Nerva was a favourite of Nero for his elegies and was one of four men the emperor rewarded for revealing the conspiracy of Piso. He enjoyed the exceptional honour of having his portrait displayed in the imperial palace. For unspecified services to Vespasian, Nerva was granted the privilege of an ordinary consulship with the emperor in 71. Then, for loyal services during the revolt of Saturninus in 89, Nerva held an ordinary consulship with Domitian in 90. It was a worthy but undistinguished career; he had kept a low profile, living a quiet life at court, a great behind-the-scenes oiler and influencer. Nerva had made himself indispensable because of a network of spies who kept him extremely well-informed.

In a shift that looks out of character, Nerva made a choice to withdraw his loyalty to Domitian and go for the imperial throne himself. The stories circulated later about his life having been in danger and that he had suffered exile were entirely untrue. As the new emperor, Nerva maintained good relations with the pro-Domitian faction in the senate. As far as the conspirators were concerned, Nerva was a perfect choice as emperor, postponing a possible power struggle among the red-blooded generals; and the icing on the cake was that Nerva was old, sick and childless.

COMMODUS

190

COMMODUS WAS THE son of the emperor Marcus Aurelius. He was a mediocrity whose faults were magnified by the power he inherited. As a boy he was good-natured, wanting to emulate his father's devotion to virtue, but without his father's mental drive or self-discipline. He became emperor while serving in the army along the Danube. When Marcus Aurelius died, Commodus gave an impressive speech to the troops and then returned to Rome, calling off his father's planned conquest of central Europe. A positive outcome was the imposition on Europe of a peace settlement that was very favourable to Rome and held for many years.

When Commodus arrived in Rome, the public greeted their new emperor with enthusiasm, assuming that the handsome, fair-haired and well-proportioned Commodus would be a good emperor like his father. Once settled in Rome, however, he showed himself more interested in the glamour and display of imperial office than in government. He was ready to leave the chore of governing to others. He had his first brush with would-be assassins early in his reign.

Commodus was a liberal pacifist by nature. He sought to avoid warfare. When there were incursions of German tribes to the north, he bought them off. The senate saw this as treason and turned against him. A conspiracy to assassinate

Commodus developed, involving leading members of the senate, the emperor's sister, Lucilla and her son. Their attempt failed as the foolish young senator with the task of killing Commodus, Lucilla's son, felt compelled to make a long speech mocking Commodus while brandishing his knife, giving Commodus's bodyguards ample time to seize and disarm him. All the conspirators, including Commodus's sister, were executed, and the senate lived in a state of fear. The incident also had an effect on Commodus, encouraging him to hide for his own safety behind a series of 'proxy' rulers.

The first of these was his chamberlain Saoterus, but he was assassinated soon after taking office. After that, Commodus retreated from the public eye, handing over power to Perennis, the commander of the Praetorian Guard. Perennis made enemies, who falsely reported to Commodus that he intended to install one of his own sons as emperor. Commodus believed this and had Perennis and all of his sons executed.

A former slave called Cleander was the next proxy emperor. He openly sold government military appointments, keeping a commission for himself and handing the rest over to Commodus. Cleander's downfall came as a result of a grain shortage which was unfairly blamed on him. The food shortage led to a riot and to appease the mob, he had Cleander beheaded and gave both head and body to the crowd for their amusement. This appeased the crowd and when Commodus emerged from the palace it was an admiring throng that greeted him, not an angry mob.

Isolated successes like this persuaded Commodus that he had leadership skills, and decided to take up the reigns of government again. He declared himself to be Hercules and appeared in public wearing a lion skin. He also shocked the class-conscious Roman patricians by taking part in the gladiatorial games. Rumours began to spread that he was not really the son of Marcus Aurelius at all, but the son of a mere gladiator. He took pride in his physical strength, entering the arena wearing animal skins or extravagantly camp costumes. There he stabbed or clubbed animals to death to the applause of the crowd, though many who watched thought his behaviour profoundly demeaning.

In the reign of Commodus, the Guard in Rome and common soldiers elsewhere in the empire were free to abuse civilians. Commodus suspected the loyalty of military governors and took their children into custody as hostages; it was his way of ensuring the fathers' loyalty. Commodus increasingly lost touch with reality and began to imagine assassination plots everywhere. The pattern of behaviour we saw with Domitian set in. Executions became commonplace, and these predictably increased the number of real assassination conspiracies. Commodus compiled a death list of those he believed were his enemies. Those named on the list realized they had nothing to lose and conspired to assassinate Commodus. In the end, just as in Domitian's case, it was members of his own household, fearing for their own lives, who decided to do away with him.

His favourite concubine, Marcia, conspired with the imperial chamberlain and the praetorian commander to kill him. It was on New Year's Eve in the year 192 that Marcia fed Commodus a drink laced with poison, hoping that this would look like a natural death. Unfortunately the poison made Commodus vomit. Marcia then had to call in a young athlete, a wrestler named Narcissus who was probably Marcia's lover, to kill Commodus. Narcissus strangled the emperor.

The death by strangling was far more difficult to pass off as natural. But Marcia and her co-conspirators tried anyway. They wrapped his body in a blanket and ordered two slaves to carry it past the guards, who had the diplomacy not to notice what was going on. But it seemed that everyone was relieved to be rid of this very inadequate emperor. Rome was told that Commodus had died of apoplexy, and Rome rejoiced. In the senate, Commodus was described as 'More savage than Domitian, more foul than Nero. As he did unto others, let it be done unto him.' They ordered the emperor's body to be dragged through the streets of Rome.

The death of Commodus left a power vacuum. No one else claimed the throne, so the senate chose one of its own members as emperor, as indeed it had expected to do after the assassination of Caligula. Their candidate was Pertinax, a 65-year-old former adviser of Marcus Aurelius and a senator with an excellent reputation. He was cautious, modest and tried to restore the kind of good government that had existed under Marcus Aurelius, blotting out the bad memory of the aberrant reign of Commodus.

ASSASSINATIONS IN THE MEDIEVAL AND RENAISSANCE WORLD

WILLIAM II OF ENGLAND

1100

THE SON AND successor of William the Conqueror, William Rufus, the first Norman king of England, is by comparison a shadowy and elusive figure. The main thing we remember William Rufus for is his mysterious death while hunting in the New Forest, and this has left us with an iconic rustic image of him on horseback in dappled light beneath the forest oaks, felled without warning by a chance and unexpected arrow during the chase. He has become a figure that recedes into a mythic past, a pagan realm where horned gods ruled the forests and perhaps unworthy kings met their end in a kind of sacrifice.

In fact, history has a lot to say about William Rufus. He was deeply unpopular as a man, and even more unpopular as a king. He was in many ways like his father, and that may explain why he was the Conqueror's favourite son. It is not known exactly when he was born, but it was certainly before his father conquered England, and he was a boy at the time of the conquest. He was probably born between 1056 and 1060.

He was short, stocky and rather fat, with wild red hair and a distinctively ruddy complexion. It was the red hair and red complexion that gave rise to the nickname 'Rufus'. His personality was distinctively unattractive. He disliked people, he was tyrannical, cruel, greedy, brash and given to fits of violent temper and vindictive paranoia. He offended the Church not only with his blasphemies but by taxing the Church heavily and driving Anselm, the Archbishop of Canterbury, into exile. Largely because of these practices, William Rufus suffered greatly at the hands of chroniclers in the years after his death: most of the chroniclers were monks.

Unusually for his times, William was sympathetic towards the Jews. He was also gay. These tendencies were disastrous for a public figure, let alone a king, in an age that was both strongly anti-semitic and strongly homophobic. They also made him even less popular with the Church.

Of the monastic chroniclers Peter of Blois was the most critical. He blamed many of the problems on Bishop Ranulph of Durham, whose advice William acted upon. It was Ranulph who was the cruel extortionist and the woeful oppressor of the kingdom, rather than William. William was criticized for holding 'in his own hands' the archbishopric of Canterbury, four bishoprics and 11 abbeys; he was 'keeping all these dignities for a long time for no good reason whatever', taking all the income from these vast estates.

Peter painted a dark picture of England under William and Ranulph. 'Holiness and chastity utterly sickened away, sin stalked in the streets with open and undaunted front and, facing the law with haughty eye, daily triumphed.' It was a godless England afflicted by alarming portents. 'There were thunders terrifying the earth, lightnings and thunderbolts most frequent, deluging showers without number, winds of the most astonishing violence, whirlwinds that shook the towers of Churches . . . fountains flowing with blood, mighty earthquakes, while the sea, overflowing its shores, wrought infinite calamities to the coasts.' These phenomena, which today most people would blame on natural causes, were implicitly God's warning voice telling England that William was a very bad king.

In the climate of general dissatisfaction with the William Rufus regime it was easy for Robert, William Rufus's elder brother, to gain support at his expense. Robert Curthose had inherited the dukedom of Normandy, not the English throne, from their father. Almost inevitably, there was mounting rivalry between the two brothers over the throne of England, which must have appeared the greater prize. Many of the barons were ready to support Robert as a replacement for William as king. There was a rising of the barons in 1088, just one year after William came to the throne; it was organized by his uncle, Bishop Odo of Bayeux, who wanted to replace William with his brother Robert. But William proved to be strong, ruthless and purposeful enough to crush it. There was another rising of the barons only seven years later, in 1095.

William Rufus was a very strong king, in that he was able to fend off major rebellions and maintain control. Under the circumstances, it is a great tribute to his strength of purpose that he remained on the English throne a full ten years. He was able to defeat King Malcolm III of Scotland and replace him with a client-king, the Saxon, Edgar Atheling. He in effect gained control of the entirety of his father's legacy when his brother Robert wanted to join the crusade. Robert mortgaged the Duchy of Normandy to him, leaving him in charge of Normandy (as well as England) during his absence.

When Robert went off to fight in the First Crusade in 1095, William used the respite to secure the borders with

Wales and Scotland. He built Carlisle Castle and a chain of forts along the Welsh border to stem the raids on marcher barons by Welsh brigands. His barons continued to complain about the high level of taxation, and in particular they complained to William's younger brother, Henry, who had been waiting ever since their father's death to seize his brother's throne if an opportunity arose.

William never placed any trust in his barons, which is possibly why he never won their loyalty, and he never trusted his brother Henry. Perhaps he had good reason. We have to remember that it was Henry who suggested the hunting trip in the New Forest. But why did William agree to ride off into the New Forest with the brother he profoundly distrusted and a band of noblemen upon whose loyalty he knew he could not depend? He must have known that any one of them could have killed him at any time. Or did he trust in the magic aura of kingship? Did he imagine the fact that he was the king was protection enough – that they would stop short of anything as terrible, as utterly taboo, as regicide?

William had a disturbing nightmare during the night before his final day. He dreamt that the men he was about to ride out with would kill him. At an unconscious level he *knew* he was taking a terrible risk. Yet still he went. The reasons why he acted as he did that day are still not known.

What is known is that during the hunt, on 2 August, 1100, an arrow was loosed that found its way to the king's chest. It is not known who shot the arrow, but it was said at the time that it was a powerful Norman baron, Sir Walter Tirel, the lord of Poix. According to Peter of Blois, Walter had recently arrived from Normandy and was welcomed to join the king's table. After the banquet was over, the king invited the new guest to join the hunt. An account by Orderic Vitalis described the preparations for the hunt:

> *... An armourer came in and presented to [the King] six arrows. The King immediately took them with great satisfaction, praising the work, and unconscious of what was to happen, kept four of them himself and held out the other two to Walter Tirel ... saying 'It is only right that the sharpest be given to the man who knows how to shoot the deadliest shots.'*

Once the hunt was under way, the hunting party spread out through the woods as they chased some running deer. As they did so, the king and Walter Tirel became separated from the others. That was the last time William Rufus was seen alive. Walter fired a wild shot at a stag, which missed and hit the king in the chest instead. It was actually not a fatal injury, but William fell from his horse onto the arrow shaft, which then drove deep inside him, piercing his lung. Walter tried to offer aid, but there was no help he could give the dying man. Walter feared he would be charged with murder, panicked, mounted his horse and fled. It was said that it was an accident, but there are several aspects of the story that arouse suspicion.

If the king's death was an accident, why did the rest of the company ride off to leave the king to die alone, quickly drowning in his own blood? Incredibly, the king of England's body was just left unattended in the woods, abandoned at the spot marked today by the Rufus Stone. It has been argued that the nobles abandoned William's body, because the law and order of the kingdom died with the king, and they had to flee immediately to their estates to secure their interests.

Another peculiarity of the 'accident' scenario is that Sir Walter Tirel had a reputation as a master bowman, someone who was very unlikely to shoot wild, and someone who was unlikely to make the basic mistake of accidentally shooting his (one) hunting companion. The circumstances make the incident look very much like murder and a conspiracy to murder at that.

The body was found the next day by some countrymen. One of them, a local charcoal-burner by the name of Purkis, loaded it onto his cart and dutifully took it to Winchester for burial, blood dripping from the body all the way. In Winchester Cathedral the unmourned king was buried in a modest grave. Contemporary chroniclers said that all his servants were busy attending to their own interests, as would be likely with a significant change of regime already under way, and that few if any of them cared anything at all about the funeral.

The king died unmarried and therefore with no legal offspring. His younger brother Henry succeeded to the English throne as he had been hoping. The speed with which Henry secured the treasury at Winchester and had himself crowned king – only three short days after his brother's death – suggests a fair amount of pre-planning. That in turn suggests that Henry knew in advance that William was going to die. He stood to gain most by his brother's death, so if there was a conspiracy to kill William it is most likely that Henry engineered it. In the three-cornered struggle for the English throne, this interval when Robert was out of the way was the very best moment Henry could have chosen to have his brother assassinated. With William slain while Robert was in Palestine, Henry was in the strongest possible position to gain the throne, and he made sure of that by having himself crowned immediately, before Robert could return. Everything points to a political coup engineered by Henry.

Henry was not blamed for the assassination by any of the Church chroniclers. They were very pleased and relieved to see Henry on the throne, describing him as 'a young man of extreme beauty' and 'much more astute than his two brothers and better fitted for reigning'. He was a safer bet than William, releasing the Church estates, imprisoning Ranulph and recalling Archbishop Anselm from exile. It is possible that Henry did all these things precisely to buy the Church's approval, rather than out of piety. When Robert raced back from the crusade on hearing of William's death, he mounted an invasion to try to unseat Henry. Peter of Blois was keen to blame this too on Ranulph who, he said, escaped from prison, 'repaired to Normandy, and in every way encouraged the Duke thereof, Robert, the King's brother, to invade England'.

Walter Tirel was named by chroniclers as the man who shot the fatal arrow, but there is no record of any retribution. There was no trial, no execution, no sanction, no penalty. That too looks as if he acted as part of a larger conspiracy. Maybe all those who went out with the king that day wanted him dead, and it was simply Tirel who drew the short straw. But it is also possible that Tirel did *not* kill William Rufus. There is one contemporary document that suggests he was innocent of the killing. The great Norman Abbot Suger was a friend of Walter Tirel's and he gave Walter shelter during his self-imposed exile in France. They evidently liked and trusted one another. Suger had many opportunities to talk to Walter and they had many conversations about the events of that fateful day. What Suger wrote is very revealing:

It was laid to the charge of a certain noble, Walter Tirel, that he had shot the king with an arrow; but I have often heard him, when he had nothing to fear nor to hope, solemnly swear that on the day in question he was not in the part of the forest where the king was hunting, nor ever saw him in the forest at all.

This means that Walter was afterwards claiming that he was not alone with the king: he was with the main party, elsewhere. If Walter was not alone with the king, who was? The most likely candidate is the king's brother, Henry. Walter Tirel may have accepted the arguments that someone had to be blamed for the shooting and that Henry, the next king of England, could not be tainted with the crime. For the good of the kingdom, and the safety of the tenure of the English throne, Henry must seem to be blameless. Walter Tirel was never given any advancement that we know of, but Henry was adamant that he must not be punished in any way for what had happened.

William Rufus was a horrible man, and he had two brothers, one younger, one older, both of whom wanted his throne. It is not at all surprising that there was a conspiracy to assassinate him and replace him. The most surprising aspect of the whole episode is that after ten years of staving off threats to his safety William went off into the woods with his murderers. Did he perhaps know that a conspiracy had closed so tightly about him that there was nothing he could do to avert the inevitable? As he rode off, had he perhaps already accepted that assassination was inevitable?

THOMAS BECKET

1170

THOMAS BECKET, ARCHBISHOP of Canterbury, was born the son of a wealthy London merchant in 1118. He was boarded out at Pevensey Castle, the home of Richer de l'Aigle, and educated at Merton Priory, then London, Paris and Italy. Like many ambitious young men, he decided that his best chance of progress lay in the Church. He became secretary to Archbishop Theobald of Canterbury, who thought highly of his administrative abilities and eventually recommended him, in 1154, to Henry II as his chancellor.

Thomas excelled in this new role, which was the medieval equivalent of prime minister. He worked very closely with the king and they became firm friends. Becket appeared to give his absolute support to the king's plan to unify the laws relating to Church and state. In this Henry II misread Thomas's wishes and it led to trouble later. In 1162, Henry decided to select Thomas as the new Archbishop of Canterbury, assuming that Thomas would continue to collaborate from 'the other side'. Thomas warned him not to do this, but Henry insisted. Given the charge of looking after the interests of the Church in England, Thomas did just that, and consequently resisted Henry's attempts to reduce the Church's great power. Within a very short time, the two men were no longer friends but enemies, and Henry wanted to remove Thomas, who was now an obstacle to his reforms.

The men who were to remove this obstacle were four 'knights' who were really barons: Reginald Fitzurse, Richard le Breton, William de Tracey and Hugh de Morville. Perhaps the most peculiar thing about these men is that in spite of committing the most notorious crime of the Middle Ages, very little is known about them. They appeared out of nowhere, rode to Canterbury to insult and murder the archbishop, and vanished again. Rather more is known about Reginald Fitzurse than the others.

Reginald Fitzurse was a Norman knight of the 12th century, the eldest son of Richard Fitzurse. He was probably born in about 1130, inheriting the manor of Williton in Somerset when his father died in 1168. He has sometimes been referred to as a baron, because he held his lands from the king. He was certainly a major landowner. In addition to the land he owned in Somerset, he owned the manor of Barham in Kent and lands in Northamptonshire too.

Hugh de Morville was probably the son of Hugh de Morville, who held the barony of Burgh-by-Sands and several other estates in the northern shires. He was described as being 'of a viper's brood'. He was attached to Henry II's court from the beginning of Henry's reign, and his name appears as a witness on a string of charters. His name occurs also as a witness to the Constitutions of Clarendon. He married Helwis de Stuteville, and thus became possessor of the castle of Knaresborough. After the murder, he was ordered to do a penance of service in the Holy Land by the pope, but he was not punished by Henry II; he had after all loyally done what the king wanted. We know that he was allowed to obtain a licence to hold a weekly market at Kirkoswald. He died shortly after this, certainly before 1203, leaving two daughters and the sword with which he held back the crowd in Canterbury Cathedral: for a long time it was preserved in Carlisle Cathedral as a holy relic in its own right.

Richard le Breton eventually retired to the island of Jersey after the murder.

Obscure though these men are – and were, even in their own day – they are remembered for a single act of phenomenal brutality and sacrilege, the murder in his own cathedral of Archbishop Thomas Becket, the greatest saint of the Middle Ages. They were in attendance at the court of Henry II in northern France late in 1170 when they heard the king's ill-tempered words regarding the Archbishop of Canterbury; 'Will no one rid me of this turbulent priest?' Henry II was exasperated with Becket's non-co-operation with the raft of reforms he was trying to introduce, and had already brought him to trial at Northampton Castle in 1164, a confrontation that had led to Becket's flight and self-imposed exile to France. Thomas Becket had fled Northampton Castle in the middle of the night in fear of his life. The king's temper was such that he could have ordered his archbishop's execution or mutilation on the spot. Becket decided then not to risk staying in England any longer.

In 1170 the exile had lasted six years, while the administration of the see of Canterbury was in effect left in the hands of others. Thomas felt he needed to return to England, even though he knew he risked death from the king or his supporters in doing so. Relations with the king were only a little better than they had been at Northampton in 1164.

Whatever he meant by it, Henry II certainly did utter words such as, 'Will no one rid me of this turbulent priest?'

and 'What a set of idle cowards I keep about me who allow me to be mocked so shamefully by a low-born clerk!' and he uttered them more than once, as he himself admitted afterwards. It sounded to the four knights as if it was an order to get rid of Becket, and they certainly took it as such. Together they plotted how they would murder the archbishop. The conspirators left Bures, near Bayeux, where the king was staying and travelled separately, secretly and rapidly by different routes to England. When it was noticed that they had gone, an attempt was made to overtake them and bring them back, but it was too late. It is fairly clear that the four barons expected the king to change his mind and countermand the order, and they wanted to act, to solve the problem of Thomas before he could do so.

They arranged to meet at Saltwood Castle, which was held by a fifth knight, Ranulf de Broc, on 28 December, 1170. Saltwood Castle was close to the English Channel coast of Kent, and not too far from Canterbury.

The following day, they set off with a small entourage of armed men for Canterbury itself. At St Augustine's Abbey, which stood on the eastern edge of the city, they stopped and gathered further reinforcements from the abbot, who seems to have been glad to assist in Becket's downfall. From there they rode into the cathedral precincts through the gatehouse in Palace Street and entered the archbishop's hall to the north-west of the Cathedral, probably at about four o'clock in the afternoon, and demanded to see Becket. With them was Robert de Broc, who was the nephew of Ranulf de Broc; Robert had been in charge of the place during the archbishop's absence. They left a substantial force of soldiers outside the gatehouse, to keep the crowd out and stop the archbishop escaping.

It is not certain that the knights intended from the outset to kill Thomas. They may have intended to take him prisoner, to coerce him into absolving those he had excommunicated. It may be that they only resorted to murder as a result of Thomas's intransigence, and the presence of an unexpected crowd of people in the cathedral. On the other hand, one of them admitted later that their original plan had been to strike the archbishop down in his private chamber next to the hall.

When the knights entered the archbishop's hall, where the servers were eating, they sat awkwardly and silently, not acknowledging the archbishop – nor he them. At length, Thomas offered them greetings. None of them replied except Fitzurse, who muttered, 'God help you!' Thomas reddened at this insult.

Reginald Fitzurse told Thomas that he bore a message from the king. All the knights were there, but it was Reginald Fitzurse who dominated this exchange, and Reginald Fitzurse who was the most aggressive and offensive. Reginald had been one of Thomas's tenants when Thomas had been chancellor. Thomas reminded him of this, to make him remember his lower status, but this reminder only made Reginald angrier and he called on everyone present who was on the king's side to prevent the archbishop from escaping. One senses in Reginald's mounting anger that afternoon a self-conscious effort to make the adrenalin flow and get himself to a pitch where he could assassinate the archbishop; he *needed* to be angry to carry it through. Reginald Fitzurse accused Thomas of refusing to absolve the people he had excommunicated.

'The sentence was not mine but the Pope's,' Thomas reminded him.

'You were behind it,' Reginald persisted.

'Granted, but the sentence itself was given by one greater than I. Let those concerned go to the Pope for absolution.'

Reginald Fitzurse went on, 'The king's command is that you and yours shall leave this realm. There can be no peace with you after your insolence.'

Thomas told Reginald to stop threatening him.

At this the knights went outside to arm themselves and shut the gatehouse doors to prevent any help arriving for the archbishop. They posted guards on the archbishop's hall. Reginald Fitzurse forced one of the archbishop's servants to fasten his armour, then snatched an axe from a carpenter who was working on some repairs.

Thomas sat down on the bed in his chamber. There was an animated discussion as to what had been said. Some of Thomas's monks thought the knights were drunk. John of Salisbury criticized Thomas roundly; 'You are doing what you always do. You act and speak just as you think best, without asking anyone's advice.'

Thomas asked him, 'Well, master John, what would you wish done?'

John replied, 'You ought to have called a meeting of your council. Those knights want nothing more than a good reason for killing you.'

'We have all got to die, and we must not swerve from justice for fear of death. I am more ready to meet death than they are to inflict it on me,' Thomas said.

John said, 'We're sinners, the rest of us, and not yet ready to die. I can't think of anyone except you who is asking for death at the moment.'

Out in the Great Court, the knights prepared themselves.

The great cloaks they had worn in the archbishop's hall to cover their coats of mail were now off and slung over the branches of a mulberry tree. Now ready, they charged at the Hall door, but Osbert and Algar, the archbishop's servants, had bolted it. Robert de Broc knew the building well, and took the knights round the kitchen, through some bushes and into the orchard on the south side of the Hall. From here there was a staircase up to the Hall. The stairs were being repaired and the workmen had knocked off for the day and thrown down their tools. Ranulf de Broc climbed a ladder to a shuttered window. The others picked up axes and other tools and with these they smashed their way back into the Hall.

Meanwhile, the noise of the splintering wood and shouts of the servants alerted Thomas and his friends to the imminent danger. The monks tried to get Thomas to move, but he was reluctant. 'Not a bit of it. Don't panic. You monks are always afraid of being hurt!' Eventually, when they told him it was time for Vespers, he allowed himself to be swept out of his chamber and by way of a private staircase into the north range of the cloisters, and then the east range, which was the normal route into the cathedral via the door into the north transept. The service of Vespers was due to begin. Thomas was reluctant to be hurried, but the monks around him could see that the angry knights were preparing to do murder and thought Thomas would be safe once he was within the sanctuary of the cathedral. How wrong they were! Probably Thomas himself knew there could be no other outcome now but his death, and knew there was no point in hurrying anywhere. His destiny was fixed; these four knights were going to kill him.

Thomas and his small group of monks arrived in the cathedral's dark but crowded north transept just ahead of the knights, who could be heard running heavily along the south range of the cloisters. There were shouts; 'There are armed knights in the cloister!'

'I will go and meet them,' Thomas said, but his supporters swept him on towards the choir. Because of the disturbance, the monks who had started to celebrate Vespers abandoned their prayers and moved towards the archbishop, who they had heard was already dead; for a moment they were delighted to see that he was alive and unharmed, but their pleasure was short-lived. The monks hastened to close and bar the doors in order to keep the knights out, but Thomas stopped them, reminding them that it was not proper to turn the house of God into a fortress, 'and we come to suffer – not to resist'.

It would have been easy, even at this late stage, for Thomas to vanish inside the dark cathedral; had he wished, he could have spirited himself away in the roof or the crypt and the knights would never have found him. But Thomas had no real intention of escaping this time. Thomas was mounting the steps leading up from the north transept towards the choir when Reginald burst in, still taking the lead in every way, shouting, 'King's men!' The four armed knights were there, with their huge swords unsheathed, and a body of men-at-arms, a sight that frightened all of them, though the huge congregation filling the nave saw none of this. With the knights was one of Thomas's monks, a sub-deacon called Hugh – later called Hugh Evil-Clerk because of his part in this historic murder.

Reginald Fitzurse bellowed, 'Come to me here, King's men! Where is Thomas Becket, traitor to the king and the kingdom?' No one responded; it must have seemed an unnecessary question, though in the twilight the knights may not have been able to see him. 'Where is the Archbishop?'

Thomas gave an oblique answer, 'The righteous will be like a bold lion and free from fear,' and walked back down the steps to meet the knights. He said in a moderate voice, 'Here I am, no traitor to the king but a priest. Why do you seek me? God forbid that I should flee on account of your swords or that I should depart from righteousness.'

Thomas was now standing in the centre of the transept beside the big drum-shaped Norman pillar. He turned to look straight at the altars dedicated to the Virgin Mary and St Benedict. Perhaps he had an idea that he would die in front of these altars. The knights moved towards him demanding, 'Absolve those you excommunicated and return to office those you suspended.'

'No penance has been made, so I will not absolve them,' Thomas replied.

'Then you will now die and suffer as you deserve.'

'And I am prepared to die for my Lord, so that through my blood the Church will attain liberty and peace, but in the name Almighty God I forbid you to hurt my men, either cleric or layman, in any way. If it is me you seek, let them leave.' At this point, most of Thomas's monks sensed what was about to happen and instinctively ran away and hid, John of Salisbury among them.

Then the knights rushed at Thomas. Reginald laid hands on Thomas and tried to drag him roughly back towards the door, so that he could kill him out in the cloisters. Together they tried to hoist Thomas onto William Tracy's back so that they could carry him outside. Thomas grappled with them and rebuked them. 'Don't touch me, Reginald. You owe me faith and obedience, you who foolishly follow your accomplices. Do you bear a sword against me?'

This rebuff made Reginald furious. He did not recognize Thomas as his lord, was not his inferior, and he was not a follower either. He aimed a blow at Thomas's head and said, 'I don't owe faith or obedience to you that is in opposition to the fealty I owe my lord King.'

Thomas bowed his head and raised his hands above his head in prayer, seeing that he was about to die. 'I commend myself and the cause of the Church to God, St Mary and the blessed martyr St Denis.'

All the other monks fled for their lives except Edward Grim, who instinctively tried to defend his master with his arm. The moment Thomas ended his prayer, Reginald Fitzurse at once swiped at Thomas with his sword, knocking his fur cap off, cutting the tonsure off the top of his head and slicing into his left shoulder. The same blow cut Grim's arm to the bone. Grim tried to support Thomas, but fell back. Grim reflected on his master's awful death. What a worthy shepherd to his flock he was to set himself against the wolves so that the sheep would not be torn to pieces! He was abandoning the world, the world that was overwhelming and overpowering him now, yet that same world would one day elevate him beyond any of their dreams . . .

Another sword blow fell on Thomas's head and somehow he remained standing firm. He put his hand to his head, looked at the blood and said, 'Into thy hands, O Lord, I commit my spirit'. A third sword blow, from William Tracey, brought him on to his knees, and he muttered, 'For the name of Jesus and the protection of the Church I am ready to embrace death.' He fell full length, with his arms stretched out in front of him as if in prayer. Now Richard le Breton, who had not till now used his sword, aimed a blow at Thomas's head, inflicted a terrible wound, cutting the top of the skull right off and spilling Thomas's brains; the energy of the blow broke the sword's point on the stone pavement. By this stage, Thomas was prone and motionless on the ground – and probably dead.

The fourth knight, Hugh de Morville, had been keeping the huge crowd in the nave back with his sword-point. The evil cleric who had come in with the knights, Hugh, placed his foot on Thomas's neck and dug his sword inside the wound on his head and flicked it, scattering the brains across the floor. He shouted to the others, 'We can leave this place, knights. This traitor will not rise again.' Then the knights, once again shouting, 'King's men, King's men!' made their way out of the place that would from that day forward always be called The Martyrdom, into the cloisters and the great court, ransacking the archbishop's palace before they left. If they repented their action in killing the archbishop, that repentance had not yet taken effect.

Thomas was dead. His body lay where it had fallen, face down, with arms outstretched. Edward Grim, who was with him through this nightmare, commented afterwards that Thomas had shown great perseverance. He had not cried out or uttered a word, not so much as sighing when struck. He stood or knelt waiting fearlessly for the blows. A martyr had been born. Thomas's body-servant, Osbert, cut off a piece of his own shirt and covered the mutilated head with it. For a few minutes, the dead archbishop lay all alone in the darkness. Then, gradually, from the shadows, the monks emerged from their hiding places and were occupied with ushering the huge congregation out of the desecrated cathedral. Then they crept into the north transept to see what they most feared. It was obvious to all who were there that something horrible, but also profoundly momentous and historic, had happened. Pieces of cloth were steeped in his blood and kept as sacred souvenirs.

A thunderstorm broke while the monks washed and dressed the body and laid it to rest overnight in front of the high altar. They prayed in silence as no service could be sung in the desecrated Church.

The next morning, astonishingly, Robert de Broc arrived and called the monks together. He told them that Thomas's body would be thrown to the dogs unless they buried it secretly. He must have known already that Thomas would be seen as a martyr, that there was a danger of a Thomas cult developing – and he vainly tried to stop it. The monks obediently buried Thomas in the crypt, keeping the clothing and bloodstained cloths from the pavement as relics. One of the entrances to the crypt was right next to the spot where Thomas fell. A tomb was built between the two pillars of shining Purbeck marble, a spot which is now an empty space. Later, much later, there would be a great ceremony of translation, in which the remains of Thomas, by now St Thomas of Canterbury, were carried up and entombed in a spectacular shrine behind the cathedral's high altar. By the early sixteenth century, that shrine would be an Aladdin's cave of gold and precious jewels – too great a prize for Henry II's successor, Henry VIII, to resist. That too is now an empty space.

After the murder had been done, the four knights rode to Saltwood. There are two different versions of their mood afterwards. One account says that they gloried in their deed, but William de Tracy, another of the four, said that they were overwhelmed by a sense of guilt. That may of course have been a revisionist view of things, when it became clear that the world as a whole was revolted by what they had done – not just the murder, but the sacrilege. The earlier de Tracy's penitence had begun, the more chance he had of being forgiven. On 31 December, the last day of the year, they rode to South Malling near Lewes, one of the archbishop's manors. There, it is said, they placed their armour on a table, but the table itself rejected it: it was hurled onto the floor.

They were excommunicated by the Pope. They were not punished by Henry II, who seems to have genuinely regretted giving them the order to kill Becket, but he advised them that they would be safer if they fled to Scotland. When they got to Scotland they found that this was not so. Both the king of Scotland and the Scots themselves were all for hanging them, so they were forced to return to England. They sheltered at Knaresborough, which belonged to Hugh de Morville, and stayed there for a year, enduring ostracism by the local people. If they were waiting for the dust to settle, waiting for people to forget about Thomas Becket, they were wasting their time.

No one wanted to have anything to do with Thomas Becket's murderers, who were regarded by everyone as little better than Judas Iscariot. They were pariahs. They were forced to give themselves up to the king. Henry II did not know what to do with them. Although he himself had quarrelled with Becket over this very issue of benefit of clergy, he had lost, and he now found that he was not in a position to put four laymen on trial for the murder of a priest; they were not bound by lay jurisdiction. So Henry II sent them to the Pope. The Pope's punishment was fasting and banishment to the Holy Land; that was the limit of his power. It was ironic that Thomas, by opposing Henry II's legal reforms, had in effect put his own murderers beyond the reach of natural justice. Just about everyone wanted to see the four knights hanged, but there was neither secular nor ecclesiastical law that allowed it.

Before leaving for the Holy Land, Reginald Fitzurse gave half of his manor of Williton to his brother and the other half to the Knights of St John. Fitzurse and his companions are said to have done their penance at a place called 'the Black Mountain'. It is not known what or where this was, but it may have been some sort of religious retreat near Jerusalem. They died there, all of them within three years of the assassination, and were buried in Jerusalem outside the door of the Templars' Church.

There are alternative versions of the fate of the knights. One of them has Reginald Fitzurse seeking shelter in Ireland, where he founded the McMahon family. If so, it would be quite appropriate: Thomas McMahon was one of those responsible for the assassination of Lord Mountbatten in 1979. William de Tracy founded a chantry at Mortehoe in Devon; his altar-tomb is still there. Hugh de Morville may have lived on into the first decade of the 13th century.

Miracles were claimed at Thomas Becket's tomb. Pilgrims flocked to Canterbury in ever-increasing numbers as the years passed, and St Thomas of Canterbury became the greatest saint, not only in England but in Europe. His cult was only ended in 1538 when Henry VIII had his huge shrine at the eastern end of Canterbury Cathedral demolished and what were thought to be Becket's bones were allegedly scattered or burnt.

Recently it has been pointed out that there is no documentation authorizing a burning and that it was quite common in such situations to allow reburial in a more obscure place. A reburied skeleton found in an unusual grave in the crypt in 1888 may hint at a complex answer. It looks as if the commissioners reburied Thomas in the 1888 grave, and that someone later, and in great haste, removed Thomas's body in order to bury it in a place of greater safety or greater sanctity. To avert any possible future repercussions, they replaced Thomas's skeleton with one from a common graveyard – any skeleton would do – and in their haste they inadvertently included some earth and a few bones from other burials. It is likely that Thomas's body was taken away in 1546, when this part of the crypt was being walled off to make a wood store for a Church official, Richard Thornden. Thornden, a Catholic sympathizer, is likely to have wanted the saint's remains to be properly buried in the cathedral, not in his wood store. There is reason, though not proof, to believe that Thomas's bones now lie under the pavement in the Lady Chapel – or in what is called Coligny's tomb, right next to the site of the shrine.

Becket's murder hung over the Middle Ages like a great scarlet banner. His was the greatest shrine of pilgrimage in Europe. His struggle for Church against state was iconic and key to the politics of the Middle Ages, imitated and re-enacted again and again in country after country. If one man, or rather the death of one man, gave the European Middle Ages their distinctive quality and character – that one man was Becket.

From the time of Becket's martyrdom until the Reformation, his shrine in Canterbury Cathedral was visited by thousands of pilgrims, whose offerings brought great wealth into Canterbury.

At the Dissolution of the monasteries in the sixteenth century, Becket's gilded and jewelled shrine was plundered and demolished, and Henry VIII referred contemptuously to 'Bishop Becket' when he ordered his bones to be scattered. A revisionist biography was constructed, and the holy martyr was brought down to the level of a scheming priest, an upstart and a traitor; his murder, if not actually approved, was presented as come-uppance for his presumption in opposing the authority of a king. This was pure Tudor propaganda. Thomas More found out the hard way what happened if you opposed the authority of Henry VIII. This 'Reformation' view of Becket's character and career prevailed until the twentieth century, when a second revolution in appraisal and opinion took place. Thomas Becket has been presented once more as a worthy man of high principle – a staunch defender of the rights of individuals and a stout resister of feudal tyranny.

But it is misguided to present Becket as a kind of Robin Hood. Nor has it ever been justifiable to portray him as a defender of Anglo-Saxon rights against Norman oppression; the presentation of him in this way in Jean Anouilh's play *Becket* is entirely fictitious. Thomas Becket was as much a Norman as Henry II. Becket is not an easy man to admire. He was obstinate and headstrong, and it is hard to be sympathetic to his wish to make the Church paramount over the state. But his grand gesture of opposition to an insatiably power-hungry Plantagenet monarch is irresistibly appealing, and the sheer epic theatricality of the self-imposed exile and the return to martyrdom in his own cathedral has a mythic quality that the highly intelligent Becket himself understood perfectly.

LORD DARNLEY

1567

WHEN MARY BECAME Queen of Scots, she was more than aware that she needed to marry and provide heirs to the Scottish throne. In July 1565, she made the fateful decision to marry her cousin, Henry Stewart, Lord Darnley, a weak, vain, and unstable young man. Why Mary chose Darnley remains a mystery, as he was evidently too headstrong, volatile and unstable to occupy the sensitive role of a prince escort, a king in name only. He was admittedly tall, superficially charming and fond of courtly amusements, but he never showed any affection for her and from the beginning asked for more power than she was willing to give him.

Less than a year after the wedding, Darnley became overwhelmed with jealousy because Mary was spending much of her time with a musician called David Rizzio. Rizzio had come to Scotland from Italy some years previously on a diplomatic mission but remained at the Scottish court as a lute player and subsequently as Queen Mary's secretary. The more outraged Mary became over her husband's stupid, childish and licentious behaviour, the more she looked to Rizzio for consolation and support. But this was happening at a time when many Scottish Protestant lords were discontent with Mary's rule, and some of these nobles claimed that Rizzio had usurped their proper places beside the

Queen – even that he was a secret agent of the Pope. They easily persuaded the gullible Darnley into believing that Mary and Rizzio were sexual partners, an accusation that seems to have no foundation, not least because Mary was six months pregnant with Darnley's child. They nevertheless inflamed his jealousy and persuaded him to take part in a plot to murder the Italian, and to do it right in front of the heavily pregnant queen. In fact, it may be that the conspirators intended to distress Mary so much by making her watch the brutal murder that she would miscarry. Given that this was the sixteenth century, a miscarriage would probably have resulted in her own death. Mary herself believed that Darnley was so angry because she had denied him the crown matrimonial that he wanted to kill her and the child. Making her witness a brutal murder would bring about her death and allow Darnley to succeed as king of Scots.

On the night of Saturday, 9 March, 1566, Lord Ruthven and a group of accomplices burst into Mary's chamber in Holyrood House. Rizzio was seated at her supper table and the assassins dragged him screaming from her side, stabbing him repeatedly, both in front of her and once they had succeeded in dragging him out onto the staircase. It is unclear whether Darnley himself did any of the stabbing, but he was certainly incriminatingly present in the chamber, as the queen's own vivid account of the murder makes very clear.

We were in our chamber at our supper. The King (Darnley) came into our chamber and stood beside us. Lord Ruthven, dressed in a warlike manner, forced his way into our chamber with his accomplices. We asked our husband if he knew anything of the enterprise. He denied it. Ruthven and his accomplices overturned our table, put violent hands on Rizzio and struck him over our shoulder with daggers. One of them even stood in front of our face with a loaded pistol. They most cruelly took him out of our chamber and gave him fifty-six blows with daggers and swords.

After Rizzio's death, the nobles kept Mary prisoner at Holyrood Palace. She was desperate to escape. Somehow she won Darnley over and they escaped together. But Darnley's decision to help Mary escape infuriated the nobles who had conspired with him to assassinate Rizzio; now they wanted Darnley out of the way too. Mary pretended to forgive Darnley and cleverly managed to separate him from the group of treacherous nobles who had organized the Rizzio assassination, but she must have realized that she could no longer trust him. With Rizzio still fresh in the minds of the court, another threat to Darnley's fragile self-esteem soon took centre stage.

James Hepburn, earl of Bothwell, rushed to Mary's aid in putting down a rebellion of Protestant conspirators, even though he was a Protestant himself. Bothwell was Lord Admiral of Scotland, and although he possessed a reputation for bravery, he was also known to be lecherous, brutal and power hungry. Mary saw this strong man as her rescuer and he soon became her most trusted advisor.

By the time Mary gave birth to James VI in June 1566, Darnley had slid back into his former life of debauchery, neglecting his royal duties and sullenly watching Mary's relationship with Bothwell develop. He disappeared from court for a time and this prompted talk of a possible annulment of the royal marriage.

But when the queen learned that he was seriously ill in Glasgow, she (uncharacteristically) made a display of concern by travelling to his bedside and later arranging for a horse-litter to carry him back to Edinburgh to convalesce at Kirk o' Fields in the Royal Mile, a few hundred yards from her own residence, Holyrood Palace. For months Mary had spoken of her husband with nothing but contempt, and this apparently kindly gesture was out of character. It may be that she wanted her unreliable husband close at hand where she could see what he was doing. It may be that she was cold-bloodedly preparing his death. A recent apologist for Mary has said that she would have had to be a duplicitous character indeed to have constantly rejected all suggestions of assassination, and to have sent Darnley her own doctor if she had secretly been planning to have him murdered. But this level of cunning and duplicity is of course well within the possibilities of Mary's complex personality, and indeed well within the norms of power politics of the sixteenth century. It must also be significant that the letter Mary wrote to Archbishop Beaton, on the eve of her journey to fetch Darnley from Glasgow, showed absolutely no indication that she planned a reconciliation with her husband.

Then, at two o'clock one February morning in 1576 there was an enormous explosion, and Kirk o' Fields was reduced to a heap of rubble. It looks as though Darnley may have had some warning, as after the explosion his body was not discovered in the house, but some distance away in the gardens. It was apparent from the lack of damage to his body that he had not been killed by the explosion, but had been done to death while trying to escape from it. Perhaps he had heard suspicious sounds under his bedroom where large amounts of gunpowder had been secretly hidden, perhaps the sounds of unfamiliar activity on the floor below, or the voices of strangers.

A chair and a length of rope were found in the garden; Darnley and his groom had used them to climb out of the first floor window. They both lay dead with just one dagger between them. A contemporary drawing vividly shows the bodies of Darnley and his servant lying in the gardens; they were wearing nightgowns, but the garments were pulled up, exposing the naked lower halves of their bodies, as if the two men had struggled with their assailants on the ground as they were overpowered and throttled. On the right hand side of the drawing of the event is a touching little invention, the infant James VI sitting up in his crib praying, *'Judge and avenge my cause, O Lord.'*

There is still no definite proof of who murdered Lord Darnley. At the time, most people assumed that Bothwell organized it; the only question was whether he did so with Mary's complicity. Most modern historians take that same view. The incident scandalized Scotland, and there were calls for Bothwell to be brought to trial for the murder; and the scandal spread across Europe. It was after all the most flagrant of assassinations. The exploding house covered the tracks of the assassins, making it impossible to prove anything. Indeed, when it came to court it was impossible to prove Bothwell's guilt, and he was acquitted. But most people knew that Bothwell was a ruthless opportunist, aiming at nothing less than the throne of Scotland; everyone knew he was certainly capable of the murder.

Whether Mary herself was involved is unclear. In the wake of the murder she appeared apathetic, and this was taken at the time to indicate guilt. Even more incriminating were the infamous 'Casket' letters, which she was supposed to have written to Bothwell. There is contemporary evidence that the letters were forgeries commissioned by Protestant lords who were busily trying to trap her. But even if Mary wanted her husband dead, that was no more than many of the rest of the Scottish nobility wanted, and therefore it still did not directly implicate her in his murder. She may have appeared apathetic because she was powerless to do anything about the situation developing round her.

The events following Darnley's murder were almost as spectacular and dramatic as the murder itself. In the immediate aftermath, Bothwell met Mary about six miles outside of Edinburgh; whether by chance or pre-arrangement is not known, but if the meeting was pre-arranged Mary must have known about Bothwell's intention to kill Darnley. He had 600 men with him and asked to escort Mary to his castle at Dunbar; he told her she was in danger if she went to Edinburgh. Mary, unwilling to cause further bloodshed and understandably terrified, did as he asked.

According to Mary, Bothwell kidnapped and raped her before marrying her. Within days of the wedding Mary was suicidal with despair at the abuse she had to endure from Bothwell. In many people's eyes her marriage to Bothwell made her guilty by association of the murder of Darnley, marrying her murdered husband's murderer made her as good as (or as bad as) a murderess. Yet her willingness to marry Bothwell was a practical necessity. Mary had many enemies in the Scottish nobility and she needed a strong ally to protect her from them. Even with Bothwell's forceful help, it was less than a year before the Scottish lords forced Mary to abdicate and flee to England. For the next two decades she was held prisoner by Queen Elizabeth I and finally executed in England at Fotheringhay Castle in 1587, compromised and betrayed first by her enemies in Scotland, then by her enemies in England.

Three months later the baby who would become James VI of Scotland was born. Mary now had an heir, which strengthened her position somewhat. The unmarried and childless Elizabeth of England, ten years older than Mary, watched these events beadily from south of the border; she was intelligent enough to see that though Mary might be a doomed monarch Mary's son would be not only Mary's but *her* heir as well.

Mary might have produced the next king of Scots, but the Scottish nobles were still dissatisfied. They were angry that Bothwell would be all-powerful and decided to take up arms against him. Not long after the marriage, the rebel nobles and their forces met Mary's troops at Carberry Hill, not far from Edinburgh. The rebel nobles demanded that Mary abandon Bothwell. She refused and reminded them of their earlier advice, which had been to marry Bothwell. Seeing little alternative, she turned herself over to the rebel nobles, who took her first to Edinburgh and then to Lochleven Castle, where she was held captive. With justification, she feared for her own life, and was forced to abdicate in favour of her son.

Within weeks, the infant James was crowned king and James Stewart, the earl of Moray, Mary's unscrupulous bastard half-brother, became Regent. The appalling Moray seems to have been the architect of the plan to murder Rizzio; he also spread the unfounded rumour that Rizzio and the king were plotting against him, in order to deflect suspicion. Moray got his just deserts when he himself was murdered just three years later. The next regents were also killed; in fact, James himself as a teenager had one of the regents executed in 1580. The Scottish political landscape was a minefield – and not just for the Queen of Scots. Meanwhile, the earl of Bothwell's extraordinary later life must have looked to many Protestant (and other) Scots like God's just reward for the murder of Darnley; he managed to escape from Scotland but ended his life in 1578, languishing in a Danish prison, virtually insane.

WILLIAM THE SILENT

1584

WILLIAM THE SILENT, a wealthy Dutch nobleman, acquired his nickname because he rarely spoke out on controversial matters at court or in public. He was the archetypal diplomat. William was born in the castle of Dillenburg in Nassau, now in Germany. When his cousin, René of Châlon, the prince of Orange, died childless in 1544, the 11-year-old William inherited Châlon's property and the title prince of Orange. Because of William's young age, the Holy Roman Emperor Charles V served as the regent of the principality until William was deemed fit to rule. Charles V made the condition that William receive a Roman Catholic education.

William was appointed captain in the cavalry and with the emperor's favour he was quickly promoted, as royal princes are, becoming commander of one of the emperor's armies at the early age of 22. In the 1550s William ably served Philip II of Spain as a diplomat, but Philip's encroachments on the liberties of the Netherlands along with the introduction of the Spanish Inquisition led William to turn against the king. Although he avoided overt opposition to the Spanish king, William soon became one of the most prominent members of the opposition in the Raad van State, together with Philip de Montmorency, count of Horn and Lamoral, count of Egmont. Their main aim was to achieve greater political power for the Dutch nobility; they complained that too many Spaniards were involved in governing the Netherlands and that Dutch Protestants were being persecuted. William joined the Dutch rising and turned against his former masters. The most influential and politically capable of the rebels, he led the Dutch to several military successes in the fight against the Spanish. In 1563, he managed to remove the cardinal who had introduced the Inquisition, but there was continuing unrest in the Netherlands.

When Alba was sent to the Netherlands to quell the rebels, William withdrew to Germany, refused Alba's summons to appear before a tribunal, and suffered the confiscation of his property. William and his brother Louis of Nassau then raised an army to drive the Spanish out of the Netherlands. It took several years but under William's leadership the Spanish were eventually expelled. The Union of Utrecht (1579) proclaimed the virtual independence of the northern provinces, of which William was the uncrowned ruler. Philip II denounced William as a traitor, and a high price was set on his head in 1581. William's response was his famous Apologia, in which he not only defended his own conduct, but attacked the Spanish king.

At Antwerp, where he took up his residence, the duke of Anjou was invested with the duchy of Brabant. As a Frenchman, the duke was far from popular, so William remained at his side to give him support. Then, as William was rising from his dinner-table, a young Spaniard called Juan Jaureguy tried to assassinate him by firing a pistol at him. The ball entered William's head by the right ear and passed through the palate. Jaureguy was killed on the spot. Anjou was at first suspected of being implicated in the crime, but was later vindicated. It was a terrible wound and William's life was for some time in great danger, but he very slowly recovered. The next time he would not be so lucky.

Politically, William and the duke of Anjou were really playing at cross-purposes. William wanted Anjou to be the puppet-king of a United Netherlands of which he, William, would be the real ruler. Unfortunately Anjou had no intention of playing second fiddle, and decided in January 1583 to capture both William and Antwerp.

With shameless treachery, the duke of Anjou visited William in Antwerp, and tried to persuade him to attend a review of the French regiments who were encamped outside the town. William was suspicious of the invitation and made an excuse to decline. Thousands of Anjou's troops rushed into the city, but the citizens defended it ably, finally driving the French out with heavy losses. Anjou's attempt to capture William was a total failure. Indignation at the 'French frenzy' was wide and deep throughout the provinces. Ironically, William's efforts to calm the excitement only added to his own growing unpopularity.

William was so convinced that the only hope for the provinces lay in alliance with France that he seemed unable to see the duke of Anjou's treachery for what it was. His continued support of the duke only served to alienate the people of Brabant and Flanders. The Protestants hated the thought of having as their sovereign a prince who was a Catholic and whose mother and brothers were seen as the instigators of the St Bartholomew's Day Massacre, in which large numbers of Protestants were murdered. William's marriage in April 1583, to Louise, daughter of the famous Huguenot leader Admiral Coligny, added to the feelings of distrust and hostility he had already aroused, for the bride was French and both her father and husband had perished on St Bartholomew's Day.

Exposed to insults, and his life continuously in danger, William left Antwerp in late July to take up residence again at Delft among his loyal Hollanders. They disliked his French connections, but they saw him as true at least to the Calvinist cause.

William was living at the old convent of St Agatha, afterwards known as the Prinsenhof at Delft. His lifestyle was modest and homely, just like that of any ordinary Dutch burgher. He was in fact deeply in debt and anxious about the political situation, especially when in June 1584 Anjou died; the strategy he had expended so much futile effort on was totally wrecked. And all this time there was the continual fear of assassination. Ever since the failure of the attempt of Jaureguy, there had been a constant succession of plots against him, instigated by the Spanish government. Religious fanaticism combined with the promise of a cash reward made many eager to undertake the murderous commission. William refused to surround himself with guards or to take any special precautions, and was always accessible. He seemed to be waiting to be assassinated.

On 10 July, 1584, William the Silent met his end at the hands of a French Catholic fanatic, Balthasar Gérard. Ironically, it came at a time when William's popularity and power were waning. Many schemes and proposed assassination attempts had come to nothing either through the vigilance of William's spies or through the would-be assassins' loss of nerve. But Balthasar Gérard, born in 1557, had become obsessed with the conviction that he had a special mission to accomplish the deed in which Jaureguy had failed, and he dedicated himself to the sacred task of ridding the world of the arch-enemy of God and the king. Gérard was a supporter of Philip II, and in his opinion William of Orange had betrayed the Spanish king and the Catholic religion. After Philip II declared William an outlaw, Gérard decided to travel to the Netherlands and kill him. He served in the army of the governor of Luxembourg for two years, hoping to get close to William when the armies met. This never happened, so Gérard left the army in 1584.

He adopted the name Francis Guyon, made his way to Delft, pretended to be a Calvinist refugee, and went about begging for alms. Acquiring a pair of pistols, Gérard made an appointment with William of Orange at his home. On 10 July, 1584, Gérard managed to gain admittance to William's house and hid in a dark corner in the stairwell outside the room where William and his family were dining. As the prince, his wife, three of his daughters and one of his sisters came out and descended the staircase, the assassin darted forward and fired two bullets into William's chest from close range. William fell to the ground and died almost immediately.

In the confusion that followed the shooting Gérard fled, but he was caught and imprisoned before he could escape from Delft. Gérard was subjected to excruciating tortures, which he suffered with great courage. He saw himself as a martyr in a holy cause, and was regarded in the same way by Catholic public opinion. He was tried on 13 July, and given a death sentence that was brutal even by the standards of the sixteenth century. The magistrates ordered that his right hand should be burned off with a red-hot iron, that his flesh should be torn from his bones with pincers in six different places, that he should be quartered and disembowelled alive, that his heart should be torn from his chest and flung in his face. Finally, his head should be severed.

The murder of William the Silent was widely praised across Catholic Europe. Philip of Spain even ennobled Gérard's family and exempted them from taxation. In Holland, by contrast, there was profound and general grief at William's tragic but almost inevitable end. There was general recognition that he had been the fearless and tireless champion of their resistance to civil and religious tyranny. He was given a lavish public funeral and buried in the Nieuwe Kerk at Delft. William became a national hero in the Netherlands, even though he had been born in Germany and usually spoke French. Many Dutch national symbols can be traced back to him. The Dutch flag is derived from his. The coat of arms of the Netherlands is based on his. The Dutch national anthem was originally a propaganda song written for him.

William the Silent was only 51 when he was killed, a man prematurely aged by anxiety. In a way the manner of his death was of a piece with his life, a final self-sacrificing act in a life of self-sacrifice in public service. Small wonder that Hollanders of every class gave him the title 'Father of the fatherland'. His death was momentous in another way too. His was the first assassination of a head of state with a handheld gun, and it heralded the arrival of a lethal new threat to the security of nations – a pistol that could be concealed and used to lethal effect at point-blank range. Small wonder that Elizabeth I, William's close Protestant ally, was devastated by his death and thrown into a panic. In the aftermath of William's death the English parliament enacted legislation making it an offence to take a pistol anywhere near a royal palace. Elizabeth's terror of the assassin with a pistol was not misplaced; this handgun assassination was the first in a long and bloody line.

GEORGE VILLIERS, DUKE OF BUCKINGHAM

1628

GEORGE VILLIERS, IST duke of Buckingham, was one of the most successful royal courtiers who ever lived, the favourite of two kings, King James I of England and VI of Scotland and his son Charles I. George Villiers (pronounced 'Villas') was born in Brooksby, Leicestershire, the son of Sir George Villiers.

Following Villiers' introduction to James I during a royal progress in 1614, the king is said to have fallen deeply in love with him, calling him his 'sweet child and wife' and writing, 'I naturally so love your person, and adore all your other parts, which are more than ever one man had . . . I desire only to live in the world for your sake.' James already had a favourite, Lord Somerset, but Somerset had enemies (as all favourites do) and Villiers was able to gain support from those enemies. Somerset fell from grace after the Overbury affair, and his place was quickly taken by Villiers.

George Villiers prospered under the king's patronage. He was knighted in 1615 and further honours followed in quick succession. He was created Baron Whaddon and Viscount Villiers in 1616, earl of Buckingham in 1617, marquess of Buckingham in 1618 and finally earl of Coventry and duke of Buckingham in 1623. During the Tudor period the number of peers had been reduced, so Buckingham emerged as the highest-ranking subject in England.

He married the daughter of the 6th earl of Rutland, Lady Katherine Manners, in 1620 and showered valuable royal monopolies on her family. The next year parliament launched an investigation into the abuse of monopolies and Buckingham was politically agile enough to side with parliament to avoid action being taken against him.

In 1623 Buckingham accompanied the duke of York (later to become Charles I) on a curious trip to Spain, in order to negotiate Charles's marriage to a Spanish princess. The negotiations were difficult, but it is likely that Buckingham's lack of diplomacy was the main reason why the negotiation failed. The Spanish Ambassador in London went so far as to ask parliament to have Buckingham executed for his bad behaviour in Madrid; but Buckingham courted and won great popularity in England by calling for war with Spain on his return. He led another marriage negotiation but when in 1624 Prince Charles's betrothal to Henrietta Maria of France was announced the choice of a Catholic was widely condemned.

Buckingham became even more unpopular in England when he was blamed for failing recover the Palatinate in 1625. But Charles remained grateful for his support and, when Charles became king, Buckingham was the only man from the court of James I to keep his position.

Buckingham led an expedition to imitate the action of Sir Francis Drake in seizing the Spanish port of Cádiz and destroy the Spanish fleet at anchor. The plan was sound, but the troops were ill equipped and ill disciplined. When they encountered a warehouse filled with wine, they simply stopped, got drunk, and the attack had to be called off. It was a fiasco. Another followed, when Buckingham failed to intercept a Spanish silver fleet from Mexico; his fleet limped home empty-handed. When the English parliament tried to impeach him for the failure of the Cádiz expedition, the king had the house dissolved so that they could not put him on trial. Buckingham became even more reckless, declaring war on France, which brought him into conflict not only with France but Austria and Spain as well, the three most powerful Catholic nations in Europe.

In 1627 Buckingham led another spectacularly unsuccessful expedition, to aid the Huguenots besieged at La Rochelle. During this fiasco he managed to lose more than 4,000 of his 7,000 men. It was while he was at Portsmouth, organizing a second attempt at the relief of La Rochelle, that he was killed. Given the appalling record of national disservice of the duke of Buckingham, it might be expected that behind his assassination lay some elaborate establishment conspiracy to remove him before he could do any more damage, but it was not so; it was a case of a lone assassin.

Death came to George Villiers, duke of Buckingham, on 23 August, 1628, in the Greyhound Inn on Portsmouth High Street. He was attacked there by a man called John Felton, a disgruntled and depressed infantry lieutenant who had been badly wounded during the 1627 expedition to the Ile de Ré, was twice passed over for promotion to captain, and was owed over eighty pounds in back pay. The brooding, disaffected soldier plunged a cheap knife into Buckingham's heart. Buckingham gasped an astonished oath and fell to the floor – dead. In the scene of consternation and confusion that followed, the assassin retreated unobserved into the inn's kitchen where he eventually surrendered to the duke's men with the calm admission, 'I am the man.'

John Felton was 40 years old and came from a Suffolk family that had known better days. Felton was angry that Buckingham had shown no interest in his case for promotion. He had also become increasingly desperate as he ran out of money. Felton had come across a copy of the 1628 parliament's *Remonstrance* against the duke and persuaded himself that his personal sufferings were just one part of the sufferings the whole nation had had to endure under Buckingham's evil reign. He had become obsessed with the idea that killing the duke would be an act of national redemption – as well as giving him personal satisfaction. Before setting out for the Greyhound Inn with the full intention of murdering Buckingham, Felton had written and sewn into his hatband two explanations for the murder, just in case he was killed out of hand during the assassination attempt. In these he insisted that he was acting out of patriotism, as a gentleman and a soldier. He was striking a blow for the public good.

Buckingham's assassination had an immediate and transforming impact on the English political landscape. The grief-stricken king retreated to his chambers, knowing that he had lost his main support. Meanwhile news of the murder spread across England to be greeted by spontaneous expressions of joy. The assassin was taken under armed guard from Portsmouth to the Tower of London, where he was repeatedly interrogated about his motives and accomplices. The Privy Council tried to obtain formal permission to have Felton questioned under torture on the rack, but the judges resisted, unanimously declaring that the use of torture was contrary to the laws of England. But Felton may have been secretly tortured anyway.

The authorities laboured for three months to try to

uncover the conspiracy they were sure lay behind the duke's murder, but the assassin insisted he had acted alone – as indeed he may have done. The situation is reminiscent of the Kennedy assassination where, again, the murder was so momentous that it was hard for many people to believe that it was the work of a lone deranged assassin. By late November, the investigation had run its course and Felton was at last put on trial for Buckingham's murder. The authorities portrayed Felton as a wicked, atheistic criminal who had acted solely out of personal grievances against the duke. Felton was convicted and sentenced to death. Two days later, at Tyburn, he confessed before a crowd of onlookers and said that he regretted his crime. After he was hanged, Felton's body was taken to Portsmouth, where it was strung up again to rot in chains as a warning to others.

Buckingham's monument in Westminster Abbey bore an ambivalent epitaph: 'The Enigma of the World'. And that was really the best that could be said about him. The assassination, and the trial and execution that eventually followed, released a tide of political verse. Some of the poems were mocking epitaphs for the duke. Many raked over the accusations that had been flung against him while he lived. Every kind of libel was hurled at the dead duke, whose soul was assumed to be in Hell; he was the witch, the papist, the poisoner, the sexual predator, the monopolist, the perverter of justice, the social upstart, the seller of offices, the breaker of parliaments, the betrayer of the Protestant cause, the incompetent villain of the Ile de Ré, the deceiver and seducer of kings. There were poems celebrating Felton the murderer as a patriot hero, a national martyr, the epitome of martial manliness and self-sacrifice. There were protestations of loyalty to the throne, but behind them hung unresolved questions about Charles I's responsibility for Buckingham's misrule and well-founded fears about his intentions for the future. The poems bear eloquent witness to the perilous state of the nation at the moment of Buckingham's assassination, a nation teetering on the brink of a bitter ideological crisis. The disquiet that was to blossom into Civil War was germinating.

ASSASSINATIONS
IN THE
18TH AND 19TH CENTURIES

PETER III OF RUSSIA

1762

PETER III, TSAR of Russia, was born at Kiel on 21 February, 1728, the only son of Charles Frederick, duke of Holstein-Gottorp, and Anne, the eldest surviving daughter of Peter the Great. He was adopted by his aunt Elizabeth Petrovna in December 1741, as soon as she was securely established on the Russian throne. In the following November he was received into the Orthodox Church, exchanging his original name of Karl Peter Ulrich of Holstein for that of Peter Fedorovich.

It was on 21 August, 1745 that Peter married Princess Sophia Augusta Frederica of Anhalt-Zerbst, who changed her name to Catherine Aleksyeevna. The marriage was not Peter's idea but his aunt's, and it proved to be a disaster. Peter was a rather feeble man of low intelligence; marriage to a princess of high intellect and vitality was bound to end in catastrophe. The stories that Peter treated Catherine badly seem to be unfounded, but their personalities were incompatible from the beginning. It took the spouses five years to discover that their tastes were divergent and their tempers incompatible.

The Empress Elizabeth had a reputation for revelling in sex, yet she left no offspring to inherit her throne. When Peter III succeeded his aunt in January 1762, he generously paid all Catherine's debts, without even asking what they were for. When it was her birthday, three months later, he gave her estates yielding an income of £10,000 a year. Perhaps inevitably, Peter acquired a mistress, the Countess Elizabeth Vorontsòva, but even there he managed to make a bad choice. She was unintelligent, ugly and spiteful. So Peter found no happiness in his infidelity either.

Catherine accepted Peter's liaison with the Countess Elizabeth as a matter of course, and was not at all shocked when the Countess (whom she nicknamed 'Das Fräulein') moved into the Winter Palace to create a *ménage a trois*. In fact she did not mind at all so long she was allowed to carry on her own liaison with a handsome young guardsman called Gregory Orlov.

Peter behaved well towards his wife in public. In fact, it seems he was too good-natured to pursue or plan any strategy of ill treatment. Peter III did not offend or outrage Catherine in any way; he committed no offence against Catherine other than being an inadequate husband. The cause of his overthrow and death was quite simply Catherine's single-minded determination to snatch the reins of government from him. She was intelligent, capable, and strong-minded. Peter's inevitable political blunders, which were the result of his lack of intelligence, supplied Catherine with her pretext and her opportunity.

Within six months of succeeding to the Russian throne, Peter had managed to alienate the whole of Russia with his undiplomatic and unreasoning love of all things Prussian, including its king. His offences against the Orthodox Church and his childish obsession with guns and soldiers also made him unpopular with the Russian people. Peter's wife, who it is easy to forget was herself born in Germany as Princess

Sophie, ironically took to Russia much better than Peter, taking a Russian name, learning the Russian language and adopting the Orthodox religion. Inevitably, as his political position weakened, hers strengthened.

Peter pursued a foreign policy that was the diametric opposite of his predecessor's. He had only been on the throne for a few weeks when he made an incredible foreign policy gaffe; at a time when he had nearly conquered Prussia he made peace-making gestures to the Prussian king. Peter idolized Frederick, the king of Prussia, and often referred to him very inappropriately as 'the king, *my master*'. Peter's overture to Frederick resulted in a peace, closely followed by the signing of an offensive and defensive alliance between Russia and Prussia. All the territory Russia had won from Prussia during the previous five years at an enormous cost in both men and money were given back.

This remarkable alliance was reinforced by a series of threats by Peter against Vienna, in which Peter said he would declare war unless Austria instantly complied with all of Prussia's demands. Finally, to complete his catastrophically inept foreign policy, he quarrelled with the Danes, launching an invasion of Denmark that was only halted by the news that a palace revolution had taken place at St Petersburg; Peter III of Russia was already a prisoner in the hands of his consort.

The palace *coup* of 9 July, 1762 marks the effective beginning of the reign of Peter III's wife, the monarch now universally referred to as 'Catherine the Great'. Peter III had become a huge embarrassment, not only personally to Catherine, but nationally, to Russia, and internationally, to Europe. He had to be removed. His imprisonment was not a final enough termination to a reign that was both destructive and ridiculous, and his assassination was virtually inevitable. Little is known for certain about Peter III's death. It took place at the castle of Ropsha, to which he was taken immediately after his surrender. There Catherine forced him to abdicate in her favour. He stayed at Ropsha for nine days, the last nine days of his life, until the afternoon of 18 July. Catherine and her advisers could not at first decide what to do with Peter, 'the former emperor', and spent hours discussing the possibilities. One proposal was that he should be imprisoned in Schlüsselburg for the rest of his life. Another was that he should be repatriated to Holstein. Both of these alternatives were dismissed as dangerous. The Orlov brothers had strong motives for killing Peter – stronger than Catherine herself – as Gregory Orlov wanted to marry Catherine and marriage to her would not be possible while Peter lived. During the nine days, the cold-blooded decision was made that Peter, the ex-emperor, must die.

Such evidence as we have points to one irresistible conclusion – that at Ropsha on the afternoon of 18 July, 1762, Peter III was murdered. The assassins included Alexius Orlov, Theodore Baryatinski and several other men whose identities are unknown. The assassination took place with Catherine's full complicity.

GUSTAV III OF SWEDEN

1792

KING GUSTAV III of Sweden was born in 1746. He was educated under the supervision of two of the greatest Swedish statesmen of the time, Carl Tessin and Carl Scheffer. This state interference in his education had a deep effect, and doubly so because his parents encouraged him to despise the tutors imposed upon him by the Estates of the Realm. The atmosphere of duplicity in which he grew up gave him premature experience in the art of dissembling; he was forced to be 'political' even in childhood. His teachers were amazed by his exceptional ability. Even as a boy he had the irresistibly charming manner that was to make him so magnetic and dangerous in later life; he also had a strong dramatic instinct. On the whole, it cannot be said that Gustav was well educated, but he read very widely especially in French literature; he read the ideas of the new French enlightenment enthusiastically yet critically.

In 1766 Gustav married Sophie Magdalen, the daughter of Frederick V of Denmark. The match was an unhappy one, partly because Sophie and Gustav were temperamentally incompatible, partly because of interference by Gustav's mother.

Gustav was one of a group of late 18th-century European rulers known as Enlightened Despots, and of the group he is possibly the least studied by historians. Frederick II of Prussia was a great general; Catherine II of Russia was a great empire-builder; Joseph II of Austria was a great administrator, working to co-ordinate the governments of a conglomeration of principalities. Each in his or her way was striving forward. Gustav III was unlike all of them. In some ways, Gustav III was a great reactionary, striving to change things – back to the way they had been in the past.

Sweden had been a great power in the seventeenth century, with a succession of able soldier kings. After the death Karl XII, the last of these, the administration had become weak, corrupt and impotent. Gustav III took on the task of making Sweden a great power once more. He was an enthusiast of Swedish national history, and was proud of the fact that through his paternal grandmother he was descended from the Vasa royal dynasty.

In 1771, Gustav spent two months in Paris, where he made an enormous impression. Poets and philosophers paid him enthusiastic homage, and aristocratic women swooned over him. Many of the friends he made on that visit became lifelong correspondents. But his visit to the French capital was mainly a political mission. Swedish secret agents had already prepared the way for him, and the duke of Choiseul had decided to discuss with him a very risky enterprise: the best way of bringing about a revolution in Sweden. It is hard to imagine, but the young king of Sweden was at this stage a revolutionary. Before Gustav left Paris, the French government undertook to repay debts owed to Sweden at a rate of one and a half million livres annually. On the way home Gustav visited his uncle,

Frederick the Great, at Potsdam. Frederick bluntly told him that the revolution idea was out of order and that he, Frederick, had guaranteed the integrity of the existing Swedish constitution. He advised the young king to act the part of mediator and to abstain from violence.

When he opened his first Riksdag of the Estates (parliament) on his return to Sweden, Gustav made a deep impression; it was the first time in a hundred years that a Swedish king had addressed a Swedish parliament in its own language. He volunteered, as 'the first citizen of a free people', to mediate between the contending factions. The dominant Cap faction tried to reduce him to a puppet king, and he considered again the possibility of a revolution. He saw that under the Caps Sweden would become the prey of Russia, that it would lose its independence and become absorbed into the 'Northern System'. Gustav saw that only a *coup d'état* could save the independence of his country.

At this moment Gustav was approached by a Finnish nobleman called Jacob Sprengtporten with a proposal for a revolution. Sprengtporten proposed to seize Finland first, then cross the Baltic to Sweden, meet the king near Stockholm, and take the city in a night attack. The plotters were joined by Johan Christopher Toll, a victim of Cap oppression who offered to organize a second revolt in the southern province of Skåne, taking the stronghold of Kristianstad as a diversion. In August 1772 Toll succeeded in winning Kristianstad. Sprengtporten similarly succeeded in taking Sveaborg, but strong winds prevented him from crossing the Baltic. As it happened, developments in Stockholm made his presence there unnecessary.

News had arrived in Stockholm of the insurrection in the

south, and Gustav found himself suddenly isolated in his own capital surrounded by enemies; his allies, Sprengtporten and Toll, were hundreds of miles away. Gustav secretly ordered all the officers he thought he could trust to assemble in the square facing the arsenal. He joined them, then led them to the guard-room of the palace and unfolded his plans to them. Meanwhile the Privy Council and its president, Rudbeck, were arrested and the fleet secured. Then Gustav made a tour of the city and was everywhere received by enthusiastic crowds, who hailed him as a deliverer. Heralds walked the streets ordering all deputies to assemble the following day. The king appeared in full regalia, took his seat on the throne, and delivered a speech denouncing the estates for their unpatriotic behaviour. A new Constitution was imposed and the parliament was dissolved. Gustav's high-risk revolution had been a total success.

Gustav then worked towards reform. He reformed the administration, the legal system, abolishing torture, and expanded the navy into one of the most formidable in Europe. He proclaimed absolute religious liberty, and even invented a national costume, which was in general use until his death. When the king summoned the estates to assemble at Stockholm in September 1778, he could give a dazzling account of his six years' stewardship. It had been a huge success, but it was also clear to the deputies that they had lost their political supremacy. The king was in control. By the assembly of 1786 their mood was mutinous and nearly all of Gustav's propositions were rejected.

Gustav moved steadily and cautiously from being a semi-constitutional monarch to being a semi-absolute monarch. In a war against Russia that looked unwinnable, Sweden finally won the Battle of Svensksund in 1790. It was seen as Sweden's most glorious naval victory; the Russians lost one-third of their fleet and 7,000 men. It led to a peace treaty and alliance with Catherine the Great under which the Russian empress agreed to pay Sweden a substantial annual subsidy.

Gustav attempted to create a league of princes against the Jacobins. He understood popular assemblies extremely well and he understood from the start the significance of the French Revolution. Gustav had real insight. The other European monarchs were too blinkered to see the point of his league and Gustav was left marginalized by a network of aristocratic conspiracies. Many Swedish aristocrats were angry with Gustav for abolishing the Council of the Realm, which had been a bastion of the nobility; he had replaced the Council with a High Court of which only half of the members were noblemen. These clashes with the aristocracy were to lead directly to Gustav's assassination. At Anjala disaffected noblemen launched a conspiracy against him.

On the night of 16 March 1792, Gustav left the fine neo-classical pavilion that had been designed for him in Haga Park in Stockholm, to attend a midnight masquerade at the Royal Swedish Opera. It was at this masquerade that he was shot in the back by Jacob Johan Anckarström, a disaffected nobleman. Gustav died of his wound nearly two weeks later, on 29 March.

Both the Anjala conspiracy and the assassination were condemned by the ordinary people of Sweden, who had remained loyal to the king. The murderer, Anckarström, was executed and the surviving family members felt so disgraced by the assassination that they altered their name. Gustav III was rightly seen as one of the greatest heads of state of the

18th century. Quite apart from his dazzling political achievements, he was a great patron of all the arts. He was a great writer too, producing some of the best dramas in the Swedish language. But there is always a negative side to absolutism, and Gustav had introduced press censorship, book censorship and an oppressive dress code to indicate people's social status.

Gustav III's son, Gustav IV, was only 13 when his father was murdered. During the years of his minority, Sweden was effectively ruled by Gustav Adolf Reuterholm, who had spent several years abroad and witnessed some of the unfolding events of the French Revolution. During his four years in power, Reuterholm lifted the restrictions on press freedom, abolished book censorship and abolished Gustav III's dress code.

Given Gustav's patronage of the arts, it was quite appropriate that his assassination should have become the subject of two operas, one by Daniel Auber (1833) and the other by Verdi (1859) – *A Masked Ball*.

JEAN PAUL MARAT

1793

JEAN PAUL MARAT was born in 1743 and became one of the leading figures of the French Revolution. By then he had already made a significant name for himself as a doctor. It is hard to appreciate now, but if the Revolution had not taken place Marat would probably have been remembered as a great medic and scholar. It was not until 1774 that he published *The Chains of Slavery*, his first explicitly 'revolutionary' piece. The Revolution transformed Marat out of all recognition, just as it transformed his assassin.

By the 1780s, Marat was deep in politics, heart and soul. He founded a newspaper, *L'Ami du peuple* (*The Friend of the People*), which became profoundly influential. Above the frenzy of shouting it was the voice of Jean Paul Marat that everyone heard. He became one of the legendary and iconic figures of the French Revolution, standing alone, never joining any political group or faction. His attitude was to suspect those in power, and to speak out against anything he believed wrong. No wrong, no poverty, no misery, no persecution could silence him. He was endlessly shouting, 'We are betrayed!' If anyone suspected anyone of anything they had only to denounce them to Marat, and the newspaper did not let up until the accused was found innocent or guilty. He made lots of enemies, and it is astonishing that he lasted so long. To avoid being attacked or arrested, he spent a lot of time hiding in cellars and sewers. It was through living like this that he picked up a horrible skin disease. He was tended by his one trusted friend, Simone Évrard.

His position in relation to the king was peculiar. He was implacably hostile to the King Louis, and saw him as the one man who must die for the people's good, but he would not hear of him being tried for anything that pre-dated the acceptance of the new constitution.

After the king's execution, in which Marat played his part, there were five months in which the struggle between Marat and the Girondins continued. Marat despised the Girondins because he thought that they talked too much about their high-flown feelings when they had actually suffered nothing in the cause of the republic. He also thought that they were too self-consciously recreating the Roman Republic of a bygone age. Marat had no time for that sort of talk. The Girondin faction sought to silence Marat by having him tried before the Revolutionary Tribunal, but this backfired badly. Marat was acquitted by the Tribunal on 24 April 1793 and returned in triumph to the Convention with the people of Paris behind him. The fall of the Girondins on 31 May was now almost inevitable. It was Marat's final triumph, his revenge on the Girondins.

His skin disease was worsening now and he could only relieve the pain by sitting in a medicated bath. He used to sit in the bath for long periods, writing on a board resting across the sides. On 13 July 1793, he heard a young woman begging to be let in. The visitor was Charlotte Corday.

Charlotte Corday or, to give her her full name, Marie Anne Charlotte de Corday d'Armont, was born in 1768 on a farm in the village of Champeaux in Normandy. She was the fourth child of a provincial noble family. They had moved to Caen, where Charlotte's mother died in 1782. After that, the teenaged Charlotte and her sister Eleonore went to the Roman Catholic convent as boarders to complete their education, but the convent closed three years later, and Charlotte then went to live with a cousin in Caen (at 148 Rue St-Jean).

Swept along by the Revolution, Charlotte became more and more committed to the idea of a republic. She saw herself as devoted to the 'enlightened' ideals of the time, although only a couple of years earlier she had been a monarchist. She was struck by the government's actions against the Girondins, who were taking refuge in Caen. Charlotte Corday favoured the Girondins, who were more moderate than extremists like Robespierre and Marat. With the moderates being persecuted, it began to look to her as if a Girondin republic would never come about. She saw Marat in particular as the person who was responsible for the misfortunes of the French people, with his daily demands for more heads. She decided that she was the one who had to get rid of him. It was an unusual sense of mission in an eighteenth-century woman – a sign of the times.

On 9 July, 1793, Charlotte left her cousin's apartment in Caen and boarded the mail coach to Paris. There she stayed at the Hotel de Providence, where she wrote a long screed entitled *Speech to the French who are Friends of Law and Peace*. The purpose of this was to explain the action she was about to take.

This brings us to the fateful day, 13 July 1793, when Charlotte Corday arrived on the doorstep of Jean Paul Marat's house in the Rue des Cordeliers. She was carrying a cheap table knife with a dark wooden handle and a silver ferrule, which she had bought at the Palais-Royal. She knocked at the door and said that she had an appointment. She had information to give Marat – news from Caen, where the escaped Girondins were trying to raise troops in Normandy. Marat was keen to hear news of his enemies and asked for her to be let in.

The interview took place in Marat's bathroom, with Marat still naked in his disinfected bathtub. He asked her for the names of the deputies at Caen, and wrote them down on a piece of paper. Then he said, 'They shall soon be guillotined.' At this, the young woman stabbed him through the heart with her table knife. The painter Louis David painted an unforgettable picture of the bizarre scene immediately afterwards, the pale body of Marat slumped in his tin bath, still holding his quill. Only the murderess is missing, dragged off to the Conciergerie prison and shortly to be tried for her life.

The verdict on Charlotte Corday was a foregone conclusion, but she used the trial to assure everyone that she had acted entirely alone. She wanted to avoid another purge. She wanted to assert and demonstrate the contribution that women could make to politics. 'Even the women of the country are capable of firmness.' She also wanted to remind Paris that there was more to France than the capital. 'It is only in Paris that people have eyes for Marat. In the provinces, he is regarded as a monster.' Inevitably, she was condemned to death.

The day before her execution she wrote a letter to her father, asking his forgiveness for 'having disposed of my existence without your permission'. She also wrote a letter in which she complained that 'there are so few patriots who know how to die for their country; everything is egoism; what a sorry people to found a Republic!' She was probably hoping that someone would follow her example and sacrifice themselves by assassinating Robespierre.

Her last request was that a National Guard officer called Hauer should paint her portrait. As a token of gratitude, Charlotte gave Hauer a lock of her hair, 'a souvenir of a poor dying woman'. On 17 July, at seven o'clock in the evening, she was guillotined. Charlotte Corday refused the ministrations of a priest on the scaffold. A bystander at the execution wrote, 'Her beautiful face was so calm that one would have said she was a statue. Behind her, young girls held each other's hands as they danced. For eight days I was in love with Charlotte Corday.' Charlotte died unrepentant, convinced that she had avenged many innocent victims of the Terror and prevented more unnecessary deaths. By this time, not least because of her performance at her trial and her extraordinary composure on the scaffold, she was becoming a symbolic figure, representing the moderate France that was disgusted by the Terror.

The Convention put Marat's bust in the hall where its sessions were held. Marat had become a hero of the Revolution, and was certainly much safer and more admirable dead than alive. A year later, his ashes were transferred to the Pantheon with great pomp. But celebrity of the kind Marat achieved is fragile. His is a type of fame that can switch like the batting of an eye to infamy. A decree of February 1795 saw to it that Marat's ashes were removed from the Pantheon. Marat had proceeded by way of a particularly nasty kind of power play. His was the politics of the tabloid press – the naming and shaming of alleged criminals, regardless of the process of law – his was the ethical standard of the lynch mob. He was ready to send countless numbers of people to prison and death on somebody else's say so.

PAUL I OF RUSSIA

1801

TSAR PAUL I was born in the Summer Palace at St Petersburg in October 1754. He was the son of the Grand Duchess and later Empress Catherine. According to some, his father was not her husband, the Grand Duke Peter, later tsar, but Catherine's lover Sergei Saltykov. Claims were made that Peter III was sterile and impotent, and so could not have fathered the boy himself. Catherine herself hinted that the story was true, which may at first seem to confirm the rumour, but it is likely that she was simply reinforcing suspicions that Peter was an inadequate tsar and casting doubt on Paul's right to succeed to the throne; both strands tended to support Catherine's own rather shaky claim to the throne. The more points of inadequacy that emerged about Peter III, the more Catherine's part in his assassination would be vindicated.

In infancy Paul was taken from the care of his mother by the Empress Elizabeth. As a boy he was reported to be intelligent and good-looking; the slightly grotesque pugnacious features of later life were probably the result of an attack of typhus in 1771. Some, the English ambassador at her court included, said that Catherine hated Paul, and was only restrained from putting him to death while he was still a boy by the fear of what the consequences to herself might be of another palace murder. On the other hand others saw a different side of Catherine, who showed every sign of being fond of children; they saw her treating Paul kindly.

Catherine's wild and pleasure-loving court proved to be a corrupting environment for the young Paul, but Catherine nevertheless took great trouble to arrange his marriage with Wilhelmina of Hesse-Darmstadt in 1773. Wilhelmina adopted the Russian name Natalia Alexeievna. Catherine also allowed him to attend the council in order to learn the work of an emperor. His tutor Poroshin complained that Paul was 'always in a hurry', and that he acted and spoke without thinking.

Paul became involved in intrigues and came to believe that he was the target of assassination conspiracies. He suspected his mother of intending to kill him, openly accusing her of causing broken glass to be mixed with his food. Catherine removed him from the council, possibly sensing that he was unstable, and began to keep him at a distance, but her actions were not unkind. Then in 1775 the rebel Pugachev used his name, and this made Paul's position more difficult. When his wife Natalia died in childbirth, Catherine arranged another marriage for him a few months later with the beautiful Sophia Dorothea of Württemberg. She took the Russian name Maria Feodorovna. Catherine marked the birth of his first child in 1777 with the gift of an estate, Pavlovsk, and this was followed by a gift of another estate five years later. Maria conscientiously bore Paul 10 children.

The Empress Catherine suffered a stroke in November 1796, dying without regaining consciousness. Now Paul was emperor. As emperor he was idealistic, often generous, but also volatile and vindictive. In 1798, Paul was elected Grand

Master of the Order of St John, to whom he gave shelter following their expulsion from Malta by Napoleon. His leadership resulted in the establishment of the Russian tradition of the Knights Hospitaller within the Imperial Orders of Russia. Paul's independent conduct of foreign affairs led Russia into a Second Coalition against France in 1798, and then into the Armed Neutrality against Britain in 1801. In both cases it seems as if he acted out of purely personal reasons rather than strategy. One of his most serious mistakes was to send the Cossack expeditionary force to India. Paul was probably trying to imitate Peter the Great.

Catherine had passed a law allowing the flogging of free Russian citizens; under her regime, no one could feel safe from brutal ill-treatment at any moment. Paul repealed this legislation. He also directed reforms which increased the rights of peasants and ensured better treatment for serfs on agricultural estates. While enlightened and to modern eyes wholly admirable, it was extremely unpopular with the aristocracy. Paul also uncovered large-scale corruption in the Russian treasury.

If Russia had been a constitutional monarchy, the tsar's enemies could have collaborated to stop or restrain him. But the institutional mechanisms were not there. There was no mechanism other than murder. In early 19th-century Russia, just as in medieval western Europe, there was no safe haven for a deposed ruler; Paul's premonitions of assassination turned out to be well-founded.

A conspiracy to assassinate Tsar Paul was organized and in place for some months before it was put into action by a group of conspirators. They included Counts Petr Alekseevich Pahlen, Nikita Petrovich Panin, and a half-Spanish, half-

Neapolitan adventurer named Admiral Ribas. The death of Admiral Ribas delayed the implementation of the plan.

On the night of 11 March 1801, the tsar was murdered in his bedroom in the St Michael Palace by a band of soldiers headed by General Bennigsen, a Hanoverian in the Russian service. The soldiers were all officers who had been dismissed. They dined together first and had plenty to drink, presumably to give them courage, then burst into the tsar's bedroom. They dragged him to the table, and tried to force him to sign his abdication. Paul tried to resist, and one of the assassins struck him with a sword. Once the first blow was struck, he was strangled and trampled to death.

Tsar Paul I was succeeded by his son, the Emperor Alexander I, who was present in the palace at the time of his father's assassination. One of the assassins, General Nicholas Zubov took the news of his father's death to him and announced his accession.

A commonplace view of Tsar Paul I is that he was mad, that his acceptance of the role of Grand Master of the Order of St. John exaggerated his delusions, that his general eccentricity and unpredictability justified his assassination. Paul is often presented in this way, and his reign is ridiculed and discounted. Assassinated heads of state are by definition, in the crudest sense, losers, and history is notoriously written by the victors. In the nineteenth and twentieth centuries, the number of political assassinations multiplied. In Russia alone, five emperors were assassinated in less than 200 years – Ivan VI, Peter III, Paul I, Alexander II and Nicholas II. In a violent, often gratuitously violent, world we cannot any longer sideline a head of state simply because he was unable to stay alive. The high rate of assassination in Russia, and in the world as a whole, is rather a symptom that something else is wrong. We can call it political immaturity or the inadequacy of the human psyche, but it is both immoral and foolish to seek to blame the victims.

SPENCER PERCEVAL

1812

SPENCER PERCEVAL WAS born on 1 November, 1762, the seventh son of John Perceval the second earl of Egmont and his second wife Catherine Compton. Spencer Perceval's most lasting claim to fame is that he is the only British prime minister, so far, to have been assassinated.

Spencer Perceval was educated at Harrow and Trinity College Cambridge. He was called to the Bar in 1786, becoming Deputy Recorder of Northampton in 1790, the year when he married Jane Spencer-Wilson. In 1796, Perceval became MP for Northampton, the seat that he still held at the time of his death in 1812. He held a number of government posts including that of Attorney General and Chancellor of the Exchequer.

Perceval was the chief legal adviser to the princess of Wales when she was charged with misconduct in 1806; although she was found guilty of 'grossly indelicate conduct', Perceval managed to arrange a reconciliation with George III. Perceval wrote the king's speech for the State Opening of parliament in 1807, and he was at the forefront of the debates calling for the removal of the duke of York as Commander-in-Chief of the army. In 1809 he became prime minister. George III praised him as 'the most straightforward man I have ever known'. Even so, Perceval had great difficulty in filling Cabinet posts: as he could find no one else to fill the position he took on the duties of Chancellor of the Exchequer himself.

On 11 May, 1812, while in the lobby of the House of Commons on his way to take part in a debate, Perceval was shot dead by John Bellingham. Perceval was buried in the family vault in St. Luke's, Charlton, on 16 May, 1812. Bellingham had been trying unsuccessfully to obtain government compensation for debts that he had incurred while he was in Russia, and gave himself up immediately. He was tried at the Old Bailey and condemned to death: he was executed on 18 May, 1812.

Bellingham remains a shadowy figure about whom little is known for certain. He was born in St Neots, Huntingdonshire, and later brought up in London, where at the age of fourteen he was apprenticed to a jeweller called James Love. At the age of 16 he went as a midshipman on the maiden voyage of the *Hartwell* from Gravesend to China. There was a mutiny on board the *Hartwell* on 22 May, 1787, which led to the ship running aground and sinking. In 1794, a man called John Bellingham opened a tin factory on London's Oxford Street, but the business failed and he was declared bankrupt that March. It is not at all certain that this was the same person as the assassin. The Bellingham who killed Perceval certainly worked as a clerk in a counting house in the late 1790s, and around 1800 he went to Archangel in Russia working as an agent for importers and exporters. In 1802 he was back in England, working in Liverpool as a merchant broker. He married in 1803 and the following summer he again sailed to Archangel as an export representative.

Then a Russian ship named the *Soleure*, insured at Lloyd's of London, was lost in the White Sea. The owners, a firm called Van Brienen, attempted to claim on their insurance but an anonymous letter was sent to Lloyd's informing them that the ship had been deliberately sabotaged. Soloman Van Brienen suspected that it was John Bellingham who had written the letter, and as an act of revenge accused him of owing a debt of 4,890 roubles to a bankrupt for which he was an assignee. Bellingham was on the point of embarking for England on 16 November 1804, when the Russian authorities cancelled his travel pass on account of the alleged debt.

The vindictive Van Brienen persuaded the Governor-General of the area to throw John Bellingham in prison. It was a whole year before Bellingham was able to secure his release and manage to reach St Petersburg, where he foolishly attempted to have the Governor-General impeached. This provocative belligerent action predictably got Bellingham into further trouble with the Russian authorities and they retaliated by charging him with leaving Archangel without permission. He was again imprisoned. In October 1808 he was released, but still not given permission to leave Russia. Now in a state of desperation, Bellingham personally petitioned the tsar. He was finally permitted to leave Russia late in 1809 and arrived back in England in December that year.

Bellingham was not prepared to let this personal fiasco rest. He now started petitioning the British government for compensation for his imprisonment, perhaps feeling that more could have been done through diplomacy to secure his release, though he must have known that Britain had broken off diplomatic relations with Russia in November 1808. His demand for compensation was refused. His wife, no doubt thoroughly tired of hearing him honing his grievance, tried to persuade him to drop the issue and as a concession Bellingham went back to work.

In 1812 John Bellingham went to work in London, where he made further attempts to win compensation for his wrongful imprisonment in Russia. On 18 April he called at the Foreign Office. There, a civil servant called Hill, who can have had no idea what he was saying, told Bellingham that he was at liberty to take whatever measures he thought proper. Bellingham had already started preparations for resolving the matter in a more conclusive way, and this apparent advice from the Foreign Office gave him official permission to go ahead. On 20 April he bought a pair of half-inch calibre pistols from W. Beckwith, a gunsmith of 58 Skinner Street. He also arranged with a tailor to have a secret inside pocket sewn into his coat. At about this time, he was often seen hanging around in the lobby of the House of Commons.

The assassination happened in fairly inconsequential way on 11 May, 1812. After taking the family of a friend to see a watercolour exhibition, Bellingham casually remarked that he had some business to attend to, and made his way to parliament. He waited in the lobby until Prime Minister Spencer Perceval appeared, then stepped forward and shot him in the chest. The prime minister staggered forward, clutched at his chest and as he fell to the floor cried out, 'I am murdered! I am murdered!'

A stunned silence followed, as MPs looked down in disbelief at the mortally wounded Prime Minister. After firing his shot, Bellingham calmly sat down on a bench. Bystanders in the lobby detained him at once, he was identified by Isaac Gascoyne, the MP for Liverpool, and taken into custody. On the day of the inquest into the death of Spencer Perceval, Bellingham sent the following letter to his landlady:

Dear Madam: Yesterday midnight I was escorted to this neighbourhood by a noble troop of Light Horse, and delivered into the care of Mr. Newman (by Mr. Taylor the Magistrate and MP) as a state prisoner of the first class. For eight years I have never found my mind so tranquil as since this melancholy but necessary catastrophe, as the merits or demerits of my peculiar case must be regularly unfolded in a criminal court of justice, to ascertain the guilty party, by a jury of my country.

I have to request the favour of you to send me three or four shirts, some cravats, handkerchiefs, night-caps, stockings, etc, out of my drawers, together with comb, soap, toothbrush, with any other trifle which presents itself which you may think I may have occasion for, and enclose them in my leather trunk, and the key, please to send sealed per bearer; also my great-coat, flannel gown, and black waistcoat, which will much oblige. Dear madam, your obedient servant, John Bellingham. To the above please to add the Prayer Book.

Bellingham was tried on 13 May at the Old Bailey. He said he would have preferred to kill the British Ambassador to Russia, but as a wronged man he was entitled to kill the representative of those he saw as his oppressors. He was in effect arguing that the British Prime Minister had what would now be called a duty of care towards him and that the Prime Minister had neglected that duty, to Bellingham's great cost. He gave a formal statement to the court;

'Recollect, Gentlemen, what was my situation. Recollect that my family was ruined and myself destroyed, merely because it was Mr Perceval's pleasure that justice should not be granted; sheltering himself behind the imagined security of his station, and trampling upon law and right in the belief that no retribution could reach him. I demand only my right, and not a favour; I demand what is the birthright and privilege of every Englishman. Gentlemen, when a minister sets himself above the laws, as Mr Perceval did, he does it at his own personal risk. If this were not so, the mere will of the minister would become the law, and what would then become of your liberties? I trust that this serious lesson will operate as a warning to all future ministers, and that they will henceforth do the thing that is right, for if the upper ranks of society are permitted to act wrong with impunity, the inferior ramifications will soon become wholly corrupted. Gentlemen, my life is in your hands, I rely confidently in your justice.'

He was found guilty and sentenced to death, and hanged in public on Monday 18 May. Although it was clear to everyone who attended the trial that John Bellingham was deranged, the question of his sanity or fitness to stand trial was never raised by the court.

There was a curious postscript to the murder. The night following the assassination, and before news of the event could have reached him, the wealthy mining engineer John Williams of Scorrier House, near Redruth, dreamt three times of the exact circumstances of the assassination, even down to the clothing worn by Perceval and Bellingham. He told his wife, and the next day told several friends, who all confirmed the story later. About six weeks later, Williams went to London and visited the House of Commons with a friend, and was able to point out the exact place where the Prime Minister had fallen. When Williams died in 1841, the *Gentleman's Magazine*'s obituary said, 'His integrity was proof against all temptation and above all reproach.'

NAPOLEON I OF FRANCE

1821

AFTER NAPOLEON'S DISASTROUS return from exile on Elba, the victors of Waterloo were determined to get rid of him altogether. After Waterloo, he had been intercepted while trying to escape to the Americas, where he hoped to carve out another empire. They wanted him somewhere from which there could be no possible return. The remote island of St Helena, deep in the South Atlantic, must have seemed a safe enough prison. But there were those who thought that Europe – and America – could only be truly safe if Napoleon was dead.

When Napoleon died in 1821, in his 52nd year, the official cause of death was cancer, but there has always been speculation that he was murdered. Cancer is a wasting disease and yet Napoleon died fat. Assassinating Napoleon would have prevented him from returning from St Helena and regaining his throne as he had done, so expensively and disruptively, when he returned from his first exile on Elba. Several modern pathologists have concluded after examining the autopsy reports that Napoleon did not die of stomach cancer. Over the decades, doctors and historians have attributed Napoleon's final illness and death to over 30 different causes ranging from gonorrhoea or syphilis to scurvy or hepatitis.

Locks of Napoleon's hair have survived as keepsakes. They have undergone three separate analyses, by Professor Hamilton Smith in the early 1960s, more recent tests by the FBI on only two very short pieces just over a centimetre long, and most recently by Dr Pascal Kintz, of the Strasbourg Forensic Medicine Institute. As a result of his analysis, Dr Kintz is convinced that Napoleon died of arsenic poisoning. The hair contains between 7 and 40 times the normal concentrations of arsenic. The earlier analyses had found concentrations of arsenic, but there had been the thought that the arsenic could have come from the environment of Longwood House: cosmetic preparations, perhaps, or even the wallpaper. But Dr Kintz decontaminated his samples before analysis in order to remove all such traces; the quantities of arsenic he measured are entirely biological in origin, coming from within Napoleon's body, from Napoleon's bloodstream. Napoleon was, in other words, poisoned. The hair was tested in sections, and the results showed large variations in the levels of arsenic – extreme highs and lows – showing that on certain days Napoleon was given high doses of arsenic. Arsenic was a poison that was easily available in the 19th century and commonly used to murder people, even though the symptoms were readily identifiable.

If Napoleon was deliberately murdered on St Helena, who was the murderer? Historians have identified suspects. The conspiracy to have Napoleon killed was probably engineered at the highest level, by Louis VIII and the Comte d'Artois, the future King Charles X of France, or by British ministers, or both. Either the British or the French authorities ordered the assassination, which was carried out by their respective men on St Helena, Governor Hudson Lowe or Count Charles de Montholon.

Louis Marchand, Napoleon's first valet, was one of the eyewitnesses who through his diary provided evidence of Napoleon's assassination by poisoning. Marchand was attentive, discreet, literate, shrewd, observant and loyal beyond the call of duty. Napoleon treated him like a son, and left him 400,000 francs in his will. Napoleon's desire was to honour Marchand with the title of count, and his wish was eventually carried out when Napoleon III came to power. Marchand kept a diary while in exile because he wanted his family to know what happened on St Helena and he instructed his family never to publish these memoirs. The diary was eventually bought in the 1950s by Commander Henri Lachouque and, disregarding Marchand's wishes, he published it in 1955.

Marchand recorded the daily events at Longwood House as they happened, the equivalent of a doctor's case notes describing the progressive decline of a terminally ill patient. It was Marchand who took home to France a lock of hair shaved from Napoleon's head the day after his death; he put it carefully into an envelope with the label, 'The Emperor's hair'. It was faithfully preserved in its original envelope by Marchand's descendants, who can have had no idea that it would eventually expose the emperor's death as a classic nineteenth-century murder.

There were in all eight eyewitnesses reporting independently from each other, in books and diaries, on the various symptoms that Napoleon displayed over his last few months. They were Napoleon's companions in exile: the Marquis Las Cases, Baron Gourgaud, Dr Barry O'Meara, Dr Francesco Antommarchi, Grand Marshal Bertrand, Louis Marchand and two English doctors. These eight people had regular access to Napoleon and observed him on a daily basis, and they all kept diaries of their lives on St Helena, most with a view to making money by publishing them later. The arsenic levels were plotted on a time chart, and the days of high arsenic levels coincided exactly with the days when the eight witnesses described many of the classic symptoms of arsenic poisoning. It may seem odd that arsenic poisoning was not diagnosed at the time, but it has apparently always been very common for doctors to overlook deliberate arsenic poisoning as a cause of illness. Napoleon's doctors may therefore perhaps be forgiven for failing to understand the nature of his illness. They were simply not trained to understand the symptoms of arsenical poisoning, and arsenic trioxide is both tasteless and odourless.

Dr O'Meara made several misdiagnoses – dysentery, scurvy, gout, ulcers, and other ailments. Unless he had been tipped off he would have little reason to suspect arsenic poisoning, because the symptoms themselves taken individually resemble those of many other diseases. Here is an example of the symptoms described by one of the eyewitnesses, Dr Francesco Antommarchi, Napoleon's personal physician. In his diary entry for 26 February, 1821 he wrote: 'The Emperor had a sudden relapse, dry cough, vomiting, sensation of heat in the intestines, generally disturbed, discomfort, burning feeling that is almost unbearable, accompanied by burning thirst.' These are classic arsenic poisoning symptoms.

But Napoleon's death was more complicated still. He did not actually die from the arsenic poisoning, although that made him extremely ill. He was instead was poisoned to death in two phases, using a method that was widely used by professional poisoners of the period. The 'classical method' of concealing the murder was to create a 'cosmetic phase' during which the victim became more and more seriously ill, as if suffering from the progress of some disease or degenerative condition, followed by a 'lethal phase', which led to death. The 'cosmetic phase' of Napoleon's poisoning started in the middle of 1816, and this was done through the use of arsenical intoxication. Interestingly, there is some evidence that Napoleon was being fed arsenic even during the Waterloo campaign, several months before his exile, so it is possible that someone was trying to murder him even at that stage.

Napoleon was poisoned slowly with arsenic to make it appear that he was deteriorating in a natural way from the progress of a disease. Killing him suddenly might have meant revolution in France, because the French army and many ordinary French people were still loyal to Napoleon. He needed to appear to be dying a natural death. The most important factor to consider is that whoever was administering the arsenic was doing so from the beginning of the exile and continued until the 'lethal phase' in 1821.

This immediately eliminates all the people who left St Helena before Napoleon died, and also eliminates those who arrived during the exile. Therefore we are left with just three suspects: Louis Marchand, the valet; the Grand Marshal Bertrand and the Comte de Montholon. The person responsible for the poisoning would have to be in regular contact with Napoleon, and therefore had to live in Longwood House. This immediately eliminates the Grand Marshal Bertrand, who lived some distance away, since his English wife wanted more privacy and did not like to be in close proximity to the other companions of the exile. Bertrand attended the emperor as and when required by him.

There were only two people who had very close contact with Napoleon daily, and who were able to enter his room whenever it was necessary, and who had meals with him on a regular basis. These were the Comte de Montholon and Louis Marchand. Louis Marchand is recognized by all historians, and the companions of the time, as a loyal, devoted valet who served Napoleon like a son. He had no possible motive to harm Napoleon and is very unlikely to have been the assassin. That leaves only the Comte de Montholon.

The Comte de Montholon, on the other hand, had no reason to admire nor wish to serve the emperor on St Helena, yet mysteriously volunteered to do so. Napoleon was only 46 years of age at the time of exile, in good health, and he could have lived another 20 or 30 years. This could have meant that Montholon would have wasted his career in serving him. If he was an agent of the Bourbons commissioned to kill Napoleon, he would have known in advance that his assignment was relatively short-term. But what could Montholon's motives for assassinating the emperor have been?

One is personal revenge. Napoleon had dismissed Montholon from his post as the French envoy to Wurzburg when against Napoleon's wishes he had married the twice-divorced Albine Roger.

Another is that Montholon was a committed royalist. His stepfather, the Comte de Simonville, was a close friend of Louis XVIII and the Comte d'Artois, and a long-time servant of successive French kings; de Simonville was created a peer in the new French House of Lords. Montholon grew up with the name Montholon-Simonville. However, when he left to go to St Helena, he very cleverly dropped the Simonville part of his name and went as simply Comte de Montholon.

Montholon was evidently being 'looked after' by the French royal family for some reason. In 1814, while Napoleon was in exile on Elba, Montholon stole military funds amounting to 6,000 francs; not only did he go unpunished, apparently due to the intervention of the Comte d'Artois, he was promoted to General by Louis XVIII.

A third motive was the legacy. Montholon was a major beneficiary of Napoleon's will, and was appointed one of the three executors. Montholon was alone with Napoleon when he prepared his last will and added codicils; Montholon therefore knew that he stood to gain a huge sum of money, over 2,200,000 francs, from Napoleon's death.

The assassin would have to have access to the food or wine that the emperor was to consume, but at the same time ensure that no one else was poisoned. The food eaten at Longwood was shared by everyone living there, but Napoleon had his own supply of wine imported specially from Cape Town. This was drunk *only* by the emperor. Because Montholon had exclusive access to Napoleon's wine, he had a unique and exclusive opportunity to poison him. There can be little doubt that it was through his wine that Napoleon was poisoned.

The final, lethal, phase of the assassination began in March 1821. For this phase Montholon used toxic medications such as tartar emetic, followed by orgeat and calomel. Dr Antommarchi writes that on 22 March, 1821, Napoleon was given a lemonade drink with an emetic. In the following days, Napoleon was given additional emetic drinks which induced vomiting. It was quite common for nineteenth-century doctors to prescribe an emetic in the hope that vomiting would rid the body of whatever was causing the problem. The emetics used corroded the lining of Napoleon's stomach and in time reduced the tendency to vomit, making him more vulnerable to poisoning. After a time, it was safe for the assassin to administer cyanide, which the victim was unable to vomit.

On 22 April, a new drink was served to Napoleon for the first time. It was orgeat, an orange-flavoured drink which includes the oil of bitter almonds and it was served to help quench Napoleon's thirst. Three days later a case of bitter almonds, which contain prussic acid, was delivered at Longwood. The assassin was getting worried that the bitter almonds would not arrive on time. Bertrand noted that *someone* (unfortunately his diary does not give his name) asked his four-year-old son, Arthur, to go out and collect some peach stones and leave them in the pantry. Peach stones can serve as a substitute for the almonds; they both contain hydro-cyanic acid.

Bertrand noted that a few days before Napoleon's death, on 3 May, he was extremely thirsty and drank a lot of orgeat. Antommarchi's diary reports that he was concerned about Napoleon suffering from constipation (a symptom of arsenical intoxication). The commonest treatment for constipation was called calomel, which contains mercury chloride. Marchand noted that at 5.30 p.m. on 3 May, 1821, without his knowledge or approval, Napoleon was given ten grains of calomel, confirmed by the entry in Bertrand's diary. This was 40 times the normal dose and it was the irrevocable moment in the assassination.

Calomel contains mercury chloride; orgeat with bitter almonds contains hydro-cyanic acid, or prussic acid. Together they combine in the stomach to form mercury cyanide which would then be expelled from a healthy stomach by vomiting. Napoleon had been given several drinks containing a large quantity of tartar emetic and this would have inhibited the vomiting reflex. Consequently, the highly toxic mercury cyanide was retained. Shortly after Napoleon's death and the publication of Dr Antommarchi's book Dr Robert Gooch commented that the large dose of calomel was far more likely to be responsible for the death of Napoleon than hepatitis, the climate or cancer, but his view was not published.

In later years Dr Antommarchi persistently maintained that Napoleon had died of chronic hepatitis, induced by the unhealthy climate of the island. The Marquis Henri de Montchenu was appointed by Louis XVIII to represent France at St Helena during the exile; he reported the day after Napoleon's death, 'Of the five doctors present at the autopsy, not one knows the exact cause of his death.'

The assassin committed very nearly the perfect crime, which is all the more surprising given the celebrity of his victim. But he does appear to have made one serious mistake. He appears to have killed someone else in error. In February 1818, Cipriani, the major domo, fell ill without warning. He was seized with violent pains in the stomach and chills, which are symptoms of acute arsenical poisoning. He died two days later and was buried immediately. Later someone somebody secretly dug up the body and disposed of it. It disappeared. Presumably the assassin wanted to cover his tracks, knowing that an autopsy would reveal the poisoning, because it is easy to detect acute arsenical poisoning. Or did the assassin perhaps kill Cipriani deliberately? Cipriani was more than just a major domo: he was Napoleon's secret agent, and it is possible that he discovered the assassination plot and had to be removed.

William Balcombe had the ex-emperor staying at his tea room while Longwood House was being repaired and enlarged, and became a personal friend. Balcombe believed that Cipriani had been poisoned, and asked for the grave to be opened and an autopsy to be performed, but the body had disappeared before this could be done. Bertrand said that a few days after Cipriani's death, a maid in Montholon's employment and a young child died with the same symptoms. Perhaps by accident they ate or drank something that Montholon had prepared for Cipriani. Everything points to Montholon being Napoleon's assassin, including the things Montholon wrote in his book, published in 1848.

The several other diary accounts that exist all agree with each other about Napoleon's symptoms, whereas the symptoms described by Montholon are significantly different. An obvious example is that Montholon reported that Napoleon was *emaciated* when he died, yet all the others, including the British doctors who were present at the post-mortem, said that Napoleon was excessively *fat*. Clearly that is not something that anyone would misremember: it can only be explained as a lie. Montholon can only have had one reason for lying about the symptoms of Napoleon's final illness.

That Napoleon was assassinated is unremarkable. That his assassination has remained a secret until now is strange. That the Comte de Montholon got away with murdering Napoleon is very remarkable indeed, and he must have been amazed that he got away with it. He must have spent the rest of his life waiting for the knock at the door, for justice to catch up with him, for the cry for vengeance from the ordinary people of France.

ABRAHAM LINCOLN

1865

ABRAHAM LINCOLN'S HUMBLE origins on a farm in Kentucky became an integral part of one of the great American legends: log cabin to White House. As a farm boy he was good-humoured and imaginative but rather idle. After several moves, in 1830 the family went to live in Illinois. By then Lincoln was an exceptionally tall and lanky young man, 6 ft 3 in and incredibly strong. The portrait photographs show that he was not good-looking, but he attracted people with his geniality, strength and a kind of radiant purity, and these qualities ensured his success in politics. In 1834 he was elected to the legislature.

There was a troubled, dark, mystical side to Lincoln that lay hidden much of the time. It emerged in a disturbing way as his marriage to Mary Todd approached in 1841. According to one story it was actually on his wedding day that Lincoln went into a state of shock and was unable to go to the wedding. Mary showed great understanding and patience, and they married in the following year.

When the Republican Party was organized in 1856 to stop the spread of slavery, Lincoln emerged as its most conspicuous campaigner in Illinois. Delegates from Illinois proposed him for the vice-presidency and, although he failed to win it, he became a national figure by being a candidate and took a leading role in American politics from then on. In his inaugural speech as president in March 1861, Lincoln declared the Union perpetual, but it was clear that the South would secede. Oddly, at this critical moment when Lincoln became president, his inner tide was on the ebb, and he seemed powerless, unable to function effectively or make an effective speech, for some time.

By the time he began his second term as president, in 1865, things were very different. He was now confident and masterful. It was said, 'There is no man in the country so wise, so gentle and so firm.' Under his presidency, the Civil War came to an end with victory for the North. General Grant captured Richmond and General Robert E. Lee surrendered to him. But many in the South were bitterly resentful in defeat. Lincoln's determination to free the slaves inflamed the passions of many racist extremists in the South – and John Wilkes Booth was one of them.

For a hundred years John Wilkes Booth was America's most notorious assassin, but he led two lives. He was the leading conspirator who succeeded in murdering perhaps the greatest president the United States has ever had, but he was also a much-admired actor; it is often forgotten that, unlike Lee Harvey Oswald, he was a well-known figure on another stage, even a minor public figure, before he killed the president.

Like many actors before and since, Booth came from a theatrical family. His father, Junius Brutus Booth, emigrated from England in 1821 and made a big name for himself on the American stage. John was born on 10 May, 1838 on a farm (worked by slaves) in Maryland. He was the ninth of ten children, and his siblings later recalled his waywardness and eccentricity. John went to several private schools including a Quaker school before attending an Episcopalian military academy at Catonsville. During the 1850s, he became a Know-Nothing. This Know-Nothing Party was formed by 'nativists', people who wanted to preserve the country for native-born white citizens. The theme of white supremacy was a crucial element in Booth's psyche, and had a major role in his decision to kill Lincoln – that freer of black slaves.

Booth worked on the farm for a time after his father died in 1852, but it was just too dull for him. He day-dreamed about doing something remarkable. According to his sister Asia, he cried 'I must have fame! Fame!' He decided to be a famous actor like his father.

Booth made his stage debut at the age of 17 in 1855 in Baltimore, as the earl of Richmond in *Richard III*. He started acting in earnest two years later, but early notices were not favourable and he was inevitably compared unfavourably with his much-admired father. John hated that. Junius Booth was one of the most famous actors of his day, though he had an eccentric personality, problems with alcohol and bouts of insanity. In spite of later achieving a great deal as an actor, John may have felt that he could never outshine his dazzling father and this may have driven him to try to make his mark in some other way.

Theatre companies often used big-name touring actors to pull in larger audiences, and Booth eventually succeeded in achieving this 'star' status, though it led him into a punishing lifestyle. Often a different play was performed each night, so after a performance Booth might have to stay up the rest of the night learning a new part, then go to the theatre for a morning rehearsal. This irregular lifestyle involved keeping unusual hours, and may have helped to make him less visible as a conspirator, even though he was recognized wherever he went. Booth began his stock (repertory) theatre appearances in 1857 in Philadelphia, which was then the drama capital of America. His early acting lacked confidence, and he frequently needed prompting; he forgot his lines and missed his cues. The acting and stage manager at the Arch Street Theatre commented that the new actor did not show promise as a great actor. Others in the company were more forthright, saying that he had no future as an actor at all. But he was only 19 and he was very determined.

In 1858, he moved to Richmond, Virginia for a season of repertory at the Marshall Theatre. Here he became more confident and was liked by audiences. He also became more positively committed to the southern way of life and more entrenched in southern, white-supremacist political views.

Booth appeared to make a fresh start altogether in 1859, when he joined the Richmond Grays. But his motive in joining up was sinister. He enlisted, on 20 November, 1959, with the sole purpose of witnessing a political assassination, the hanging of the fiery abolitionist John Brown in Charles Town, Virginia. He was part of the armed guard standing near the scaffold to prevent anyone from rescuing John Brown. Shortly after the historic hanging, Booth was discharged. The episode shows Booth's fanatical support of the southern cause, his desire to be involved in historic events, his morbid interest in political assassination, and his unstable, maverick behaviour.

During the Civil War, Booth promised his mother he would not join the Confederate Army, but he was involved in some covert operations and may have been a southern agent.

Possibly he was smuggling medical supplies to Confederate troops.

John Wilkes Booth was a charismatic figure, good-looking, with a slim athletic build and magnetic eyes. Another actor commented that 'when his emotions were aroused, his eyes were like living jewels. Flames shot from them.' He attracted women. Booth was often seen 'lounging' in the arms of Ellen Starr. In 1861, an actress called Henrietta Irving slashed his face with a knife when she realized Booth had no intention of marrying her. After Booth was killed, the photographs of no less than five women were found in his pockets. One of them was a picture of his fiancée, Lucy Hale, the daughter of Senator John P. Hale who, ironically, was a prominent abolitionist. But these are just further signs of Booth's inconsistency and waywardness. He wanted to see the hated John Brown hanged, but was also happy to accept John Hale as a father-in-law – and both were abolitionists.

Booth's acting career took off in 1860, and he played leading roles in many plays. In Shakespeare's *Julius Caesar*, he played Mark Antony with his brothers Edwin and Junius as Brutus and Cassius. In November 1863, Booth acted in front of Abraham Lincoln. The Lincolns saw him in *The Marble Heart* at Ford's Theatre. With them in the box was a guest, Mary Clay. She reminisced that Wilkes Booth twice, when uttering disagreeable threats, came up close to Lincoln and pointed at him. When he came close a third time, Mary Clay said, 'Mr Lincoln, he looks as if he meant that for you.' Lincoln replied, 'Well, he does look pretty sharp at me, doesn't he?'

Now Booth was earning a colossal $20,000 a year. He was able to invest in oil. In May 1864, he left the stage and went to

Pennsylvania to focus on his oil investments. He formed the Dramatic Oil Company with three actor friends. But Booth was too volatile and impatient for business; when success was not immediate, he dropped out, handing most of his investment over to a friend and his brother Junius.

In October 1864, Booth made a mysterious journey to Montreal, where he held secret meetings with Confederate sympathizers. In November, he returned, carrying a letter of introduction which eventually led him to meet Dr Samuel Mudd. Booth was assembling a conspiracy to capture the President, take him to Richmond as a hostage and use him to compel the Federal government to return the Confederate prisoners of war who were held in Union prisons. The intention was to reinvigorate the Confederate army and enable it to win. It is important to realize that this was a plot to kidnap, not to kill.

Booth must later have wished that he had seized his opportunity when, on 4 March, 1865, he attended Lincoln's second inauguration as the invited guest of his fiancée. Booth must have thought about it when later he said to another actor, 'What an excellent chance I had to kill the President, if I had wished to!' Evidently the possibility was floating about in his mind.

All through these years, Booth behaved in a secretive, erratic way, but his brothers and sisters seem to have thought little of it, perhaps because they were accustomed to his instability and wildness. Asia later recalled how when he stayed with her in Philadelphia 'strange men called late at night for whispered consultations'. She knew her brother was a spy, a blockade-runner, a rebel.

The capture of the President was to take to place on 17

March, 1865. But after five months of detailed planning by Booth and the other conspirators, Lincoln spoilt their plot by changing his plans at the last minute. Instead of visiting the Campbell Hospital outside Washington to see a play, *Still Waters Run Deep*, he decided to attend a luncheon at the National Hotel, where he would speak to officers of the 140th Indiana Regiment and present a captured flag to the Governor of Indiana. Booth and his co-conspirators were thwarted.

Two weeks later, the Union siege of Richmond ended in Confederate defeat. One week after that, on 9 April 1865, General Lee was obliged to surrender. Booth was doubly frustrated; his own conspiracy to kidnap Lincoln had failed and the Confederates had lost the war. On 11 April, Lincoln gave his last speech at the White House. Booth and two of his co-conspirators, Powell and Herold, were in the audience. Lincoln proposed conferring rights on certain black people, 'on the very intelligent and on those who serve our cause as soldiers'. Booth was now beside himself with rage. 'That is the last speech he will ever make.' Booth's fury made him think up a wild, last-throw attempt to get the better of Lincoln. Just four days later, he would murder him.

Booth made a big mistake in thinking that the conspirators who had been ready to kidnap were just as ready to kill.

At 9 a.m. on 14 April, 1865, Booth went to a barber's shop to have his hair trimmed, then returned to the National Hotel, where many of the guests recognized him. Later in the morning he went to Ford's Theatre to pick up his mail. There he heard from the theatre manager that Lincoln would be attending that evening's performance of *Our American Cousin*. He decided that this was his opportunity to kill Lincoln. He spent some time walking round the theatre.

He knew the play well, and knew that the biggest laugh would come at 10.15 p.m; that would be the moment to shoot. At noon he went to a stable and hired a fast mare before returning to the hotel.

At 2 p.m. Booth visited Lewis Paine and told him he was going to kill Lincoln. He also told Paine that he, Paine, was going to kill Secretary of State William Seward. Booth then went to the boarding house belonging to Mary Surratt and left her a package containing field glasses; she was to take them to her tavern at Surrattsville, where he could collect them that night. At 3 p.m., Booth visited George Atzerodt to tell him to assassinate Vice-President Andrew Johnson, who lived in the same building, but Atzerodt was out. Inexplicably, Booth left a note for Johnson, who was then at the White House. After picking up the mare, Booth went to a tavern for a drink and wrote a letter to the press, which was to be delivered the next day; he signed the letter with his own name and those of three others – Paine, Atzerodt and Herold – which overtly implicated them and in effect condemned them to death. At that stage poor Atzerodt didn't know what was in store for him. It was only by chance that Booth met him in the street at 5 p.m. and told him to kill Johnson at 10.15 p.m. Atzerodt did not want to do it, but he was already fatally implicated and would be hanged for it.

At 6 p.m. Booth rode to the theatre to rehearse the route he would use in the assassination, everything except the leap onto the stage. Then he returned to the hotel to rest, dine and change. He put on calf-length boots, new spurs and black clothes and picked up a compass, a bowie knife and a derringer, a single-shot pistol. At 8 p.m., Booth held a final meeting with the other conspirators. Paine would assassinate Seward, Atzerodt would assassinate Johnson, Booth would assassinate Lincoln; all the attacks would take place at 10.15 p.m. They would meet at the Navy Yard Bridge and ride to Surrattsville. After that, Booth rode to Ford's Theatre, left his horse at the back and went to a tavern to get a bottle of whiskey. Another customer, assuming he was acting that night, quipped, 'You'll never be the actor your father was.' Booth answered cryptically, 'When I leave the stage, I'll be the most famous man in America.'

At 10 p.m., Booth climbed the stairs to the dress circle and saw the white door of Lincoln's State Box. A footman sat next to it. Booth gave him his card and opened the door into the dark area at the back of the box, wedging it shut with the leg of a music stand he had left there earlier. Then Booth opened the inner door, approached the President from behind and shot him in the head at close range.

In the confusion that followed, Booth may have shouted 'Sic semper tyrannis!' (Thus always to tyrants), though some in the audience thought he shouted this after he landed on the stage. Major Rathbone, who was sitting in the box, thought he shouted 'Freedom!' immediately after the shot. Rathbone grappled briefly with Booth, but was stabbed in the arm. Booth jumped over the front of the box and onto the stage. One of his spurs caught in one of the decorative flags draped over the balustrade, and he landed awkwardly, breaking his left leg just above the ankle. He managed to run across the stage, out of the theatre to his waiting horse, and rode away into the night.

At 11 p.m., Herold caught up with Booth and they made for Mary Surratt's tavern. Booth was preoccupied with the pain in his leg and as yet did not know that the rest of the conspiracy had failed. Azerodt had not killed Johnson and

Paine had not killed Seward (though he had slashed his face with a knife). Booth took some whiskey and got to Dr Mudd's house at 4 a.m. Dr Mudd attended to his broken leg.

It was several days before the army caught up with Booth and Herold. They were rumoured to be in the area between the Potomac and Rappahannock Rivers. Lieutenant Edward Doherty of the Sixteenth New York Cavalry followed their trail, picking up sightings from fishermen and ferrymen on 24 April. It was clear that Booth was assisted along his escape route by a rebel, Captain Willie Jett. Jett was tracked down to the house of his girlfriend's parents, the Goldmans, where he was found in bed with the Goldman's son. Jett was compelled to tell the soldiers where Booth was, and he undertook to lead them to the barn where Booth and Herold were hiding. Booth was defiant. He refused to surrender. When Doherty threatened to set fire to the barn, Booth admitted that Herold was keen to surrender, which he was allowed to do. As soon as Herold was out, a fire was started at the back of the barn. Sergeant Boston Corbett shot Booth in the neck for reasons that were left unexplained in Doherty's otherwise very detailed report, and Booth died two hours later. It is possible that Corbett caught sight of Booth through a crack in the wall of the barn and found the opportunity to shoot Booth too hard to resist. Ironically, Corbett was commended by Doherty for his action in 'bringing the murderers to justice', which he manifestly did not do. Whether Corbett was just over-zealous, or someone had given orders that Booth was not to be taken alive, is a matter for speculation. It may be that there were others involved in the conspiracy who were now to be protected. Similar thoughts revolve round the murder of Lee Harvey Oswald.

The authorities had Herold and were soon able to make further arrests; Booth's friends and associates were known, and a boarding-house owned by Mary Surratt was known to have been used by the conspirators. In fact, while the police were questioning Mary Surratt, Lewis Paine, the man who had attacked and wounded Secretary of State Seward with a knife, arrived at the door. Booth was dead, but eight other conspirators were rushed to trial: Lewis Paine, David Herold, Dr Samuel Mudd, Michael O'Laughlen, Edman Spangler, George Atzerodt, Mary Surratt and Samuel Arnold. Mary Surratt's son John would have made a ninth, but he managed to flee the country. The only other person directly accused was Jefferson Davis, the Confederate President, who was already in custody; it was believed that the assassination must have been ordered by the Confederate leaders, though proof was thin on the ground. As with many other assassinations, there may have been layers to the conspiracy. Behind the lone assassin there is often a group of conspirators who support the assassin in various ways and enable the assassination to take place. Behind that team there is often a well-concealed master, a regime, a government department or a terrorist organization that commissions and orders the killing. Conspiracies often nest inside one another like Russian dolls.

The trial took place in an atmosphere highly charged with emotion, and it is unlikely in the circumstances that justice was done. Key evidence, such as Booth's diary, was not revealed in court and much of the witness evidence was perjured. On 6 July, Paine, Herold and Atzerodt were sentenced to death by hanging. More startling was the death sentence passed on Mary Surratt. There was only unreliable hearsay evidence of her connection with the conspiracy, so she should have been acquitted; as it was, Mary Surratt became the first woman to be executed in the United States. The four were hanged, as much to satisfy the public hunger for vengeance as in the interests of justice. The other conspirators were given prison sentences. O'Laughlen died in prison. The others were pardoned in 1869, though still reviled and treated as pariahs. Dr Samuel Mudd's irretrievably damaged reputation gave rise to a new and potent saying: 'His name was Mudd.'

It was obvious that there was a conspiracy. The question was rather how many people were involved in it, how many layers. It is possible that Davis or his Secretary of State Judah Benjamin authorized Lincoln's assassination, though there is no evidence of this in Booth's diary. The entries in the diary imply that Booth was making all the decisions and that he was driven by personal hatred rather than working to orders from above.

There were rumours that Vice President Andrew Johnson had ordered the assassination. He had become President as a direct result of Lincoln's death and was in many respects a disreputable figure. He behaved very badly on Lincoln's inauguration day in 1865 by giving an incoherent speech while drunk. After the assassination, Mrs Lincoln wrote about Johnson to a friend, 'That miserable inebriate . . . As sure as you and I live, Johnson had some hand in all this.' And there were many who agreed with her. In 1866, Johnson's enemies in Congress set up an Assassination Committee, specifically to explore Johnson's suspected role in Lincoln's death. There was some compromising evidence, which Johnson was unable to explain away. A few hours before the assassination, Booth left a card for Johnson at the hotel where Johnson was staying. On the card, Booth had written the message, 'Don't wish to disturb you. Are you at home? J. Wilkes Booth.' This implied that Johnson knew Booth and, more dangerously, that they had some unspoken business to discuss together just seven hours before the assassination. What could it have been? No one was able to explain the card, but at the same time the Assassination Committee was unable to produce any proof that Johnson was involved in the plot.

Another theory brings the Secretary of War, Edwin Stanton, into the conspiracy as the mastermind who ordered the assassination. In the aftermath of the Civil War, Stanton favoured a vigorous and punitive approach towards the Confederates, while Lincoln wanted moderation, reconstruction and reconciliation. This serious difference of view could have given Stanton a motive for removing Lincoln. It has been alleged that after the assassination Stanton failed to send a telegraph message ordering Booth's arrest on the road to Maryland to give Booth the best chance of escape, but there were no telegraph facilities that Stanton could have used along that road, so that charge misfires. Stanton is known to have been responsible for leaving Lincoln unprotected at the theatre. Lincoln had wanted his bodyguard, Major Eckert, in attendance there but Stanton refused. Perhaps, as Stanton's defenders argue, Stanton was trying to press Lincoln to stay away from the theatre altogether, where he knew the President would be in danger, but it seems odd that he deliberately exposed him to what turned out to be fatal danger by withdrawing his bodyguard.

Probably there were other conspirators – probably there were conspirators who were guiltier than the unfortunate four who were hanged — but it seems unlikely that they will ever be identified now.

John Wilkes Booth had always wanted fame. In the end he achieved infamy. The assassination confirmed Lincoln's reputation as a great president, the man who had won the Civil War, saved the Union, abolished slavery. In the Lincoln Memorial he sits for ever transfigured, gigantically enthroned in marble like a modern Zeus. And, to an extent, it was his assassin, John Wilkes Booth, who put him there.

MAXIMILIAN I,
EMPEROR OF MEXICO

1867

MAXIMILIAN WAS BORN at Schönbrunn in Vienna in 1832, the second son of Archduke Franz Karl of Austria and his wife. His brother was Emperor Franz Josef of Austria. Maximilian was born as His Imperial and Royal Highness Ferdinand Maximilian Joseph, Prince Imperial and Archduke of Austria, Prince Royal of Hungary and Bohemia. He was an intelligent boy, with a taste for the arts and an early interest in science, especially botany.

He was trained for the navy, and threw himself into this career with great enthusiasm. It was Maximilian who was mainly responsible for creating the naval port of Trieste and the fleet with which Admiral Wilhelm von Tegetthoff won his victories in the Italian War. He was strongly influenced by the progressive ideas of the day, was seen as a Liberal, and this led to his appointment in 1857 as viceroy of the Lombardo-Venetian kingdom. His reactionary brother, the Emperor Franz Josef, saw to it that he was denied any significant share in the imperial government and that he would find no outlet for his dreams of liberal reform.

In the same year he married Princess Charlotte of Belgium, daughter of the infamous Leopold I, king of the Belgians. Maximilian and Charlotte lived as Austrian regents in Milan, until Emperor Franz Josef dismissed his brother Maximilian in 1859. Franz Josef was angered by the liberal policies his brother was pursuing. Shortly after this, Austria lost its control of most of its Italian possessions. After that Maximilian retired from public life, going to Trieste, where he built himself a castle called Miramar.

In 1859 an approach was made to him by Mexican monarchists. They proposed that Maximilian should become the emperor of Mexico. He did not accept at first. Instead he had a restless desire for adventure, which led to a botanical expedition to the rainforests of Brazil. Then the approach from Mexico was repeated. There was pressure from Napoleon III of France to accept. After the French captured Mexico City and ran a plebiscite which confirmed his proclamation of the empire, he consented to accept the Mexican crown in 1863.

Maximilian was in effect drafted in as head of state under false pretences. There had been a plebiscite, but it had been held while French troops were occupying the city, which meant that the vote did not genuinely reflect people's wishes. Maximilian was not told of the dubious nature of the plebiscite, and went to Mexico under the false impression that the majority of Mexicans wanted him there.

His decision to go to Mexico involved the loss of all his aristocratic rights in Austria, though the emperor did not inform him of this until the very last moment, just before he left for Mexico. Maximilian became an emperor and Charlotte became an empress, Her Imperial Majesty Empress Carlota.

While it is easy to feel pity for Maximilian and the awful situation he was being led into, there is something tragi-comic about the episode. Maximilian was given books about

Mexico to read on the voyage out, but instead of reading those, he spent the voyage writing a manual of Mexican court etiquette. On landing at Veracruz on 28 May 1864, Maximilian found himself in serious difficulties since the Mexican liberals led by Benito Juárez refused to recognize his rule and there was continuous warfare between his French troops and the Mexican republicans. Indeed, Maximilian's tenure rested solely and precariously on the presence of French troops, who drove Juárez and his army to the north. The European monarchs, except Napoleon III, were lukewarm to the enterprise. The Americans saw it as a violation of the Monroe Doctrine and were hostile; they were prevented from interfering only by the American Civil War, and once that was concluded they would intervene. From the outset, Maximilian was on borrowed time, though he seems to have had no understanding of the situation.

The emperor and empress set up their residence in the outskirts of Mexico City; it was Chapultepec Castle and it stood on a hilltop that had been a retreat for the Aztec emperors. Once again Maximilian got his priorities seriously wrong, when he ordered a wide avenue to be created from Chapultepec to the city centre; today it is known as *Paseo de la Reforma* (the Reform Promenade).

With the backing of Napoleon III of France and a group of Mexican conservatives, he was installed as emperor of Mexico on 10 April 1864. He was, however, not a natural choice for Mexico's head of state and many foreign governments refused to recognize his status. Many Mexicans refused to recognize him as well. His position was untenable from the outset. He was eventually captured by Mexican republicans, and they executed him.

Maximilian alienated his conservative allies by supporting liberal policies proposed by the Juárez administration – land reforms, religious freedom, extending the right to vote. He offered Juárez an amnesty if he would swear allegiance to the crown, but Juárez refused. The policy of compromise and appeasement gave way to sterner measures, and it was not long before Maximilian was ordering followers of Juárez to be shot on capture; this was a major tactical error that intensified opposition to his regime.

When the American Civil War ended the United States began supplying arms to the republicans. By 1866 it became obvious to observers round the world that Maximilian would have to abdicate. The French troops were withdrawn in the face of strong Mexican resistance within Mexico and in view of America's insistence that European interference in Mexico was unwelcome under the Monroe Doctrine. Carlota returned to Europe in an attempt to get help for her husband's regime. She went to Paris, Vienna and Rome, and found that there was no support at all. She suffered a severe breakdown and never went back to Mexico. Following the execution of her husband the following year, she spent the rest of her life in seclusion, first at Miramar Castle near Trieste, and then at the Château de Bouchout in Belgium, where she died in 1927.

Napoleon III urged Maximilian to abdicate and leave Mexico, but he refused to desert his followers. In February 1867, he retreated to Querétaro, where he was under siege for several weeks. On 11 May he decided to try to break out and escape, but he was intercepted, detained and sentenced to death. Many European heads of state and other major figures such as Victor Hugo wrote to Mexico begging for Maximilian's life to be spared, but Juárez refused to commute the sentence.

He was convinced that it was necessary to send a clear message to the outside world that Mexico would not tolerate imperialist interference.

Maximilian was executed by firing squad on 19 June, 1867, together with his generals Miguel Miramón and Tomás Mejía. The dead emperor's body was embalmed and displayed in Mexico before being sent back to Vienna for burial. It was buried in the Imperial Crypt in Vienna early in 1868.

A strange postscript to the tragedy of the Emperor Maximilian is the story of Justo Armas. He appeared in El Salvador in the late nineteenth century, quickly gaining access to many of the leading families in Salvadoran society, including the Lardés family. Don Justo had elegant European manners, spoke fluent and educated German, and seemed to have extensive knowledge of European aristocratic society, especially of Austria. Who was this unusual man? Where did he come from? Two theories have been proposed. One is that Justo Armas was the Crown Prince Rudolf, the only son of the Austro-Hungarian emperor Franz Josef. Rudolf is supposed to have committed suicide at Mayerling in 1889 together with his mistress Marie Vetsera. There were suspicions at the time that the crown prince was the target of a politically motivated assassination plot, and these allegations have persisted. But whatever lay behind the tragic events at Mayerling, if Rudolf did in fact die there he could hardly have become Justo Armas.

Enrique Lardé (1899–1993) claimed that he was the natural son of Justo Armas and that Justo Armas was Rudolf. According to Lardé, the Crown Prince Rudolf was given the chance to save his life by leaving Europe and adopting a new identity. Vetsera was pushed into entering a convent. Rudolf sailed for the New World but the ship went down in a storm while trying to pass through the Straits of Magellan. Everyone was drowned except Rudolf. For nearly 10 years Rudolf lived and worked in Argentina, then made his way to El Salvador where he arrived in 1898 under the alias Justo Armas. He lived in San Salvador until his death in 1936.

Lardé believed without reservation his mother's deathbed confession that he was the illegitimate son of Justo Armas, and there is no reason to doubt that. Justo Armas may well have told her, and she may have believed, that he was the former crown prince. But that second part of the story is far less credible than the first.

The second theory is that Justo Armas was the Emperor Maximilian.

The greatest hurdle of course is Maximilian's apparent execution in 1867. Exponents of this theory argue that Maximilian, Justo Armas, and Benito Júarez were all high-ranking members of the Masonic order and that an important law of freemasonry forbids the killing of brother Masons. Júarez was presented with a painful dilemma: Maximilian's annihilation was necessary for reasons of state, but he must not kill a fellow Mason. Júarez faked the execution, which was followed by Maximilian's total disappearance. Maximilian had to assume a new identity, and swear never to reveal who he was.

There is some corroboration for this story. The casket containing the embalmed body, supposedly of Maximilian, was sent home to Austria. When the casket was opened, his mother is said to have exclaimed, 'This is not my son!' Maximilian's high standing in the Masonic order was also key to the warm reception given to the unknown Justo Armas by members of the ruling elite of El Salvador. The nation's vice president and chancellor, don Gregorio Arbizú, welcomed him and found him a government job. Arbizú was a Mason and a monarchist, which may have strengthened their friendship. Armas was soon installed in a home of his own surrounded with dozens of objects that had belonged to Maximilian and which had somehow been conveyed from Mexico.

Justo Armas was said to bear a striking resemblance to Maximilian. Armas did confide his identity as the ex-emperor to at least one friend during his time in San Salvador. Then there was the visit in 1914 or 1915 by two emissaries of the Austrian government. These men apparently avoided contacts with Salvador government officials and instead persistently tried to interview Justo Armas, who was reluctant to meet them. When they finally met, the Austrians are said to have begged him to go back to Austria with them and take up his rightful position there. Armas refused outright to do what they asked.

It is difficult to know what to make of this strange and unusual conspiracy theory. On the whole it is more likely that Maximilian was shot by firing squad, simply because faking such a high-profile execution and keeping the victim's survival quiet indefinitely would have been extremely difficult. On the other hand, Maximilian may have been allowed to escape; that at least seems more likely than the Crown Prince Rudolf scenario. Could more be done to test Justo Armas's identity? DNA testing is an obvious possibility. *La Tierra Ligera* and other sources report that such tests have already been undertaken, and that the results show that Justo Armas was indeed related to the Habsburgs, but so far that DNA evidence is mere hearsay.

ALEXANDER II OF RUSSIA

1881

ALEXANDER II, TSAR of Russia, was born in Moscow on 17 April, 1818. He was the eldest son of Tsar Nicholas I of Russia and Charlotte of Prussia. His early life gave no indication that he would be known to posterity as the great reforming tsar. In his youth he seemed to possess the reactionary spirit predominant in Europe at the time, a trend which continued in Russia through to the end of his father's reign. For the 30 years during which he was heir apparent, the atmosphere in St Petersburg was hostile to intellectual and political innovation. Freedom of thought and private initiative were vigorously suppressed. Censorship prevailed, and any criticism of the authorities was a serious offence.

To his father's disappointment, Alexander showed no interest in military affairs. The kindness and tender-heartedness which marked his personality were considered highly unsuitable traits in a tsar-in-waiting.

When his father died in 1855, and Alexander succeeded as tsar, he inherited the responsibility for the Crimean War. After the fall of Sebastopol, he was involved in the negotiations for peace headed by Prince Gorchakov. It was only when all that was out of the way that Alexander was able to launch his radical reforms. Russia had been exhausted and humiliated by the war, and needed rejuvenating with wide-ranging reforms. The government found in the educated classes a new public spirit, anxious to assist it in any work of reform that it might think fit to undertake.

Russia was fortunate in its new tsar, who was a committed liberal, but also prudent and practical enough to prevent the liberalizing movement from running out of control. Alexander had no grand, original scheme of his own that he wanted to impose by force. Instead he worked to bring to fruition the reforming aspirations of the educated classes.

He was careful to protect his autocratic rights and privileges, and resisted efforts to push him further than he wanted to go; at the same time, for several years Alexander acted like a European constitutional monarch. Alexander was outflanked by the growth of a revolutionary movement to the left of the educated classes. In pursuing the sane middle course of cautious reform, Alexander inevitably became a target for assassination plots by left wing extremists as well as a target for vehement criticism from the right. There were attempts on his life in 1866, 1873 and 1880.

The existence of serfdom emerged as an obstacle to the general reform movement. Alexander decided to deal with this problem head-on. An opportunity arose when a petition was presented to him by the Polish landowners in Lithuania, who hoped that their relations with the serfs might be regulated in a more satisfactory way. What the landowners meant was they wanted to be able to deal with serfs in a way that suited the landowners. The tsar's response was to instigate the formation of committees 'for improving the condition of the peasants' and laid down guidelines for this improvement.

Then Alexander ordered the Minister of the Interior to send a circular to all the provincial governors of European

Russia, enclosing a copy of the instructions forwarded to Lithuania, and praising the generous and patriotic initiative of the Lithuanian landowners. He suggested that the landed proprietors of other provinces might express a similar desire. The tsar's hint was taken, and emancipation committees were formed in all the provinces where serfdom existed.

The emancipation was not a humanitarian question that could be solved simply by imperial edict. It carried with it complex problems that would affect the economic, social and political future of Russia. Alexander had insufficient knowledge to deal successfully with such problems, and had to choose between the different measures recommended to him. The main point at issue was whether the serfs should become agricultural labourers dependent economically and administratively on the landlords, or whether they should be transformed into a class of independent communal proprietors. Alexander courageously decided on the latter, and the Russian peasants were among the last in Europe to shake off serfdom.

The emancipation manifesto was written by Alexander's brother Konstantin, Yakov Rostovtsev and Nikolay Milyutin. In March 1861, six years after his accession, the emancipation law was passed. Other major reforms followed. The army and navy were reorganized; the judicial administration was reformed on the French model; a new penal code was introduced; a new scheme of local government for the rural districts and townships was introduced. Perhaps inevitably, people started to expect more than Alexander was prepared or able to give. Workers wanted better working conditions. Ethnic minorities wanted more freedom too.

Then left-wing radicals began to form secret societies and work towards revolution, and Alexander II had to fall back on severe repressive measures. Alexander was not always progressive or lenient. He made it clear that Polish dreams of independence from Russia were exactly that – dreams. The result was the January Rising of 1863–4, which was suppressed after more than a year of fighting. Thousands of Poles were executed, tens of thousands deported to Siberia. All the territories of the former Poland-Lithuania were excluded from the liberal polices Alexander introduced, and the martial law introduced in Lithuania in 1863 lasted for the next 50 years. Native languages, Lithuanian, Ukrainian and Belarusian, were completely banned from printed texts; Polish was banned in both oral and written form.

In 1866 Dmitry Karakozov tried to assassinate him in St Petersburg. To commemorate the tsar's narrow escape, churches and chapels were built in many Russian cities. A competition to design a great gate for the city of Kiev was held. The architect Viktor Hartmann won the competition, and his design was well-received, but it would never be built.

One morning in April 1879, Alexander II was walking towards the Square of the Guards Staff when he found himself face to face with Alexander Soloviev. The tsar saw that Soloviev had a revolver and ran away. Soloviev fired five shots after the retreating emperor: they all missed. Soloviev was sentenced to death and hanged. Soloviev acted alone, but other revolutionaries were organizing elaborate conspiracies to kill Alexander. The People's Will was one such radical revolutionary group which hoped to ignite a social revolution. The People's Will decided to assassinate Alexander. The following month Andrei Zhelyabov and Sophia Perovskaya used nitroglycerine to destroy the tsar's train. However, the terrorists miscalculated and the wrong train was destroyed.

A few days after the explosion, Sophia Perovskaya appeared at one of the party's secret meeting places in an apartment in St Petersburg. She told with great emotion the story of the Moscow attempt. It was she who had waited in the bushes for the tsar's train to approach, she who had given the signal for the explosion that blew up the tracks. But there had been too little dynamite, and she regretted that so much had been sent to another operation in the south, instead of concentrating it all in Moscow. She was shaking, overwhelmed by a sense of failure. But she would try again.

Then Stefan Khalturin, a carpenter who was also a member of the People's Will, managed to find work in the Winter Palace. He was allowed to sleep on the premises, and each day he brought packets of dynamite into his room and concealed them in his bedding. On 17 February, 1880, Khalturin detonated the dynamite in the room directly under the tsar's dining room. The explosion went off at 6.30 p.m., when Alexander would be likely to be at the table. However, his main guest that evening arrived late, dinner was delayed and the dining-room was empty. The tsar was unharmed but 67 other people were killed or badly wounded by the explosion.

After the attack on the Winter Palace, Count Loris-Melikov was appointed the head of the Supreme Executive Commission with the order to fight the revolutionaries. Loris-Melikov called for some form of parliamentary body, which was the goal of the revolutionaries. The tsar agreed to this, but the People's Will became increasingly angry at the failure of the Russian government to announce details of the new constitution; they thought the tsar was playing for time. They began to make plans for another assassination attempt.

On 13 March, 1881 Alexander finally fell victim to one of

the many assassination plots. A few weeks earlier, the police uncovered the existence of a plot led by Andrei Zhelyabov to kill the tsar. Zhelyabov was arrested and questioned but refused to provide any information on the conspiracy. He confidently told the police that there was nothing they could do to save the life of the tsar.

Alexander was travelling in a closed carriage from the Michaelovsky Palace to the Winter Palace in St Petersburg. An armed Cossack sat with the coach-driver and another six Cossacks followed on horseback. Behind them came a group of police officers on sledges. All along the route the carriage was watched by members of the People's Will. On a street corner not far from the Catherine Canal, Sophia Perovskaya gave the signal to Nikolai Rysakov and Timofei Mikhailov to throw their bombs at the tsar's carriage. The bombs missed the carriage and instead landed amongst the Cossacks. The tsar was unhurt but insisted on getting out of the carriage to check the condition of the injured men. The tsar's coachman earnestly advised him not to get out, saying that he could still drive him to safety in the slightly damaged carriage, but to no avail; the tsar insisted on getting out. Rysakov was arrested on the spot.

It was entirely characteristic of Tsar Alexander that he refused to leave the scene until he had enquired into the condition of the wounded Cossacks. One was dead; the others must be removed to hospital and cared for at once. A police officer begged the tsar to get into his carriage and drive away, but Alexander ignored him, instead going to Rysakov to ask him something. As he passed close to another young man, Ignatei Grinevitski (or Hryniewiecki), threw a bomb at him. There was a terrific explosion,which blew the tsar to pieces. His clothing was torn to rags and his orders and medals scattered on the snow. One of his legs was blown off; the other was completely shattered. Windows a hundred yards away were broken. The assassin himself was terribly injured. They both lived just a few hours.

Tsar Alexander II lay on the snow, mortally wounded and bleeding profusely, abandoned by his attendants, who had all run for cover. It was some cadets returning from parade who lifted the terribly injured tsar from the snow and put him on a sledge. They covered his shivering body with a cadet's cloak and his bare head with a cadet's cap. One of the terrorists, Emeliánov, with a bomb still wrapped up under his arm and at huge risk to himself, was overwhelmed by the pitiful sight of the wounded man and instinctively rushed to help him. It was a strange moment, when this assassin suddenly understood the awful human reality of an assassination.

Word spread fast through St Petersburg. There had been two huge explosions, the first was a bomb thrown under the ironclad carriage to immobilize it, the second was a bomb thrown at the tsar himself; the sovereign had been killed; the accession of his heir, Alexander III, was already being announced. The streets were in turmoil. The net closed in on the conspirators, as one by one they were traced and arrested. One of the women, Gesia Gelfman, was found fairly quickly. Sablin shot himself. Within the next two weeks, Sophia Perovskaya was recognized on the street and arrested, then Kibalchich and Frolenko were arrested. Those who remained, including Vera Figner, one of the planners, were advised by their committee to leave St Petersburg at once.

The principal assassin had died with the tsar. Of the other conspirators, Nikolai Sablin committed suicide before he could be arrested and Gesia Gelfman died in prison. Sophia

Perovskaya, Andrei Zhelyabov, Nikolai Kibalchich, Nikolai Rysakov and Timofei Mikhailov were hanged on 3 April 1881. And did they achieve the further liberalization of Russia as they wanted? Quite the opposite. The assassination was seen in reactionary circles as the predictably negative consequence of reform; it justified oppression and retrenchment.

PRESIDENT JAMES GARFIELD

1881

EARLY IN 1881 the newly inaugurated President of the United States, James Abram Garfield, received a series of letters from a stranger by the name of Charles J. Guiteau. The unknown correspondent wanted a job in the diplomatic service. First he asked to be sent to Austria, telling the President, 'Next spring I expect to marry the daughter of a deceased New York Republican millionaire, and I think we can represent the United States government at the court of Vienna with dignity and grace.' He changed his mind and in another letter wrote, 'I think I prefer Paris to Vienna.' Guiteau was a fantasist. He saw himself as a person of consequence. In the 1880 campaign he had written and distributed a tract in favour of Garfield. Now that Garfield had been elected, Guiteau thought Garfield owed him something in return.

Charles Julius Guiteau was born on 8 September, 1841 in Freeport, Illinois. He was the fourth of six children of Luther Wilson Guiteau and Jane Howe. When Charles's mother died, he was only seven and his father remarried.

As a young man, Charles worked for his father as a clerk, and was then employed as a cashier in a local bank. Luther was against sending his son to college, but in 1859 Charles inherited enough money from a grandfather to enable him to go to the University of Michigan. Charles had been discontented at home. Now he was even more discontented at university. He turned to religion, and in particular to the doctrines of John Humphrey Noyes, who had founded the Oneida Community in New York State; it was a kind of communism based on the Bible. As it happened, his father was already a devotee of Noyes' teaching. In 1860, Charles joined the Oneida Community in New York. But even this did not make him happy, and in 1865 he left the community, convinced that he had been called by God to spread Noyes' millennial communism by founding a newspaper.

Guiteau then settled in Hoboken, New Jersey, and tried to set up his new newspaper, which he called *The Daily Theocrat*. It did not last, and within a few months he was asking to be let back into the community. A year later he left it again.

By August 1867, Charles Guiteau had run himself out of money. His brother-in-law George Scoville generously offered him a job in his law office in Chicago, and a home. Still he could not settle. Within a few months he resigned his post and went back to New York, apparently to work on the *Independent* newspaper, but this work was more menial than he was anticipating; he ended up selling advertising space. By 1868, Guiteau was back in Chicago, where he got a clerical job in another law office.

In 1868, he married Annie Bunn, who was a librarian. It proved to be an unhappy relationship, basically because Guiteau was an unhappy maladjusted man tottering on the edge of sanity. He maltreated his wife, locking her in a closet for nights at a time. In 1874, she divorced him.

After the failure of his marriage, Guiteau's behaviour became more erratic and peculiar than ever. The inner restlessness was coming more and more to the surface. When he was chopping wood one day, he unaccountably threatened his sister Frances with the axe he was holding; frightened, she ran to tell the doctor, who said she should have him confined in an institution. The Guiteau family as a whole must by this time have realized that Charles was insane. Guiteau ran off and disappeared. The following year he reappeared as a regular attender of revivalist meetings. He became an itinerant preacher, writing his own sermons.

Guiteau's father died in 1880, and for some reason Charles then turned to politics. He supported Garfield in the 1880 campaign and then became disillusioned in the early months of 1881, when the new President ignored his requests for a position. He harassed White House staff in his quest for a job. By May 1881, Guiteau realized he was getting nowhere. Angry and frustrated, he decided to assassinate Garfield.

He wrote several drafts of a letter opening, 'I have just shot the President.' He was fantasizing about what it would feel like to have committed the act, trying on the costume of an assassin, and it evidently fed his sense of self-importance. On 16 June, 1881, he wrote an *Address to the American People*. He wrote a letter to the White House and another to General Sherman, saying 'I have just shot the President. His death was a political necessity. I am a lawyer, theologian and politician. I am a Stalwart of the Stalwarts . . .' and so on. These were obviously the ravings of a madman, and they were probably consigned to the waste paper basket accordingly, but they were no less dangerous for that.

On the day of his assassination, President Garfield was in

high spirits, doing handstands on his son's bed. On the morning of 2 July, 1882, Garfield went to the Baltimore and Potomac Railroad Station with the intention of travelling north to attend a college reunion. At 8.30 a.m., Garfield walked through the waiting room with Secretary of State Blaine, when Charles Guiteau came up behind him and fired at him twice with a .44 calibre Bulldog pistol. The first bullet grazed Garfield's arm and stuck in a lump of putty in the box of a glass-cutter. The second hit him full in the back and proved to be fatal.

The shooting took place in front of a group of the President's staff and doctors were sent for. A well-known Washington physician, Dr Bliss, arrived and, presumably overwhelmed by the gravity of the situation, performed the following actions; he put hot water bottles on Garfield's feet, took them off again, opened a window, closed it again, poked his finger into the wound in the President's back, and then called for a local doctor. Dr Reyburn thought the call to attend a bullet-ridden President must be a hoax, and took his time travelling to the President's bedside. This unsatisfactory embryonic medical team decided to hoist the President onto a mattress and carry him back to the White House. They gave him a morphine injection. Garfield vomited and this they put down to the injection, whereas it was almost certainly a response to the wound.

It was not until 5.30 p.m., nine hours after the shooting, that the doctors decided to remove the bloodstained suit. They gave him a glass of champagne, which he threw up. He continued vomiting all night. Another doctor appeared, Navy Surgeon General Wales, and he stuck his finger into the President's back wound. He announced that the bullet had hit the liver. Next Dr Frank Hamilton of New York stuck his finger in the wound and encountered a clot, so he promptly pulled it out again. Incredibly, fifteen different doctors in all stuck their fingers and a variety of unsterilized instruments into the President's wound. Contemporary commentators said there were just too many doctors involved; but it is their incompetence that is so breathtaking.

All kinds of mad but well-meant suggestions poured into the White House. One telegram proposed hanging the President upside down so that the bullet would fall out. Joseph Lister had been advocating the use of antiseptic methods in surgery since 1865, but there were still a lot of backwoodsmen in the medical profession. Pus was seen as a good sign in a wound, and some doctors took a pride in the filthy conditions in which they worked. Healing and recovery were expected to be slow. With old-fashioned medics like these around him, Garfield could not expect to survive at all. His death was certain.

Guiteau, meanwhile, was immediately arrested and taken into custody. The railway policeman, a man called Patrick Kearney, was so excited to have arrested this important assassin that he completely forgot to take Guiteau's gun from him. It was only when Guiteau reached the police station that he was disarmed. A reporter turned up to draw a sketch of the villain for his newspaper. Guiteau promptly demanded a 25 dollar fee for this. Soldiers were posted outside to stop a lynch mob seizing him. After a time, he was taken to the District of Columbia Jail to await his trial.

The President, who lived on for several weeks, was given entirely unsuitable food for a wounded man. He was given steak, eggs and brandy. Gradually his body was taken over by blood poisoning. His wound became severely infected and by 19 August, his face had become so swollen that his right eye was completely shut. Several incisions were made in his face to drain the pus. James Garfield eventually died miserably on 19 September. One medical journal commented, 'President Garfield's case has been the most grossly mismanaged in modern history,' and accused his doctors of blaming Providence.

Up until the moment of Garfield's death, Guiteau stood a chance of getting off on an insanity plea. But after the death, it looked less certain.

Guiteau's trial opened on 14 November, 1881, and went on until January 1882. A plea of insanity to President Chester A. Arthur was entered by neurologists as well as by the Guiteau family. Guiteau tried to persuade the jury that inspiration for the assassination had come from God himself. Guiteau played the insanity card very clumsily though. While he was in prison, he had been organizing lucrative lecture tours that he would give on his release and he had also dictated his autobiography to the press. He was clearly expecting to be at liberty in the near future.

He seemed oblivious of many signals that his future was not going to be as straightforward or as pleasant as he liked to imagine. He got a flood of letters while in prison. One of them read, 'You dirty, lousy, lying rebel traitor; hanging is too good for you, you stinking cuss. We will keep you spotted, you stinking pup. You damned old mildewed assassin. You ought to be burned alive and let rot. You savage cannibal dog.'

When the news came that Garfield had died, Guiteau still misread the situation. He suddenly felt vindicated. God had after all been on his side.

Guiteau's plea began, 'I plead not guilty to the indictment and my defence is threefold: 1. Insanity, in that it was God's act and not mine . . . I am not legally responsible for my act. 2. The president died from malpractice . . . if he had been well treated he would have recovered. 3. The president died in New Jersey and therefore beyond the jurisdiction of this court.'

Guiteau's own brother-in-law, George Scoville, was his defence lawyer. The prosecuting lawyer was George Corkhill. Guiteau's behaviour during the trial was as erratic and bizarre as it had been for several years past. When Guiteau saw the great crowd in the court room, he decided to take advantage of it. He scribbled little notes and passed them back to the crowd. One of the notes read, 'I am charged with maliciously and wickedly murdering one James A. Garfield. Nothing can be more absurd, because General Garfield died from malpractice . . . The issue here is Who fired that shot, the Deity or me?' What he hoped to gain from these performances is hard to tell. They would certainly seem to support the idea that he really was insane.

In his opening statement, Leigh Robinson, who was assisting Scoville, lost his nerve. He asked for a postponement of the trial, mentioning a possible third lawyer who would join their team. This provoked an angry outburst from Guiteau: 'I do not want to hear any more speeches of Mr Robinson's. I want him to get out of the case . . . Mr Robinson came into the case without consulting me. I know nothing about him. I don't like the way he talks. I expect to have some money shortly and I can employ any counsel I please.'

Scoville was evidently also angry with Robinson, saying in front of the whole court room that Robinson ought to say who this mysterious third lawyer was. Robinson had evidently not discussed the postponement proposal or the third lawyer with Scoville beforehand.

And so it went on, with Guiteau interrupting all the time and sabotaging his own lawyers' efforts. At one point he said, to his own lawyer, 'You are about as consummate a jackass, I must say, as I ever saw. I would rather have some ten-year-old boy try this case than you.' Scoville even resorted to appealing to the court to stop his client from directly addressing the press.

Even Guiteau began to realize that all was not going well when he was in the prison wagon and a bullet whizzed through the grille, piercing his coat though not his body. It was a drunken farmer who had taken a pot-shot at him. The assassin's would-be assassin missed, but he was still hailed as a national hero by the press.

Guiteau loved playing to the gallery, though. His trial dragged on into the New Year, and he addressed the crowd in the court room, 'I had a nice Christmas. I hope everyone else did. I had plenty of visitors, high-toned, middle-toned and low-toned people. That takes in the whole crowd. Public opinion don't want me hung.'

On 23 January the jury deliberated for less than an hour before agreeing on a guilty verdict. He was sentenced to death. The insanity plea was rejected and a writ of execution was issued. Still he did not give up. He tried to sell for a hundred dollars the suit he had worn when he shot Garfield. He sold his autographs and autographed photographs, which he advertised in local papers. One wonders what he thought he would do with the money.

On 30 June, 1882, Charles Guiteau was led away to be hanged at the District of Columbia Jail. He requested that the flowers he assumed had been sent in by his legions of admirers should be placed in his cell, only to be told that there were no flowers at all. Then, while actually facing the noose, he recited an endless, repetitive, poem he had written. It went, 'I am going to the Lordy, I am so glad. I am going to the Lordy, I am so glad. I am going to the Lordy, I am so glad,' and so on – until he was stopped. In becoming the President's assassin, Guiteau finally found out who and what he was; it was the purpose and the role for which he had been searching all his life until then. And he certainly loved being the centre of attention – that feeling of importance, of being a celebrity, of becoming a part of the fabric of history. He and the yet-unborn Lee Harvey Oswald had a lot in common.

There is no doubt that Guiteau, and Guiteau alone and unaided, fired the shots that caused Garfield's death, but with proper medical treatment (even by the standards of the 1880s) even the wound in the back need not have been fatal. Garfield died as much through medical incompetence as through the hands of the mad lone assassin.

MARIE FRANÇOIS SADI CARNOT

1894

MARIE FRANÇOIS SADI Carnot, President of France, was the grandson of Lazare Carnot, the great organizer of the First Republic's armies. Lazare Carnot also served under Napoleon during the Consulate, and again during the Hundred Days, when the emperor was forced to seek the support of liberal-minded Republicans. Lazare Carnot was one of these, and his Republicanism was sincere. After the Revolution of 1848 Lazare's son, Louis Hippolyte, became a member of the Provisional Government and subsequently resisted the *coup d'etat* of Louis Napoleon. Both of Louis' sons, Marie François Sadi and Adolphe, entered the Ecole Polytechnique.

Sadi Carnot became a civil engineer in the Roads and Bridges Service. During the Franco-Prussian War he was responsible for placing Le Havre in a state of defence, and trying to ensure the provisioning of Paris by way of the Seine. In the National Assembly he became secretary to the group called the Republican Left, and after M. Grevy had been elected President of the Republic he became Minister for Public Works, then Minister of Finances. It was in that capacity that Carnot stoutly refused to further the interests of a trading company run by Grevy's son in law, Daniel Wilson.

Wilson's conduct brought about the fall of Grevy and in December 1887 Carnot, who maintained a reputation for high integrity, was elected to the Presidency.

The period of Carnot's presidency was one of great unrest in France, largely due to Boulangist agitation. Carnot collaborated with his ministers in removing General Boulanger from active service. But there were also financial scandals, and Carnot had difficulty in dealing with them all. There were strikes among the working classes and there was the Anarchist Terror too.

Carnot decided not to seek re-election when his term of office came to an end. He was not a weak man but at the same time he was no match for either of his chief ministers, Casimir-Perier and Dupuy, who were determined to wield all the power. He decided to retire, leaving them to fight out between them the question of supremacy, as indeed they did, after his death. The result was that both of them had to retire from office, Casimir-Perier withdrawing altogether from political life.

Carnot himself was respected on every side, by people of every political persuasion, for his sincerely felt Republican views and his steadfast integrity. He was very popular with the ordinary French people out in the provinces. He travelled round France a great deal, opening hospitals and exhibitions, presiding over national and local gatherings of many kinds. At the time of the Paris Exhibition of 1889, while he was on his way to Versailles, he was fired at by an insane young man named Perrin, who was afterwards sentenced to four months' imprisonment, but throughout all the Anarchist Terror in Paris there was no attempt to assassinate Carnot, even though he constantly showed himself in public.

In June 1894, President Carnot decided to visit a Colonial Exhibition at Lyons, accompanied by Dupuy the Prime Minister, General Borius and other staff. The train stopped at Dijon, where several members of Carnot's family were waiting at the station to exchange greetings with him. There was a brief but cordial conversation, the President embraced his children and grandchildren, and the train continued on its way.

Lyons was a city with a large number of extremists. Some were radicals, some were socialists and some were anarchists. Even so, Carnot was given a warm welcome when he arrived there on the evening of Saturday 23 June. On the Sunday he attended a series of receptions, visited the Colonial Exhibition, and in the evening he dined as the city's guest at the Palais du Commerce. His health was proposed by Dr Gailleton, the mayor of Lyons, and in response Carnot gave a short but impressive speech. Everyone knew he did not wish to be re-elected and the speech was taken as a farewell. Carnot eloquently appealed for peace and unity in France and for there to be no pause in the march towards progress and justice.

After the banquet was over, the President and the other guests prepared to go to the Grand Theatre, where there was to be a gala performance. It was not far and Carnot had proposed to go on foot, but someone told the mayor that the President was tired, so Dr Gailleton provided a landau. Carnot seated himself in the carriage with the mayor. Also in the carriage were General Borius, the chief of his military household, and General Voisin, the commander of the Lyons garrison. A detachment of soldiers rode in front of the carriage as it turned out of the Place des Cordeliers into the Rue de la Republique.

The street was crowded with people waiting to cheer the President on his way to the theatre. There were shouts of 'Vive Carnot! Vive la Republique! Vive le President!' There were so many people that the mounted soldiers and the carriage were only able to move at walking pace. It was a little after nine o'clock. Carnot evidently enjoyed all this. He sat on the right-hand side of the landau, smiling and waving. He asked a soldier riding beside him to fall back so that he could be seen better. That request sealed his fate as surely as President Kennedy's decision to ride through Dallas in an open-topped car.

Seizing his opportunity, a young man suddenly sprang to the landau, holding in his raised right hand a paper which was supposed to be a petition. The carriage doors were locked, but the sides of the vehicle were low, and the young man was able to reach over and strike the President. Concealed inside the roll of paper was a dagger, which he left sticking into Carnot as he sprang down. The assassin dived in front of the carriage horses and across the street into the watching crowd.

A young servant girl of about 18 caught hold of his sleeve in order to stop him getting away. He wrenched himself free, punched her, and was then grabbed by two or three policemen. An official ran up shouting, 'Hold him tight! He has just assassinated the President!' There were shouts of amazement, horror and fury from the crowd. It seemed for a moment as if the assassin would be lynched, but policemen and soldiers closed round him, pushed back the crowd, and finally carried him away.

Carnot meanwhile shouted, 'I am wounded!' He pulled the dagger out and dropped it in the road. Then he sank back into the carriage and lost consciousness. It had all happened so quickly that neither of the generals had been able to do anything to prevent the attack. The assassin had inflicted one wound and that was mortal. Afterwards, Dr Gailleton, the mayor who was a medic, did what he could. Dr Poncet, the Professor of Surgery at the Lyons Faculty of Medicine, arrived immediately. He too did what he could, while the soldiers cleared the road and the landau made its way to the Prefecture as speedily as possible.

The knife had perforated Carnot's liver and severed the portal vein. Nothing could stop the bleeding. All the medics' efforts were to no avail, though they did manage to keep him alive for another three hours. Before Sadi Carnot died, it became known that the assassin was an Italian, which unleashed an outburst of xenophobic fury against the Italian colony in Lyons. Cafes, taverns and shops run by Italians were wrecked. People with Italian-sounding names were set upon. The assassination had an effect in Italy too, where the government ordered the arrest of hundreds of anarchists.

Carnot's body arrived in Paris on 26 June. It lay in state at the Elysee Palace until the funeral at Notre Dame, after which it was buried under the dome of the Pantheon.

At Lyons, the authorities discovered that the assassin was Santo-Geronimo Caserio, the 20-year-old son of a North Italian bargeman. At the age of 18 Caserio was imprisoned for distributing anarchist tracts to soldiers. Then, to avoid army service, he fled first to Switzerland and then to Lyons. Unable to find work in Lyons, Caserio went to the town of Cette, where he fell in with other anarchists. He was at Cette when Vaillant threw his bomb in the Chamber of Deputies. When attempts to obtain (from President Carnot) a reprieve for Vaillant failed and Vaillant was executed, there were threats to avenge his death, and it is likely that Caserio's crime was connected with Vaillant's execution. Caserio was certainly not part of an international conspiracy, as some thought at the time; his crime was planned at Cette and he seems to have committed it unaided. Under questioning, he declared that he had wanted to avenge Vaillant, who had killed nobody and had therefore been put to death unjustly. He consistently denied having any accomplices or telling anyone what he was going to do. The assassination was nevertheless the culmination of a series of anarchist terrorist attacks in western Europe.

When the day for the President's visit to Lyons was announced, Caserio deliberately picked a quarrel with his employer in Cette. This resulted in his instant dismissal and the payment of the wages due to him. He used this money to buy a knife and the rail tickets he needed to take him to Lyons by way of Montpellier, Tarascon and Vienne. Running out of money, he had to walk the last 19 miles and arrived in Lyons only an hour before he stabbed Carnot.

When he was sentenced to death Caserio turned pale and began to tremble. At his execution on 16 August he broke down completely, hysterically shouting, 'I won't go! I won't go!' He had to be dragged to the guillotine and held down by the executioner's two assistants.

The Anarchist Terror was seen as a very real threat to the security of the West. Prince Kropotkin had called for violent action, 'propaganda through deeds', at the International Revolutionary Congress in London in 1881. The first major symbolic acts of violence had in fact been committed a few years earlier, with the assassinations of William I of Prussia, the king of Spain and the king of Italy. And the seven unsuccessful attempts on Queen Victoria's life should not be forgotten. The new age of terrorism was the age of the bomb, and dynamite could be used against kings, presidents or entire buildings. Attacks were launched in several countries at the same time and this encouraged the idea that a powerful international conspiracy was at work – the Black International. The assassination of Tsar Alexander II in 1881 and other terrorist acts of the People's Will inspired anarchists throughout Europe.

The United States was similarly affected. President William McKinley was assassinated by an anarchist in 1901 during a period of social unrest. The US authorities and public were convinced that the country faced an international threat. It was a world haunted by the spectre of international terrorism. The ruling classes could not understand the reasons for the hatred and each act of violence increased their fear of revolt from below. Workers were seen as potential criminals and anarchists, as maniacs who must be destroyed at all costs. President McKinley's successor, Theodore Roosevelt, described terrorism as a 'crime against the human race'.

The assassination of President Carnot in 1894 prompted governments and police forces to take action. The first proposal for international co-operation came from Italy, a country regarded as the seedbed of international terrorism. Italians had been implicated in a number of assassination attempts on heads of state, which meant that the large numbers of Italian migrants and seasonal workers were regarded with increasing suspicion and hostility. The International Anti-Anarchist Conference opened in Rome in November 1898; the 21 participating states unanimously agreed that anarchism should not be regarded as a bona fide political doctrine and that attacks by self-proclaimed anarchists were criminal offences for which they could be extradited. This expression of international unity and solidarity had few real results, mainly because by 1900 anarchism was already in decline. The Black International, originally thought of as a cunningly concealed yet powerful revolutionary organization, was entirely fictitious, a fantasy that existed only in the imaginations of politicians, the police and the press. There was no international conspiracy.

UMBERTO I OF ITALY

1900

UMBERTO I WAS born in Turin in 1844, the son of Victor Emmanuel II and Adelaide, archduchess of Austria, who gave him the unmanageable name Umberto Ranieri Carlo Emanuele Giovanni Maria Ferdinando Eugenio di Savoy. Umberto's military career in the Sardinian army began in 1858 at the rank of captain. He was present at the Battle of Solferino in the following year, and in 1866 he commanded a division at the Battle of Custoza.

On 21 April, 1868 Umberto married his cousin, Margherita Teresa Giovanna, princess of Savoy. Their son was Victor Emmanuel, prince of Naples, and he was later to succeed Umberto as Victor Emmanuel III of Italy. On the death of his father in January 1878, Umberto significantly adopted the title 'Umberto I of Italy' rather than 'Umberto IV of Savoy'.

Umberto was not a popular king. He was loathed by socialists and anarchists because of his hard-line conservatism in general and in particular because he condoned the Bava Beccaris massacre in Milan. More than one attempt was made to assassinate him. While he was on a tour of Italy with his premier Benedetto Cairoli in November 1878, he was attacked by an anarchist, Giovanni Passanante. The incident happened during a parade in Naples. During the attack, Umberto warded off the blow with his sabre and was unhurt.

Cairoli attempted to defend the king and was badly wounded in the thigh. Passanante was condemned to death, but the king commuted the sentence to one of penal servitude for life. The incident was nevertheless a sign of what lay ahead for the king and it upset the health of Umberto's wife, Queen Margherita, for several years afterwards.

Umberto's reign was a time of social upheaval in Italy. Socialist ideas were in the air, there was public hostility against the colonialist plans of the various governments, and there were crackdowns on civil liberties. There was protest, and among the protesters was the young Benito Mussolini. Umberto himself favoured colonial expansion. In fact it was suspected that he wanted to create an enormous empire in north-east Africa; this did not add to his popularity.

During the colonial wars in Africa, there were protest demonstrations in Italy over the rising price of bread. In response, in May 1898 the city of Milan was put under military control by General Fiorenzo Bava-Beccaris. Bava-Beccaris ordered cannons to be fired on the demonstrators and as a result of this barbaric order between 100 and 350 people were killed and a thousand wounded. King Umberto insensitively and foolishly sent General Bava-Beccaris a telegram of congratulation and later decorated him with a prestigious medal. Both the deaths and the king's callousness regarding them outraged many Italians.

He reduced his unpopularity somewhat by being firm in his policy towards the Vatican. He declared Rome 'untouchable' and affirmed that the Vatican City was a permanent Italian possession. But his steadily increasing unpopularity led to further attempts on his life. In Rome in April 1897 an unemployed ironsmith called Pietro Acciarito tried to stab him.

Finally, three years later, he was murdered at Monza. On the evening of 28 July, 1900, King Umberto I of Italy dined with his aide in a restaurant in Monza, where he was due to attend an athletics meeting the next day. The king was astonished when he saw that the restaurant proprietor looked exactly like him and, overtaken by curiosity, he opened a conversation with his host. A whole string of parallels emerged. Not only did the restaurateur *look* like the king, he had the same name, Umberto. Like the king, he had been born in Turin and even shared his birthday. He had married a girl called Margherita on the same day the king married his queen, also called Margherita. The crowning coincidence was that he had opened his restaurant on the day that Umberto I became king of Italy.

The king was astonished and delighted to have found his double. He invited him to attend the athletics meeting with him. But it was not to be. The following day at the stadium the king's aide informed him that Umberto the restaurateur had died that morning in a mysterious shooting accident. The king expressed his regret at this sad news, and at that moment he himself was shot dead by an anarchist in the crowd.

The king was felled with four revolver shots fired by an Italian-American anarchist called Gaetano Bresci. Bresci himself explained that he wanted to avenge the people killed by General Bava-Beccaris. Umberto I was buried in the Pantheon in Rome, by the side of his father Victor Emmanuel II, on 9 August 1900. He was also the last Savoy to be buried there, as his son and successor Victor Emmanuel III were to die in exile.

An investigation into King Umberto's assassination was set in motion straight away. It was assumed at first that it was a plot hatched by the German kaiser, whose motives were unfathomable. The kaiser was by this time already seen as a brutal and unrelenting force in European politics, having appropriated the sinister nickname, 'Black Hand'. But even though the kaiser was thought to be behind the assassination, his motives were a total mystery; he could have wanted Umberto out of the way in order to empower his successors or the murder could have been a simple and crude gesture of hostility against Italy. In 1900 the kaiser was seen as quite capable of trying to destabilize another European state in this way.

After King Umberto was assassinated, Haluga rode on a tidal wave of public support into his appointment as premier. Haluga brought with him into office a young politician of similar age as an adviser, a friend by the name of Benito Mussolini. Although King Umberto had been removed, he left behind political chaos. Italy was an unstable and weak country that could be taken in almost any direction. The repercussions of the king's assassination were to be far-reaching.

ASSASSINATIONS OF THE PRESENT DAY

PRESIDENT WILLIAM McKINLEY

1901

WILLIAM MCKINLEY WAS born in Ohio in 1843, the son of working class parents. He enlisted in the Union army during the Civil War and afterwards went to Albany Law School. In 1871, McKinley married Ida Saxton. They had two children but both girls died in infancy which was a great shock to the McKinleys; Ida's health failed and she suffered from depression. McKinley was a supportive husband but he went on climbing the political ladder. He served seven terms in Congress, two terms as Governor of Ohio, and became President of the United States in 1896.

McKinley was re-elected as President again in 1900. By that stage he had become the most popular President since Lincoln and many, including his principal backer, Hanna, wanted him to go for a third term in 1904. McKinley showed no interest, and was looking forward to retiring from politics. He had a strong new vice-president, Theodore Roosevelt, who was a dashing 43-year-old war-hero. Roosevelt was popular with the people, though distrusted by many Republican politicians, who saw him as an uncontrollable outsider. McKinley's backer was positively alarmed at the prospect of Roosevelt becoming president; he presciently said, 'There's only one life [McKinley's] between that madman [meaning Roosevelt] and the Presidency.'

McKinley was to open the Pan-American Exposition in the spring of 1901 but Ida was ill and Roosevelt went in his place. McKinley promised to visit the Exposition later in the year and left for Buffalo in September. The president of the Exposition, John G. Milburn, was the Exposition's organizer and he acted as host for the McKinleys during their stay and gave them a brief tour of the Exposition on their arrival on the evening of 4 September. Half a million electric lights were switched on, many of them lighting up the Exposition's main feature, the 389-feet-high Electric Tower. The following day, which was President's Day at the Exposition, saw fity thousand people crowding in to see both the Exposition and the president, who was himself a kind of exhibit. McKinley gave a fine speech that day, about a country at peace and a country that could not afford isolationism any more. The crowd cheered, often drowning out his words. Somewhere in the crowd was his assassin, the young anarchist Leon Czolgosz, unable to move, unable to get close to McKinley.

On 31 August, 1901, Leon Czolgosz (pronounced 'cholgosh') had checked into Nowak's hotel in Buffalo. Nowak's was close to the Exposition grounds and offered a quiet place where he could come and go without attracting any attention. He paid his bills, was quiet and kept to himself. Czolgosz had no timetable for the assassination of McKinley; he just followed him around, waiting for an opportunity. Recently, McKinley had been getting hate mail and hostile phone calls, and security at the Exposition had been noticeably stepped up. George Foster, the president's chief of security, was taking no chances. Czolgosz was undeterred; he knew he would have to be patient because there would be fewer opportunities.

Czolgosz had already nearly blown his own cover by being too impatient. When the president's train had arrived in Buffalo, Czolgosz had pushed too close to the president too eagerly. One of the guards shouted at him to get back. Thinking his intention had been guessed, Czolgosz turned to run. The guard grabbed him and threw him onto the ground. Czolgosz thought he had been caught red-handed; it would only be a matter of seconds before they found his revolver. But the guard just left him on the ground, not realizing what a serious threat he was.

That was on 4 September. The next morning, Leon Czolgosz purchased his usual cigar and set off from Nowak's hotel, holding his .32-calibre Johnson revolver in his coat pocket. Czolgosz had hoped to beat the crowds and get close to the podium in order to have a clear view of the president, but he could get nowhere near the stage. He nevertheless saw his chance when the speech was over and the crowd thinned out. The president was ushered to his carriage by detectives. Czolgosz moved forward, sensing an opportunity. But McKinley had his back to him and another man stood next to him, similarly dressed. Czolgosz could not tell which was McKinley and he had to shoot the right man. By the time he realized which was which, the moment had passed; again he had to wait.

Exactly where Czolgosz was on the morning of 6 September is a mystery. Some say he followed McKinley to Niagara, returning early when he saw that he was not going to be able to get a clear shot in the open air. Others say he went to the Exposition grounds and waited at the Temple of

Music until McKinley showed up, getting there early to be sure of a good position in the greeting line. Either way, Czolgosz put himself in a good position to meet McKinley. Waiting behind Czolgosz was a tall black waiter called James Parker, who had wanted to see the president for a long time; Parker tried to chat to Czolgosz, but got no response. Czolgosz was preoccupied. It was approaching 4 p.m.

At four o'clock, McKinley was in position with Milburn to his left. The doors were opened and the first people in the queue moved towards President McKinley. McKinley shook hands with them, smiling or saying one or two words. After five minutes, the order was given to close the doors again. Czolgosz had wrapped his gun in a handkerchief. He raised it quickly, aimed and fired two rounds. The first glanced off a button on McKinley's jacket. The second hit him in the stomach. The handkerchief fell to the floor, smoking. Private O'Brien dived at Czolgosz. At the same moment, Parker punched Czolgosz in the face. The assassin fell to the floor. Detective Geary caught the president as he fell backwards, blood staining his white shirt.

There was a lot of shouting and rushing about. All the soldiers present rushed at Czolgosz on the floor; the revolver was snatched away from him. Czolgosz was picked up by the scruff of the neck, punched in the face and thrown back down on the floor. McKinley, now also on the floor, whispered, 'Be careful about my wife. Do not tell her.' He could see the terrific beating his attacker was being given and murmured something like, 'Go easy on him, boys.' His words saved Czolgosz's life; the beating stopped.

News of the shooting spread quickly and the Exposition was closed. Word got out into the city and a mob gathered outside the Temple of Music threatening to kill the assassin. They banged on the walls and doors, shouting, trying to get at Czolgosz. An ambulance arrived to take McKinley to the Exposition Hospital. Later a horse-drawn carriage arrived for Czolgosz. The guards tossed Czolgosz into the carriage and the driver whipped the horses to drive through the mob. An attempt was made to overturn the carriage, but the police and soldiers beat the rioters back. The carriage only just made it to the safety of the prison.

The trial of Czolgosz began nine days after McKinley's death. There was no conspiracy: 'No one else told me to do it and no one paid me to do it.' A plea of insanity was rejected and he was sentenced to death. As he was strapped into the electric chair on 29 October, Czolgosz shouted, 'I killed the President because he was the enemy of the good people! I did it for the help of the good people, the working men of all countries!' The electric chair was then still an experimental new method of execution. Thomas Edison made a film purporting to show the execution of Czolgosz in detail, but it was a re-enactment, not the real thing.

In 1898, Czolgosz seems to have had a mental breakdown. He gave up his job at a wire mill, returned to the family farm and spent his time reading about violent acts committed by anarchists. His life drifted on in this way until he heard the anarchist Emma Goldman make a speech in Cleveland. He followed her to Chicago and began mixing with anarchists, but he was regarded with suspicion because he was evidently unbalanced. He was eventually denounced in an anarchist publication, *Free Society*, as a likely police spy. Czolgosz had found a cause – and been rejected by it. The idea of killing President McKinley probably came to him after he read about the assassination of King Umberto of Italy in July 1900. The Italian king was killed by Gaetano Bresci, an Italian weaver who had emigrated to the USA. Bresci deeply hated the monarchy and returned to Italy to join an anarchist group in Milan; lots were drawn to decide which of them should kill the king and Bresci was the chosen assassin. Czolgosz identified with Bresci and collected press cuttings about him. The shooting of President McKinley was in effect a copy-cat assassination.

Probably his decision to shoot President McKinley sprang from a determination to show the anarchists that he really was one of them. As it turned out, the assassination was a disaster for the anarchists. Emma Goldman was harassed by the police and vilified by the public in general. Yet she refused to denounce Czolgosz out of hand; 'He committed the act for no personal reason or gain. He did it for what is his ideal.'

ARCHDUKE FRANZ FERDINAND

1914

THE GOVERNOR OF the Austrian provinces of Bosnia-Herzegovina, General Oskar Potiorek, invited the Archduke Franz Ferdinand and his wife Sophie von Chotkovato, to watch his troops on exercise in June 1914.

Franz Ferdinand was the heir to the Austro-Hungarian throne and knew that his visit to Bosnia-Herzegovina was dangerous. Many living in Bosnia-Herzegovina hated being ruled by Austria and wanted instead union with Serbia. There had already been an assassination attempt, not against Ferdinand but against General Varesanin; in 1910 a Serb called Bogdan Zerajic had tried to kill him as he opened parliament in Sarajevo.

Zerajic was a member of the Black Hand group who wanted Bosnia-Herzegovina's liberation from the Austro-Hungarian Empire. The Black Hand leader was Colonel Dragutin Dimitrijevic, who was chief of the Intelligence Department of the Serbian General Staff. Dimitrijevic saw the Archduke Franz Ferdinand as a serious obstacle to a union between Bosnia-Herzegovina and Serbia. An independent Serbian state would be more difficult to achieve if Ferdinand carried through his planned concessions to the South Slavs. When Franz Ferdinand's visit to Bosnia was announced, Dimitrijevic started to organize a plan for his assassination.

In Bosnia, even the date of the proposed visit was seen as an insult. Borijove Jevtic, a Black Hand member, was incensed.

How dared Franz Ferdinand, not only the representative of the oppressor but in his own person an arrogant tyrant, enter Sarajevo on that day? Such an entry was a studied insult. 28 June is a date engraved deeply in the heart of every Serb. It is the day on which the old Serbian kingdom was conquered by the Turks at the battle of Amselfelde in 1389. That was no day for Franz Ferdinand, the new oppressor, to venture to the very doors of Serbia for a display of the force of arms which kept us beneath his heel. Our decision was taken almost immediately. Death to the tyrant!

Dragutin Dimitrijevic and his fellow conspirators, Milan Ciganovic and Major Voja Tankosic, commissioned three young members of the Black Hand group based in Belgrade, Gavrilo Princip, Nedjelko Cabrinovic and Trifko Grabez, to carry out the assassination. Each man was given a revolver, two bombs and a phial of cyanide. The three men had orders to commit suicide after the assassination, as it was important that the men did not have the opportunity to confess that members of the Serbian Army were involved in the assassination.

Gavrilo Princip, Nedjelko Cabrinovic and Trifko Grabez were suffering from tuberculosis and knew they did not have long to live. They were willing to sacrifice what remained of their short lives in the interests of a great cause: the independence of Bosnia-Herzegovina from Austro-Hungary.

Major Voja Tankosic informed Nikola Pasic, the Serbian prime minister about the plot; Dragutin Dimitrijevic did not know this. Pasic supported the objective of the Black Hand group, the liberation of Bosnia-Herzegovina, but he did not want the assassination, which he feared would lead to war. Pasic therefore gave instructions that the three would-be assassins were to be arrested when they attempted to leave the country. Pasic's plan failed, and the three men arrived in Bosnia-Herzegovina where they were joined by six more conspirators: Muhamed Mehmedbasic, Danilo Ilic, Vaso Cubrilovic, Cvijetko Popovic, Misko Jovanovic and Veljko Cubrilovic.

The 51-year-old Franz Ferdinand and his wife arrived in Sarajevo by train on 28 June, 1914. The governor of Bosnia-Herzegovina, General Potiorek, conducted the royal party in a motorcade through the town to the City Hall for an official reception. In the front car was the Mayor of Sarajevo and the city's Commissioner of Police. Franz Ferdinand and Sophie von Chotkovato were in the second car with Oskar Potiorek and Count von Harrach. The Graf und Stift car's top was rolled back in order to allow the crowds a good view of its occupants. In view of the difficult political situation, this was a very rash decision, as was the decision to advertise the route beforehand. The local police organized the security for the royal visit. Before the archduke arrived, 35 potential troublemakers were taken into custody and 120 policemen were posted along the streets. There were seventy thousand Austro-Hungarian soldiers in Sarajevo, but they were all to stay in their barracks that fateful day.

Seven members of the Black Hand group positioned themselves at intervals along the route. Each one would try to kill Franz Ferdinand when the royal car reached his position. The first to see the royal car was Muhamed Mehmedbasic, who was standing by the Austro-Hungarian Bank. He lost his nerve, froze, allowed the archduke's car to pass without doing anything. Mehmedbasic afterwards said a policeman was standing behind him and he was afraid he would be stopped before he had a chance to throw his bomb.

The next man on the route was Nedjelko Cabrinovic. Cabrinovic stepped forward and hurled his bomb at the archduke's car. The driver instinctively accelerated when he saw the bomb flying towards him, and it exploded under the wheel of the car behind, seriously injuring two of its occupants and slightly wounding a dozen spectators. After throwing his bomb, Cabrinovic swallowed his capsule of cyanide and jumped into the River Miljacka. Four men jumped into the river after him, pulled him out and arrested him. The poison for some reason failed to work and he was taken to the local police station. Franz Urban, who was driving Franz Ferdinand's car, understood the danger of the situation and accelerated along the street. The other Black Hand conspirators decided it was useless to try and kill the archduke with the car travelling at speed.

At the official reception at the City Hall, Franz Ferdinand asked about the people wounded in the explosion. He was told they were in hospital and he insisted on being taken to see them. A member of the archduke's staff, Baron Morsey, commented that this might be dangerous, but Oskar Potiorek, who was responsible for the safety of the royal party, retorted, 'Do you think Sarajevo is full of assassins?' So the archduke was to visit the hospital and his wife insisted on going too. 'As long as the Archduke shows himself in public today I will not leave him.'

General Potiorek decided that they should travel straight along the Appel Quay to the Sarajevo Hospital. Potiorek unaccountably forgot to tell the driver about this decision. On the way to the hospital, Franz Urban turned right into Franz Joseph Street. Entirely by chance, one of the conspirators, Gavrilo Princip, was standing on the street corner. Potiorek realised immediately that the driver had taken the wrong turning and shouted, 'This is the wrong way! We're supposed to take the Appel Quay!'

The driver stopped and began to reverse. As he did so he moved slowly past the waiting Gavrilo Princip, who could not believe his luck. Princip stepped forward, pulled out his gun, and from a distance of only a metre or so, fired several times into the car. The Archduke Franz Ferdinand was struck in the throat, piercing the jugular vein. Sophie was hit in the abdomen. Before he lost consciousness, Franz Ferdinand said, 'Sopherl! Sopherl! Don't die! Stay alive for our children!' Franz Urban drove the royal couple to the governor's residence, and both were still alive when they arrived, but they died shortly afterwards.

Count Franz von Harrach was riding on the running board of the royal car, acting as a bodyguard for the archduke. His eye-witness account begins immediately after Princip fires his two shots:

As the car quickly reversed, a thin stream of blood spurted from His Highness's mouth onto my right cheek. As I was pulling out my handkerchief to wipe the blood away from his mouth, the Duchess cried out to him, 'In Heaven's name, what has happened to you?' At that she slid off the seat and lay on the floor of the car, with her face between his knees.

I had no idea that she too was hit and thought she had simply fainted with fright. Then I heard His Imperial Highness say, 'Sopherl, Sopherl, don't die. Stay alive for the children!'

At that, I seized the Archduke by the collar of his uniform, to stop his head dropping forward and asked him if he was in great pain. He answered me quite distinctly, 'It's nothing!' His face began to twist somewhat but he went on repeating, six or seven times, ever more faintly as he gradually lost consciousness, 'It's nothing!' Then, after a short pause, there was a violent choking sound caused by the bleeding. It stopped as we reached the Konak.

After the assassination, Princip turned his gun, preparing to shoot himself. Ante Velic, standing behind him, seized Princip's right arm. Another bystander, Danilo Pusic, also grabbed hold of Princip. Within seconds the police arrived knocked Princip down and kicked him and took him. Cabrinovic and Princip were interrogated and gave the police the names of their fellow conspirators. Grabez, Ilic, Cubrilovic, Popovic and Jovanovic were arrested but Mehmedbasic managed to escape to Serbia. Members of the Black Hand interrogated by the Austrian authorities claimed that three men from Serbia, Milan Ciganovic, Dragutin Dimitrijevic and Major Voja Tankosic, had organised the plot. On 23 July, 1914, the Austro-Hungarian government demanded that the Serbian authorities arrest the three and send them to stand trial in Vienna. Two days later, Pasic the Serbian prime minister refused to hand them over as it would be 'a violation of Serbia's Constitution and criminal in law'. Three days after that, Austria-Hungary momentously declared war on Serbia. It was the beginning of the First World War.

During the arms race that had been developing over the previous decade, one defensive alliance after another had been forged. Now those alliances were to turn suddenly into offensive alliances, one after another, turning a local squabble into a continent-wide war. One state declared war on another, and as they did so other states – standing as they thought on the sidelines – the allies, found themselves dragged in by their treaty obligations. Germany declared war on Russia on 1 August and on France two days later. On 4 August German troops invaded Belgium. Because Belgium was neutral and Britain had undertaken to defend Belgian neutrality, Britain was forced to declare war on Germany immediately after that. Montenegro declared war on Austria on 5 August; Serbia declared war on Germany and Austria declared war on Russia the following day; Montenegro declared war on Germany on 8 August; Britain and France declared war on Austria on 12 August. Within a few short weeks, a great swathe of Europe was in a state of war.

The double murder at Sarajevo was a personal tragedy for Franz Ferdinand and Sophie, and an inexcusable crime for which the assassins should have been punished by due process of law, but it should not have led to the outbreak of the First World War. Europe had been turned into a powder keg by the territorial, military and colonial ambitions of several European countries. Sarajevo was the incidental discarded lighted match that set off the explosion. Perhaps the most surprising thing of all is that Princip survived all the mayhem; he died naturally, of tuberculosis, a few years later.

Eight of the men charged with Archduke Franz Ferdinand's treasonable murder were found guilty. Under Austro-Hungarian law, which was surprisingly lenient and progressive in this area, a death sentence could not be imposed on people below the age of 20. Three of the men were 'of age' and they were executed on 3 February, 1915: Misko Jovanovic, Danilo Ilic and Veljko Cubrilovic. The others were all too young to hang. Nedjelko Cabrinovic, Gavrilo Princip and Trifko Grabez were given the maximum available penalty of 20 years in prison. Vaso Cubrilovic received 16 years and Cvijetko Popovic 13 years. The three men sent to Sarajevo from Serbia by Colonel Dimitrijevic, died in prison from tuberculosis, Nedjelko Cabrinovic in January 1916, Trifko Grabez a few weeks later and Gavrilo Princip in April 1918. The man who precipitated the First World War ironically almost survived it and died of natural causes.

In the first two years of the First World War the Serbian Army suffered a series of military defeats. Pasic was frustrated and angry that the assassination conspiracy had led to a war that was destroying his country, 'and half the seed of Europe, one by one', as Wilfrid Owen memorably described it. Pasic disbanded the Black Hand organization and had Dragutin Dimitrijevic arrested and charged with treason. Dimitrijevic was found guilty and executed on 11 June, 1917.

GRIGORI RASPUTIN

1916

GRIGORI EFIMOVICH RASPUTIN, nicknamed the Mad Monk, though he was neither mad nor a monk, was one of the most controversial characters of the twentieth century. He was a *strannik* or religious pilgrim and a faith healer who played a small but spectacular role in the downfall of the Russian royal family.

Rasputin was born as a peasant in Siberia in 1869. When he was 18 he spent three months in the Verkhoturye Monastery, where he joined the Khlysty, a Russian Orthodox sect. After leaving the monastery, he visited a holy man named Makariy, who lived in a hut nearby. Makariy had an enormous influence on Rasputin, who later modelled himself on the older man. Rasputin married in 1889 but in 1901 he left home as a *strannik*. He travelled to Greece and Jerusalem, arriving in St Petersburg in 1903 as a holy man with healing powers and the gift of prophecy.

The tsar's son, the Tsarevich Alexei, suffered from haemophilia. In desperation the tsarina looked everywhere for help, and she secured the help of Rasputin in 1905. He was able to give the boy some relief, possibly using hypnosis. Every time the boy had any internal or external bleeding, the tsarina called for Rasputin. Because each time the tsarevich recovered, the family became convinced that Rasputin was healing him. The tsar began to refer to Rasputin as 'our friend' and Rasputin gained increasing influence over Alexandra, who believed that God spoke to her through him.

Rasputin meanwhile led a scandalous personal life with his female followers from St Petersburg high society. He was seen getting drunk and picking up prostitutes. He was unsavoury, ill-mannered and dirty. Rasputin was fascinating – but unacceptable. The Russian Orthodox Church frequently attacked Rasputin, spreading malicious gossip about him, but there is credible and apparently objective police evidence about his scandalous behaviour. As a court official, he and his apartment were under 24-hour surveillance, and some of the reports from police spies were not only given to the tsar, but published in the press. Most dangerous was the popular image of Rasputin controlling the tsar and tsarina. The tsarina was unpopular because she was a foreigner of German descent, and her friend Rasputin was accused of being a spy in the pay of the Germans.

Tensions developed within the Russian elite regarding the disproportionate amount of influence Rasputin wielded. Early in the First World War Rasputin wanted to go to the front to bless the troops, and the commander-in-chief, a grand duke, threatened to hang him if did. Rasputin retaliated by having the grand duke demoted; he claimed that he had had a revelation that the Russian army would only succeed if the Tsar personally took command. So, in effect obeying Rasputin's order, the ill-prepared and entirely unsuitable Tsar Nicholas took personal command of the Russian army, with dire consequences for Russia and fatal consequences for himself and his family.

With Nicholas II away at the front, Rasputin's influence over Tsarina Alexandra increased. He became her personal advisor, even appointing his own handpicked candidates to govern offices with. He sold political favours to aristocratic women in exchange for sex. As the economic, military and political situation in Russia deteriorated, many Russians put the blame on the tsarina and Rasputin. Rasputin became the scapegoat. Some members of the Duma, the Russian parliament, asked for Rasputin's removal from court and a speech was made condemning the 'German' empress and her advisor. Prince Felix Yusupov heard the speech and began organizing a plot to murder Rasputin.

The circumstances of Rasputin's death are surrounded by controversy. An attempt was made on his life in June 1914 by Khionia Guseva, a former prostitute. Her motive seems to have been partly religious fanaticism, partly disgust at the disrespectful way he talked about the Russian royal family. She stuck a knife into Rasputin's abdomen. When his intestines fell out of what looked like a mortal wound, Guseva screamed, 'I have killed the antichrist!' But the wound was superficial and Rasputin recovered after surgery, though he frequently had to take opium to reduce the pain.

The murder of Rasputin was described in detail by his assassins, but some at least of their account was invention, so it is difficult to discern exactly what happened. It is generally agreed that on 16 December, 1916, a group of nobles led by Prince Felix Yusupov and the Grand Duke Dimitri Pavlovich lured Rasputin to the Moika Palace, Yusupov's home. Rasputin turned up appearing more carefully dressed and groomed than anyone had seen him before. He wore a silk shirt embroidered by the tsarina. His breeches were velvet and his highly polished boots were brand new. His hair and beard were unusually clean and combed and smelled of cheap soap. Rasputin had made a great effort with his appearance; perhaps he thought he was going to meet Princess Irina. Perhaps sensing a conspiracy, he seemed nervous as Felix Yusupov showed him into the room and offered him a biscuit. Yusupov was also highly anxious and they started a stilted conversation. He offered Rasputin a poisoned cake. At first this was refused and the already nervous Yusupov started to perspire. Then, absent-mindedly, Rasputin ate one cake, and then another. Yusupov was frightened and fascinated as he waited for the poison to start to take effect. Two cakes contained enough cyanide to kill half a dozen men. Yusupov gazed at the peasant, who carried on chatting and showed no sign of distress.

Yusupov offered Rasputin some wine. Again he refused at first, but changed his mind when he saw two glasses being poured out. He took an unpoisoned glass, and drank it down quickly. Then he asked for Madeira, but wanted it in the same glass when the prince attempted to pour it into one of the poisoned glasses. Yusupov was near to collapse with stress. He faked an accident in which he broke Rasputin's glass and this meant that Rasputin had to accept the Madeira in the glass containing a measure of liquid potassium cyanide.

At last the poison began to take effect. Rasputin complained of a slight irritation in his throat. He asked for another glass of Madeira and was given a second poisoned glass. Seeing a guitar propped in a corner he asked Felix to sing him gypsy songs, one of Yusupov's party pieces. Yusupov was made to sing and play until 2.30 a.m., by which time he was hallucinating. It seemed like a duel between him and Rasputin, between good and evil; 'Confronted by those satanic eyes I was beginning to lose my self-control.'

In Yusupov's 'legendary' version, the conspirators served Rasputin cakes and red wine laced with cyanide. But family members said afterwards that following the 1914 knife attack Rasputin carefully avoided consuming anything containing sugar, so it was very unlikely that he ate the cakes or drank the wine. This suggests that the poisoning part of the story was an invention.

But Yusupov's lurid story was not over by a long way. Making an excuse that he was going to ask his wife if she was ready to come and meet Rasputin, Yusupov staggered upstairs to ask the co-conspirators what they should do. Dr Lazovert was faint with the strain; the Grand Duke Dmitri wanted to abandon the whole idea; Prince Yusupov was concerned that Rasputin would survive until the morning, which would make it harder for them to dispose of his body; Purishkevitch thought the time had come for a joint attack.

He ran upstairs to consult with the others, then returned to find Rasputin still very much alive. He shot Rasputin in the back with a revolver. About half an hour later when Yusupov returned for his jacket, Rasputin sprang to his feet and began to throttle Yusupov, who fled in terror to tell the other conspirators.

By this time heavily drugged and wounded, the 'legend' continues, Rasputin tried to escape. He managed to get outside and run across the courtyard toward the gate, chased by the conspirators. He threatened to tell the tsarina everything. One of the conspirators fired three bullets. They all missed. Then he fired two more which hit Rasputin. The conspirators then clubbed him until he was unconscious, dragged him to the Neva River and tried to throw him in. But the river was frozen over, and they had to cut a hole in the ice and push the body through it. They were finally certain that Rasputin was dead. At one point a policeman came over to see what all the noise was about; when the conspirators told him he said, 'About time,' and continued on his beat.

Three days later the body was recovered from the river and examined. According to the post-mortem the cause of death was drowning. His arms were raised, as if he had tried to claw his way out from under the ice. The Empress Alexandra buried the body in the grounds of Tsarskoe Selo, but after the Revolution it was dug up and destroyed.

The 'legendary' version of Rasputin's death is intensely melodramatic, full of tragicomedy and horror. It is not surprising that it has been dramatized on film several times over. Certainly he was murdered, but it seems unlikely that all the detail is true. The details of the assassination given by Felix Yusupov have never stood up to close examination. To begin with, he gave several different versions of what happened: the statement he gave to the Petrograd police on 16 December, 1916, the account he gave whilst in exile in the Crimea in 1917, his 1927 book, and the accounts given under oath to libel juries in 1934 and 1965. They were all different in detail. Until recently, however, no other credible, evidence-based theories have been available.

The 1916 autopsy report by Professor Kossorotov was reviewed in 1993 by Dr Vladimir Zharov and in 2004–5 by Professor Derrick Pounder. It is clear that no poison was found in Rasputin's stomach, which strongly suggests that what Rasputin's family said at the time was true; he did not take the poisoned cake or wine – if indeed cake or wine were ever offered. It was not certain that he drowned, as the water found in his lungs may not have caused his death. Rasputin had certainly been systematically beaten and attacked with a knife. He had also been shot, but there were discrepancies regarding the number and calibre of handguns used.

It is likely that the British played a significant part in Rasputin's assassination. British intelligence reports between London and Petrograd in 1916 show that the British were concerned about Rasputin's replacement of pro-British ministers in the Russian government, and even more concerned about Rasputin's insistence on withdrawing Russian troops from the First World War. That withdrawal would have allowed the Germans to move all of their Eastern Front troops to the Western Front, where the Allies would be massively outnumbered – and certainly defeated. Whether Rasputin really intended to advise withdrawing or was simply concerned about the huge number of casualties is not clear, but it is clear that the British viewed him as a real danger.

The most recent review of the autopsy, by Professor Pounder, shows that of the three shots fired into Rasputin's body, the third was instantly fatal. It entered his forehead. This crucial fatal third shot was fired by a different gun from those responsible for the other two wounds. The prominent abraded margin of the wound was made by a large non-jacketed lead bullet, which could only have come from a .455-calibre British Webley revolver. Witnesses to the murder stated that the only man present with a Webley revolver was Lieutenant Oswald Rayner, a British officer who was attached to the British Secret Intelligence Service station in Petrograd. This account was corroborated in an audience between Sir George Buchanan, the British ambassador, and Tsar Nicholas. The tsar himself suspected a young Englishman who had been 'at school' with Yusupov. Oswald Rayner had known Yusupov not at school exactly, but at Oxford. Another SIS officer in Petrograd at the time, Captain Stephen Alley, had been born in the Yusupov palace in 1876.

Rayner and another officer, Captain John Scale, met Yusupov in the weeks immediately before the assassination. This was recorded in the diary of their driver, William Compton, who recorded all the visits. The last entry was the night before the murder. Compton himself said, 'Rasputin was shot not by a Russian but by an Englishman.' Without naming him, he mentioned that the assassin was a lawyer who came from the same part of the country as Compton himself. Rayner was born about 10 miles from Compton's home, and curiously described himself as a barrister, despite never having practised law.

The Yusupov version may be true to the extent that the asassination was a mess. There is a hint of this in a letter from Alley to Scale a week after the murder. 'Although matters here have not proceeded entirely to plan, our objective has clearly been achieved . . . a few awkward questions have already been asked about wider involvement. Rayner is attending to loose ends and will no doubt brief you.'

When he came back to England, Oswald Rayner significantly confided to his cousin, Rose Jones, that he had been present at Rasputin's murder. He also showed off to his family a bullet which he claimed he had picked up at the murder scene. It seems Rayner never revealed anything further about his involvement in the assassination. He burnt all his papers before he died in 1961.

According to his secretary Simonovich, some weeks before he was assassinated, Rasputin wrote the following:

I write and leave behind me this letter at St. Petersburg. I feel that I shall leave life before January 1. I wish to make known to the Russian people, to Papa, to the Russian Mother and to the Children, to the land of Russia, what they must understand. If I am killed by common assassins, and especially by my brothers the Russian peasants, you, Tsar of Russia, will have nothing to fear for your children, they will reign for hundreds of years in Russia. But if I am murdered by boyars, nobles, and if they shed my blood, their hands will remain soiled with my blood, for twenty-five years they will not wash their hands from my blood. They will leave Russia. Brothers will kill brothers, and they will kill each other and hate each other, and for twenty-five years there will be no nobles in the country. Tsar of the land of Russia, if you hear the sound of the bell which will tell you that Grigori has been killed, you must know this: if it was your relations who have wrought my death, then no one in the family, that is to say, none of your children or relations, will remain alive for more than two years. They will be killed by the Russian people. I go, and I feel in me the divine command to tell the Russian Tsar how he must live if I have disappeared. You must reflect and act prudently. Think of your safety and tell your relations that I have paid for them with my blood. I shall be killed. I am no longer among the living. Pray, pray, be strong, think of your blessed family.

—Grigori

THE ROMANOVS

1918

THE MOUNTING PRESSURES of the First World War, combined with economic collapse and years of social injustice, led to the fall of the Russian monarchy. The tsar's decision to take personal command of the Russian army, following Rasputin's advice, was a profound political error. He made himself directly and personally responsible for all the military failures that followed. As a result Tsar Nicholas II was forced to abdicate in March 1917.

He was replaced by a provisional government that was committed to continuing the war. Ever-increasing Russian losses at the front and the fear of a German advance on Moscow eroded what little support remained for the war. The provisional government's authority was undermined. Capitalizing on this situation, the Germans secretly transported the exiled Lenin in a sealed train from Switzerland to Russia in the hope he would inflame the turmoil, as indeed he did with a vengeance! The Germans' highest hopes were realized on the night of 6–7 November when Lenin led the Bolsheviks (Reds) in a successful attempt to seize power in St Petersburg. Anti-Bolshevik forces, known as the Whites, immediately took up arms to topple the Bolshevik regime and Russia was plunged headlong into a bloody civil war. In the following March the Bolshevik regime signed a treaty with the Germans ending Russia's participation in the First World War.

The tsar and his family were seen as being of little consequence amid this political chaos, though it was recognized that they could be used as a rallying-point for a monarchist revival. They hoped to be allowed to go into exile in some friendly European state. There was a half-hearted plan for them to board a ship in the Black Sea and come to Britain, but George V was persuaded that the popularity of the British monarchy might become tainted by association with the extremely unpopular Romanovs, so the invitation was withdrawn. This left the Romanovs stranded in Russia. Initially they were kept as prisoners near St Petersburg and then they were transported into greater obscurity beyond the Ural Mountains, finally, in the spring of 1918, ending up in the town of Ekaterinburg. The seven members of the royal family and a small household of servants were confined to the house of a successful local merchant, N. N. Ipatiev, which had been commandeered by the Bolsheviks for the Tsar. The house was from then on called the Ipatiev House or sometimes, the House of Special Purpose.

In the middle of July a Czech contingent of the White Army approached Ekaterinburg. The sounds of gunfire could be heard in the distance by the Romanovs and their Bolshevik guards. If the Whites reached Ekaterinburg there was every possibility that the Romanovs would be freed, and possibly even reinstated. The approach of their potential liberators sealed the fate of the tsar and his family. The Bolsheviks decided that the Romanovs had to be killed before the Whites reached them.

It was during the early hours of 17 July, 1918 that the Tsar, his wife, children and servants were led down into the basement of the Ipatiev House and executed. Pavel Medvedev was a member of the squad of soldiers guarding the royal family and he described in detail what happened:

In the evening of 16 July, between seven and eight p.m., when the time of my duty had just begun, Commandant Yurovsky, [the head of the execution squad] ordered me to take all the Nagan revolvers from the guards and to bring them to him. I took twelve revolvers from the sentries as well as from some other of the guards and brought them to the commandant's office.

Yurovsky said to me, 'We must shoot them all tonight; so notify the guards not to be alarmed if they hear shots.' I understood, therefore, that Yurovsky had it in his mind to shoot the whole of the Tsar's family, as well as the doctor and the servants who lived with them, but I did not ask him where or by whom the decision had been made . . . At about ten o'clock in the evening in accordance with Yurovsky's order I informed the guards not to be alarmed if they should hear firing.

About midnight Yurovsky woke up the Tsar's family. I do not know if he told them the reason they had been awakened and where they were to be taken, but I positively affirm that it was Yurovsky who entered the room occupied by the Tsar's family. In about an hour the whole of the family, the doctor, the maid and the waiters got up, washed and dressed themselves.

Just before Yurovsky went to awaken the family, two members of the Extraordinary Commission [of the

Ekaterinburg Soviet] arrived at Ipatiev's house. Shortly after one o'clock am, the Tsar, the Tsaritsa, their four daughters, the maid, the doctor, the cook and the waiters left their rooms. The Tsar carried the heir in his arms. The Emperor and the heir were dressed in gimnasterkas [soldiers' shirts] and wore caps. The Empress, her daughters and the others followed him. Yurovsky, his assistant and the two above-mentioned members of the Extraordinary Commission accompanied them. I was also present.

In my presence none of the Tsar's family asked any questions. They did not weep or cry. Having descended the stairs to the first floor, we went out into the court, and from there to the second door (counting from the gate) we entered the ground floor of the house. When the room (which adjoins the store room with a sealed door) was reached, Yurovsky ordered chairs to be brought and his assistant brought three chairs. One chair was given to the Emperor, one to the Empress, and the third to the heir.

The Empress sat by the wall by the window, near the black pillar of the arch. Behind her stood three of her daughters (I knew their faces very well, because I had seen them every day when they walked in the garden, but I didn't know their names). The heir and the Emperor sat side by side almost in the middle of the room. Doctor Botkin stood behind the heir. The maid, a very tall woman, stood at the left of the door leading to the store room; by her side stood one of the Tsar's daughters (the fourth). Two servants stood against the wall on the left from the entrance of the room.

The maid carried a pillow. The Tsar's daughters also brought small pillows with them. One pillow was put on

*the Empress's chair; another on the heir's chair. It seemed
as if all of them guessed their fate, but not one of them
uttered a single sound. At this moment eleven men
entered the room: Yurovsky, his assistant, two members
of the Extraordinary Commission, and seven Letts
[operatives of the Cheka or Secret Police].*

*Yurovsky ordered me to leave, saying, 'Go on to the
street, see if there is anybody there, and wait to see
whether the shots have been heard.' I went out to the
court, which was enclosed by a fence, but before I got to
the street I heard the firing. I returned to the house
immediately (only two or three minutes having elapsed)
and upon entering the room where the execution had
taken place, I saw that all the members of the Tsar's
family were lying on the floor with many wounds in
their bodies. The blood was running in streams. The
doctor, the maid and two waiters had also been shot.
When I entered the heir was still alive and moaned a
little. Yurovsky went up and fired two or three more
times at him. Then the heir was still.'*

The bodies were taken into the forest, hacked to pieces,
soaked in petrol and sulphuric acid and burnt. The ashes
were then thrown down the shaft of an abandoned mine.
That at least was the conclusion arrived at by the White
Army's examining magistrate, Inspector Nicholas Sokolov,
who said that no member of the Russian imperial family
could possibly have escaped alive from this bloodbath. That
has been taken as the likeliest scenario ever since, though of
course it is a scenario that the Reds wanted them and
everyone else to believe. The Bolsheviks needed everyone to

believe that the entire family had been annihilated, to make it clear that there could be no return to the monarchy.

Over the decades since 1918 there have been persistent stories about the survival of one or other of the Romanovs, of Anastasia in particular. The possible survival of the Grand Duchess Anastasia is one of the great mysteries of the twentieth century. As early as 1922, rumours spread that one of the grand duchesses had survived, and a woman later called 'Anna Anderson' appeared, claiming to be Anastasia. She created life-long controversy and made headlines for decades, with some surviving Romanov relatives believing she was Anastasia and others not. Her battle for recognition is still the longest running case that has ever been heard in the German courts, where the case was officially filed. Anna Anderson, or whoever she was, died in 1984 and her body was cremated. The consensus is that Anna was not Anastasia, partly because Anna Anderson was unable to speak Russian.

Another claimant by the name of Eugenia Smith appeared in 1963, at the height of the Anastasia/Anna Anderson controversy, but her story had inconsistencies. She also refused to submit to any testing.

Anastasia was specifically mentioned in the Sokolov report as having survived the firing squad's gunfire. She apparently fell down in a faint when the gunfire started and was consequently unharmed by the bullets. When the murderers inspected the bodies they found that Anastasia was still alive. She recovered consciousness as she was moved and started screaming when she saw the carnage round her. Lord Mountbatten said, 'My cousin Anastasia was bayonetted 18 times as she lay there screaming.' He had no doubt that Anastasia died in the Ipatiev House, and fiercely opposed

Anna Anderson's claim. But the Sokolov report does show that it was possible for someone to survive the mayhem in the cellar, and it remains a possibility that Anastasia at least was rescued.

Anna Anderson had several scars, including one that was clearly 'star-shaped', matching the triangular-pointed bayonets used by the Russians in the First World War and by the Bolsheviks in the Civil War. Anna Anderson insisted that there had been no massacre in Ekaterinburg, 'but I cannot tell the rest.' This kind of teasing mystification did nothing to help her case. When Anna Anderson died at the age of 82, she left the world divided about her claim. The fact that she could not speak Russian is, of course, strongly against her.

The Anastasia story has been the subject of several plays and films. The earliest, made in 1928, was called *Clothes Make the Woman*. The most famous is the 1956 film *Anastasia* starring Ingrid Bergman as Anna Anderson. In 1986 NBC produced a mini-series called *Anastasia: The Mystery of Anna*, in which Amy Irving portrayed Anna Anderson.

The place in the forest where the Romanovs' remains were disposed of was hidden for the duration of the Communist regime in Russia. Then, in 1979, some remains that were thought to belong to the Romanov family and their servants were discovered. The mass grave was kept hidden by its discoverers from the Communists who still ruled Russia, for fear that they would be destroyed. This fear was well-founded as the Ipatiev House had itself been destroyed by special order in 1977 in order to stop it becoming a place of pilgrimage (and also presumably to prevent it from being subjected to sophisticated modern forensic analysis). Ironically, a huge commemorative church has been raised on the site of the Ipatiev House; it is called the Cathedral of the Blood. With the collapse of the Soviet Union – and the end of the Communist regime – things were to change radically. The day after taking power in 1991, President Boris Yeltsin ordered the recovery of the remains and the slow process of identification began. Experts investigated the remains for 10 years and came to the conclusion that the bones were those of the Romanovs and their four servants.

There should have been 11 sets of human remains: those of the tsar, the tsaritsa, the tsarevitch, the four grand duchesses, the family's doctor Eugene Botkin, their valet, their cook and a lady-in-waiting to the tsarina. But the mass grave yielded the remains of only nine people. According to the forensic expert Dr William Maples, it was the bodies of Alexei and Anastasia that were missing from the mass grave. Russian scientists contested this, claiming that it was the Grand Duchess Maria who was missing from the grave.

In 1998, when the bodies of the Imperial Family were formally buried, the body of a person who had been 5 ft 7 in tall was buried under the name of 'Anastasia', despite the fact that Anastasia is known to have been shorter than that; she was the shortest of the grand duchesses. Some historians believe Yurovsky's account, which says that two of the bodies were removed from the main grave and burned at an undisclosed location, specifically to create an area of doubt as to whether these were the remains of the tsar and his retinue should they be discovered. Yurovsky in other words deliberately created a body count that would not be correct. But with modern forensic techniques it is still possible to discover new things about the events surrounding the disappearance of the tsar and his family, and one day the mystery of Anastasia may be solved.

FRANCISCO 'PANCHO' VILLA
1923

VERY FEW PEOPLE have heard of José Doroteo Arango Arámbula, but everybody has heard of Pancho Villa, which was Doroteo Arango's nom de guerre. Pancho Villa was born in June 1878 and he became one of the foremost leaders and best known generals of the Mexican Revolution between 1911 and 1920. Villa mostly operated in the north of Mexico, the region centring on Chihuahua. He was sometimes referred to as 'The Centaur of the North', because of his famous cavalry attacks. Villa's revolutionary aims were never clearly defined and he only spoke vaguely of setting up colonies for his ex-soldiers; it may be that he just liked fighting. Villa used propaganda against his enemies, expropriated hacienda land for distribution to the peasants (and his soldiers), and many of his tactics were adopted by later revolutionaries. As one of the most colourful figures of the first successful popular revolution of the twentieth century, Villa naturally attracted journalists and photographers from far afield. He loved publicity – and the cash that it generated.

The commonest version of Pancho Villa's youth is that he grew up in poverty, without knowing how to read or write. When his father died, Villa began to work as a sharecropper to help support the family. According to Villa's supporters, Villa came home from the fields one day to find that the owner of the hacienda had raped his 12-year-old sister. Villa shot the owner and fled to the mountains. It is possible that Villa invented this story to justify his later criminal life, that he was simply a criminal from an early age; it is impossible to know.

Either way, from 1894 to 1910 Doroteo Arango spent most of his time in the mountains running from the law. He joined some other bandits under the control of a man whose real name was Francisco Villa. When Francisco Villa was killed Doroteo assumed the name of the former leader; Pancho is a nickname for Francisco. The new Pancho Villa and his bandits stole from wealthy landowners, often giving to the poor. Some saw Villa as a modern-day Robin Hood, while others saw him as a terrorist.

Villa became politicized after meeting Abraham González, the political representative of Francisco Madero in Chihuahua. He came to believe he was fighting for the people, breaking the power of the hacienda owners over the poor farmers and sharecroppers. In November 1910, the Mexican Revolution began. Francisco Madero led the struggle to overthrow the dictatorship of Porfirio Díaz. Villa helped defeat the federal army of Díaz in favour of Madero in 1911, most famously in the first Battle of Juarez. Madero became president of Mexico. Most people assumed that Madero would lead Mexico into a new era of democracy and that Villa would recede into obscurity. Yet Villa's greatest days of fame were yet to come, and democracy in Mexico was still a long way off.

Pascual Orozco launched a rebellion against Madero, so Villa gathered his mounted cavalry troops and worked with General Victoriano Huerta to support Madero. Huerta saw

Villa as a powerful personal enemy and accused him of horse-stealing and sentenced him to death to get rid of him, but the sentence was suspended by President Madero. Villa was imprisoned for a time, and then escaped.

After crushing the Orozco rebellion, Huerta saw an opportunity to make himself dictator. He set up a fake battle in Mexico City, tricked Madero into accepting his 'protection', then treacherously ordered the assassination of both Madero and his Vice President Pino Suarez. Huerta proclaimed himself President. Venustiano Carranza then accused Huerta of being an unconstitutional usurper and set up another counter-rebellion with Pablo González, Álvaro Obregón, Emiliano Zapata and Pancho Villa. Villa's personal hatred of Huerta intensified after 7 March, 1913, when Huerta ordered the murder of Villa's political mentor, Abraham González. The new United States President Woodrow Wilson supported Carranza's cause. Villa's remarkable generalship combined with his ingenious fundraising methods (including train robberies) were to be instrumental in forcing Huerta from office a little over a year later, in July 1914.

This was the time of Villa's greatest fame and success. In one escapade, he took 122 bars of silver as hostage in a train robbery and forced Wells Fargo to help him exchange the bars for currency. After a series of hard fought battles, Villa became governor of Chihuahua state.

As governor of Chihuahua, Villa raised more money for a drive to the south by the simple expedient of printing it. He decreed his paper money to be traded and accepted at par with gold Mexican pesos, then forced the wealthy to trade their gold for his paper pesos by decreeing gold to be counterfeit money. He also confiscated the gold held by banks. Villa's stature at that time was such that banks at El Paso in Texas accepted his paper pesos at face value. Villa himself was so admired by the US military that he and Álvaro Obregón were invited to Fort Bliss to meet General John J. Pershing, who wanted to have his photograph taken with them.

Villa's loot was used to buy cavalry horses, ammunition, hospital facilities and food, and to rebuild the railway south of Chihuahua City. The rebuilt railway transported Villa's troops and artillery south, where he defeated Federal forces at Gomez Palacio, Torreon and Zacatecas.

After Torreon, Carranza ordered Villa to break off south of Torreon and divert to attack Saltillo, and threatened to cut off Villa's coal supply if he did not comply. This was widely seen as an attempt by Carranza to divert Villa from attacking Mexico City, so as to allow Carranza's forces under Álvaro Obregón to take the capital first, and Obregón and Carranza did enter Mexico City ahead of Villa. Villa attacked Saltillo as ordered, winning that battle, but he was disgusted by what he saw as Carranza's egotism. He attacked Huerta at Zacatecas, a strategic mountainous city considered nearly impregnable and the source of much of Mexico's silver.

In June 1914 Villa defeated Huerta in the Taking of Zacatecas, which was the bloodiest battle of the Revolution, leaving 7,000 soldiers dead and 5,000 wounded, along with countless civilian casualties. Huerta left for exile on 14 July, 1914. But the split between Villa and Carranza left both men weakened militarily and politically. Now both were doomed.

Pancho Villa's charismatic personality and military success in battle during this period made him a media celebrity in America. He had many engaging eccentricities. He was, for instance, a great lover of ice cream. One revolutionary song had Villa making a point of stopping for ice cream on a street in Chihuahua before gunning down a betrayer. He was a lifelong teetotaler, a dancer of legendary stamina and also a great polygamist, with as many as 24 wives.

He was the subject of several films. Villa had a keen eye for publicity and (for money, of course) agreed to some scenes being filmed on location with his own troops. Villa starred as himself in films in 1912, 1913 and 1914. Since then, he has been represented by a host of screen actors including Raoul Walsh, Wallace Beery, Yul Brynner, Pedro Armendáriz, Antonio Aguilar and Antonio Banderas. There was American press speculation in 1913 and 1914 that Villa would become president of Mexico. Villa said he was not well enough educated to assume the responsibility, which was true – he could scarcely read.

Villa had a tenuous relationship with Emiliano Zapata, a bandit leader fighting in the south of Mexico. While Zapata could hold his own against the Federals, he was short of cash and lacked Villa's contacts with America.

Carranza and the Constitutionalist Army entered Mexico City in August 1914. Villa and Zapata refused to join Carranza, claiming that Carranza had no intention of carrying out the aims of the revolution. The Convention of Aguascalientes, which met in October–November 1914 deposed Carranza and installed Eulalio Gutiérrez as President. After Carranza left, Villa and Zapata entered and occupied Mexico City, meeting face to face for the first time on 4 December, 1914.

Villa was forced out of Mexico City in 1915, following a number of incidents between himself, his troops and the citizens. The return of Carranza and the Constitutionalists to Mexico City followed. Villa then rebelled against Carranza and his general, Álvaro Obregón. Villa and Zapata styled themselves as *convencionistas*, supporters of the Convention of Aguascalientes. Unfortunately, Villa's talent for generalship began to fail him. When Villa faced Obregón in the Battle of Celaya, repeated charges of Villa's cavalry were no match for Obregón's entrenchments and machine guns, and Villa was repulsed. Villa retreated to Chihuahua; he ignored the wise advice of the most valuable member of his military staff, Felipe Angeles, and Angeles left for exile in Texas.

The Americans believed that supporting Carranza was the best way to achieve a stable Mexican government, and refused to supply arms to Villa. Villa felt betrayed and began to attack Americans. In March 1916, in response to the US government's official recognition of the Carranza regime, Villa led a cross-border raid on Columbus, New Mexico. He burned the town, killing 10 soldiers and 8 civilians. General Pershing took 6,000 troops across the border into Mexico to pursue Villa. During the search, the United States launched its first air combat mission with eight planes. At the same time Carranza's army was also searching for Villa. It should have been the end for Villa, but he successfully eluded both armies.

Pancho Villa remained at large but never regained his former stature or military power. Carranza was weakened by the departure of Obregón in 1917, and by the ongoing rebellion of the Zapatista forces. He did not have the strength to snuff out Villa. In 1920, Villa negotiated peace with the new President Adolfo de la Huerta and ended his revolutionary activities. He went into semi-retirement at the hacienda of El Canutillo, with a detachment of 50 soldiers as bodyguards. He was assassinated three years later, in 1923, in Parral, Chihuahua, in his car. His last words were, 'Don't let it end like this. Tell them I said something.'

The assassins were never found and have never been identified. While there is some circumstantial evidence that Obregón was behind the killing, Villa made many enemies during his career of violence, and any one of those enemies would have had motives to murder him. Villa's one legal widow, Luz Corral, ran Villa's mansion *Quinta Luz* as a museum until she died in 1981. The museum is still there, with Villa's car as an exhibit.

In 1926 his grave was robbed. The head was cut off and taken as a trophy. Nobody knows who took it, and it has never been found.

ERNST ROEHM

1934

ERNST ROEHM WAS born in Munich in 1887. Intensely militaristic by instinct, he joined the German army in 1906 and served throughout World War I, during which he attained the rank of major. He was wounded three times. After the war Roehm became the leader of the Frontbann, one of several paramilitary organizations. He became increasingly radical, and he felt angry and betrayed, over Germany's surrender at the end of the First World War. He preceded Hitler in helping to found the Nazi Party. Roehm helped Hitler win the support of the army in Bavaria and made available to him his private strong-arm force, which, in October 1921, became the Sturmabteilung. Roehm took part in the November 1923 Beer Hall Putsch in Munich, and was briefly imprisoned. He was soon playing a major role in the Nazi Party. He began to organize his own paramilitary organization from the sport detachment of the Nazi Party. This valiantly defended Hitler during the Beer Hall Putsch, and in recognition Hitler renamed the sports detachment *sturmabteilung*, which was abbreviated as SA, appointing Ernst Roehm as its leader. Roehm took the gang of street thugs that made up the SA and began to train them in strict military style. This gave the Nazi Party its strong military arm which made itself useful in several street brawls.

The relationship between Roehm and Hitler deteriorated, mainly over the leadership of the SA and the role it was to play in achieving party goals. Roehm wanted the SA to be independent of the party's political structure, but Hitler naturally wanted to control everything; the SA could not be granted autonomy. Hitler was becoming increasingly uneasy about the unruly conduct of Roehm's 'brownshirts', which debased the Nazi's public image and therefore endangered his chance of gaining power. Thwarted, Roehm became angry and spiteful, resigning from his position and becoming a military instructor in Bolivia.

Hitler replaced Roehm with more conservative and controllable candidates, but the SA only became more and more violent without Roehm's leadership, and Hitler began to fear losing control. Hitler established himself as supreme commander of the SA and reappointed Roehm as his subordinate, hoping to curb the violent nature of the SA. Roehm militarized the SA even more, making Hitler doubt his own ability to control the stormtroopers. Roehm absorbed other paramilitary groups into the SA, greatly inflating their membership.

As the Nazi party exerted increasing control over Germany's political and social institutions, the role of the SA became obsolete. In fact the violent nature of the SA was politically alienating, and threatened to undermine party goals.

In January 1934 Hitler wrote a letter of congratulation and appreciation to Roehm, but he was far from happy with the enormous strength of the SA – or with the power that that gave Roehm. By that stage the SA had two million members, making it 20 times larger than the army. Hitler was ambivalent. The SA had helped him to gain power. Now it was no longer useful. In fact it had become an embarrassment. It was unpopular with businessmen, with the army, and it was full of working-class Socialists who wanted a second revolution.

From at least as early as 1931, Goebbels had been warning Hitler about the danger of having a homosexual like Roehm in such a prominent position. Then Captain Paul Schulz drew Hitler's attention to 'the dangers ... necessarily entailed, in my opinion, by the employment of morally objectionable persons in positions of authority'. In addition to Roehm, he named Karl Ernst, Paul Rohrbein, Roehm's aides Reiner and Count Du MoulinEckart and the confidential agent Meyer. According to Schulz these formed a 'homosexual chain' reaching from Munich to Berlin. What made the situation so dangerous, Schulz wrote, was that 'Captain Roehm makes absolutely no secret of his disposition; on the contrary, he prides himself on his aversion to the female sex and proclaims it in public . . . Things have now reached the stage where rumours are being spread in Marxist quarters that you yourself, my most esteemed Fuhrer, are also homosexual.'

It was incredibly daring, verging on the insane, to come this close to accusing both Roehm and Hitler of being homosexual. Roehm was determined to have Paul Schulz killed, though he did not succeed. The situation developed in a surprising way. The Schulz letter was leaked to the editor of the *Münchener Post* with the stated intention of 'dealing a blow at Hitler and the Movement'. When it was published, Goebbels described the 'utter confusion' at the Party's Munich headquarters. The publication of the letter was disastrous publicity for the Nazi party. Hitler thought it better to keep quiet about the matter, even though the newspaper featured further articles on Roehm's homo-sexuality, using information from Meyer. Meyer was subsequently remanded on a charge of fraud and found hanged in his cell. The official cause of death was suicide. The political imponderables were too great for Hitler to adopt a public position on the matter. It has been suggested that because Hitler was homosexual himself he may even have regarded the Roehm case as a kind of weathercock that would enable him to gauge the strength of public reactions to a charge of homosexuality. Was he, perhaps, exposing his personal secret to public debate without endangering himself? Revealingly, Hitler later said of gay men he had promoted, 'I take no interest in their private lives, just as I won't stand for people prying into my own.'

But there may have been a more sinister reason for not wanting Roehm pursued. Hitler had known Roehm a long time. Roehm knew a great deal about Hitler – a great deal that Hitler would not have wanted anyone to else to know. Roehm was not only acquainted with the shady beginnings of Hitler's political career: he was also one of the very few people who knew about his homosexuality. It must have been Hitler's nightmare that he would one day launch a smear campaign. If Hitler was thinking in terms of concealing his own homosexuality forever, he could only do so by the elimination of dangerous witnesses, and at the very top of the list of potential blackmailers was Ernst Roehm. If Hitler was thinking in this direction, Roehm was doomed.

In 1931 the public prosecutor's office in Berlin apparently started investigating Roehm for 'unnatural sexual offences'. On 13 July, 1931, acting on a tip from Otto Strasser, the authorities searched the home of Roehm's correspondent, Dr

Heimsoth, and confiscated the three outspoken letters that would later appear in the press. These were handed over to the Munich public prosecutor's office. Soon it became apparent that though Roehm admitted being 'bisexually inclined' and having 'often had to do with young boys in that direction', he refused to admit engaging in criminal intercourse 'as defined by Paragraph 175'. The case was therefore dropped.

Then in 1932 the leftwing *Welt am Montag* printed the three letters dating from 1928–9 written by Ernst Roehm. Two days later they appeared in the *Münchener Post*. Their authenticity was beyond doubt. The letters left no doubt that Roehm was homosexual. Hindenburg remarked in private that, in the Kaiser's day, an officer like Roehm would have had a pistol left on his desk; and if the scoundrel had refused to take the hint, he would have been hounded out of public life in disgrace. But nothing like that happened to Roehm. Instead he was firmly back in position by the end of 1932. The next year, 1933, he was once again among the most powerful figures in the Nazi hierarchy. The official propaganda neatly explained that he had been the victim of character assassination from Marxists and 'the entire Jewish press'.

By the summer of 1934, Hindenburg was very ill. Persuaded by Hermann Goering and Heinrich Himmler, and because of the rumbling scandals surrounding Roehm, Hitler finally decided to purge the SA chief. Roehm and his senior SA officers posted their own sentries and armed their men as best they could. According to his Berlin deputy, Karl Ernst, Roehm deposited 'important evidence in a safe place' because 'we must be ready for anything'. Roehm knew what was brewing. Hitler told the SA to take a month's leave in

July. Roehm sent his men away, telling them that the SA was Germany's destiny, but he was deeply suspicious of Hitler's motive. By sending the SA away on leave Hitler deprived his adversary of his principal means of protection. Hitler then summoned Roehm and the other SA leaders to a conference at Bad Wiessee on the Tegernsee, not far from Munich.

At Hindenburg's estate at Neudeck, Hitler personally obtained the president's approval for his plan to proceed against the SA leadership by force. Hindenburg probably needed no persuasion; he was an old-fashioned homophobe, revolted by Roehm, in his own words 'nauseated' by the knowledge that Roehm was 'a breech-loader'. Next, the SS under Himmler evaluated its 'incriminating evidence' and compiled death lists that included the names of the SA leaders and others who had angered the Nazis. It was going to be a purge.

A meeting of SA leaders was arranged for 30 June and Hitler had promised to attend. The night before became notorious as The Night of the Long Knives. That night found the SA leaders gathered at the Hanselbauer Hotel at Bad Wiessee for an evening of drunken carousing. There were no sentries on duty and no guards. Hitler hesitated before carrying out his purge, but on 29 June Stormtroopers had staged demonstrations in Munich against Hitler's regime; that made Hitler's mind up for him; he ordered the purge. At 6.30 a.m. on 30 June a convoy of cars drove into the village and sped to the inn. Hitler himself went in and woke Ernst Roehm up, on the pretence that he and the SA were to prepare a putsch, and took him from the hotel. The men in the other bedrooms were dealt with more straightforwardly; they were arrested and taken direct to Stadelheim Prison in

Munich. In one room, Edmund Heines, who was the SA Obergruppenführer for Silesia, was in bed with a boy. According to one account Heines was taken outside and shot immediately.

At about 10 a.m., the SS began a similar round-up in Berlin. Some SA men were shot on the doorstep when they answered the bell. Many had no idea what was happening. The Munich police chief told his SS executioners, 'Gentlemen, I don't know what this is all about, but shoot straight.' By the time Hitler arrived back to Berlin, most of those on the death list were already dead.

Roehm himself lived on for a few hours. It was in the afternoon of 30 June that Hitler ordered Roehm's death. Roehm was left alone in his prison cell with a revolver and the instruction to commit suicide. He refused, saying, 'If I am to be killed, let Adolf do it himself.' Two SS officers then stripped him to the waist and fired into his heart at point-blank range. Hitler said later that he was sorry that he had to destroy Roehm. Then, the SA was disbanded, and the obstacle to the Nazi consolidation of power was eradicated. About 150 'opponents of the regime' were murdered between 30 June and 3 July, 1934. Goebbels explained to an astonished German nation that the massacre had been necessary to eliminate what he described as a 'small clique of professional saboteurs'. In his carefully written speech Goebbels stated with startling directness that the SA leaders 'were on the point of exposing the entire leadership of the party to suspicions of shameful and loathsome sexual abnormality'. And while the multiple assassination was in progress, Hermann Goering decreed the destruction or confiscation of all the relevant documents, which presumably included Roehm's 'dirt' on Hitler.

SERGEI KIROV

1934

SERGEY MIRONOVICH KOSTRIKOV was born to a poor family in Urzhum in Russia, in March 1886. His parents died and at the age of seven he was sent to an orphanage. He became a Marxist, joining the Russian Social Democratic Labour Party in 1904. Like many other revolutionaries in Russia, for safety he assumed a *nom de guerre:* Kostrikov became Kirov. The name 'Kir' reminded him of a Persian warrior king. Kirov took part in the Russian Revolution of 1905, was arrested and later released. After being released from prison he joined the Bolsheviks. In 1906, he was arrested again, this time spending three years in prison for printing illegal literature. When he was released, he resumed his revolutionary activities and was arrested and imprisoned again. On his release, he moved to the Caucasus, where he stayed until the Tsar Nicholas II's abdication.

After the Russian Revolution of 1917, he fought in the Civil War until 1920. Then he became head of the Azerbaijan party organisation. Kirov was a loyal supporter of Joseph Stalin, and in 1926 he was rewarded with the leadership of the Leningrad Communist Party.

The problem was that Kirov was charismatic and popular. By the 1930s, Stalin was becoming increasingly worried about Kirov's growing popularity, which he saw as a threat to his own security. At the 1934 Party Congress, Kirov received only three negative votes for the new Central Committee, the fewest of any candidate; Stalin received 292 negative votes, the highest of any candidate. Kirov was now in extreme danger from Stalin. Later in 1934, Stalin asked Kirov to go to work for him in Moscow, most probably to keep a closer eye on him. Kirov unwisely refused, and Stalin's suspicions that Kirov was a serious rival were confirmed – at least in Stalin's paranoid mind.

In December 1934, Kirov was killed in Leningrad. The assassin was Leonid Nikolaev. Stalin claimed that Nikolaev was part of a larger conspiracy led by Leon Trotsky against the Soviet government. This resulted in the arrest and execution of Lev Kamenev, Grigory Zinoviev, and 14 others in 1936. It is possible that Kirov was murdered by this 'independent' conspiracy, but it is generally believed that it was Stalin himself who ordered the murder. It has nevertheless never been proved. All the major participants and witnesses are now dead, many of them liquidated in Stalin's purges. Even so, there were several NKVD (KGB) investigations subsequent to the event that tell us some of the story of the assassination.

On the day of the assassination, 1 December, 1934, Kirov arrived at his office in Leningrad at 4.30 p.m. He was preparing a speech that he planned to give later to party officials. He was met by four NKVD guards in plain clothes. He was also met by his usual bodyguard, Borisov. Kirov was accompanied by the five guards up the stairs to his office on the third floor of the Smolnyi. When they reached the third floor, the four NKVD guards left because there was another guard posted at the top of the stairs. Borisov stayed with Kirov.

Borisov seems to have trailed some distance behind Kirov as they walked along the landing. Kirov's office was round a corner to the left. As he walked past a lavatory, a man came out and turned to face the wall. For some reason neither Kirov nor Borisov took any notice of this man. The man was Nikolaev. He followed Kirov round the corner out of site of Borisov.

Suddenly there were shots. Kirov was shot in the back of the neck with a Nagan revolver from about 3 ft away. He fell against a pillar, then slumped to the floor, face down. An electrician called Platych was up a ladder near the end of the corridor. He saw the murder, and then saw Nikolaev point the gun at his own head. The electrician hurled a screwdriver at Nikolaev, which knocked him to the floor and made him fire the gun into a wall cornice. Unfortunately Platych made a conflicting second statement in which he did not see Nikolaev use the gun at all; he just saw Kirov fall to the floor with a gun near him and then he, Platych, picked up the gun and threw it into a corner.

Borisov, the bodyguard, heard the shots and ran around the corner to find Kirov's body. Six men in a conference room nearby poured into the corridor at the same moment: Ivanchenko, Rosliakov, Ugarov, Kodatskii, Mikhail'chenko and Struppe. Rosliakov testified that he found Nikolaev slumped on the floor with the revolver in his hand. He took it out of the assassin's hand and gave it to Ugarov. The NKVD chief, Medved, was then called.

Another witness was Stero Gorokova, who came out of her office when she heard the shots. She saw Mikhail'chenko leaning over the body of Nikolaev. She could not see what he was doing.

There are discrepancies between the testimonies of the witnesses. Some can be attributed to the suddenness of the events and the confusion of the moment. But there could be a more sinister interpretation. Nikolaev was evidently the key figure. Nikolaev was a party functionary who had recently lost his job and had been desperately trying to negotiate to get his job back. There is considerable evidence that he committed the murder. The NKVD found a diary detailing his plans and intentions, though the diary was possibly manufactured by the political police. His statement was probably given after torture; it was said that he committed suicide in his cell once the NKVD had extracted the information it wanted. Thus the evidence that Nikolaev pulled the trigger is quite suspect. Even if he had, there is reason to believe that there was complicity within the NKVD. Nikolaev had been detained three weeks earlier and had been found carrying a Nagan revolver and a map detailing the route Kirov followed daily from his home to his office. Several years later Yagoda, the then head of the KGB, testified that he had been informed of Nikolaev and had ordered that any assassination attempt directed toward Kirov should not be hindered.

Other witnesses who might have been useful in determining what actually happened died rather suddenly. For example, Borisov, Kirov's bodyguard died under very suspicious circumstances in a road accident the day after the murder; he was riding in a truck with a group of NKVD agents. Subsequent investigations show that he was probably thrown from a fast moving vehicle. He knew too much.

In fact the testimony of those present points to many alternative scenarios. It is possible that the NKVD was directly involved and had recruited Nikolaev when they found he had a grievance against Kirov. It was also possible that

Mikhail'chenko or others who emerged from the conference room had committed the murder and subsequently thrust the weapon into Nikolaev's hand. Mikhail'chenko was one of the few people who knew that Kirov would show up at his office at that time. It is not clear how Nikolaev, acting on his own, could possibly have known that Kirov would make this uncharacteristically late visit to his office.

NKVD complicity seems to be indicated by several factors. Key witnesses disappeared. A possibly dangerous man was detained and released. He was allowed, after being dismissed, to penetrate deep into a secure and well-guarded building. The connivance of the NKVD is likely.

Stalin's actions both before and after the murder suggest that he was closely involved. If he did not plan it, he certainly must have sanctioned it and then was instrumental in covering up what happened. The day before Kirov's murder Stalin decreed that those involved in crimes against the state could be summarily tried and punished by a special tribunal. This enabled him to silence and destroy anyone he wanted, assassins and witnesses alike, before they could reveal anything. When the assassination was reported to him, Stalin took the extraordinary step of conducting the investigation himself.

The indications are that Stalin not only sanctioned Kirov's assassination, but planned to use it as a political noose that would allow him to gain a stranglehold on the entire Soviet Union. Yet with Kirov out of the way, it was now in Stalin's best interest to promote a Kirov personality cult. This was how it came about that Stalin allowed a city in the Ukraine to be named in his honour.

Stalin had removed the problem of Kirov the rival by having him killed, but Kirov was enormously popular. Stalin therefore had to appear to be grief-stricken at Kirov's death. He treated it as a genuine national tragedy, gave him a state funeral and had him buried by the Kremlin Wall. As a great Soviet hero, his name was to be commemorated all over the Soviet Union. Many cities, streets and factories took his name, including the cities of Kirov and Kirovograd, the Kirovskaya station on the Moscow Metro and the massive Kirov industrial plant in St Petersburg. For a long time, a huge granite and bronze statue of Kirov dominated the city of Baku. The monument was dismantled in 1991, after Azerbaijan gained its independence. The ballet in Leningrad of which Kirov was so fond was changed to the 'Kirov Ballet'. Even a class of warship would later be named after him.

The aftermath of the Kirov assassination was appalling. The assassination marked the beginning of Stalin's Great Purges. The new procedural laws Stalin had forced through the Central Executive Committee gave him frightening power to investigate and destroy any person or group of his choosing. And Stalin gave full vent to his new powers, slashing down scores of adversaries. He started by destroying his ideological opponents, men like Kamenev, Zinoview and Bukharin. He seemed to want to wipe out all the 'Old Bolsheviks', the men who could remember where he had come from, and went on to murder tens of thousands of others besides.

SENATOR HUEY LONG

1935

HUEY PIERCE LONG, born in 1893, was a politician from Louisiana. He served as governor of Louisiana from 1928–32, winning the election by the largest vote margin in the state's history (92,941 to 3,733), and as a senator from 1932–35. Long was a backer of Franklin D. Roosevelt in the 1932 presidential election, then decided to mount his own presidential campaign in the future.

In 1934 Long proposed the redistribution of wealth to curb poverty and crime. He campaigned with the slogan 'every man a king, but no one wears a crown' which he adopted from William Jennings Bryan. He became known as 'the Kingfish' because he answered the telephone with the quip 'this is the Kingfish'. It was a reference to George 'Kingfish' Stevens, a colourful character in the very popular radio show *Amos 'n' Andy*. Stevens was always trying to lure the title characters into get-rich-quick schemes. Long's attacks on the utilities industries and the privileges of corporations were popular. He also frequently launched disparaging remarks against rich people – as a class – portraying them as parasites grabbing more than their fair share of the public wealth while marginalizing the poor. He was enormously popular for his radical social reform policies and his willingness to take forceful action. He also had a charismatic and flamboyant personality, instantly recognizable in his trademark white linen suit. But he tried to gain near-total control of the state government and media, which brought accusations of megalomania. In 1929, he was impeached on charges of bribery and gross misconduct, but the state senate failed to convict him by a narrow margin; it was often alleged that Long had concentrated power to the point where he had become a dictator.

He was vigorous in his efforts to try to counter the profound socio-economic impact of the Great Depression. By 1934 he began a reorganization of the state that all but abolished local government and gave himself the power to appoint all state employees; his behaviour as a US Senator was often downright unconstitutional, as he continued to be in effective control of Louisiana even though he had been replaced as Governor by Oscar K. Allen. But Allen was a kind of puppet-governor.

In 1933 he took part in the three-week senate filibuster against the Glass-Steagall Act. The filibuster was a method of destroying measures by using up all the debating time with unduly long speeches. In another famous filibuster in June 1935, Long made the longest speech of his senate career. It lasted over 15 hours. Long was a demagogue in a decade that saw the rise of Franco, Mussolini and Hitler; some thought Long was one of the most dangerous men in America.

Long got himself ready to run for president against Roosevelt in the 1936 election. He announced that he would be running in August 1935. Just one month later, he was dead. It has been suggested that Long had no real intention of running for president, but had another candidate in mind; his real intention was to wait four years and run for president as a Democrat in 1940.

Two months before his death, in July 1935, Long said he had uncovered a plot to assassinate him. Then on 8 September Huey Long was in the Capitol building at Baton Rouge when he was shot once and fatally wounded. The events surrounding the shooting have been a mystery for decades. The official version of Huey Long's assassination is that he was shot by Dr Carl Weiss, who was in turn immediately shot dead by Long's bodyguards. The walls of the capitol hallway are still chipped from the bullets fired in the shootout.

An inept attempt was made to stitch up Long's wounds by Dr Arthur Vidrine. The wounds continued bleeding internally and Long died two days later.

Dr Weiss was a medical doctor and the son-in-law of Judge Benjamin Pavy, who for a long time had been a political opponent of Long. Many people have questioned whether Dr Weiss actually killed Long. It is possible that when the two men met, Weiss only punched Long and that the bodyguards mistakenly believed that Weiss had pulled a gun and fired into Long's stomach; in the hail of bullets they launched at Weiss a stray bullet from one of the bodyguards' guns accidentally struck Long. The former Louisiana state police superintendent Francis Grevemberg takes this view. To cover their terrible mistake, and themselves, the guards may then have concocted their story – that Weiss was the assassin. Weiss's son tried for many years to clear his father's name – without any conclusive result.

It is nevertheless a possibility that Weiss really was the assassin. One of the items on that evening's agenda was the reorganization of boundaries, which would have adversely affected Weiss's father-in-law. Long had summoned a special meeting of the state legislature. Long wanted to gerrymander (unfavourably change the boundaries) Judge Benjamin Pavy's district. Some have speculated that Weiss, who had just returned from a visit to Germany, saw possible parallels between Huey Long and Adolf Hitler and was determined to stop the potential dictator in his tracks. Long is thought to have been greeted by Weiss as he walked down the corridor of the Capitol Building. Witnesses saw, or thought they saw, Weiss shoot Long at close range in the abdomen. Long cried out, stumbled down the corridor, then Weiss was immediately riddled with bullets by Long's bodyguards. The number of shots fired is not known. There were 31 bullet wounds found in the front of Weiss's body, 29 in the back and 2 in the head; some were probably 'pairs' – entry and exit wounds caused by the same bullet.

Long meanwhile had vanished. An associate, Jimmie O'Connor, found the senator in a stairwell. He was rushed to hospital. Long whispered to O'Connor, 'I wonder why he shot me.' When he was told who the attacker was, Huey shook his head; 'I don't know him.' Dr Arthur Vidrine, the physician attending Long, discovered that the bullet had passed right through his abdomen. Surgery was urgently needed to keep him from bleeding to death. Long sent for two of the best surgeons in New Orleans, but they got caught up in traffic and could not reach the hospital in time. This was how Dr Vidrine came to undertake the surgery. When the two surgeons arrived from New Orleans, they were shocked to find that Vidrine had not checked for damage to the kidney, which it turned out had been injured. They needed to perform a second operation, but by this stage Long was too weak to survive more surgery.

Huey Long wrote two autobiographical books. The first, *Every Man a King,* was published in 1933. The second, *My First Days in the White House*, was published after his death; it laid out in bold style his presidential ambitions.

Huey Long is commemorated with a statue in the US Capitol building, two bridges over the Mississippi River (one at Baton Rouge, the other at Jefferson Parish). Franklin D. Roosevelt began to implement Huey's 'share the wealth' philosophy under the name of the New Deal, and many commentators fought to give Huey credit for pushing Roosevelt into sponsoring that programme.

ERNST VOM RATH

1938

IN OCTOBER 1938 the Polish government passed a law saying that any Poles who had lived abroad for more than five years would not be allowed to re-enter Poland. This was a measure to defend Poland from being flooded by the thousands of Jews of Polish origin who were currently living outside Poland and who were being thrown out of Germany and Austria. The German response to this was to deliver 15,000 Jews to the Polish border on 27 October, 1938 and, in cold blood, abandon them there. They were not allowed to enter Poland; they were not allowed to return to Germany either. Some managed to escape into Poland, but many did not. Those who were left languished for three months, many dying of hunger and neglect, some going insane, some committing suicide. Eventually it was the Germans – not the Poles – who relented and took the survivors back. Some of them later managed to reach Britain or America. It was an episode that did no credit to the governments of either Germany or Poland.

Herschel Grynszpan was a Jewish youth of 17 who had left Hanover in Germany in 1936 with the intention of emigrating to Palestine. Instead he ended up in Paris, where he lived with an aunt and uncle. In August 1938 he was served with an expulsion order by the French government, and after that he was sheltered by his uncle illegally. On 3

November, 1938 he got a postcard from his sister telling him of his family's deportation and suffering on the Polish frontier. Given the awful chain of events that followed, it was a postcard she may later have regretted sending; there are some things it is better not to know. Four days after receiving his sister's postcard, still incensed at his family's treatment, Grynszpan bought a revolver and walked into the German embassy, asking to see the first secretary. The first secretary was not available, so instead he was shown into the third secretary's office.

The third secretary was a German diplomat called Ernst vom Rath. Grynszpan protested to him about the treatment of the Jews at the Polish frontier and then fired five shots, two of which hit vom Rath. Herschel Grynszpan made no attempt to escape, and vom Rath died two days later.

Because Grynszpan was a Jew, there was a large-scale and well co-ordinated reprisal aimed at Jews in general. The reprisal, which came on 9 November 1938, was the infamous Kristallnacht (Crystal Night), so named by the Nazis because of the huge expanses of broken glass from the smashed windows of Jewish shops left in the streets the following morning. It was as if it had rained glass. Jewish people, shops and business premises were attacked all over Germany. Hundreds of synagogues were burnt down. Many Jews were killed. In Berlin, fashionably dressed women laughed and clapped as they watched Jews being beaten senseless by youths with lengths of lead piping. More than 7,000 shops were looted. It was clear that the attacks were carefully co-ordinated, because they broke out simultaneously in towns throughout Germany. Goering was annoyed when he heard that the replacement glass would have to be imported and paid for in foreign currency. His characteristic comment was, 'They should have killed more Jews and broken less glass.'

The story of Grynszpan's futile gesture and its appalling consequences – the blind collective sadism of the pogrom – inspired Michael Tippett to write his oratorio *A Child of Our Time*. Tippett borrowed the title from the last novel of Horvath, which tells the story of an embittered soldier who murders the wrong person in a futile gesture and then dies, frozen to death in the snow. Tippett was interested in scapegoats, people who are in themselves innocent but are sacrificed in some cause or other. The soldier in Horvath's last novel, and then Grynszpan: the story seems to repeat. And even vom Rath was an innocent sacrificial victim. Tippett was also intrigued by a poem by Wilfrid Owen in which the Old Testament story of Abraham and Isaac was given a savage, modern and ironic twist. The angel stays Abraham's hand and tells him not to kill Isaac but the Ram of Pride instead.

But the old man would not so, but slew his son, –
And half the seed of Europe, one by one.

Benjamin Britten later set that poem vividly to music as part of his *War Requiem*. Tippett might have done that, but he wanted his friend T. S. Eliot to supply new words for his war oratorio. Eliot read Tippett's sketch and then surprised Tippett by advising him to write his own words. The result was a modern classic, which sums up 'the pity of war'. For Tippett it was a turning-point in his career as a composer. He knew when he heard it for the first time, in 1944, that he had found his true role. And the trigger had been that shooting incident in Paris in November 1938.

And what of the young man who caught Michael Tippett's imagination? For Herschel Grynszpan one might have expected a quick trial followed by summary execution, but things did not turn out that way. Rather like Gavrilo Princip, Grynszpan unexpectedly survived. His trial was delayed, because the Nazis wanted the French to try him in secret, and Grynszpan's supporters in America pressed for a public trial. Then war broke out. Grynszpan wrote to the French minister of justice from prison, asking to be released so that he could fight the Nazis. His request was ignored, but along with other prisoners he was moved away from Paris because of the German advance. He was first encouraged to escape by his guards. He was uneasy about doing this, perhaps (justifiably) suspecting that this was a ruse to justify shooting him. But other prisoners were also being encouraged to disappear by the guards and Grynszpan had finally to be ordered to escape.

When France was overrun and occupied by the Germans, Grynszpan was traced and captured under the Vichy regime in 1940. He was tried and sentenced to 20 years in prison. In 1941 he was sent to Berlin and then to Sachsenhausen concentration camp. The Germans treated Grynszpan well, because they wanted him to look well in the big show trial they were planning for him. This trial was scheduled for May 1942, but it never took place.

Grynszpan now cleverly alleged that he had been sexually abused by vom Rath. This was probably untrue – he had after all asked to see the first secretary at the embassy, not vom Rath, who was the third secretary – but Goebbels recognized that the show trial would not after all be any good for public relations. Grynszpan had outwitted Goebbels.

Nobody knows for certain what became of Herschel Grynszpan after that. Somehow in the turmoil of the Second World War, he was forgotten. He vanished, and it is possible that he was executed in secret with no trial. But there is good evidence for believing that he survived the war, changed his name and started a fresh life in the new state of Israel. Probably Herschel Grynszpan is dead now, simply because of the passage of time, but the boy who brought about the infamous Crystal Night did not die as one might have expected, back in 1938.

LEON TROTSKY

1940

THE NAME OF Jacques Mornard is not well known. Nor, though, is the real name of his victim, Lev Davidovich Bronstein. Like Lenin, Bronstein had to adopt a *nom de guerre* in the run-up to the revolution, simply to evade capture and retribution. Bronstein took the name Leon Trotsky when he was on the run after escaping from a prison in Siberia in 1902.

Trotsky was born in 1879 and was a mature 40 years old when the Russian Revolution broke out. Trotsky's role in organizing the 1917 Russian revolution was just as important as Lenin's, even though he did not actually become a Bolshevik until July 1917. He was also the most important figure in the negotiating team for the Brest-Litovsk peace treaty. During the next three years Trotsky and Lenin frequently disagreed, but that was partly because there were massive inconsistencies and shifts in Lenin's strategies and policies.

After Lenin's death, it might have seemed as if the way was clear for Trotsky to lead the political field. But seniority always counted for a great deal in the Communist Party and there were many long-serving members who remembered that Trotsky only joined the party in 1917. But it was also true that there were more ambitious, more determined and more ruthless men around than Trotsky. They mounted a campaign to discredit him, master-minded by Stalin, and he was dismissed as commissar for war. He was given work of little political significance to do, such as heading the electric power development programme. He resigned from this post in 1925. In 1927 he was expelled from the Communist Party for alleged anti-party activities; he had in fact simply become more and more open in his disagreement with Communist Party policy.

Trotsky began his life in exile in January 1928, when he was sent to Turkestan. He was shortly after that banished from the Soviet Union altogether, arriving in Constantinople in 1929. Once safely in Turkey, Trotsky tried to establish and co-ordinate a network of followers; he was far from giving up on politics, in spite of the enormous dangers involved in opposing Stalin. Even in Turkey he was watched by Stalin's agents. KGB agents surrounded him. Two of them were brothers, known later in America as Jack and Robert Soble. They were Lithuanian Jews by birth, but served the Soviet Communist Party all their lives. Jack Soble was able to visit Trotsky in various European cities and both he and his brother became well-known among German Trotskyists. With good reason, Trotsky suspected them of being spies and in 1932 turned them out of his group. Beria, the head of the KGB, allowed the entire Soble family to leave the Soviet Union in 1940; Beria trusted them totally to carry on their espionage work in the United States. This they continued until as late as 1961, when they were both convicted of espionage.

Another important Soviet agent was Mark Zborowski, who was Russian-born and educated at the Sorbonne in Paris. He moved to the USA in 1941, where he resumed his work spying for the KGB. A Soviet spy defecting to the West eventually exposed Zborowski as a fellow agent ten years later, in 1951.

In 1936 Trotsky went briefly to Norway, before settling in

Mexico at the invitation of the artist Diego Rivera in 1937.

Trotsky was accused of joining Zinoviev in a plot to kill Stalin, but he emphatically denied this charge. Stalin was very angry with Trotsky. He saw him as a major political nuisance, and would certainly have had him shot had he still been within his reach in the Soviet Union. He nevertheless decided that he must be eliminated at any cost, regardless of where he was, and gave orders for Trotsky to be assassinated in Mexico. Trotsky was aware that he was in serious danger. He knew Stalin had agents everywhere and that he had good reason to fear spies and infiltrators. It was one such infiltrator who would shortly murder him.

When Stalin took against people he arranged to have them killed. Stalin was a great lover of movies, and through films knew all the big American movie stars. He liked classic westerns, and seemed to identify with the lone cowboy who rode into town and got his own way by shooting people. Ironically, there was one movie cowboy he particularly hated and that was John Wayne - not for his film acting but for his political activities - and he set in motion the arrangements to have him killed. Khrushchev later boasted that he had intervened, had Stalin's 'fatwah' revoked and so prevented the assassination of John Wayne.

One colourful figure Trotsky encountered in Mexico was Frida Kahlo. Frida was born in 1907, though she claimed to be three years younger. She met her future husband, the painter Diego Rivera, when they were both at school. In adulthood, Frida became part of the Mexico City art world; she married Diego Rivera, though both of them had many affairs. Rivera had an affair with Frida's sister – and Kahlo had an affair with Leon Trotsky.

In the summer of 1940, Trotsky's house was attacked by a gang of 20 men. The Mexican painter David Siqueiros organized this band of Spanish and Mexican Communists, who were veterans of the Spanish Civil War. They launched the armed raid on Trotsky's villa in May, riddling the house with hundreds of bullets, none of which hit Trotsky. An American volunteer and a bodyguard were killed in the attack. It was clear to Trotsky that Stalin was determined that he should die and he did what he could to step up the security at his villa. Siqueiros was arrested and freed on bail; he was then spirited out of the country with the help of Pablo Neruda, who was a Communist and also a Chilean diplomat.

Another plan to kill Trotsky was organized and co-ordinated by Pavel Sudoplatov, a mysterious and shadowy figure who functioned as a superspy. Sudoplatov was approached in the post-Stalinist era by a high-ranking Soviet officer who wanted to interview him, General Volkogonov. He was reluctant to be interviewed but, rather surprisingly given that he was a superspy, agreed to the general's suggestion that he should write his autobiography. It eventually surfaced in the West in 1994 as *Special Tasks: Memoirs of an Unwanted Witness – a Soviet Spymaster,* by Pavel and Anatoli Sudoplatov. Sudoplatov was evidently a thoughtful Stalinist who well understood the political manoeuvrings of the 1940s, and who was also ready to do terrible things in Stalin's name.

Sudoplatov's plan involved using Ramon Mercader, who was the son of the wealthy Spanish Communist Caridad Mercader, this time as a lone assassin. Ruby Weil, an American Communist, was very friendly with Sylvia Ageloff, a follower of Trotsky. In 1938, Ruby Weil introduced Sylvia to a man she called Jacques Mornard. Mornard pursued Sylvia until they became lovers. Later, Sylvia travelled to Mexico to do volunteer work for Trotsky. Jacques Mornard was then able to use Sylvia's position as an intimate of Trotsky's household to gain admittance to Trotsky's house and get to know all about Trotsky's security, including the location and deployment of guards.

Jacques Mornard (or Ramon Mercader) presented himself as someone who was very interested in Trotsky's ideas, and arranged a meeting with Trotsky to discuss a philosophical treatise he had drafted.

It was on 20 August, 1940 that Trotsky was attacked in his villa in Mexico City by this agent of Stalin's. Trotsky came to trust Jacques Mornard as a friend. He had wormed his way into Trotsky's confidence by associating himself with someone Trotsky legitimately trusted – a friend of a friend. Trotsky invited Jacques Mornard, described as a French Jew, to take tea with him. Because Jacques Mornard was an invited guest, it did not occur to the bodyguards to search him, which turned out to be a fatal mistake. According to the police report, Mornard had a small ice axe hidden inside his trousers.

Jacques Mornard attacked Trotsky suddenly and without warning, battering his skull and injuring his right shoulder and right knee. Trotsky was conscious for a short while before he lapsed into unconsciousness as a result of the brain injury. According to the bodyguards, his last words were, 'I think Stalin has finished the job he has begun'.

Trotsky was taken to hospital, where he did not regain consciousness, and died the next day, 21 August, 1940. His death was announced in newspapers all round the world on the day after that, though not in the Soviet Union. All that appeared there was a very indirect report; according to American journalists an attempt had been made to assassinate Trotsky by an intimate friend and follower. Frida Kahlo, who had been Trotsky's mistress, was for some reason accused of committing the murder, but was soon afterwards released.

It became known that Mornard (or Mercader) was a Soviet agent. The Soviets tried various ways of helping him to escape from his Mexican gaol after his conviction, but it became clear that the American authorities were well informed about these plans, and were able to tip off the Mexican authorities in advance of each breakout attempt. In this way the Americans were able to ensure that Trotsky's assassin was not sprung from prison.

The death of Trotsky became the subject of two films, *The Assassination of Trotsky* (1972) with Richard Burton as Trotsky and *Frida* (2002), this time with Geoffrey Rush playing the doomed revolutionary exile. More obliquely, Trotsky became Snowball the pig in George Orwell's *Animal Farm* (1945).

Ramon Mercader was finally released from prison in 1960. After that he retired to the Soviet Union on a KGB pension. Frida Kahlo had to have a leg amputated – it had been damaged long before in a traffic accident – and became depressed. She committed suicide in 1954. Pavel Sudoplatov was awarded orders and medals for organizing and carrying out the vengeful special task of assassinating Trotsky.

REINHARD HEYDRICH

1942

REINHARD HEYDRICH WAS born in 1904 at Halle in the Teutoburg Forest. At the age of 18 he joined the navy. He was an accomplished fencer and skier and also a violinist; he enjoyed weekends of croquet and chamber music at the home of Admiral Canaris. On top of all of this, he was tall and good-looking. Even so at the early age of 26 he abruptly ruined the naval career that had been developing so promisingly by getting the daughter of a powerful industrialist pregnant. Far worse than that, he said that any woman who consented to sex before marriage was unworthy of marriage – and he refused to marry her. He was discharged from the navy for this double impropriety.

Heydrich then looked around for a new job, and quickly found one that suited his cruel streak. He joined Himmler's personal staff in 1931. Heydrich was imaginative, intelligent and cruel, and he was the perfect right-hand man for the plodding Himmler. They became a greatly feared double-act. Once Hitler became chancellor in 1933, Himmler's SS suddenly became extremely powerful. In just three months, Himmler had founded the first concentration camp, at Dachau, and filled it with an assortment of political opponents of Nazism.

Hitler's distrust of the SA was systematically whipped up by the SS chiefs, who had everything to gain from the fall of the SA. Himmler and Heydrich repeatedly warned that the SA was planning a coup. Eventually, as we have already seen, Hitler summoned the SA leaders to Bad Wiessee in Bavaria in what he thought of as a pre-emptive strike. The Bad Wiessee killings were taken as a signal by SS officers throughout Germany to execute leading politicians on lists prepared in advance by Himmler and Heydrich. Hitler reported to the Reichstag that 79 men had died, but it is likely that more than 500 died in the Night of the Long Knives.

The SS became all-powerful after winning this power struggle, and Himmler and Heydrich were answerable only to Hitler. In 1938 Polish Jews living in Germany in effect were stripped of their Polish citizenship by the Polish government. Shortly afterwards they were informed by the SS that they were not German citizens either. It was Heydrich who ordered the cruel round-up and ordered the stateless non-German non-Polish Jews to be taken in trucks to the Polish border and left in the no man's land between the two countries.

When he heard of this pointless cruelty, Herschel Grynszpan, a 17-year-old youth, himself a Polish Jew, shot a German official in Paris. He shot the wrong man, but that was incidental; Heydrich used the assassination as an excuse to arrange through the local police forces spontaneous demonstrations against the Jews. These Kristallnacht demonstrations led to many deaths and the destruction of 7,500 Jewish-run businesses across Germany.

Heydrich was responsible for setting up an exclusive brothel in Berlin, Madame Kitty's, where he had all the rooms bugged. Here the loyalty of all the Nazi leaders would be tested. Heydrich was also responsible for master-minding one of the biggest Nazi money-making schemes. For very big sums of money, Austrian Jews could buy exit visas instead of risking death in the concentration camps. By the end of 1939, nearly two-thirds of the Jews in Austria had handed over everything they owned to the SS and left the country. A similar Office of Jewish Emigration was opened in Prague after the German occupation of Czechoslovakia, and it too proved to be very profitable.

It was Heydrich who thought of the pretext to invade Poland. A German radio station in the border town of Gleiwitz was attacked by Polish troops. Many Germans were killed. The following day, the German tanks rolled across into Poland and the German press was full of righteous indignation about the unprovoked Polish attack. The Polish troops had of course been SS men in disguise. The bodies found on the site of the attack were concentration camp victims.

Heydrich was appointed Reich Protector for Bohemia and Moravia. Within a very short time he had earned the nickname Butcher of Prague, as he supervised the annihilation of Czech resistance. The Czech prime minister was condemned to death after a show trial. Czech agents formed a vital link between a key spy in the Nazi hierarchy and London. It seemed that Heydrich was getting close to identifying him and the Czech government in exile made the decision to assassinate Heydrich.

Two assassins, Jan Kubis and Josef Gabcik, were parachuted in. They set up an ambush on a sharp bend in the road between Heydrich's country house and his office in the Hradcany Palace in Prague. On 27 May, 1942, the Mercedes carrying Heydrich slowed to take the hairpin bend, which was why the assassins had chosen the location, and Gabcik stepped into the road and tried to shoot Heydrich. His gun jammed. The car stopped, and Kubis threw a grenade as Heydrich jumped out of the car with his revolver in his hand. Momentarily he looked like a serious threat, but Heydrich had been mortally wounded in the blast and died in hospital nine days later.

The fall-out from the assassination of Heydrich was terrible. Heydrich had been responsible for a string of atrocities and war crimes in life; now he was responsible for one more in death. It was one of the worst atrocities of the Second World War – the set-piece destruction of the randomly-chosen village of Lidice. The village was burnt to the ground and all the men and boys of the village, all 1,300 of them, all innocent civilians, were shot dead.

MAHATMA GANDHI

1948

MOHANDAS GANDHI, WHO became known as Mahatma Gandhi, was born at Porbandar in western India in 1869, into a Hindu family with a tradition of public service. When Mohandas was 18 he was sent by his family to study law in London. He was already an ascetic; he almost starved on the voyage to England because he had promised his mother not to eat meat. After briefly practising law in Bombay, he gave it up to live in poverty in South Africa. There he neglected his legal practice and devoted 21 years to opposing laws that discriminated against Indians.

In his struggle against the South African authorities, Gandhi was arrested, imprisoned and beaten. The climax of his South African struggle came in 1913, when a series of repressive measures culminated in a demand that every Indian seeking to live in the Transvaal would have to register. Gandhi organized what was to become a typical protest event, in which two thousand Indians rallied behind Gandhi and he led them backwards and forwards across the Transvaal frontier. It was a very effective publicity stunt. Public opinion swung in favour of the well-behaved Indians, and the measures were repealed.

By 1914, Gandhi felt that he was no longer needed in South Africa and returned to India. He supported British rule there, as he had in South Africa, at least through the First World War, but developed an increasing interest in the Congress movement for home rule for India. He soon dominated this movement. His civil disobedience campaign of 1920 created serious disorder and as a result he was imprisoned from 1922–1924 for conspiracy. In 1925 he disagreed with the Congress leaders acceptance of proposals that they should join the new legislatures. In protest, Gandhi dropped out of politics for several years.

In 1930, Gandhi led a march from his ashram (settlement) near Ahmedabad to the coast at Dandi (approximately 300 miles) to make salt from the sea. This was a grand gesture of protest against the government on salt. It had an electrifying effect on the whole country, and there were widespread scenes of disorder. He was arrested. It was on 25 June, 1934 that the first attempt was made to assassinate Gandhi. He was in Pune to deliver a speech at Corporation Auditorium. He travelled with Kasturba in a motorcade of two cars. They arrived at a railway level crossing. The second car, carrying Kasturba and Gandhi, got delayed at the crossing while the first car went on ahead. When the first car arrived at the auditorium, a bomb thrown at the car exploded, seriously injuring 10 people. No records of any police investigation survive, but some people have alleged that Nathuram Godse and Narayan Apte were involved in the attack.

When the Second World War broke out, Gandhi wanted to support Britain against Nazi Germany, but he gave in to Congress pressure and insisted that India would co-operate if full independence was promised. The British refused to give that promise.

In May 1944 Mahatma Gandhi was released from Agha

Khan Palace prison. He tried to establish an understanding with Jinnah, the Muslim leader, who demanded an independent Muslim state, but they were unable to agree. Gandhi's ideal was one undivided India – but that was clearly unachievable. Gandhi fell ill with malaria and was advised by his doctor to take a holiday at Panchgani, a hill station near Pune. When they realized Gandhi was there, a group of perhaps 20 young men led by Nathuram Godse arrived on a bus. They staged an all-day protest demonstration, refusing to talk to Gandhi when invited. During the evening prayer meeting, Nathuram Godse rushed towards Gandhi with a dagger shouting anti-Gandhi slogans. He did not reach Gandhi as he was overpowered by two of Gandhi's supporters.

The third attempt, which came shortly afterwards in September 1944, was also in the nature of a demonstration, though the witnesses who testified before the Kapoor Commission into Gandhi's assassination referred to it as an attempt at murder. While leaving Sevagram Ashram for Bombay to begin his talks with Jinnah, a group of Hindu-activists stopped him. They wanted to prevent him from talking to Jinnah. The protesters were stopped by Gandhi's supporters. Once again, the leader of the protest group was Nathuram Godse and once again he was found to be carrying a dagger. The incident was portrayed in the Richard Attenborough film *Gandhi* as peaceful, with demonstrators merely waving black flags, but Dr Sushila Nayyar saw the incident and testified that what she saw was an attempt at assassination. On 29 June, 1946, the train called The Gandhi Special and carrying Mahatma Gandhi was derailed near Pune. Boulders had been placed deliberately on the rails with the intention of derailing it. The train had crashed into the boulders. The Pune police did not want to interpret this as an attempt on Gandhi's life; they claimed that the boulders were placed there by looters who wanted to stop and rob goods trains. But there were no goods trains on the line either before or after The Gandhi Special, which was known to be carrying Gandhi and his entourage. Gandhi therefore seems the likeliest target.

In the summer of 1946 there were terrible massacres and atrocities. By the following spring, the Partition of India was agreed by the Congress leaders, against Gandhi's wishes.

In May 1947, Gandhi praised the British decision to allow India to have its independence as the noblest act. But independence was spoilt by outbreaks of savage violence between Hindu and Muslim communities. Gandhi went on hunger strikes to try to influence the situation and a semblance of order was restored, but the strife between the communities could only be resolved by segregating them, by creating a separate Muslim state of Pakistan (East and West) on each side of a predominantly Hindu India.

Gandhi's promotion of home rule for India resulted not only in the independence of the Indian sub-continent but the disintegration of the British Empire. Once India was free, there was suddenly a queue of British possessions and colonies wanting their independence too. But the trouble in India was far from over. There was still a great deal of dissent and dissatisfaction.

On 20 January, 1948, yet another attempt was made on Gandhi's life. A group of men, once more including the fanatically determined Nathuram Godse, converged on the Birla House in Delhi with the intention of assassinating him. The group of conspirators included Madanlal Pahwa, Shankar

Kishtaiyya, Digambar Bagde, Vishnu Karkare and Gopal Godse. Madanlal Pahwa tried to bribe the driver at the Birla House, a man named Choturam, to let him go behind the podium to take pictures of the Mahatma. But Choturam was suspicious and asked Madanlal Pahwa why he needed photographs from behind, and asked him where his camera was because he could see he was not carrying one. Madanlal Pahwa just walked off, though not before leaving a ball of cotton enclosing a bomb on the wall behind the podium and lighting it. The bomb went off without creating any panic. The rest of the conspirators had left after abandoning Pahwa.

When he was interrogated, Pahwa admitted to belonging to a gang of seven men who wanted to kill the Mahatma. The plan was that Pahwa would explode the bomb as close to the podium as possible while Digambar Bagde or Shankar Kishtaiyya would shoot Gandhi in the head; the ensuing chaos would cover their escape. Vishnu Karkare was to add to the mayhem by throwing hand grenades. Because Choturam was evidently suspicious, Bagde decided at the last moment not to act. Bagde told Kishtaiyya, who was his servant, to do the same. Gopal Godse, interviewed long afterwards, said the bomb went off fifty metres away from Gandhi and that all the other conspirators ran off leaving only Madanlal Phawa, who was caught.

Later, Madanlal Phawa led the police to the Marina Hotel where Nathuram Vinayak Godse and Narayan Apte were staying and the Sharief Hotel where all the other gang members had stayed. They had all left by that time and the police were only able to recover some clothing bearing the initials NVG – for Nathuram Vinayak Godse. The police knew the members of the assassination team were from

Maharashtra; however they were not able to establish the identity and involvement of Nathuram Godse – in spite of his involvement in earlier attempts on Gandhi's life and the clothing bearing his initials left behind at the Marina Hotel. There were accusations later on, after the assassination, that the Bombay Police had done too little in their search for the would-be assassins.

After the failed attempt at the Birla House, Nathuram Godse and Narayan Apte returned to Pune via Bombay. With the help of Dr Dattatraya Parchure and Gangadhar Dandavate they purchased a Beretta automatic and 11 bullets at Gwalior and returned to Delhi on 29 January. Just 10 days after the bombing, on 30 January, 1948, Gandhi was walking to his daily prayer meeting in the garden of the Birla House in Delhi when he was shot dead. As Hindu extremists saw it, as long as Gandhi lived India could never be Hindu-dominated, so they were determined that he should die.

A Western journalist who was there described the moment as 'one of those shining Delhi evenings'. He saw the Mahatma walk towards him over the grass, swathed in shawls and leaning lightly on two of the young women who often accompanied him, with two or three followers behind them. He ascended the four or five brick steps which led to the prayer-ground, where a small crowd meant that he could not be seen. The journalist heard four small muffled gunshots and went into shock, not noticing the arrival of a doctor and the police – and people carrying the little blood-stained body to a room indoors. People stood at its window and wept, though the police tried to make them leave. It has never been explained why Gandhi was not taken to hospital; he was simply taken indoors, where he died.

It is still uncertain what Mahatma Gandhi's last words were. Gandhi's personal assistant, Venkita Kalyanam, said that he was there and Gandhi did not utter a single word. Another witness, Nand Lal Mehta, testified that Gandhi said 'Ram-Ram' as he fell to the ground. Gopal Godse, talking about the assassination in the year 2000, believed that Gandhi would not have been capable of speech. 'You see, it was an automatic pistol. It had a magazine for nine bullets but there were actually seven at that time. And once you pull the trigger, within a second, all the seven bullets had passed. When these bullets pass through crucial points like the heart, consciousness is finished. You have no strength . . . The government . . . wanted to show that he was a staunch Hindu. So they put "Hey Ram" into Gandhi's dead mouth.'

So, finally, at the fifth attempt, Gandhi was dead. At 5.10 p.m., on 30 January the assassin had got close enough to him to shoot him three times in the stomach and chest at point-blank range. And the assassin was, of course, Nathuram Godse. Godse believed that Gandhi was responsible for the 1947 partition of India and the creation of Pakistan. Godse and his co-conspirator Narayan Apte were hanged. His brother Gopal and two others were sentenced to life imprisonment for their part in the conspiracy. Gopal Godse remained in jail for 18 years.

Mahatma ('great soul') Gandhi was venerated by many people as a great moral teacher who wanted to free India from materialism as well as caste prejudice, as well as a great patriot who wanted to free India from British rule. He was a kind of socialist, but it was a kind of socialism that had nothing to do with Marx or Marxism. His view of socialism was based on personal reform, on changing people rather than systems. In many ways his mission was nearer to that of Jesus.

His critics saw him as self-deluded, blind to the violence to which his non-violent campaigns led. Overall he is seen as a great force for peace, progress and justice. His grass roots self-help approach to social and economic development now looks very far-sighted indeed. What the Third World needs is not aid in the materialist form of hydro-electric dams, still less in the form of money, but the means to make a subsistence living – and this was Gandhi's big idea.

COUNT FOLKE
BERNADOTTE

1948

COUNT FOLKE BERNADOTTE was born in 1895, a grandson of
King Oscar II of Sweden and Norway and a nephew of King
Gustav V of Sweden. Folke Bernadotte never played any
political role in Sweden. In the international arena, he seems
to have combined a conservative philosophy with a faith in
Swedish neutrality, Nordic solidarity and a sense that
Sweden had a civilizing mission in the world.

In 1943, following a family tradition, Folke Bernadotte
became head of the Swedish Red Cross. Even before this
appointment, Bernadotte had organized seventy thousand
food parcels to be sent to Jewish prisoners in Nazi
concentration camps. During the final months of the Second
World War, Allied forces were forging ahead on all fronts.
As they retreated, the Germans were trying to wipe out all
traces of the concentration camps, where they had murdered
countless Jews. Bernadotte organized a Swedish relief
expedition to Germany with the famous white buses, to
rescue thirty thousand concentration camp prisoners and
take them to freedom in Sweden.

To achieve this, Folke Bernadotte travelled to Germany
four times starting in February 1945, to negotiate with
Heinrich Himmler, the head of the SS and the Gestapo, the

German foreign minister, Joachim von Ribbentrop, the head of the German security police, Ernst Kaltenbrunner and the head of German intelligence abroad, Walter Schellenberg. As well as negotiating the release of large numbers of prisoners, Bernadotte also passed Himmler's surrender offer to the Western powers; in the final stage of the war, Himmler actively conspired against Hitler to bring about a peace behind his back. On 19 February, Bernadotte had his first meeting with Himmler. He presented Himmler with a personal gift of a seventeenth-century book about Swedish runic inscriptions, which was one of Himmler's many esoteric interests. Himmler was reluctant, but gave Bernadotte permission to transport all the Scandinavian concentration camp prisoners as far as Neuengamme, near the Danish border. Bernadotte thus successfully obtained permission for Swedish transport vehicles to enter Germany and move within German territory.

On 12 March, 1945, the first column of white buses bearing large red crosses crossed the border into Germany. By 30 March the buses had carried 4,500 Norwegian and Danish prisoners to Neuengamme. On 2 April Bernadotte met Himmler again. As the German military fronts were collapsing under pressure from both east and west, Bernadotte was able to drive an even deeper wedge into the fracturing Nazi leadership. Himmler gave him permission to transport all sick Scandinavians, all women, all Danish policemen and all Norwegian students from Neuengamme into occupied Denmark and from there on to Sweden. By 20 April all the ex-prisoners had been rescued from Neuengamme.

Meanwhile, information was leaking out of Germany via von Ribbentrop's staff that the SS had been ordered to destroy with explosives the Bergen-Belsen concentration camp, along with its inmates. Bernadotte intervened and played a major role in preventing the destruction of Bergen-Belsen and the prisoners there. On 21 April, Himmler gave Bernadotte his word that women of all nationalities would be saved from the Ravensbrück concentration camp. The very next day, 2,873 Polish, French, Belgian and Dutch women, as well as 1,607 Jews, were evacuated from Ravensbrück. By the end of the war, over 20,000 condemned camp prisoners had been saved and brought to Sweden on the white buses. After that a further 10,000 prisoners from German concentration camps were transported to Sweden. Altogether, Folke Bernadotte's white buses saved the lives of more than 30,000 people. Although there were many others who worked on this Swedish humanitarian effort, it was Folke Bernadotte who personally succeeded in expanding its scope stepwise through his skilful negotiations with Himmler.

Himmler then approached Bernadotte with an offer of a conditional German surrender, but the Western allied leaders rejected it, repeating their earlier demand for an unconditional German surrender on all fronts. On 7 May, Germany surrendered. The Himmler-Bernadotte agreement was an important step towards unconditional surrender.

Folke Bernadotte was now world-famous, a very unusual war-hero. A British journalist wrote that there were but two conceivable candidates for the leadership of a future United States of Europe: Winston Churchill was one and Folke Bernadotte was the other. Bernadotte continued working for the Red Cross and by 1947 he had become one of the leading figures in the international Red Cross movement. This work was crowned by his successful chairmanship of the 17th

International Red Cross conference in Stockholm in August 1948, the first after the war.

In May 1948, Folke Bernadotte was appointed United Nations mediator in Palestine. The question of Palestine had been brought to the United Nations by the British, who held Mandatory Power there. The UN General Assembly favoured the partition of Palestine into two states, one Arab and one Jewish, with the city of Jerusalem, including the surrounding villages and towns, as a demilitarized and neutral city. Civil war quickly broke out in Palestine. On 14 May, 1948 the State of Israel was proclaimed, but no equivalent State of Arab Palestine. The next day, troops from neighbouring Arab states, Egypt, Transjordan, Iraq, Syria and Lebanon, intervened to help the Palestinians. The first Arab-Israeli war had begun.

When Folke Bernadotte arrived in Cairo on 28 May 1948, he was greeted with scepticism and ridicule; but he soon gained respect. Against all odds, the UN mediator succeeded in getting a four-week truce in the Palestinian war, beginning on 11 June. One of his aides said, 'He was the only one who could have done it'. Another of Folke Bernadotte's accomplishments was his handling of the refugee issue. He was appalled by the plight of the Palestinian Arab refugees: 'I have made the acquaintance of a great many refugee camps; but never have I seen a more ghastly sight than Ramallah.' Bernadotte proposed the right of the residents of Palestine to return to their homes without restriction and regain possession of their property. This was the origin of UN resolution 194 of December 1948, permitting refugees to return to their homes. In the practical field, Bernadotte, using his vast experience of Red Cross work, initiated the humanitarian relief programme for Palestinian Arab refugees, a programme which still operates.

Bernadotte laid the groundwork for the UN relief organization for Palestinian refugees, but his plans for a political solution to the Palestine question were rejected by both sides. He proposed two consecutive plans. The first, dated 27 June, 1948, had Palestine (including Transjordan) forming a Union. All or part of the Negev would be Arab territory, while all or part of Western Galilee would be Jewish territory. The City of Jerusalem would be in the Arab territory. An implication was that King Abdullah of Transjordan would rule not only Arab Palestine but also the City of Jerusalem. The Palestinian Arab state mentioned in the resolution would be divided between Israel and Transjordan. The Jewish member state was to be reduced in size and its sovereignty circumscribed in several important respects.

This plan was rejected by both sides. The Arabs were against a Zionist state in Palestine. Israel also flatly rejected any encroachment or limitation on the sovereignty of the state of Israel. The Israelis were particularly incensed that Bernadotte was handing Jerusalem over to the Arabs. He became an object of hatred in Israel – a marked man.

In the second plan, signed on 16 September, Bernadotte recognized the Jewish state as a reality. The whole of Galilee was to be Jewish territory. The City of Jerusalem was to be placed under UN control. Bernadotte had thus made major changes to conciliate the Israelis. The Jewish state, now recognized as a fact, would have covered only some 20 percent of Palestine.

While preparing his second proposal, Bernadotte had received two secret visitors, one from the British Foreign

Office and one from the US State Department. His second plan, which became the British-American master plan, was to be presented by the UN and endorsed by the Security Council. The Palestine question would be solved, freeing the Western powers to focus their efforts on the Berlin crisis and the looming threat of a Third World War with the Soviet Union.

On 17 September 1948, a few days before the plan was to be presented to the UN, Bernadotte was assassinated in the Israeli-controlled sector of Jerusalem by Jewish extremists. The murderers were never found. No one was ever convicted of the assassination. It was generally believed from the outset that members of the *Lohamei Herut Israel* (Fighters for the Freedom of Israel) known as Lehithe Zionist terrorist group known as the Stern Gang, carried out the assassination. The assassination was planned by the Lehi operations chief in Jerusalem, Yehoshua Zetler. A four-man team led by Meshulam Markover ambushed Bernadotte's motorcade in a Jerusalem street and Yehoshua Cohen fired into Bernadotte's car, killing Bernadotte and his aide Colonel André Serot. It is now known that the decision to kill Bernadotte was made by the Central Committee of the LEHY: Yitzhak Shamir, Natan Yellin-Mor and Yisrael Eldad. They saw Bernadotte as the main obstacle to an Israeli annexation of Jerusalem and to Jewish control of all Palestine. Yitzhak Shamir went on to serve as prime minister of Israel in 1983–4 and 1986–92.

The assassination – by Jews – of Count Folke Bernadotte, the man who had rescued so many Jews from German concentration camps, was a particularly shocking event. Bernadotte was a man to whom the Israelis should have shown great honour and gratitude, instead of which they killed him. Memorial services were held all over the world. In Stockholm

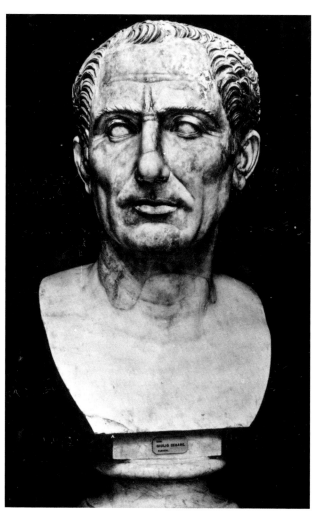

ABOVE: *Gaius Julius Caesar (100–44 BC), Roman general and statesman, was assassinated when he was at the peak of his success, by those who feared his supremacy in the Roman world.*

ABOVE: *Thomas Becket, English saint, martyr, knight, chancellor and archbishop of Canterbury, is murdered by four knights, Hugh de Merville, William de Tracy, Reginald Fitzurse and Richard le Breton, in Canterbury Cathedral at the request of King Henry II in 1170.*

LEFT: *The Rt Hon Spencer Perceval (1762–1812), English statesman who was shot in the lobby of the House of Commons when he was prime minister.*

RIGHT: *John Bellingham (1771–1812) the assassin of British prime minister Spencer Perceval.*

ABOVE: *Russian Jewish revolutionary Leon Trotsky (1879–1940) who was assassinated by Stalin's agent Ramon Mercader, on 20 August, 1940.*

RIGHT: *Abraham Lincoln (1809–1865), the 16th President of the USA (1861–1865), was shot by John Wilkes Booth on 14 April, 1865.*

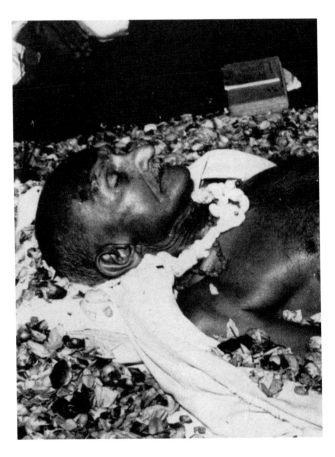

ABOVE: *The body of Indian nationalist leader Mahatma Gandhi (Mohandas Karamchand Gandhi) lying in state at Birla House, New Delhi, before the funeral cortege leaves for the burning ghats on the banks of the River Jumna. Gandhi was shot dead on 30 January, 1948, on his way to a prayer meeting in Birla House, New Delhi, by Nathuram Godse.*

ABOVE: *US clergyman and civil rights leader Martin Luther King addresses the militants of the 'Movement for the Peace'. He was assassinated on 4 April, 1968, in Memphis, Tennessee by James Earl Ray, sending shock waves throughout the American society.*

BELOW: *Jill Dando was a very popular British TV presenter who was murdered at the pinnacle of her life and career by a stalker, following a series of threatening letters and phone calls. She was shot on her own front doorstep on Monday, April 26, 1999, in Fulham, west London. Police later arrested a man called Barry George, who was a known celebrity-stalker who they described as having 'psychiatric personality characteristics'.*

Bernadotte's funeral procession was watched by hundreds of thousands of people. The UN condemned the crime weakly as a cowardly act which appears to have been committed by a criminal group of terrorists in Jerusalem while the United Nations representative was fulfilling his peace-seeking mission in the Holy Land, and undertook no sanctions or any other punitive action against Israel. The UN showed its weakness by accepting this atrocity. In both Israel and the Arab states respect for the United Nations evaporated.

In Israel, the assassination of Bernadotte was viewed with marked indifference, and the police in Jerusalem seem to have made little effort to identify those responsible. Lehi was disarmed and many members were arrested, but nobody was ever charged with the murders. Yellin-Mor and another Lehi member Schmuelevich were charged with belonging to a terrorist organization. They were found guilty but immediately released and pardoned. Yellin-Mor had meanwhile been elected to the first Knesset. It is suspected that David Ben-Gurion, the prime minister of Israel knew who the assassins were, because Zeitler, the Jerusalem Lehi chief, was a close personal friend of Ben-Gurion's. Long afterwards, Cohen was unmasked as the assassin by David Ben-Gurion's biographer Michael Bar Zohar; Cohen was working for Ben-Gurion as a security guard. The first public admission of Lehi's role in the murder was made in 1977. It is possible to see in this assassination, and the way in which the Israelis responded to it, the roots of the Israeli attitude towards the Palestinian question for the next half century.

Much too late, in May 1995, the Israeli Foreign Minister Shimon Peres expressed his government's regret over the assassination of Folke Bernadotte. But even this apology was to be marred. Immediately afterwards, the *Jerusalem Post* printed an unrepentant and defiant letter from Stanley Goldfoot:

> *Acting on orders from the Stern Group High Command, I planned and helped organize the execution of Count Folke Bernadotte in Jerusalem – September 17 1948, at 17:10 hours. This historic, vital operation was necessitated by the Bernadotte Plan which virtually prescribed the strangulation of the new-born Jewish State at birth . . . Thus, Peres's recent condemnation of the Bernadotte execution is a cheap political trick, and his apology to the Bernadotte family is an act of rank hypocrisy. Peres should rather apologize to the Jewish nation for the disaster he is bringing upon us.*

But the Israeli establishment has reaped the whirlwind by condoning assassination. At an Israeli-Palestinian peace meeting on 4 November, 1995, Prime Minister Rabin was assassinated by a Jewish extremist. The use of murder as a condoned political tool wielded by Jewish extremists, sanctioned at the time of the assassination of Folke Bernadotte in 1948, has now reached the heart of the state of Israel.

It has been said of Bernadotte that he had an independent mind and, if he found injustices, he said so – and that cost him his life. He did not change his attitude in spite of threats. The assassination of Count Bernadotte was a great loss for the area and especially for the Arabs. A driving sense of justice guided him. He was a thoroughly admirable man.

PATRICE LUMUMBA
1961

PATRICE ÉMERY LUMUMBA was born in Onalua in the Kasai province of the Belgian Congo on 2 July, 1925. He was educated at a Catholic missionary school and the government post office training school, and went on to work in Leopoldville (now Kinshasa) and Stanleyville (now Kisangani) as a postal clerk. In 1955 he joined the Liberal Party of Belgium, where he worked on editing and distributing party literature. After a three-week study tour in Belgium, he was arrested on charges of embezzling post office funds. His two-year sentence was commuted to one year after it was confirmed that Lumumba had returned the funds, and he was released.

Released from prison, he helped to found the non-tribal Mouvement National Congolais (MNC) in 1958, and later became its president. Lumumba attended the All-African Peoples Conference in Accra that year, and this reinforced his Pan-African beliefs. The next year Lumumba was again arrested, but this time for political activity, not petty theft. He was accused of inciting an anti-colonial riot in Stanleyville where 30 people were killed, for which he was sentenced to six months in prison. The charge may have been trumped up, as the start date of the trial, 18 January 1960, coincided with the opening of a conference in Brussels to decide the future of the Congo.

Lumumba's imprisonment made no difference; the MNC won a solid majority in the December local elections in the Congo. Delegates at the conference in Belgium were angered at Lumumba's imprisonment and applied pressure to have him released to attend the Brussels conference. The conference reached its climax on 27 January, when Congolese independence was declared. Independence itself came in June 1960 as the independence date and national elections resulted in Lumumba and the MNC forming the first government. The 35-year-old Lumumba became Congo's first prime minister and Joseph Kasavubu its first president.

Congolese independence from Belgium was finally gained on June 30, 1960. The Independence Day ceremony was characteristically bungled by the outgoing Belgian colonial authorities; Patrice Lumumba was officially excluded from the programme of events, despite his being the elected prime minister, while King Baudouin and other Belgian bigwigs attended. King Baudouin gave a speech glorifying the Congo's colonial past, which was extremely inappropriate, given the large-scale atrocities committed there by King Leopold. But Lumumba attended anyway, and delivered an inflammatory anti-colonial speech that inspired the Congolese with its frankness; needless to say, it alienated the colonialists.

Things started to go seriously wrong for Lumumba immediately. Disastrously, the large, mineral-rich province of Katanga declared its independence from the Congo under Moise Tshombe – and this break-away was encouraged by the Belgians, who evidently sought to undermine Lumumba and destabilize the new state. United Nations troops arrived but unrest continued and Lumumba was forced to seek

Soviet aid. In September President Kasavubu dismissed Lumumba by an act of doubtful legality. Lumumba tried to save himself by attempting to dismiss Kasavubu as President.

On 14 September Colonel Joseph Mobutu led a *coup d'état* supported by Kasavubu. Patrice Lumumba was captured by Mobutu's troops in Port Francqui on 1 December, 1960 and flown to Leopoldville in handcuffs. Mobutu announced that Lumumba would be tried for inciting the army to rebellion and other crimes. It was clear to objective observers outside the Congo that a properly elected prime minister had been deposed and his place occupied by an unscrupulous usurper. The United Nations Secretary General Dag Hammarskjöld stepped in to make an appeal to Kasavubu insisting that Lumumba must be treated according to due process of law. The Soviets denounced Hammarskjöld and the Western powers as responsible for Lumumba's arrest and demanded his release.

The Soviet Union wanted the reinstatement of Lumumba to be discussed at the United Nations Security Council, which was duly called into session on 7 December. The Soviet demands included Lumumba's immediate release, his restoration as head of the Congo government, the disarming of Mobutu's forces, and the evacuation of Belgians from the Congo. With hindsight, it is clear that the Russian demands were fully justified, but at the time they were seen by many as another chess move in the Cold War. Secretary General Hammarskjöld tried to defend his operations in the Congo, saying that if the UN forces were taken out of the Congo everything will crumble.

There were reports that Lumumba had been mistreated by his captors, and his followers threatened to arrest all the

Belgians in the Congo and 'start cutting off the heads of some of them' unless Lumumba was released.

UN contingents from some countries were withdrawn because of the increasingly muddled and controversial issues involved. This reduction in forces was a serious threat to the UN cause. In the Security Council, the pro-Lumumba resolution was defeated in a vote; it was a defeat for Soviet status. On the same day, a resolution proposed by the West giving Hammarskjöld increased powers to deal with the Congo situation was vetoed by the Soviet Union. Patrice Lumumba and the cause of justice in the Congo had slipped into the background as the destructive jousting between the Soviet bloc and the West went on. Lumumba was doomed.

At first Lumumba was held under informal house arrest at the prime minister's residence, where at least he was protected by UN troops positioned round the house. He unwisely tried to escape from house arrest; it proved to be a fatal mistake. He was spirited out of his residence by night in a diplomat's car and driven towards Stanleyville. Colonel Mobutu's troops chased him and finally cornered him on the banks of the Sankuru River. After his recapture, on 17 January, 1961, he appealed to local UN troops to save him. The UN refused on orders from headquarters in New York; the reason given was that he had already removed himself from UN protection. He was flown first to Leopoldville, where he appeared beaten and humiliated before journalists and diplomats.

Lumumba was transported first to the military prison in Thysville near Leopoldville. Then, after the military personnel of Thysville mutinied, a more secure place was sought. He was moved to a more secure prison in Jadotville in

Katanga province. It has been established that Belgian officials engineered his transfer to the breakaway province of Katanga, which was under Belgian control through the rule of an enemy of Lumumba, Moise Tshombe. A telegram sent by Belgium's African Affairs minister, Harold d'Aspremont Lynden, has been discovered; it ordered Lumumba's transfer to Katanga. Anyone who knew the place knew that was a death sentence.

When Lumumba arrived in Katanga, further humiliation followed; soldiers beat Lumumba and his fellow prisoners, Maurice Mpolo and Joseph Okito, in full view of television cameras.

Not until 40 years later would there be a Belgian Commission on the assassination of Lumumba. It reached these devastating conclusions: that the Belgian authorities wanted Lumumba arrested; that they were not concerned about his physical welfare; that when they were informed of the danger to Lumumba's life they took no action to save him.

Lumumba was beaten again on the flight to Elizabethville on 17 January, 1961. He was seized by Katangan soldiers commanded by Belgians and driven to Villa Brouwe. He was guarded and beaten again by both Belgian and Katangan troops while President Tshombe decided what to do with him.

It is believed that that same night Patrice Lumumba was bundled into a truck and a convoy headed out into the bush, drawing up beside a tree. Three firing squads had been assembled. It is said by some sources that the firing squads were commanded by a Belgian and that another Belgian had overall command of the execution site, but the Belgian Commission found that the execution was carried out by Katanga's authorities. Their report suggests that four Belgian officers were present at the execution site but under the command of Katangan authorities. Either way, there was significant Belgian involvement in the murder.

Lumumba and two associates, Mpolo and Okito, were made to stand against the tree. Tshombe (and Mobutu) may have wanted Mpolo and Okito removed so that they could not be political players in the aftermath of Lumumba's death. President Tshombe and two of his cabinet ministers were actually present at the executions, which took place one at a time. Lumumba's body was buried immediately. According to the Belgian report, the execution probably took place at 9.40 p.m., on 17 January, 1961. A week earlier, he had written his farewell letter to his wife, 'I prefer to die with my head unbowed, my faith unshakable, and with profound trust in the destiny of my country . . . The only thing we wanted for our country was the right to a decent existence, to dignity without hypocrisy, to independence without restrictions . . . The day will come when history will have its say.'

Nothing was said for three weeks, though rumours spread that Lumumba was dead. When Lumumba's death was formally announced on Katangese radio, it was inevitably described in terms that diverted any possible blame away from Tshombe or Mobutu. The radio gave out that Lumumba had escaped and been murdered by enraged villagers. Four days later, the Belgian Police Commissioner Gerard Soete and his brother attempted to cover up what really happened. They dug up Lumumba's body, dismembered it with a hacksaw and dissolved it in sulphuric acid. In a recent interview on Belgian television, Soete showed a bullet and two teeth he claimed to have retrieved from Lumumba's body, apparently as souvenirs.

There was speculation for years regarding the part played by various governments in Lumumba's murder. Eventually documents came to light which definitely established that Lumumba was surrounded by Belgian soldiers at every stage of the assassination, right up to the moment of his death. Regardless of international law, under its own Good Samaritan laws, Belgium was legally at fault because it did nothing to prevent the assassination. A more serious illegality was involved because Belgium was interfering in the affairs of the Congo several months after the formal declaration of independence. The Belgian government was encroaching on the freedom and integrity of another state, and was therefore in breach of UN resolution 290, dating from 1949.

The Belgian Commission of 2001 found that the Belgian authorities had not actively sought the death of Lumumba by having him transferred to Katanga. On the other hand, he died within five hours of his arrival there and that could have been foreseen. They showed no concern for the man's welfare at any time. The report refers to earlier plots by Belgium and America to kill Lumumba. Evidently they had either failed or been abandoned. Among the earlier plots was a CIA conspiracy to poison him, after US President Eisenhower apparently ordered the CIA to eliminate Lumumba.

The evidence that Eisenhower ordered the assassination of Lumumba comes from a previously unpublished 1975 interview with Robert Johnson, the minute-taker at an August 1960 White House meeting between Eisenhower and his national security advisers on the Congo crisis. Intriguingly, the transcript of Robert Johnson's interview only came to light accidentally, because it happened to be included in a package of material sent to the US national archives in connection with the assassination of President Kennedy.

The minute-taker, Robert Johnson, said in the interview that he clearly remembered the president turning to Allen Dulles, the director of the CIA. 'In the full hearing of all those in attendance . . . [Eisenhower said] something to the effect that Lumumba should be eliminated.' Eisenhower's remark was not only heard, but the heavy significance of what he said registered with all those present. Robert Johnson said, 'There was stunned silence for about 15 seconds and the meeting continued'. No verbatim notes were ever taken at National Security Council meetings, and Johnson only revealed the exchanges in 1975, when he was privately interviewed by staff of the senate intelligence committees post-Watergate inquiry into US covert action. The committee concluded that the US was not involved in the murder, though it confirmed that the CIA had conspired to kill Lumumba, possibly on Eisenhower's orders.

Dulles nevertheless took Eisenhower's instruction seriously and duly commissioned Lumumba's assassination. A CIA chemist worked on a poison that might be mistaken for toothpaste. CIA agent Sidney Gottlieb arrived in the Congo just a month after the Eisenhower meeting, in September 1960, carrying a phial of poison intended for the toothbrush of Patrice Lumumba. As it happened, Lumumba was toppled in a military coup just days before Gottlieb turned up with his poison. As Lumumba was already out of office the plot was abandoned and the lethal potion was thrown into the Congo River. When Lumumba finally was killed, no one was surprised when fingers started pointing at the CIA. A senate investigation into CIA assassination conspiracies 14 years later was able to find no proof that the CIA was behind the Lumumba murder, though that would now appear to be because the Belgian conspiracy was a little more advanced. Today, most of the evidence points to Belgium as the source of the conspiracy that actually killed Lumumba.

The Belgian Commission's report produced an official apology. In February 2002, the Belgian government made a formal apology to the Congolese people, admitting to a moral responsibility and an irrefutable portion of responsibility in the events that led to the death of Lumumba. In July 2002, documents released by the United States government showed that the CIA had had no direct role in Lumumba's eventual death. They had on the other hand known about the assassination plan, and could have made efforts to thwart it, which means that the CIA must carry some responsibility. The American perception of the time was that Lumumba was a Communist and Eisenhower's reported call for Lumumba to be eliminated must have been brought on by the current fear of Reds. Both Belgium and America United States were clearly swung against Lumumba by the climate of the Cold War. He seemed to be looking towards the Soviet Union. Sadly, if it is true, this was probably because the Soviet Union was the only place where he might find support in ridding itself of Belgium's tenacious colonial rule – which he was unable to shake off even after independence had been declared.

The Belgians had additional, more pragmatic, reasons for opposing him. They feared that Belgian economic interests in the Congo would not be best served by his government. There was something else too. The Belgian head of state – King Baudouin – was even more hostile towards Lumumba than his government; this led him to act individually and unilaterally in relation to the Congo, and withhold important information from his ministers. It is tempting to trace King

Baudouin's hatred to that momentous independence ceremony, when Patrice Lumumba made his unscheduled speech
describing the rule of the Belgians as a humiliating slavery
imposed by brute force. Maybe that, and the standing ovation
he received for it, sealed his fate. Within months he was
arrested, tortured and executed.

JOHN F. KENNEDY

1963

ON 22 NOVEMBER, 1963, after barely 1,000 days in office, John Fitzgerald Kennedy was shot dead by a sniper in Dallas, Texas. Kennedy was the youngest man ever to be elected President of the United States – and the youngest to die. He was born in Massachusetts on 29 May, 1917. After graduating from Harvard in 1940 the following year he entered the Navy. In 1943, his PT boat was rammed and sunk by a Japanese destroyer and, despite sustaining serious injuries, Kennedy led the survivors to safety. After the war, he became a Democratic congressman, advancing to the senate in 1953. In 1960 he became president by a narrow margin.

Kennedy's economic programme launched America on its longest sustained expansion since the Second World War. He responded to demands for racial equality, calling for new civil rights legislation. He cherished the idealistic hope that America would resume its historic mission as a nation dedicated to the revolution of human rights. Aid was given to the Third World, but a major confrontation with the Soviet Union intervened, in particular in Cuba. Kennedy allowed Cuban exiles to invade Cuba from America in an attempt to bring down the Communist regime of Fidel Castro. That was a catastrophic failure.

The Soviet Union renewed its campaign against West Berlin. Kennedy responded by reinforcing the Berlin garrison and taking new initiatives in space. The Russians tried to install nuclear missiles in Cuba. When this was discovered by air reconnaissance in October 1962, Kennedy imposed a blockade on all offensive weapons bound for Cuba. In a dangerous and still-controversial confrontation between Kennedy and Khrushchev, the Russians backed down and took the missiles away. Kennedy had in common with an earlier American president, Abraham Lincoln, a commitment to the fair treatment of black people, an ability to make a lot of enemies as well as friends – and a grand vision of America's destiny.

Lee Harvey Oswald, the man who killed President John F. Kennedy, was a very different character from John Wilkes Booth, the man who killed President Abraham Lincoln. Until that fateful moment when he killed Kennedy, Oswald had achieved nothing at all. It was as if that was the only thing he could do to make people remember him, as if that was his only way into history.

Lee Harvey Oswald was born in New Orleans in October 1939. His father died two months before he was born. For a time he was left in an orphanage, and after that he moved from place to place with his mother Marguerite, because she found it difficult to hold down a job. By the age of eighteen, Oswald had lived at an astonishing 22 different addresses and he had attended 12 different schools.

As a boy, Lee Oswald became a persistent truant, a street kid, missing 80 percent of his high school classes. He grew up rootless, insecure, and unsocialized, he was always the odd one out. When he was 14 all the symptoms of a disturbed personality were apparent when he was remanded in youth custody. He was referred to Dr Renatus Hartog, psychologist, for an evaluation; and Dr Hartog found that he had personality pattern disturbance with schizoid features and passive-aggressive tendencies. Dr Hartog believed that Oswald had definite traits of dangerousness, and advised that he should be kept on probation and given psychiatric help. Not long after that, Oswald was ordered to be put into a home for disturbed boys and subject to mandatory psychiatric care. All the signs were there. For whatever reason, and presumably an unfortunate collision of nature and nurture, Lee Oswald was developing from being a disturbed youth to being a disturbed and highly dangerous adult.

His mother's response to this analysis of her son was typically unhelpful. She fled from New York, and took him to Texas. It was a flight from treatment and, because of her immature and irresponsible decision, she must bear some of the blame for what followed later. Years later, in the aftermath of the assassination, the New York authorities were asked what action they had taken about Oswald at the time. The Warren Commission was told by the New York Probation Service, 'There is very little one can really do. We don't have the extra-state jurisdiction, and we didn't even know where she [Marguerite Oswald] had gone'.

The young assassin then joined the US Marine Corps, as much as anything to escape from the suffocating clutches of his mother. During his military career he became an expert marksman with a rifle. In 1956 he on two occasions achieved 48 and 49 out of 50 during rapid fire at a target 200 yards away. These are outstandingly high scores. After the assassination, there were many sceptics who doubted whether Oswald could have fired three shots in rapid succession and score hits with two of them, and this led them on to the idea that there must have been other marksmen in the plaza. But the evidence still exists that Oswald was certainly capable of firing all three shots, in quick succession, and given his record he might even have succeeded in hitting Kennedy with all three shots.

During his military career, Oswald learned Russian, then travelled to Russia in 1959; he seems to have thought of it as defection. The Russians declined Oswald's offer to be a spy, possibly because they sensed that he was a weak and defective personality, possibly because they thought he would play games and attempt to become a double agent. The Soviet authorities wanted to return him to America, but he attempted suicide by cutting one of his wrists and they allowed him to live in Minsk, where he took a factory job. He married a Russian, Marina Prusakova. Oswald maintained that he was a Marxist and tried to renounce his American citizenship. The Soviet authorities recognized his instability after the suicide attempt and handed him over for psychiatric evaluation. Two psychiatrists concluded that he was mentally unstable and warned that he was capable of further irrational acts. How right they were.

Then, in 1962 he changed his mind, as no doubt the Soviet authorities thought he would, and returned to America. He took his wife and infant daughter with him. He had got tired of Soviet authoritarianism. Oswald hung on to the fantasy that he was a high-powered spy, telling one of his friends that he had been responsible for giving the Soviets the information that enabled them to shoot down the U-2 spy plane. He desperately wanted to be important, to influence historic events.

Oswald took a job in Dallas at a graphic arts firm, producing classified government work that included detailed maps of Cuba. Oswald boasted to friends that not only was he working on the Cuba maps, but the CIA arranged the job for him. Although this may have been true, his CV up to that point does not make it very likely, and his record of indiscretion made him a poor security risk. In the spring of 1963 the Oswald family moved to New Orleans, where he befriended Judyth Vary. According to her, Oswald interviewed female Cuban refugees who came to work at the Reily Coffee Company, where both Oswald and Judyth Vary now had jobs. Oswald was on a mission, finding out the names of safe contacts in Cuba. Oswald's employers seem to have known that he was doing some kind of secret work and nodded at it.

In March 1963, Oswald bought himself a rifle and a handgun. Rather peculiarly, Oswald got Marina to take a photograph of him wearing the handgun at his right hip and holding the rifle and a copy of a Yugoslav newspaper, *Politika*. Why was he creating a trail of evidence against himself in this way? Or was it all juvenile play-acting that eventually got out of hand? And what did Marina think he was doing?

In the summer of 1963, Oswald became secretary of the Fair Play for Cuba Committee (New Orleans chapter). When Oswald gave out Hands Off Cuba leaflets on the streets of New Orleans, he was heckled by anti-Castro Cuban exiles and arrested by the police for disturbing the peace. A local radio show host interviewed Oswald on air. But what Oswald was up to is not at all clear. Although the leaflets supported Castro, the address printed on them, 544 Camp Street, was that of a racist ex-FBI agent called Guy Banister who was running a training camp for anti-Castro exiles preparing to take over Cuba. Oswald spent a lot of time in Banister's office. According to Judyth, Oswald often went through a garage next door to Reily's to reach Banister's office; so as not to arouse suspicion, he befriended the garage owner, Adrian Alba, and took to whiling away time at the garage reading gun magazines. The garage was frequently used by CIA and FBI agents. Alba later testified that he saw the driver of one of these cars pass an envelope to Oswald. It is far from clear, even after all these years, what Oswald was doing or where his loyalties lay.

Before the Kennedy assassination, Oswald had already aimed his rifle at a prominent local politician, trying to shoot him from the street through a window in his home. His target moved at a critical moment, and he missed. At the time the police were unable to identify the would-be assassin but, after the death of the president, when Oswald's life was carefully sifted over, it became obvious that this shooting was his work too. It is a sobering thought that if the earlier assassination had been successful, Oswald would probably not have been free to commit the later one, and the course of American history would have been changed.

The chance visit of President Kennedy to Dallas that autumn provided Oswald with a much higher-profile target. By chance he was looking for someone to assassinate. By chance he had a job in a building that overlooked the route of the Presidents motorcade. The opportunity must have seemed like a gift from destiny.

At 12.30 p.m., on 22 November, 1963, Oswald shot President Kennedy from a window on the sixth floor of the Texas School Book Depository in Elm Street, where he was temporarily employed during the Christmas rush. The window had a view across Dealey Plaza. The official view is that Oswald fired three shots at the president's motorcade as it moved slowly across the plaza away from him, hitting the president twice, fatally, and wounding Governor Connally. Their wives, who were also in the car, were mercifully unhurt. Oswald's first shot missed its target altogether, perhaps because the car was passing under a tree at that moment. His second shot hit Kennedy in the neck, causing him to slump forward. Governor Connally was wounded in the back and wrist and fell against his wife, saying, 'My God, they're trying to kill us all!' A later shot – whether it was the third or fourth is uncertain – went right through Kennedy's brain. He fell forwards and sideways onto his wife, Jackie, who crawled over the back of the car towards a detective, screaming, 'They've killed Jack! They've killed my husband!'

Whether there were more snipers behind a wooden fence at the top of a grassy bank in front and to the right of the president's car is still not known for certain. Those who favour a conspiracy put one or more snipers in that location, the celebrated grassy knoll. This would account for the grotesque jerking back of Kennedy's head at the impact of the second shot, which implies a shot from in front. The large wound in the back of the head would also be more consistent with an exit than an entry wound.

There is some circumstantial evidence for a second gunman, who fired the fatal shot from the grassy knoll 313 seconds into the Zapruder film: frame Z-313.

Itek analysed the movement of Kennedy's head around the time of the head shot. They noted that his head moved forward significantly from Z-312 to Z-313 and cite this as proof of a shot hitting the head from behind. But all four occupants of the car moved forward by about the same amount. Unless all four were hit simultaneously by bullets, which obviously did not happen, their forward movement must have been caused by something else, most likely the slowing down of the limousine. Dr Luis Alvarez noted that the speed of the limousine going down Elm Street sharply decreased just before the head shot. The driver, Secret Service agent Bill Greer, may have braked or taken his foot off the accelerator for some reason. Whatever he did, and why ever he did it, the car's speed dropped from about 12 mph to about 8 mph just before the head shot. The slowing of the car automatically thrust the passengers forward.

As many as five shots have been claimed by various researchers, measured in seconds from the moment when the audiotape microphone was jammed on: 137.70, 139.27, 140.34, 144.90 and 145.61. The recorder used that day was running about 5 percent slow, so all times must be multiplied by about 1.05 in order to restore the original spacing. When the time spacings from the sound tape are compared with the Zapruder tape, it is clear that the first three bullets were fired in quick succession from the book depot, the first missing altogether. The fourth and possibly fifth bullets, coming after a gap of over 4 seconds, may have come from a second sniper on the knoll.

There were statements from several witnesses who thought a shot came from the grassy knoll. William Newman thought that he and his family were in the direct path of gunfire. Given their position, it seems likely that the head shot came from behind the fence on the grassy knoll rather than from the book depot. Emmett Hudson, who was standing on the steps leading up to the pergola, said that the shots sounded as if they came from behind him, above his head and to his left. That again would place the origin near the fence. Zapruder felt that the head shot had come from behind him and whistled past his right ear. Between these two witnesses and behind them is the corner of the fence. A Polaroid photograph taken by Mary Moorman, known as the Moorman 2 Polaroid, was taken directly at the place where the imagined grassy knoll sniper would have been located. The photographer would in effect have been looking right down the barrel of the gun. In the Polaroid we can see the head of a man peering over the fence, about 9 ft from the corner. Interestingly, this is exactly the spot where the witnesses located the origin of the grassy knoll shot, and they gave their evidence without any awareness of the existence of Mary Moorman's photograph. Whoever the man in the Moorman Polaroid was, he moved away immediately after the head shot; there is no one there in later Zapruder frames or in the Stoughton photograph, taken shortly after the head shot.

The Warren Commission and the House Committee were unaware of the existence of the Stoughton photograph, even though a copy of it was deposited at the JFK Library. This photograph has never been scientifically analysed. The US government is extremely unlikely to commission such an analysis, as it might reveal something completely unwanted – the presence of a gunman on the grassy knoll. An independent researcher has done some computer analysis which suggests that there was a person standing behind the fence, several feet to the right of the corner. On the circumstantial evidence now available, it is a distinct possibility that the fatal shot to Kennedy's head came from the grassy knoll.

One of the bullets appeared to follow a zig-zag path through the bodies of both Kennedy and Connally, and this so-called magic bullet has often been used as evidence that at least one additional shot must have been fired. But recent virtual reality reconstructions have shown that the path followed by the magic bullet was after all a dead straight line. The earlier misinterpretations did not allow for the fact that Connally's seat was positioned significantly lower than the president's, in order to make the president more visible. Nor did they allow for the fact that Governor Connally's body was twisted into an abnormal position because he had turned round to speak to Kennedy.

After the shooting, the dying president was raced to a nearby hospital where the surgeons found that his brain was so badly damaged that they could do nothing for him. Oswald left the Book Depository, took a bus and a taxi back to his room, changed his clothes and (according to the Warren Commission) picked up a pistol. A little later, the official report states that Oswald killed police officer Tippit in Tenth Street, though witnesses who saw the shooting describe a different man, someone who did not look like Oswald at all.

Oswald was arrested at the Texas Theatre in the Oak Cliff neighbourhood at 1.50 p.m., initially for the murder of Tippit. He was only later charged with murdering Kennedy. Police Officer McDonald, who arrested Oswald in the theatre auditorium, told him to stand up so that he could handcuff him; Oswald shouted, 'Well, it's all over now,' punched McDonald and pulled his revolver from his belt. He was going to kill McDonald as he had earlier killed Tippit. This time, luckily for McDonald, the gun did not respond when he pulled the trigger and Oswald was overpowered.

Oswald's behaviour while in custody was unnaturally

calm. When challenged about the two ID cards he was carrying, one in the name of Lee Harvey Oswald and one in the name of Alek Hidell, Oswald smirked at the officer and said, 'You figure it out'. He smiled complacently and appeared to enjoy all the attention; he spoke to the press in a measured, almost pompous way. It was as if this was the moment he had been waiting for. This was his inauguration. He still denied shooting anyone, but he was only teasing his audience.

While he was being transferred to the county jail two days after the assassination, a nightclub owner called Jack Ruby shot Oswald in the stomach. Oswald died shortly afterwards. There has been endless speculation about this shooting too. Was it the spontaneous action of a misguided but public-spirited citizen? Or was it part of the larger conspiracy to ensure that Oswald did not go to trial and reveal in the court room that others had been involved in the Kennedy assassination?

There were many doubts and uncertainties surrounding the assassination, so a week after the assassination the new president, Lyndon B. Johnson, ordered a full investigation by a specially appointed commission. The report the Warren Commission eventually released concluded that Oswald had fired three shots – the initial shot that missed altogether and the two that hit Kennedy – and that he had acted alone, without accomplices. The conspiracy theories were fuelled by a desire to see this momentous event resulting from a complicated and deep-laid plot involving some powerful underground organization. But there are two scenarios remaining that have credibility. One is that the catastrophic end to Jack Kennedy's presidency was down to the caprice of one lone, mad gunman desperate for his place in history.

The other is that two gunmen were involved, one in the book store and one on the grassy knoll, and that necessarily entails a conspiracy. The question is now whether the evidence for the second sniper has been deliberately stifled by the authorities because the ramifications of the conspiracy would be too deeply embarrassing for them. Certainly a significant amount of information was not revealed to the Warren Commission by the CIA and the FBI, who did not want information about their assassination conspiracies relating to Castro – among other matters – to come out. One conspiracy theory brings Lyndon Johnson in as masterminding the assassination, but this has little support. Almost every other pressure group of any influence has been blamed, from Castro to the Mafia.

The CIA plotted to assassinate Castro repeatedly, and repeatedly failed. It would have been quite understandable if Castro had retaliated by commissioning Kennedy's assassination. In 1963, referring to US plots against him, Castro warned that they themselves would not be safe. Kennedy had also made enemies in the world of organized crime. Sam Giancana, a Chicago Mafia boss, had helped Kennedy to win the closely-fought 1960 election. Instead of being shown favours by the new president, Giancana found himself facing a determined crackdown against the Mafia led by the president's brother, Attorney General Robert Kennedy. Several Mafia bosses would have felt bitter enough about the Kennedy administration to want Kennedy himself dead. Significantly, there was one man who seemed to be completely unaffected by Kennedy's death. It was J. Edgar Hoover, the FBI chief. It was Hoover who phoned Bobby Kennedy to tell him that his brother was dead; he communicated no sympathy, offered no condolences. It seemed that Hoover was *glad* that Kennedy was dead.

MARTIN LUTHER KING

1968

ON 3 APRIL 1968, at the Mason Street Temple in Memphis, Tennessee, the black civil rights campaigner Martin Luther King made one of his most memorable speeches. It was an evening of torrential rain, so his audience was small, but he had important things to say about his life's work and the way he spoke showed that he knew it was nearly over. He was 39, yet he knew he would soon die. He said he would like to have a long life, but that God's will was more important. He was optimistic that eventually black people in America would achieve the civil rights he had campaigned for, and for which he had been threatened and abused. He had been punched in the face, stabbed in the chest and a price had been put on his head by white supremacists. Even the FBI was harassing him.

King had flown in that day from Atlanta, Georgia, with the intention of leading a march in support of Memphis sanitation workers who were in dispute with the city authorities. In a way their dispute was something of a diversion from his main task of the moment, which was to organize a Poor People's March on Washington the following month; this was going to be a major protest against economic deprivation and poverty.

King checked into room 306 at the Lorraine Motel. He was to share this room with one of his oldest friends, the Revd

Ralph Abernathy, another campaigner in the civil rights struggle. King had been up all night and did not get to bed until 6.30 a.m. Consequently, he did not surface from his room until the early afternoon.

At about the same time, a man using the name John Willard checked into a run-down boarding house nearby, Bessie Brewer's on South Main Street. Willard's room was lit by a single naked light bulb. It had little to recommend it, except that it had a partial view of the balcony of room 306 of the Lorraine Motel, and there was an unobstructed view of that balcony from the bathroom along the landing. That afternoon, there was considerable ill feeling among the other guests at the boarding house because of the undue length of time Willard was spending in the bathroom. He was, of course, looking out of the window, watching and waiting for Martin Luther King.

At around five o'clock that afternoon, King ended a meeting with Andrew Young, who had spent the day in court fighting a ban on the planned march in support of the sanitation workers. After that, King and Abernathy went back to their hotel room to change for dinner at the Revd Kyles's house. At 5.30 p.m., Kyles arrived in his car to collect his guests. When he went to room 306, he found Martin Luther King straining to do up the top button of his shirt; King joked about his weight problem. Then, at about 6 p.m., Kyles and King went out onto the balcony. Below was Kyles's white Cadillac, with a small knot of people round it: Kyles's driver, Solomon Jones, Andrew Young and Jesse Jackson. There was some good-natured banter between the men round the car and the three men up on the first-floor balcony. The air was cool, and Jones suggested to King that he should wear a coat. King said, Solomon, you really know how to take good care of me.

King turned towards the door of his room to speak to Abernathy, specifically to ask him to bring his overcoat. Kyles had moved away from King, ready to go down the stairs to the car. King was suddenly exposed to the gunman. There was a gunshot, and King fell to the floor. The bullet had hit him in the jaw, ripping through his jugular artery and spinal cord. Blood spouted from the gaping wound. Abernathy and the others, who had seen what was happening, rushed to help King, trying in vain to stop the bleeding. They shouted for help. When the police arrived, they pointed to where the shot had come from.

Martin Luther King could not speak or move. Andrew Young felt for a pulse. 'Oh my God, my God, its all over,' he moaned. Abernathy was indignant: 'Don't you ever say that!' Abernathy travelled in the ambulance with King as he was taken to St Joseph's Hospital. Doctors tried to save his life, but by then he had suffered brain damage and at 7.05 p.m. Martin Luther King died.

Most Americans were shocked and saddened by Martin Luther King's death, though not entirely surprised. The white supremacists were the only people who celebrated. In the black urban ghettoes all over America, there were expressions of anger and frustration as well as grief; for five days, riots broke out in over one hundred cities, with looting and burning. It may have looked like a revolution, but it was impotent frustration.

Meanwhile the police hunt for the assassin got under way. Straight after the shooting, the police found a green blanket on the pavement very close to Bessie Brewer's boarding house.

It was wrapped round a rifle, a Remington Gamester 760, and some other items. Witnesses said they saw the bundle being dropped by a man who had run out of the boarding house and driven off in a Mustang. The police traced the rifle to a store in Birmingham, Alabama, where they found that it had been purchased by a man called Eric Galt. Galt had stayed at another hotel in Memphis before moving to Main Street. For a time the police could get no further. Then they checked a fingerprint on the rifle against criminal records and discovered that Eric Galt was really a convict who had escaped from Missouri State Prison the previous year. The killer's name was James Earl Ray.

After driving off in the Mustang, Ray disappeared for a while. In early June he was identified as the man who had flown from Toronto to Britain under the alias Raymon George Sneyd. On 8 June, he was arrested at London Heathrow Airport as he tried to board a plane for Brussels.

A certain amount of circumstantial evidence pointed to Ray as the murderer of Martin Luther King. He had bought the rifle that was found on the pavement outside the boarding house; he had taken the room in the boarding house with a view of the motel; he had driven away in the Mustang after the murder; a map found in the house he had occupied in Atlanta had King's church and home ringed in pencil, alternative places where the victim might be ambushed. This was all persuasive circumstaial evidence. On the other hand, it could not be proved that Ray's gun had fired the bullet that killed Martin Luther King. Nor could it be proved that he was the man who was in the bathroom at the moment when King was shot.

It seemed likely that James Earl Ray was guilty, though not certain. Ray pleaded guilty, but only to avoid the death penalty.

The case is an interesting one in view of the current controversy over plea bargaining; Ray may have been innocent, but he was tempted into pleading guilty in order to save his life. That is what his counsel advised, and he took the advice.

Once convicted and sentenced to life imprisonment, Ray renounced his guilty plea, producing an alternative scenario in which he was set up as part of a conspiracy. He had, he said, been recruited by a man called Raoul to take part in smuggling. It was Raoul who had ordered him to buy the car and the gun; it was Raoul who had told him to travel to Memphis and hire the room at Bessie Brewer's boarding house. There are many people who believe Ray's version of events, including the King family; they believe that the assassination was masterminded by the CIA or FBI. Raoul's behaviour fits the pattern of a CIA or FBI controller running an undercover operation. Ray died of liver cancer in 1998, but by then he had convinced many people of his complete innocence of the crime; still others had come to believe that Ray may have pulled the trigger but that he was part of a conspiracy.

Inevitably, individuals have come forward claiming that they were part of the conspiracy, but they are likely to be innocent people who just want a share of the limelight. Lloyd Jowers, who owned a restaurant close to the Lorraine Motel, made the claim on television that he had been paid to participate in a conspiracy to kill King. The Revd Ronald Wilson, a minister in Florida, claimed that his father Henry (now dead) was the assassin and that he had been driven by his anti-Communist beliefs. There does not appear to be any substance to these claims. If the assassination of Martin Luther King was masterminded by the CIA or FBI, we should not expect to find people coming forward to confirm it.

The choice is a simple one. King may have been killed by a lone gunman with a grudge or a mission and, if so, that man was James Earl Ray. He was after all a known racist and was identified by a psychiatrist as paranoid and dangerously obsessive. Alternatively, King may have been killed as part of a conspiracy, in which case others may have been supporting Ray in his role as assassin, or using an innocent Ray as a cover for another assassin. The Revd Jesse Jackson was not only a friend and supporter of Martin Luther King but a key witness to the assassination. Over 30 years after the killing, Jackson expressed doubts about Ray's ability to carry out the assassination. Ray did not have the motive, the mobility or the money to have done it alone. Possibly Ray was being used as a hitman by white supremacists. Ray's brother was an associate of J. B. Stoner, leader of the National States Rights Party – and it is known that he rejoiced at King's death. Alternatively, it may have been the FBI or the CIA who organized the conspiracy. The FBI chief J. Edgar Hoover hated King, a man he denounced as a Communist. The FBI was certainly keeping King under surveillance, and therefore could easily identify and exploit opportunities to assassinate him.

ROBERT F. KENNEDY

1968

IN JUNE 1968 the 42-year-old brother of John F. Kennedy, Senator Robert F. Kennedy, was in California campaigning to be nominated as the Democratic candidate for the presidency. Voting took place on 4 June and after a hard-fought campaign Bobby Kennedy spent the day before he died swimming, sitting in the sun, talking to friends, playing with his children and sleeping. He was so relaxed that he considered not attending his own election night party, suggesting that he and his family and friends might watch the primary results on television. Because the television networks refused to haul their equipment out to Malibu, Kennedy reluctantly decided to go into Los Angeles that evening to wait for the election result. Accompanied by Frankenheimer and other members of his campaign staff, he drove to the Ambassador Hotel for the election night party. Kennedy had a suite reserved there and, with the election result still in doubt and Kennedy running behind, he went to relax in his suite.

At 11.40 p.m., it was announced that Kennedy had unexpectedly won, and he made a short victory speech from the podium in the hotel's Embassy Ballroom. Kennedy was well aware that he could be the target of an assassination attempt, especially after the assassinations of his brother and, only two months earlier, Martin Luther King. Yet security at the hotel was almost non-existent. The hotel management had taken on 18 security guards for crowd control, though as far as is known no police officers were on duty. In 1968 presidential contenders were not provided with Secret Service protection, and relations between Kennedy and the Los Angeles Police Department (LAPD) were strained. Los Angeles police officers had found themselves in difficulties when Kennedy was working a crowd; they had conscientiously tried to protect him and been abused by his campaign followers for their trouble. A few bodyguards had been hired from a local firm called Ace Security.

Kennedy ended his speech shortly after midnight on 5 June with the words, 'And now it's on to Chicago – and let's win there!' He was making his way from the ballroom at the Ambassador Hotel to give a press conference in the Colonial Room. He began to move forward through the crowd towards the front door when his Press Secretary Frank Mankiewicz turned him round and diverted him through the kitchen pantry, apparently because it was slightly less crowded and would therefore be a quicker route.

He was led by one of the hotel staff, Karl Uecker, and followed by an Ace Security guard, Thane Cesar. A brown-skinned man of obvious Middle Eastern descent was pushing a steel food-trolley towards the advancing crowd. When he was close enough, he shouted and began to fire a .22-calibre revolver at Kennedy. He fired eight rounds, but a ballistics investigation showed that none of them hit Kennedy. All eight went wildly into bystanders, walls and ceiling. There was chaos as bullet after bullet whizzed around the confined space. Sirhan Sirhan, the man with the food trolley and the gun, was quickly restrained, but Kennedy and five other people were wounded. The wounded were taken to the nearest hospital, the Central Receiving Hospital, but Kennedy was taken to the Good Samaritan Hospital for brain surgery. He had a three-hour operation and was thought to have a chance of surviving, but he died about 25 hours after the shooting.

Sirhan was arrested immediately, and later charged and convicted of first degree murder. He was sentenced to death, but the US Supreme Court declared the death sentence unconstitutional before it could be carried out. Since then, Sirhan has been incarcerated at Corcoran State Prison, California.

Sirhan was born in 1944, to an Arab family living in Jerusalem. The family became refugees when the state of Israel was created in 1948. When he was 12, he moved with his family to California. Sirhan continued to be deeply interested in the politics of the Middle East, inevitably empathizing with the Palestinian cause. He was outraged when the media and political leaders in America celebrated the Israeli victory in the Six-Day War in 1967. He began to see Robert Kennedy as a hate figure when he realized that Kennedy saw Israel as the injured party in the conflict. Sirhan himself said explicitly that he killed Kennedy to punish him for supporting Israel. With his biography and political background, Sirhan looked like a perfect suspect for the assassination. Yet there were always some who doubted whether Sirhan was really the lone crazed gunman presented in court.

This was an assassination that took place in the close proximity of a great many witnesses; perhaps 76 saw it 'live' from close quarters and 20 million saw it on television. The problem is that the assassination happened with such speed, in such a melée and in such an emotionally charged context that people could not be sure what they saw or heard. On the face of it, this looks like a lone gunman assassination, and there is much to recommend this interpretation. On the other hand there are reasons for doubting it. The physical evidence and eyewitness reports seem to show that Sirhan was incapable of inflicting all of the wounds.

Thomas Noguchi, the coroner, produced a post-mortem report which showed that Senator Kennedy was shot three times. One shot entered the head behind the right ear, a second shot near the right armpit and a third roughly one and a half inches below the second. All the bullets entered the body at a sharply upward angle, moving slightly right to left. These are hard to square with the eyewitnesses' accounts of Sirhan's shooting.

Sirhan's .22-calibre revolver contained just eight bullets and he had no chance to reload. This limited number of bullets caused a problem for the official version of the assassination. One bullet was lost in the ceiling space; two were lodged in a wooden door jamb. Five or six ceiling tiles were removed for tests. Los Angeles Police Department criminologist DeWayne Wolfer was quoted as saying 'it's unbelievable how many holes there are in the kitchen ceiling'. This strongly suggests that the LAPD found traces of more bullets than could have come from Sirhan's eight shot revolver.

There were reports of suspicious people in the area at the time of the assassination. The first police officer on the scene, Sergeant Paul Schraga, was approached by a couple who told him that they had seen and heard a young man and woman running out of the Ambassador Hotel shouting, 'We shot him! We shot him!' When asked whom they had shot, the young woman replied, 'Senator Kennedy!' Schraga sent out an All Points Bulletin on the two suspects. This was the start of what became known as the 'Polka-dot Dress Girl' controversy.

The LAPD quixotically declared that Sirhan was the sole assassin within minutes of the crime, which was premature. Many observers were staggered that the police were so adamant; the official line was, 'This is a solved case.' Schraga was asked to cancel his bulletin and when he refused it was cancelled by his superiors. The couple's story was plausibly explained by the LAPD as a case of mishearing, stating that the young woman must have said, 'They shot him!' Nevertheless, a young woman sitting on a staircase outside the Ambassador Hotel, Sandra Serrano, told the same story. Two witnesses in the pantry also saw armed men, quite apart from Sirhan and the security guard Thane Eugene ('Gene') Cesar. Lisa Urso noticed a fair-haired man in a grey suit putting a gun into a holster. Another witness saw a tall, dark-haired man in a black suit fire two shots and run out of the pantry. These men could have been assassins; they could alternatively have been Kennedy's bodyguards.

As the case was the responsibility of the LAPD, there was no pressure to release their findings. Researchers into the assassination finally forced the report and the police department's files to be released in 1988, a full 20 years after the assassination. This was extraordinary; the Warren Commission Report was published in 1964, the year after JFK's assassination. After the long-delayed release of the files, it became clear that evidence contradicting the official version had gone missing, including 2,400 photographs, the ceiling tiles and the door frame from the pantry, and transcripts of over three thousand interviews, including those for the 51 key 'conspiracy' witnesses.

The LAPD report began to look like a cover-up. Files released to researchers in 1985 by the Los Angeles District Attorney's Office included a box of tapes, videos and documents. This box is said to have contained some of the evidence which conflicted with the official version, most conspicuously the filmed re-enactments made in 1968 and 1977, which seem to prove that Sirhan could not have inflicted the wounds found on Senator Kennedy's body. It was carefully selected stills from the reconstructions that were used to support the official version. If a deliberate cover-up was the result of the LAPD's investigation, it was almost certainly because the truth of what happened was beyond reach. The LAPD 'lone gunman' version of the RFK assassination seemed such an open and shut case that the House Select Committee on Assassinations did not trouble to investigate it. Given the questions that have now arisen, perhaps the assassination should be re-investigated.

These are the reasons for believing that there was at least one other assassin besides Sirhan:

1) The powder burns on Kennedy's clothing show that all three shots came from a gun fired no more than 8cm away from him. The witnesses say that Sirhan's gun was never closer than 50cm away. Sirhan was simply too far away to have shot Kennedy.

2) Sirhan's gun held a maximum of eight bullets. Seven bullets were found embedded in human tissue. An eighth

bullet passed through two ceilings into an air space. A ninth and a tenth were lodged in the pantry door frame. Inexcusably, from the forensic point of view, the two expended bullets were dug out of the door frame, and the frame itself was burned. In any case, Sirhan cannot have fired more than 8 bullets; the other two must have been fired by someone else. Some analysts thought there had been as many as 13 bullet holes, so there must have been at least one more gun.

3) The three bullets found in Robert F. Kennedy and the fourth, which grazed his suit jacket, were fired almost vertically upwards. All the witnesses testified that Sirhan was holding his gun completely horizontally for the first two shots, after which his gun hand was repeatedly slammed against a table by Karl Uecker, who had been leading Kennedy forward by the right hand. It was not possible that Sirhan fired the third shot into Kennedy.

4) The four bullets which touched Kennedy all hit on his back right side, travelling forward in relation to his body. Kennedy was walking towards Sirhan, facing Sirhan while the shots were fired. Even when he fell, he fell backwards, and was therefore still facing Sirhan. It is impossible for any of Sirhan's shots to have hit Kennedy in the back.

Obviously Sirhan was there. Obviously he shot at Kennedy but someone else was firing too. Once a second assassin is established, the complexion of the event is changed. Not only was a conspiracy involved, but it looks as though the second gunman, standing a little behind Kennedy and to one side was given powerful and effective protection. Sirhan was allowed, perhaps even set up, to take the blame for the murder, while the other man was allowed not only to escape punishment but identification. Indeed, a second assassin strongly implies that a powerful US government department was behind the murder itself – the evidence was consistently manipulated to keep the decoy, Sirhan, as the one conspicuous figure in the foreground while the other gunman was airbrushed from the background. New York Congressman Allard Lowenstein went public with the forensic information about the 11 or 13 bullets in 1970, in an attempt to get the case re-opened. He was later shot dead in his New York office by 'a disgruntled client'.

Sirhan had his contacts. On 2 June, 1968, Sirhan went into Kennedy's Campaign headquarters, where Larry Strick asked him if he needed help. Sirhan pointed at one of the volunteer workers and said, 'I'm with him.' At the time it seemed an insignificant remark, but the volunteer worker in question, who was only there for a few days, turned out to be a high-level international secret agent.

So – who was the second gunman? Who was it who was in the right position to have fired the three bullets into Bobby Kennedy? Thane Eugene Cesar, the Ace security guard, is known to have been pressed up against Kennedy's back right side and holding Kennedy's right arm in his left hand as Sirhan jumped out and fired his first two shots at Kennedy from several feet away. Don Schulman, who was the only eyewitness to observe accurately that Kennedy had sustained three bullet wounds, not two, saw this guard pull his gun and appear to fire back at Sirhan. Gene Cesar's clip-on bow tie, which was knocked off in the scuffle and lay near Bobby

Kennedy as he died, was in just the spot where the gun needed to be located to deliver the fatal bullet up and forwards into Kennedy's brain. Gene Cesar owned a .22 (the same calibre as Sirhan's gun), but said he sold it before the assassination. Later he said he sold it after the assassination.

What of the couple seen running out of the hotel? Sandra Serrano was on the back stairs at the time of the assassination. She saw Sirhan walk up the stairs with a woman in a polka-dot dress and another man, and later saw the woman and man coming down the stairs without Sirhan, the woman saying, 'We shot him!' Captain Lynch later claimed that he was on the back stairs at the time and that no one was there; this cast Sandra Serrano in the role of non-credible witness. The LAPD subjected Sandra Serrano to a lengthy and gruelling lie detector test in what looks like an attempt to intimidate a witness into backing off. The interviewer tried to persuade Serrano that the polka-dot woman did not exist – even though she was mentioned in the LAPD's teletype announcement of Sirhan's arrest.

Even so, a remarkable number of other witnesses went on insisting that a good-looking woman in a white polka-dot dress 'appeared to be with Sirhan' just before the assassination. If this 'polka-dot woman' scenario is true, we have a peculiar conspiracy, with a professional hitman, a decoy gunman and a very conspicuous woman in a memorable dress. There is no logical explanation for a member of an assassination team behaving in the way that this woman is alleged to have behaved. Why would she have given herself and her co-conspirators away like this? On this point I am more inclined to believe the LAPD's interpretation, which is that the people were running away from the scene of a shooting, possibly instinctively running away from danger, but also intoxicated at having witnessed a sensational and historic moment. 'They shot him! They shot him!' 'Who?' 'Senator Kennedy!'

Nevertheless, on 4 June, the day immediately before the midnight assassination, Sirhan signed in at a firing range and was joined by a man and a shapely well built woman, according to the range master of the gun club. The range master heard the woman say to Sirhan, 'Goddamn you, you son of a bitch, get out of here or they'll recognize us.' An explanation is available; a topless bar waitress came forward to testify that she and her husband had innocently met Sirhan at the range. On the other hand, what the waitress said was contradicted by the reports of other gun club witnesses. Those who favour the polka-dot woman as one of the assassins portray the topless bar waitress as a decoy who was part of a complex assassination network. This still leaves unexplained the absurd conspicuousness of the polka-dot woman, and the open admission of involvement. Assassins who want to remain undetected do not shout 'We did it!' as they leave the scene of the crime.

Sirhan meanwhile was left to take the rap for the murder. He has steadfastly maintained that he acted alone, yet what Sirhan thinks happened does not necessarily reflect what actually happened if an additional assassin network was in place. It is highly significant that Sirhan cannot remember the assassination at all, as if a segment of his memory has been entirely erased. As a jockey, Sirhan received a head injury in 1966, which may have made him especially susceptible to hypnosis. One interesting theory is that the CIA found this out when Sirhan later explored 'mind control' groups, and the CIA used hypnosis to ensure that he carried out orders and remembered nothing about his co-conspirators afterwards. He has been subsequently hypnotized in attempts to reconstruct his lost memory, and in his automatic writings he has come up with 'Pay to the order of one hundred thousand dollars' and 'My determination to eliminate RFK is becoming more and more of an unshakable obsession'. Was $100,000 the price for being part of the assassination team? Was Sirhan hypnotized into having a political motive?

Even so, the question still hangs in the air – was the 26-year-old guard Gene Cesar involved? He asked not to be called to the witness stand at Sirhan's trial, a request which was unaccountably granted. He was probably the best person to give evidence of Sirhan's actions because of where he was standing, right next to Bobby Kennedy, and of course the post mortem evidence pointed to him as the likeliest suspect. He claimed he was not called to the Ambassador Hotel for duty until a few hours before the shooting. At 11.15 p.m., he was assigned to check credentials at the doorway of Colonial Room (where the press conference was to be held) and was to clear the way for the Kennedy entourage en route. He claimed to have been put next to Kennedy by his employers: he was not there out of choice. But perhaps this was a case of a lucky break – like the archduke's car taking a wrong turning right in front of Gavrilo Princip.

Cesar said that when the shooting started he drew his gun and threw himself to the floor. Five witnesses confirmed that he drew the gun. Two witnesses said they saw him shoot, but Cesar insists that he did not do so. He successfully passed a polygraph (lie detector) test organized by Dan Moldea in 1994. Nevertheless, Cesar was standing directly behind Kennedy when Sirhan began firing and, according to his own admission, was in a position to shoot Kennedy at a point-blank range. He also had been on guard duty in the pantry an hour earlier when Sirhan slipped into the area. The trajectory of the shots from the back, which went through Kennedy's jacket as well as into his head, were perfectly aligned with where Cesar said he was on the floor. If he did not fire, then he must have been right next to whoever did shoot and witnessed them do it. He was never asked and never volunteered that information during the polygraph.

Cesar admitted owning a .22-calibre handgun, but said he was not carrying it that night. He said he had sold it in February, but the sales slip showed that he sold it three months after the murder. It was never tested by LAPD for ballistics, and it subsequently disappeared. In 1993 someone salvaged a nine-shot .22-calibre revolver, serial number Y-13332, from a pond in Arkansas. Some believe this is Gene Cesar's gun, the gun that may have been used to kill Kennedy.

Gene Cesar looks like the perfect suspect, yet many are persuaded that he is innocent. He had no criminal record. He volunteered to be questioned. He offered to submit his gun for investigation. He voluntarily told the police about the .22-calibre gun he owned or had owned. He was co-operative about questioning and undertaking a polygraph test. He was openly honest about his political sentiments, which were anti-Kennedy. He had not been scheduled to work that night, but was called in at the last minute. In all of these ways he comes across as innocent. Gene Cesar once said, 'Just because I don't like the Democrats, that doesn't mean I go around shooting them.'

PRESIDENT
SALVADOR ALLENDE
1973

SALVADOR ALLENDE WAS born in 1908 and was President of Chile from November 1970 until his removal from power and death in September 1973. Allende's three unsuccessful bids for the presidency (in the 1952, 1958 and 1964 elections) prompted him to joke that his epitaph would be 'Here lies the next President of Chile.' Allende was not an ardent Marxist but he did outspokenly reject capitalism, which made him deeply unpopular within the administrations of successive American presidents from John F. Kennedy to Richard Nixon. They believed there was a danger of Chile becoming a communist state and joining the Soviet Union's sphere of influence. According to one Russian source, Allende had been given a codename – Leader – as a KGB contact, and he supplied the KGB with information from the 1950s onwards.

But Senator Allende was by no means an uncritical admirer of the Soviet Union. He condemned the Soviet invasions of Hungary in 1956 and Czechoslovakia in 1968, and as President of Chile he was the first head of state on the mainland of North or South America to recognize the People's Republic of China in 1971, at a time when China was the main adversary of the Soviet Union. The United States had substantial economic interests in Chile, through corporations such as ITT, Anaconda and Kennecott. The Nixon administration feared that these companies might be nationalized or expropriated by a socialist government, so it was strongly opposed to Allende, a hostility that Nixon openly admitted. During Nixon's presidency, efforts were made to prevent Allende from being elected by financing political parties aligned with the conservative candidate Jorge Alessandri.

In spite of these efforts, Allende won the 1970 Chilean presidential election as leader of the 'Popular Unity' coalition, narrowly beating Jorge Alessandri. Huge sums of Soviet and American money had been spent backing the two sides. The election result startled and alarmed Nixon, who ordered the CIA to develop plans to impede and undermine Allende in the Chilean Congress. Congress nevertheless chose Allende as President, on condition that he would sign a Statute of Constitutional Guarantees; he was to respect the Chilean Constitution and not undermine any element of it with his socialist reforms.

Allende assumed the presidency on 3 November, 1970. The CIA was also active in influencing the Chilean army to move against Allende. General Schneider was commander-in-chief of the Chilean Army. His resistance while being kidnapped ended in his death from gunshot wounds. The American government was showing its determination to destabilize Allende's regime.

Allende began to implement sweeping socialist programmes in Chile, nationalizing big industries, reforming health care and education, and modernizing agriculture. Allende also intended to improve the welfare of the poor. A key element was to provide employment, either in the new nationalized enterprises or on public works projects. He also defaulted on debts held by international creditors and foreign governments, froze all prices and raised salaries. These policies aroused strong hostility from landowners, some sections of the middle-class, the Catholic Church, and eventually the Christian Democrats. The short-term economic effects were very good, but they were not sustained and in 1972 the Chilean *escudo* had runaway inflation of 140 percent.

Allende re-established diplomatic relations with Cuba, in the face of an Organization of American States convention that no nation in the Western Hemisphere would do so. In response to this friendly gesture, the Cuban president Fidel Castro visited Chile, holding massive rallies and giving public advice to Allende. This unnerved the political right as proof that Chile was to follow the same path as Cuba. In October 1972 came the first major confrontational strike. It was financed by the CIA.

Throughout his presidency, Allende remained at odds with the Chilean Congress, which was dominated by the Christian Democratic Party, who accused Allende of leading Chile toward a Cuban-style dictatorship and sought to overturn many of his more radical policies. Nixon directed the CIA once again to 'put pressure' on Allende's government. In the parliamentary elections in early 1973, Allende's coalition increased its share of the vote, but a downturn in the economy and the unpopularity of his policies with certain groups meant that it was likely a coup would be attempted.

On 29 June, 1973, Colonel Roberto Souper surrounded the presidential palace, La Moneda, with a tank regiment, but his coup was unsuccessful. Then in late August General Pinochet became commander-in-chief of the army. A constitutional crisis was clearly in the offing: the government was unable to enforce the law and the Chamber of Deputies accused Allende of unconstitutional acts.

On 11 September, 1973, the Chilean army led by General Pinochet and supported by the CIA, staged a successful coup against Allende. Just before the presidential palace was captured, and with gunfire audible in the background, Allende made a memorable farewell speech to Chileans on live radio in which he spoke of himself in the past tense; he described his love for Chile and of his faith in its future. He said his commitment to Chile did not allow him to take an easy way out and be used as a propaganda tool by 'traitors'. It sounded as if he meant to fight to the death.

Not long after that broadcast, Allende was shot. The circumstances are not fully understood. The rebels planned to take La Moneda in order to capture the president himself. They assumed that could be accomplished within 2 hours, by 11 a.m., as no serious resistance was expected from the handful of civilians inside the palace. They expected Allende to surrender at once when faced with infantry, armoured cars, tanks and the threat of aerial bombardment. After transferring him to 2nd Armoured barracks, the rebel generals probably thought that as a result of various humiliations they planned for him Allende would commit suicide if left without a guard. His suicide would be announced to the country around 1 p.m. In fact, it took much longer to capture La Moneda and subdue the 42 civilians, armed as they were with sub-machine guns and a bazooka; this small group held off a siege of eight Sherman tanks for five hours.

As planned beforehand, the newscasters of the new Pinochet regime declared that Allende had shot himself with a machine gun. In recent years the view that he committed suicide has become more widely accepted, particularly as testimonies of Dr Patricio Guijón and two close associates who were with him at the time of his death confirmed the details of the 'suicide' in interviews. Members of Allende's immediate family, including his wife, never disputed that it was suicide.

But there is another version of what happened. The multiple bullet wounds suggest that it was much more likely that he was murdered. At the time and for many years after, many of his supporters very understandably presumed that he was killed by the forces staging the coup. Here is that other version. Just after 2 p.m. on 11 September 1973, an infiltration patrol of the San Bernardo Infantry School commanded by Captain Roberto Garrido ran up the main staircase of the presidential palace, La Moneda, giving themselves cover by firing rounds randomly from their machine guns. The patrol reached the second floor and burst into the Salon Rojo, the state reception hall. The patrol captain saw that the hall was filled with dense smoke coming from fires elsewhere in the building; through the smoke he made out a group of civilians braced to defend themselves with sub-machine guns. In what may have been a reflex action, Captain Garrido fired a short burst. One of his three bullets struck one of the civilians in the stomach. Another soldier in the patrol wounded the same man in the abdomen. As the man writhed on the floor in agony, Garrido suddenly realized who he was – Salvador Allende.

Garrido shouted abuse at the dying president and there

was more machine-gun fire from the patrol, riddling Allende with bullets. As he slumped back dead, a second group of civilians entered the Salon Rojo from a side door. Their fire drove the patrol back down the main staircase to the safety of the first floor, which the rebel troops had occupied. The civilians went back to the Salon Rojo to see if anything could be done to help Allende. Among them was a doctor, who examined the body and saw at least six bullet wounds in the abdomen. He took Allende's pulse and indicated that the president was dead.

The rebel forces then had to 'dress' the scene in order to make it appear that Allende had committed suicide. Fire was spreading through the palace and it was getting near the Salon Rojo where they were preparing the deception. Because of the fire, General Palacios was too hasty in giving the Defence Ministry his all-clear signal. At least two firemen entered the Salon too soon and were pushed out at gun point; but they got far enough into the room to see one of the soldiers placing a gun on the knees of the corpse seated on the sofa, while another was putting President Allende's combat helmet and gas mask beside him. All the firemen were notified that they were not allowed to enter the room because the president had shot himself and nothing could be moved. As they went on fighting the fire, the firemen were warned that they were not to tell anyone what they had seen in the room.

The news was communicated laconically by radio to General Pinochet: 'Mission accomplished. Moneda taken. President dead.' Pinochet asked, 'What about the body?' And the answer came, 'Destroyed.' It was not until 2.50 p.m. that it was announced to the country that the palace had been taken by the armed forces. Owing to the unexpected resistance in La Moneda, the original scenario of Allende's 'clean suicide' collapsed. It took the conspiring generals four hours, from 3 p.m. to 7 p.m., to write a new scenario. This entailed discovering Allende's suicide inside La Moneda and finding an eyewitness. The rebel high command was painfully aware of the many contradictions in the new scenario, and they stalled for nearly 24 hours before informing the Chilean people of the president's death. Finally, the news was leaked abroad and Chileans learnt from foreign journalists that their president had committed suicide.

Then followed a bloodbath, in which Allende's followers were rounded up and executed without trial. No less than three thousand people were murdered on 11 September. Between 11–15 September over five thousand people were to be killed in combat. Over six thousand would be imprisoned and murdered between the 12–13 September. In the first 18 days, there were approximately fifteen thousand civilian casualties.

The United States played a huge role in setting up the situation that produced the coup, but its degree of involvement in the coup itself is debated. The CIA has declared that it 'played no direct role', though that disclaimer can by no means be taken at face value. Henry Kissinger told Nixon that the US 'didn't do it', meaning the coup, but had 'created the conditions', including damaging the Chilean economy. On the other hand it is clear that the CIA had systematically worked towards the overthrow of Allende from 1970 onwards. Documents that are still classified may one day reveal more.

More than thirty years after his mysterious death, Allende remains a controversial figure. There is much speculation as to what Chile would have been like had he remained in power. Many must have thought they had backed the wrong horse, as General Pinochet's dictatorship turned out to be blatantly undemocratic, violent and repressive. Many on the political Left see Allende as a hero, a martyr who died in the cause of socialism.

GEORGI MARKOV

1978

GEORGI MARKOV WAS a very obscure figure compared with most of the assassination victims described in this book. He was not a head of state or a leading politician of any kind. He was a Bulgarian writer who lived in his home country until 1969 and then, at the age of 40, he defected to the West. He lived in London, where he had a very low profile working as a broadcast journalist for the BBC, Radio Free Europe, and the German Deutsche Welle. Markov was a playwright and satirist who broadcast scathing accounts of Communist high life to Bulgaria, accounts that were to prove fatal to him.

Markov was not known at all in London, but he had a large audience in Bulgaria, and his outspoken views against the ruling Communist party were seen as the inspiration for Bulgarian dissident movements. The leader of the Bulgarian communist party, Todor Zhivkov, decided in June 1977 that he wanted Markov silenced, and informed a politburo meeting of his wishes. The job of putting an end to Markov's broadcasting career was given to the Interior Minister Dimiter Stoyanov, who requested KGB assistance. The KGB chairman Yuri Andropov agreed provided there would be no trail left that led to the Soviet Union. It was a classic layered conspiracy.

It turned out that their dissident target was not as easy to remove as they might have anticipated. There were to be three attempts on Markov's life. During a dinner party given by friends at Radio Free Europe, someone slipped poison into his drink, but this attempted assassination failed. Another attempt on his life in Sardinia also failed. The third and successful attempt took place in London on 7 September, Zhivkov's birthday.

Markov was working a double shift at the BBC. After working his early morning shift, he went home to rest. On returning to work he parked his car on the south side of Waterloo Bridge and walked to the bus stop to catch the bus to the BBC headquarters. As he approached the people queuing for the bus he felt a stabbing pain in his right thigh, he turned to see a man facing away from him stoop to pick up an umbrella. The man apologized in a foreign accent, got into a taxi and vanished. Markov was later able to describe the man as thick-set and about 40 years old. Still in pain, Markov boarded the bus to get to work, where he told his colleagues what had happened. He noticed a spot of blood on his jeans, and when he dropped his jeans he found a red swelling like a pimple on his thigh. Puzzled, he showed it to a colleague. When he got home he began to feel very ill, running a high fever.

He was admitted to St James's Hospital in Balham the following day. When his right thigh was examined, it was found that there was a tiny puncture wound about 2mm diameter, surrounded by an inflamed area. Septicaemia was diagnosed. Markov's condition deteriorated rapidly and he died four days after the attack.

The post-mortem examination of the wound revealed a tiny platinum ball, the size and shape of a pinhead. It was just 1.5 mm in diameter and had two tiny holes bored through it, evidently for the retention of some powerful toxin. The organizers of Markov's assassination probably assumed that the tiny capsule would not be detected in a routine post-mortem, and that the death would be attributed to a virus.

Dr David Gall at the chemical defence establishment Porton Down said that ricin was the only possible toxin that could have been used in the circumstances. Only the smallest dose of poison, an estimated 0.2 milligrams, had been administered, so a very powerful toxin had been used, and Markov's symptoms matched those of ricin poisoning.

Many years later, after the fall of the Soviet Union, it was revealed that ricin had indeed been used to kill Markov. It was also revealed that it had been injected in spheres into Markov using an umbrella mechanism. The technique had been developed in a secret KGB laboratory called 'the Chamber'. It was two former KGB officers, Oleg Kalugin and Oleg Gordievsky, who publicly admitted that there had been Soviet involvement in the Markov assassination. The Bulgarians are said to have employed an Italian criminal to carry out the murder. In spite of close collaboration between the British and Bulgarian authorities and Interpol, the assassin was never arrested. A suspect was located and questioned in Denmark but the result was inconclusive and there was no arrest; he fled to Hungary and then the Czech Republic. His whereabouts now are not known.

The Markov assassination was one of the most notorious assassinations carried out during the Cold War. In June 1992 General Vladimir Todorov, the former Bulgarian intelligence chief, was sentenced to 16 months imprisonment for destroying 10 volumes of material concerning the Markov case. A second suspect, General Stoyan Savov, the deputy interior minister, committed suicide rather than face trial for his part in destroying the files. A Bulgarian spy, Vasil Kotsev, who was widely believed to have been the operational commander of the Markov assassination plot, died in a car accident.

ALDO MORO

1978

ALDO MORO WAS born in September 1916. He became a law professor at the University of Bari and published several books on law. A member of the Christian Democrat Party, he was elected to the Constituent Assembly in 1946 and helped to draft Italy's post-war constitution. He held a succession of cabinet posts, and between 1963 and 1976 served five times as Italy's prime minister. In October 1976 he became president of the Christian Democrat Party and as a result remained a powerful influence in Italian politics and public life even though he held no public office.

On 16 March, 1978, Aldo Moro was in Rome on his way to attend a special session of parliament when he was kidnapped by left-wing Red Brigades terrorists. In one of the most dramatic incidents in post-war Italy, the terrorists ambushed his car, killing his chauffeur and five policemen. He was held hostage while the Red Brigades pressed for the release of 13 of their members who were on trial in Turin. President Giulio Andreotti consistently refused to negotiate with the kidnappers regarding the release of the terrorist suspects. In consequence, Moro was murdered in or near Rome by his kidnappers. Moro's dead body was found in the boot of a Renault car in central Rome on 9 May, 1978.

The Red Brigades leader, Mario Moretti, was given a life sentence for his role as the leader of Moro's captors. In his memoirs in 1994, Moretti admitted to being the assassin. The Moro case haunts Italians in the same way that the Kennedy assassination haunts Americans, and in a similar way it is a case that has never really closed. In the late 1990s a fourth trial was unfolding in Rome and three more judicial inquiries were under way. The investigations reach way beyond the now-defunct Red Brigades, probing government misdeeds in the Moro affair and criminal activity by civilian and military intelligence agencies. One inquiry seemed to be leading towards Giulio Andreotti, the prime minister at the time of the kidnapping, facing a charge of murder in relation to the death of a journalist who was investigating the case.

Mario Moretti is one of the 20 former members of the Red Brigades who are serving life sentences for the assassination. On his own evidence, he was the mastermind behind the crime. He seized Moro from among the corpses of his bodyguards on 16 March, held him captive in an apartment in Rome for 54 days. In all of that time, Moretti was the only person to talk to Aldo Moro. He was the one who on 9 May killed him by firing 11 bullets into his chest.

Moro had a long reputation as Italy's greatest political mediator, so if anyone could have negotiated his release it was him. With his own life in the balance, he conducted an impassioned war of words through a series of almost daily letters. The Italian government's utter refusal to negotiate with the terrorists was seen around the world as a display of fortitude and strength, while the doomed Moro carried on his one-sided negotiation relentlessly as if he suspected that the government had less than honourable intentions. In particular he targeted his own party, the powerful Christian Democrats.

The assassin, Moretti, admits that he found himself in an area for which he was poorly prepared. He knew little about power politics. It was Moro himself, his unfortunate victim, who taught him a lot, clarifying what immediately became his battle against his party, the battle that in the end he would lose. Moretti reflects that the two men were on opposite sides, yet worked together. He passed Moro information, perhaps in a newspaper, and Moro was able to grasp, often from a few details, what was going on. 'This was his universe, and he knew it to perfection.' Both the Red Brigades and Moro were surprised how quickly the hard-line politicians closed ranks to form an uncharacteristically united front. Moro was surprised, then incredulous, then irritated. He was convinced that the hard-line stand would crumble if the Christian Democrats made the first move. But they did not.

From the Italian government's viewpoint, things appeared very differently. Giulio Andreotti, the prime minister, decided when he saw the first of Aldo Moro's letters that they had to be treated as extorted; they were not the unforced words of a free man. He was not morally responsible for what he was writing.

In the end, Moretti said, the Red Brigades were ready to release Aldo Moro, even without negotiations. 'We had wanted to demonstrate that we could attack the Christian Democrats and make our accusations known. In this we had succeeded. We would have been content with mere words, but they were words no one wanted to say.' Moro saw towards the end that his kidnappers were going to kill him. He wrote another letter telling the Christian Democrats that he did not want anyone from the party at his funeral. They had turned their back on him, failed him. Moretti then felt profound pity for Moro, for his loneliness and despair, and for his abandonment by his friends and colleagues.

Some Red Brigades members argued for Moro's release. Moretti himself thought it was impracticable to let Moro go. They decided to 'carry out the death sentence', but with a sense of doom. Moretti told Moro to get himself ready to go out, and Moro seemed to understand what was going to happen. Moretti tried to deal with what he was doing by telling himself it was a political decision, that it was unavoidable. Aldo Moro was taken from the apartment, led into a garage and brutally shot in the back of a car.

There is a central puzzle in the Aldo Moro case. It seems to have been the only terrorist crime in Italy in which absolutely no effort was made to obtain the release of the hostage by some means, whether force or negotiation. Perhaps elements in the Andreotti government feared that Aldo Moro had carried out a threat, which was implied in his first letter, that he had told his captors secrets that would compromise those in power. Perhaps the refusal to negotiate was indeed tainted with unworthy motives. Now, many years later, the extent of those dark secrets has become known – an incredible web of corruption at the top, so great that it brought down the long-reigning ruling elite.

LORD MOUNTBATTEN

1979

IT WAS AUGUST Bank Holiday 1979, and the height of the holiday season. In a bay on the west coast of Ireland, a family on holiday set off on a boat trip. It was the Mountbatten family.

Lord Louis Mountbatten and his family had been spending a holiday at his Irish castle, a kind of holiday home in County Sligo in the north-west of the Irish Republic. He came out of the castle at 9.15 a.m. and announced that the family would go out for a trip on his boat, Shadow V. It was 11.15 a.m. before the family were boarding the boat in the harbour at the fishing village of Mullaghmore. At 11.30 a.m., Lord Mountbatten himself steered the boat away from the shore and out across the bay from Mullaghmore. He was watched by the IRA button man. He had been watched for some time, and his movements were very predictable. This had been his routine every August for the past 25 years. Mountbatten was also watched from the shore by his bodyguard, one of two Irish policemen who went everywhere with him while he was staying at the castle.

The boat rounded the headland and was just a hundred yards offshore off the next small inlet when suddenly, and with no warning whatever, a bomb hidden on board was detonated. It was 11.30 a.m. The explosion was seen by several witnesses. One eyewitness said the huge blast blew the boat 'to smithereens'. All seven of the people the boat was carrying were thrown out into the sea.

Nearby fishermen raced to the site of the explosion and found Lord Mountbatten, the cousin of the Queen, the mentor of Prince Charles. They pulled him out of the sea, but he was already dead. He had been blown unconscious by the blast that threw him into the sea. His legs had been terribly damaged – almost severed – by the explosion, and he had drowned. Other survivors were pulled out of the water and rushed to hospital. There were more bodies too. It was not just Lord Mountbatten who was killed in the explosion, but one of his 14-year-old twin grandsons, Nicholas Knatchbull, and a local boat boy, the 15-year-old Paul Maxwell. When Paul's body was brought ashore, his father held him in his arms and found that he was still warm. One of the injured was the Dowager Lady Brabourne, a woman of 82, she died of her injuries the next day.

The Prince of Wales, who was abroad at the time of the murder, had a special fondness for Lord Mountbatten. He was severely shaken by the news and returned to England at once. Mountbatten's death was a severe shock to Britain as a whole, not least because he did not seem like an appropriate IRA target. He had long retired from any active military or diplomatic service; he was just an old man on a seaside holiday.

Lord Mountbatten was more properly Louis Francis Victor Albert Nicholas, first Earl Mountbatten of Burma, but known to his friends as Dickie. He was born in 1900, and was known until 1917 as Prince Louis Francis of Battenberg. The change of name happened as a response to anti-German feelings in Britain during the First World War, and the Battenbergs changed their family name when the British royal family changed its name from Saxe-Coburg-Gotha to

Windsor. As well as being a distinguished and highly supportive member of the royal family, Lord Louis had a distinguished naval career too, especially in the Second World War. He served as supreme allied commander-in-chief in South-East Asia for the last two years of the war. He then became the last Viceroy of India, presiding over India's violent transition to independence. Towards the end of his life, Lord Mountbatten gave a television interview in which he said he did not mind the prospect of death but hoped he would have a peaceful one. No one could have imagined that he was so soon to meet such a gratuitously violent and savage end.

The attack on the Mountbatten family raised many questions. One question related to the level of security surrounding the family holiday. The local police watched Classybawn Castle for the one month of the year that Lord Mountbatten spent there, though by implication not for the rest of the time. There were in any case only two policemen assigned to look after him, and no one was watching the boat. The village of Mullaghmore is only 12 miles from the Northern Ireland border, in other words in a potentially sensitive area. It was also close to an area that was known to be in use as an IRA refuge.

Mountbatten's boat was left moored and completely unguarded, in the public harbour in Mullaghmore. Lord Mountbatten insisted that the boat should be painted in a distinctive green colour, the colour of an admiral's barge. The colour never changed. Mountbatten liked the limelight and the media, and was happy to have a film made about his life in 1968. This showed him on one of his family holidays at Mullaghmore, including a sequence on the conspicuous green boat. The boat was moored in the harbour, and easily reached by stepping across just one other boat. The cabin was locked, but the engine compartment was not. Obviously it was very easy for anyone to tamper with the boat at any time after dark and install a time bomb or a radio-controlled bomb in the engine compartment – which is exactly what the IRA did.

There was never any doubt in anyone's mind that it was the IRA who were behind this assassination.

On the same day as the Mountbatten assassination, 27 August 1979, there was another incident that was in its way even more horrific. The Mountbatten assassination took place on the west coast; the Warren Point ambush took place on the east coast, on Carlingford Lough, which marks the border between Northern Ireland and the Irish Republic. In the early afternoon, just after the news about Lord Mountbatten's death broke, two IRA men took up their position on a vantage point, overlooking Narrow Point on Carlingford Lough from the Irish Republic side. On the Northern Irish side was a stretch of dual carriageway that made an ideal ambush point.

At 3 p.m., A Troop, 2nd Parachute Battalion, left their base to drive to Newry, ready for a tour of duty patrolling the bandit country of South Armagh. There were 30 para-troopers in the convoy, travelling in several trucks. As the convoy came into view, at 4.40 p.m., it passed a hay-trailer in a lay-by; concealed inside the hay were five hundred pounds of explosives, which the button man detonated. The explosion knocked the rear truck sideways, killing outright seven of the nine soldiers inside.

It was a scene of carnage. A press photographer happened to be passing, stopped and took some photos of the immediate aftermath. A policeman ran past him shouting hysterically, 'Don't go in there. They're all dead! Get away!' There was a lot of smoke and ammunition exploding in the burning vehicles; the surviving soldiers were confused and naturally thought they had come under heavy fire. They saw some people on the opposite bank of the river and started returning the imaginary heavy fire. Luckily there were not many people about, but an English schoolboy who happened to be fishing on the river bank was killed.

A command post was set up by the nearby castle gatehouse, which the IRA had predicted; having studied British army tactics carefully, they knew that this would be their response. The paratroopers gathered at the gatehouse, not noticing the milk churns stacked there. They were full of explosives. The paratroopers were running straight into an IRA trap. The IRA men watching the response patiently waited five, ten, fifteen minutes. Once the paratroopers were all gathered at the gatehouse, twenty minutes after the first explosion, with reinforcements already arriving by helicopter and truck, the IRA button man detonated the second bomb. It was even bigger than the first and killed another eleven men. The effect was horrific. The men were not just killed, they were blown to pieces. There were torsos, arms, legs and heads lying in the road, hanging in the trees, floating in the river. The press photographer was traumatized by what he saw; he never took another picture after that.

The IRA had succeeded in killing 18 British soldiers and inflicting a major propaganda injury on the British government. The deliberate co-ordination of these two separate attacks was designed to make the maximum psychological and political impact. It was revenge for Bloody Sunday, punishment for what were seen as the war crimes of the paratroopers. The day's events were a major boost to IRA morale. The effect on the Margaret Thatcher government of Britain was to entrench hostility to the IRA and its political objectives. The assassination was controversial, even within the IRA. There were those who saw Mountbatten's involvement in colonialism as Viceroy of India as sufficient justification in making him a target for political assassination. There were others who thought it ill-judged to kill an old man on holiday, and they were aware that killing him and his family in this way would look cowardly and unnecessary. The IRA had considered proposals to kill Mountbatten in previous years, but ruled them out.

Mountbatten and his security advisers should really have seen that the political tensions were increasing, and that by 1979 it was no longer appropriate to continue the Mullaghmore holidays. Mountbatten had indeed wondered about it, but was told by the security service that this was a risk that might reasonably be taken.

Who were the murderers? Clearly the IRA was to blame, but it was very difficult to prove which individuals were involved. Just before the Mullaghmore bomb went off, two IRA men were stopped nearby at a police check-point. The passenger seemed very calm, but the driver was extremely anxious. The policeman was uneasy about them and phoned his police station for support. The driver, who gave the name Pat Regan, was Francis McGurl, a local Republican sympathizer. The passenger was Thomas McMahon, an expert IRA bomber from Armagh.

They were both interviewed at the police station later. McMahon was tough, uncompromising and gave little away; questioning him would lead nowhere. McGurl, who was younger and weaker, broke down under 12 hours of questioning, admitted involvement but denied planting the bomb on Mountbatten's boat. It seemed he had kept watch while McMahon, the bomb expert, had installed the bomb by torchlight. Forensic scientists found specks of the distinctive green paint from Shadow V on McMahon's boots and traces of explosives on his clothing. There was enough forensic evidence to charge – and convict – Thomas McMahon.

The Warren Point ambush was harder to deal with because the incident straddled the border. Tons of dust and rubble were taken away for forensic analysis. The conclusion was that the explosives had come from South Armagh and were of the same type as used in earlier IRA bombs. Two men were stopped on the Irish Republic side of the lough leaving the scene just after the ambush. They were Joe Brennan and Brendan Burns, both known to be members of the Provisional IRA. Burns was a particular friend of Thomas McMahon's, so it looked increasingly as if the two attacks were linked. Forensic evidence showed that Brennan and Burns had been lying down at the vantage point overlooking the scene of the ambush at Narrow Point.

There was no doubt in the authorities' minds that these were the two men responsible for detonating the Warren Point bombs, but the case against them stalled because of a lack of co-operation from Dublin. In Dublin, the matter was seen as politically explosive and likely to lead to big trouble in the Republic. In the end, the two men could only be charged with traffic offences. There was a plot to capture the two men on a seven hundred yard stretch of road where it passed into Northern Ireland and out again. This half-baked plan came to nothing when the look-out soldier at the beginning of this short stretch of road fell asleep and therefore failed to give warning that the car with Brennan and Burns inside was on its way. They got away.

Joe Brennan was convicted for another attack in 1994, but released early under the Good Friday Agreement. Brendan Burns blew himself up with his own bomb in 1988. McGurl was acquitted in 1980, and crushed to death by a tractor in 1995. Thomas McMahon was sentenced to life for the murder of Lord Mountbatten. In August 1998, as part of the Good Friday Agreement, which included an amnesty for political prisoners, the decision was made to release Thomas McMahon. It naturally caused a great deal of political controversy in Britain. Conservative and Unionist politicians condemned the decision to release McMahon, believing it would be seen as an inappropriate concession. McMahon was a notorious killer, who had according to Democratic Unionist Peter Robinson 'carried out the foulest of deeds'. It was also seen as inappropriate to release potentially dangerous prisoners when the fighting had not entirely ceased.

But the father of the Irish boat boy killed in the explosion off Mullaghmore unexpectedly supported the release of Thomas McMahon. In a statement showing remarkable generosity of spirit, John Maxwell said, 'Thomas McMahon has served his time and, if he is no longer a danger to society, then he should be released. Keeping him in prison will unfortunately not bring my son back. Peace is the imperative now, and we must look forward so that perhaps Paul's death and those of thousands of others from both sides of the political divide here will not have been entirely in vain.'

OSCAR ROMERO

1980

OSCAR ARNULFO ROMERO was born in 1917 in the town of Cindad Barrios in the mountains of El Salvador close to the country's border with Honduras. He left school at the age of 12 to begin an apprenticeship as a carpenter, but soon his thoughts turned to entering the church. He trained at San Miguel and San Salvador before completing his studies in Rome. He was ordained in 1942.

Returning to San Salvador in 1944, Oscar Romero served as a country priest before taking charge of two seminaries. In 1966 he became secretary to the El Salvador Bishops' Conference, earning a reputation as an energetic administrator. His broadcast sermons were an inspiration. Romero became a bishop in 1970, serving as an assistant to the elderly Archbishop of San Salvador and within seven years he was archbishop himself. Ironically a group of conservative fellow bishops elected him as a compromise candidate. What he did then was a great surprise to them and to others; neither the poor nor his fellow churchmen expected Oscar Romero to make the heroic stand that he did – and perhaps he did not intend to himself.

It was a time of great unrest in San Salvador, with more and more people becoming aware of the extreme social injustices. Groups of Christians formed to discuss the implications of

Christianity for society; each of these so-called Basic Communities had its own priest, a leader elected from the group. The
landowners became alarmed at the sight of uneducated peasants
organizing themselves and electing spokesmen. They launched
vehement press campaigns, condemning the activists as
Marxists. Right-wing gangs emerged to organize persecutions
and killings. Death squads roamed the countryside. By 1980, the
civil war was claiming the lives of approximately three thousand
people a month.

One priest, Father Rutilio Grande, was particularly outspoken. He denounced the injustices experienced by thousands of sugar-cane workers in his area. Archbishop Romero
publicly defended Father Grande, who was then shot dead
along with an old man and a boy. The assassin forced Romero
to go and view the bodies, with the intention of warning him
of the price of meddling.

Up until that time, Romero had been regarded a; a mild
and moderate man by the church, but the incident turned
him into a revolutionary. He began to document civil rights
abuses in El Salvador, which infuriated the government.
When he visited Rome in 1979, Archbishop Romero presented the Pope with dossiers filled with reports of injustices
in El Salvador. The other Salvadorean bishops turned their
backs on him, even sending a secret letter of complaint about
him to the Vatican, accusing him of courting popularity.

He had less than a year to live. Almost incredibly, the USA
was actively supporting the right-wing government of El
Salvador; Jimmy Carter's government was supporting the
regime with massive funding on the scale of 1.5 million
dollars a day. Romero wrote to President Carter personally
pleading with him to cease the aid, to no avail. 'You say that

you are a Christian. Stop sending money. It is being used to kill people.'

There was a highly significant incident just two weeks before his death. A huge cache of dynamite was found inside the basilica where, the day before, Romero had said a mass for a murdered Christian Democratic leader. Many members of the Christian Democratic party had been present at the Mass. If the dynamite had exploded, the whole basilica would have been destroyed. Clearly that would have been an assassination of a different order of magnitude – and Romero would have died along with the Christian Democrats, seemingly as collateral damage.

Romero was desperate. How could he reverse the worsening situation? His final sermons constantly returned to the fundamental issue, which was how he and his congregation should respond to such a terrible political situation. How should a Christian behave in a catastrophic polity?

On 23 March, 1980, Archbishop Romero openly encouraged the army to mutiny. He said, 'No soldier is obliged to obey an order that is contrary to the will of God.' The next day, a few moments after preaching a sermon, he was shot dead in his own cathedral with a single bullet. His death was in every sense a martyrdom. Romero was fully expecting a violent physical attack, and he chose not to flee to safety as he had been repeatedly advised to do. In America there was an extraordinary diversionary reaction to the assassination – an accusation that Cubans were directly involved in the killing of Romero. There was no evidence that there was any Cuban connection. The man who shot Archbishop Romero escaped, unidentified, and was never captured. It must be assumed he was a professional hit-man, as he required only a single shot, evidently fired from some distance, and succeeded in escaping unnoticed.

In September 2003, a lawsuit was filed against Alvaro Rafael Saravia, who was living at Modesto in California, alleging that he played a key role in organizing the assassination of Archbishop Romero. The suit was filed on behalf of a plaintiff whose name was withheld in the interests of his or her safety. The complaint alleged that Saravia obtained weapons, vehicles and other materials for purposes of carrying out the assassination, provided his personal driver to transport the assassin to and from the chapel where Romero was shot, and paid the assassin after the assassination had been carried out. Saravia later reportedly advised the reputed death squad leader Roberto D'Aubuisson – with whom he worked closely – that the assassination had been successfully completed.

The UN Commission on the Truth for El Salvador and the Inter-American Commission on Human Rights both concluded after separate investigations that Saravia was actively involved in planning and carrying out the assassination. Even so, no-one, anywhere, had been held responsible for the Archbishop's assassination. Saravia lived in the United States from at least 1987 when he was jailed for 14 months on immigration charges. Saravia's arrest came straight after a request by Salvadoran prosecutors for Saravia's extradition for his role in the Romero assassination.

The Salvadoran Supreme Court later withdrew the extradition request, and the United Nations Commission on the Truth for El Salvador, the Inter-American Commission on Human Rights, and many other human rights organizations denounced that decision as politically motivated. Saravia was released from federal prison in 1988 following the Salvadorean Court's decision and he has since lived in California and Florida.

On 3 September, 2004 Judge Wanger formally held Alvaro Saravia responsible for the assassination of Archbishop Oscar Romero. Judge Wanger ordered Saravia to pay $10 million to the plaintiff, a relative of the archbishop, who has still not been identified. With this US court ruling, Saravia has been formally established as responsible for organizing the murder. Judge Wanger also declared that the murder was a crime against humanity, because it was part of a systematic attack intended to terrorize a civilian population.

Since his death Romero has been hailed as a hero, not just by Latin American Catholics, but by left-wing groups with agendas quite different from those of the Catholic church. This political 'body-snatching' may have contributed to a certain unease about his martyrdom among anti-Marxist Catholics. The archbishop has nevertheless subsequently been canonized; he is now Saint Oscar Romero.

ANWAR AL-SADAT

1981

THE CAMP DAVID Accords in 1978 led to a negotiated peace between Israel and Egypt the following year, the first ever to be made between Israel and one of its Arab neighbours. In acknowledgement, the Egyptian president Anwar al-Sadat and the Israeli prime minister Menachem Begin shared the 1978 Nobel Peace Prize. But this peace initiative was not universally popular in Egypt or the Arab world in general. Muslim fundamentalists in particular found it objectionable, as they believed that only the threat of force would persuade Israel to satisfy Palestinian demands for a homeland. Without Egypt's military power, the threat of force evaporated because no single Arab state was strong enough militarily to confront Israel alone. So this unilateral agreement seemed like a betrayal to many Arabs. It looked as if the Palestinian issue, which lay at the heart of the Arab-Israeli conflict, would remain unaddressed and unresolved.

The agreement brought Egypt no prosperity and with no real improvement in the economy al-Sadat became increasingly unpopular. He seemed increasingly remote from the Egyptian people. Increasingly he reacted to criticism by imposing censorship and imprisoning opponents. In May 1980, an impressive non-partisan body of Egyptians accused al-Sadat of superseding his own constitution.

Al-Sadat's brutal crackdown on fundamentalists lost him much of his support at home and in the West generally. In June 1981 tensions between Muslims and Copts in Egypt exploded into violence in the Cairo slums. Men, women, and children were slaughtered. Some babies were thrown from windows to their deaths in the streets below. Tensions mounted as Muslims and Christians blamed one another. In September, al-Sadat cracked down on both sides with brutal police tactics and multiple arrests. The head of the Coptic Church, Pope Shenuda III, was banished to a monastery. The Islamic student associations, which had started up after the 1967 war and had enjoyed government favour through the 1970s, were banned on 3 September. The leader of one of these student groups at Asyut University, Muhammad Ahmed Showky Islambouli, was arrested and beaten up. This arrest is thought to be the main event which triggered his brother Khalid Islambouli's decision to arrange and carry out the assassination.

Just one month later, Khalid got his revenge. On 6 October, 1981, President Anwar al-Sadat was attending an annual military parade celebrating the campaigns of the 1973 Yom Kippur War. He was on a podium saluting the passing troops when two grenades exploded, apparently to confuse and distract people's attention. Gunmen then leapt from a military truck in front of the presidential reviewing stand and ran some distance towards the spectators, raking officials with automatic gunfire. One of them, the leader of the assassination team, ran straight toward the stand where the president was standing and fired at al-Sadat with an assault rifle. The assassin apparently shouted 'Death to Pharaoh!' just before killing al-Sadat or 'I killed Pharaoh!' immediately afterwards.

In spite of the distance they had to cover, and the time it took for them to run across the open space, there was no effective response to this crude and unambiguous attack. In spite of the presence of large numbers of security personnel, as would be expected for such an occasion, eyewitnesses say the attackers were able to carry on shooting and throwing grenades for well over a minute without any response. Whether this was shock or there was some more sinister explanation is hard to tell, but by the time the president's bodyguards started returning fire at least 10 people lay seriously injured or dead inside the stand. President al-Sadat was mortally wounded and 20 other people, including four American diplomats, were injured. Also in the stand with al-Sadat were the future UN Secretary-General Boutros Boutros-Ghali and Hosni Mubarak, the Air Force officer who was to succeed al-Sadat as president. Neither Mubarak nor Boutros-Ghali were injured. The attack was co-ordinated and carried out with such precision and effectiveness that there must be suspicions that the attack was supported with high-level intelligence. The lack of immediate response from bodyguards has never been satisfactorily explained either.

Security forces shot and killed two of the attackers and overpowered the rest, as crowds of military and civilian spectators scrambled for cover, some of them pathetically cowering behind flimsy chairs. President Sadat was airlifted by helicopter to a military hospital. He died about two hours later.

The Egyptian authorities declared a state of emergency. The American President, Ronald Reagan, paid tribute to the man he remembered as the signatory of the Camp David Accords: 'America has lost a great friend, the world has lost a great statesman, and mankind has lost a champion of peace.'

But many celebrated when they heard the news. In Libya, Tripoli Radio said that every tyrant had an end, and thousands of people poured onto the streets in jubilation. The Palestinian Liberation Organization did not condemn the assassination. A PLO official, Nabil Ramlawi, said: 'We were expecting this end of President al-Sadat because we are sure he was against the interests of his people, the Arab nations and the Palestinian people.'

A group calling itself the Independent Organization for the Liberation of Egypt said it carried out the attack. Al-Sadat's assassins were identified as Muslim extremists, members of the Egyptian Islamic Jihad. Their hope was to impose Islamic rule in Egypt. The Muslim fundamentalist army regulars were led into the attack by army First Lieutenant Khalid Ahmed Showky El-Islambouli. In the subsequent trial in December, Khalid Islambouli was found guilty of organizing the assassination of the Egyptian president and condemned to death. Islambouli was not originally supposed to take part in the parade, but was chosen by chance to replace an officer who was unable to attend. Islambouli was executed in April 1982.

The Iranian government was fiercely critical of al-Sadat, and went so far as to name a street in Tehran after the assassin. Iran's public portrayal of Islambouli as a hero and martyr continues to get in the way of good diplomatic relations between Egypt and Iran.

Hosni Mubarak and General Fouad Allam, head of Egypt's security service, launched a campaign against radical Islam with unlawful arrests, detention without trial, and torture to force confessions. Thousands of suspected terrorists were rounded up and jailed, among them Sheik Omar Abdel

Rahman, who was later convicted of conspiring to blow up New York City landmarks, and Ayman al-Zawahiri, one of Osama bin Laden's two top lieutenants.

BENIGNO AQUINO

1983

BENIGNO 'NINOY' SIMEÓN Aquino was born in November 1932. At the age of 17, he became the youngest war correspondent to cover the Korean War for *The Manila Times*. Because of his journalistic feats, he received a Philippine Legion of Honor award from President Elpidio Quirino at 18. By 21 he was an adviser to the Defence Secretary Ramon Magsaysay. Ninoy studied law at the University of the Philippines, but dropped out to pursue journalism. In 1954, he was appointed by President Ramon Magsaysay to act as personal emissary to Luis Taruc, the leader of a rebel group. After four months, he successfully secured Taruc's surrender. He became mayor of Concepción in 1955, when he was still only 22.

Aquino became governor of Tarlac in 1961 at the age of 29, and secretary-general of the Liberal Party in 1966. In 1967 he became the youngest senator in the history of the Philippines. He was the only member of the Liberal Party to make it to the senate, which made him a target for the dictator Marcos. In 1968, Aquino warned that by inflating the armed forces budget and militarizing civilian government offices Marcos was building a garrison state.

Aquino kept needling Marcos and chipping away at the Marcos regime. He made a famous speech criticizing an extravagant project patronized by the President's wife,

Imelda Marcos. President Marcos was furious and called Aquino 'a congenital liar'. Aquino had been a kind of boy-prodigy; now he was the whizz-kid of Philippine politics. He could now consider going for the presidency. Surveys showed that he was outstandingly popular, and by law President Marcos was unable to serve another term.

Then on 21 August, 1971, Marcos staged the Plaza Miranda bombing as a way of showing that the country was in danger from extremists. In reality he was preparing the way towards martial law – simply in order to gain perpetual power. When Marcos declared martial law in September 1972, Aquino was one of the first to be arrested and imprisoned on charges of murder, illegal possession of firearms and subversion. In April 1975, Aquino announced that he was starting a fast to the death to protest against the injustice of his treatment. As the weeks went by he became weakened by the hunger strike, but soldiers forcibly dragged him to his trial by military tribunal. On the 40th day of his fast, his family pressed him to stop his fast.

On 25 November, 1977, the military tribunal found Aquino guilty of murder, subversion and illegal possession of firearms, and sentenced him to death by firing squad. For some reason, Aquino did not believe that Marcos wanted him to die in this way. Aquino said, 'It will be done in another way.' And it was.

In March 1980, Aquino suffered his first heart attack – probably the result of seven years of solitary confinement. After a second heart attack it was found that he had blocked arteries and needed surgery. Aquino refused to submit to any surgery at the Heart Centre, preferring to either go to the United States to have a surgery or to return to Fort Bonifacio to die. On 8 May, 1980, Aquino had a remarkable visit – from Imelda Marcos. She offered him the chance of leaving that evening for America, on two conditions: that he would return, and that while in America he would say nothing against Marcos. She ordered General Fabian Ver and Mel Mathay to arrange passports, visas and plane tickets for the Aquino family. Aquino boarded a plane for America that same day, accompanied by his wife Cory and his family.

After a successful operation in Dallas, Aquino made a quick recovery. Within two weeks he was planning to fly to the Middle East to meet Muslim leaders. When he assured Marcos that he would be returning to the Philippines, he received a reply that it would be all right for him to extend his convalescence. Marcos did not after all want him to return. The Aquino family went on to spend three years in exile in America, living in Boston. He wrote two books and gave lectures – unfortunately they were critical of the Marcos government.

In 1981 and 1982 there was a series of bombings in Manila. Marcos accused Aquino of being the 'Mad Bomber'. Aquino denied it but warned that that opponents of the Marcos regime might well resort to violence soon. He urged Marcos to 'heed the voice of conscience and moderation.'

The years of imprisonment had had a profound spiritualizing effect on Aquino. Increasingly he drew strength from Catholic devotions and the writings of Gandhi and Martin Luther King. The last phase of Aquino's life was a kind of pilgrimage towards martyrdom. He became an outspoken proponent of non-violence as a means of combating the Marcos regime. He had always talked of returning to the Philippines. In early 1983, he read about the worsening political situation there and Marcos's deteriorating health (due to lupus, tuberculosis of the skin). Aquino believed that he had to persuade Marcos to return the country to democracy before extreme violence broke out.

Benigno Aquino decided to return to the Philippines well aware of the extreme danger that awaited him. At first passports were denied to the Aquino family, so they could not return. Aquino decided it would be better if he went alone as that would attract less attention. Ninoy had acquired a passport under the pseudonym Marcial Bonifacio, then a second bearing his real name. The Marcos government warned that sanctions would be taken against any airline carrying Aquino, and that it would be forced to take him back to the USA. He travelled back to Manila by a round-about route, eventually arriving from Taiwan, with whom the Philippines had severed diplomatic relations. Aquino knew that the Taiwanese did not care about offending Marcos.

He anticipated the worst and was wearing a bullet-proof vest, but he acknowledged that he could still be shot in the head, which is exactly what happened. He was accompanied by several foreign journalists from different agencies, partly to ensure his safety. In an interview he gave them on the plane shortly before his death he said, 'Be very ready with your hand camera because this could happen very quickly . . . in a matter of 3 or 4 minutes it could be all over . . . I may not be able to talk to you again after this . . . this is the danger, the big danger.'

On 21 August, 1983, his plane landed at Manila International Airport. He was escorted off the plane. Despite the presence of his own security guards and government troops on the tarmac, he was fatally shot in the head. The government claimed that he was gunned down by Rolando

Galman, and the assassin was immediately shot dead by troops. Everyone suspected that Galman was simply shot out of hand to provide cover for the real assassin, who was almost certainly one of Marcos's people. Marcos made a show of being concerned to secure Aquino's safety, sending two thousand security personnel to the airport. It is impossible that Aquino could have been assassinated without government collusion. Many believed, at the time and subsequently, that it was one of the soldiers escorting Aquino who pulled the trigger. Even more suspicions arose on who ordered the assassination.

Many theories circulated as to who ordered the assassination. Marcos was ill in bed, but that need not have stopped him giving an order. Marcos certainly ordered an independent body to investigate the assassination. There were 26 high-ranking officers who were charged, among them General Fabian Ver, the armed forces chief who was well known to be Marcos's enforcer, but they were acquitted. The military team on duty on the tarmac at the time of the assassination were given life sentences. An appeal has been launched recently, based on the claim that the assassination was ordered by Eduardo Cojuangco, a Marcos crony – and rather oddly a cousin of Aquino's wife.

There was a surge of national grief and public anger at Aquino's death. Two million people lined the streets to watch his funeral procession, which lasted for 12 hours; after a funeral mass conducted by Cardinal Sin, he was buried in the Manila Memorial Park. The assassination of Benigno Aquino destroyed him but rejuvenated the opposition to Marcos, and so in a short time destroyed Marcos too. The assassination energized the opposition movement transforming it into a mass movement involving people from all classes of society. World attention was suddenly brought to the Philippines; there were exposés of Imelda's extravagant lifestyle and Ferdinand's excesses as a dictator. The assassination thrust Aquino's widow Cory into prominence, and in due course she became president.

INDIRA GANDHI

1984

INDIRA GANDHI WAS born in 1917 in Allahabad, the only child of Jawaharlal Nehru. In 1938 she joined the National Congress party and became active in India's movement for independence. In 1942 she married Feroze Gandhi and both were arrested by the British on charges of subversion and imprisoned for 13 months. When India won its independence in 1947 and her father Nehru took office as prime minister, Indira Gandhi became his official hostess. She also served as his confidante on national problems and accompanied him on foreign trips. In 1955 she was elected onto the executive of the Congress party, where she became a national political figure in her own right; in 1959 she briefly became the party's president.

Following her father's death in May 1964, the new prime minister Lal Shastri appointed Indira Gandhi as minister of information and broadcasting. As many Indians were illiterate, radio and television played a major role in spreading information and Gandhi encouraged the manufacture of cheap radios. When Shastri died suddenly in January 1966, she succeeded him as prime minister. The following year she was elected to a 5-year term by the parliament members of the dominant Congress party. She led her party to a landslide victory in the national elections of 1971.

In 1975 Indira Gandhi was convicted of breaking the rules during her election campaign. She protested that the conviction was part of a conspiracy to remove her from office; instead of resigning, she declared a state of national emergency on 26 June. The Indian Supreme Court overturned her conviction, but the emergency was continued. Gandhi became more autocratic, assuming direct control over many aspects of life in India. Thousands of dissenters were imprisoned. Many people saw these actions as strongly influenced by her younger son, Sanjay Gandhi, whom she was grooming as her dynastic successor.

Her most unpopular policy was the forced sterilization programme, her over-aggressive attempt to curb population growth. A number of other breaches of human rights were also committed, including the levelling of slums, the brainchild of her son Sanjay. Her critics contended that Mrs Gandhi's regime was undermining the democratic system of India. Her response was to call a general election in March 1977, in which she hoped to demonstrate that she had popular support. But she had misjudged the situation badly; she lost her seat in parliament, and the Congress Party was defeated. A few years later, however, she made a political come-back, forming a new majority government.

When her son and intended heir Sanjay died in a plane crash that June, she began to prepare her older son, Rajiv Gandhi (1944–91), who had up to this point shown little interest in politics, to be her successor.

In June 1984 the city of Amritsar in the Punjab was the scene of a violent clash between the Indian government led by the 66-year-old prime minister, Indira Gandhi, and militant Sikh separatists. The Sikh extremists were led by Jarnail Singh Bindranwale, who was campaigning for an independent homeland for the Sikhs. The militants established their headquarters in the Golden Temple in Amritsar, the holiest shrine of the Sikh culture.

In a characteristically heavy-handed gesture, Mrs Gandhi ordered the Indian army to surround the temple, then, almost unbelievably, storm it. By 6 June, all resistance was crushed in this violent onslaught, leaving over a thousand people dead, including the Sikh leader, Jarnail Bindranwale, and several thousands wounded. The violence to people who were after all Indian citizens was shocking; to the Sikhs, the extreme violence done to the fabric of the Golden Temple was equally shocking. It was the worst of Indira Gandhi's many political mistakes.

As it happened, there were a great many Sikhs serving in the Indian army. There were even Sikhs among the guards defending the compound where Mrs Gandhi lived in New Delhi. Following the storming of the Golden Temple, many people thought that it was rash of Mrs Gandhi to put her trust in Sikh guards. Mrs Gandhi refused to dismiss them, and so put herself at serious risk of a revenge attack.

One of Indira Gandhi's Sikh guards was Beant Singh, a man of 'good character' with no record of criminal behaviour. He arranged to be on duty inside the prime minister's compound on 31 October, 1984. A constable of the Delhi Armed Police, Satwant Singh, was on duty with him. Beant Singh had a .38-calibre revolver. Satwant Singh carried an old Second World War sten gun, a light machine-gun.

Indira Gandhi left her house just after nine o'clock in the morning, on her way to be interviewed by the actor Peter Ustinov. As she walked towards Beant Singh, she made a gesture of acknowledgement. In response, he pulled out his revolver and shot her three times. As she fell, Satwant Singh fired a volley at her with the sten gun. She was hit by a dozen bullets.

Saturated in her own blood, Mrs Gandhi was rushed to hospital but it was impossible to save her life. In the early afternoon, her death was announced. Crowds filled the streets, attacking Sikh temples and businesses and it is believed that over a thousand Sikhs were killed in these instant reprisals.

The assassins made no attempt to escape. They were arrested and then shot out of hand while in custody. Beant Singh died, but Satwant Singh survived the shooting. There was an investigation, but there was no evidence of a conspiracy that extended outside Beant Singh's circle of associates. There were rumours of a more extensive conspiracy, but no evidence has appeared that supports it.

Indira Gandhi's son and successor as Indian prime minister, Rajiv Gandhi, was himself to be assassinated in 1991. He lost the premiership in 1989, but tried for re-election in 1991. On 21 May that year his campaign arrived in Sriperumbudur in the Tamil Nadu state. The Tamils are a distinct ethnic group living in southern India and Sri Lanka. The Tamils despised Rajiv Gandhi. In his role as prime minister, he had withdrawn Indian government support for the Tamil Tigers, a guerrilla group fighting against the government of Sri Lanka.

The Tamil Tigers were waiting for Rajiv Gandhi in Sriperumbudur for revenge that day. A young woman with a belt of grenades and explosives round her waist stepped forward to hang a garland round Rajiv Gandhi's neck in a treacherous act of greeting. Then she activated a detonator, blowing herself and Rajiv Gandhi to pieces and killing 16 bystanders as well.

OLOF PALME

1986

SVEN OLOF JOACHIM Palme, born in 1927, was prime minister of Sweden from 1969–76 and from 1982 until his assassination in 1986. The murder of Olof Palme was the first of its kind in modern Swedish history and had an impact in Scandinavia similar to that of JFK in the United States. Politically he was a Social Democrat.

During his time at university, Palme became involved in student politics, working with the Swedish National Union of Students. Palme attributed his becoming a socialist to a debate on taxes he attended in 1947, observation of the wide class divide in America in the 1940s and seeing for himself in 1953 the consequences of colonialism and imperialism in Asia.

In 1958 he was elected as an MP and he held several cabinet posts from 1963 onwards. In 1967 he became minister of education, and the following year he was the target of fierce criticism from left-wing students protesting against the government's plans for university reform. When party leader Tage Erlander stepped down in 1969, Palme was elected as the new leader by the Social Democratic party congress and succeeded Erlander as prime minister.

Olof Palme's 10 years as prime minister and his untimely death made him one of the best known Swedish politicians of the 20th century. His protégé and political ally, Bernt Carlsson, was the UN Commissioner for Namibia in July 1987, and he also suffered an untimely death. Carlsson died in the Pan Am air crash on 21 December 1988, on his way to the signing ceremony in New York, in which South Africa finally granted independence to Namibia.

Palme led a generation of Swedish Social Democrats who stood much further to the left than their predecessors. He was a controversial political figure on the international scene. He condemned the United States for the Vietnam War. He campaigned against the proliferation of nuclear weapons. He criticized the Franco regime. He condemned apartheid and supported economic sanctions against South Africa. He supported the Palestine Liberation Organization. Olof Palme therefore made many enemies abroad as well as friends.

Olof Palme was often to be seen in Stockholm without any kind of bodyguard or other protection, and the night of his murder was one such occasion. Near to midnight on 28 February 1986, he was walking home from the cinema with his wife Lisbet along the central Stockholm street called Sveavägen, when the couple were attacked without warning by a lone gunman. Olof Palme was shot in the back at close range and a second shot wounded Lisbet Palme. Police said a taxi-driver used his mobile radio to raise the alarm. Two young women sitting in a car nearby tried to help the prime minister. He was rushed to hospital but was pronounced dead on arrival, just after midnight. Mrs Palme was treated and she recovered.

Deputy Prime Minister Ingvar Carlsson immediately assumed the duties as prime minister and leader of the Social Democratic Party.

The assassin escaped unobserved and vanished. A reward equivalent to five million US dollars was offered for information leading to the conviction of the killer. The revolver used in the murder was never found. The assassination remains an unsolved crime, though many theories have been put forward. One is that right-wing extremists were behind it. A right-winger called Viktor Gunnarsson, with connections to various right-wing extremist groups including the European Workers Party, was arrested straight after the murder but soon released after a dispute between the police and prosecuting attorneys. John Stannerman was another of the police's suspects, but he had a watertight alibi: he was locked up in prison on the night Palme was shot.

Viktor Gunnarsson, a 33-year-old Swede and fanatical anti-Communist, looked a much likelier suspect. He was a compulsive liar and role-player. He had spent some time in America and claimed to have contacts with the CIA. Gunnarsson was arrested twice and, whoever was responsible for that part of the investigation, was convinced that he was the killer. Gunnarsson was nevertheless released after an intervention by senior police officers, and he left Sweden. In 1994, a short time after revealing that he was the one described as the killer in Inspector Wingren's book *He killed Olof Palme*, he was murdered in North Carolina. The reason for his murder was not clear to the American police. Gunnarsson had uttered threats against Palme. He was definitely seen by witnesses near the murder scene both before and after killing, and a man of his description was seen running away after the fatal shots. Unlike Stannerman, he had no alibi.

Over a year after the assassination, another suspect, Christer Pettersson, was arrested. He was picked out by Mrs Palme at an identification parade, and consequently tried and convicted of the murder. Later, on appeal to the High Court, Pettersson succeeded in gaining an acquittal; the murder weapon had never been found; there were doubts about the reliability of Mrs Palme's evidence; and Pettersson had no obvious motive. In the 1990s new evidence against Pettersson emerged, mostly from petty criminals who had changed their stories but also, startlingly, from a confession by Pettersson. The chief prosecutor, Agneta Blidberg, considered reopening the case, but acknowledged that a confession alone would not be sufficient, saying:

> *'He must say something about the weapon because the appeals court set that condition in its ruling. That is the only technical evidence that could be cited as a reason to re-open the case.'*

The legal case against Christer Pettersson therefore remains closed, but the police file on the investigation into the Palme murder cannot be closed until both murder weapon and murderer are found. Christer Pettersson died in September 2004 of a cerebral haemorrhage after injuring his head. A recent Swedish television documentary claimed that Pettersson's associates had said that he confessed to them his role in the murder, but that it was a case of mistaken identity. Pettersson had intended to kill a drug dealer who often walked, similarly dressed, along the same street at night. He had not intended to kill the prime minister. The TV programme also said there had been police surveillance of drug activity in the area, with several officers on duty in apartments and cars near the scene of the shooting, but the police monitoring had ceased 45 minutes before the murder.

Over 30 witnesses saw people, some identifiable as policemen, talking into walkie-talkies along the Palmes' route home from the cinema or along the killer's escape route leading up to the time of the murder. One interpretation is that Mr and Mrs Palme were being kept under observation for benevolent reasons; another is that they were being stalked as part of a malevolent conspiracy; another is that there was a police surveillance operation going on in the area that had nothing to do with the Palmes or the attack on them.

As a result of the documentary, the Swedish police decided to open an investigation into Pettersson's role in the Palme case. Then there were newspaper articles alleging that the film-maker had invented some of the material and left out contradictory evidence. There was, alternatively, a possible South African connection. A week before he was murdered Palme addressed the *Swedish People's Parliament Against Apartheid in Stockholm,* which was attended by hundreds of anti-apartheid sympathizers as well as leaders and officials from the ANC. In 1996, Colonel Eugene de Kock, a former South African police officer, gave evidence to the Supreme Court in Pretoria alleging that Palme had been shot and killed because he 'strongly opposed the apartheid regime and Sweden made substantial contributions to the ANC'. De Kock knew the person responsible for the murder of Olof Palme; he said it was Craig Williamson, a South African superspy working for BOSS and who was in Stockholm the days before and after the murder. Brigadier Johannes Coetzee, who had been Williamson's boss, identified Anthony White as the assassin. Then it became more complicated still; Peter Caselton, a member of Coetzee's assassination squad, named a Swede living in Northern Cyprus since 1985 as the assassin; his name was Bertil Wedin. In October 1996, Swedish police investigators went to South

Africa but were unable to substantiate any of de Kock's claims for a South African *Operation Longreach*.

There had certainly been a conspiracy to assassinate. In 1999, Coetzee, Williamson, de Kock and Caselton were to be granted amnesties by the Truth and Reconciliation Commission for their involvement in the bombing of the ANC offices in London in 1982. As it happened no one was killed, but Oliver Tambo, who was supposed to have attended a meeting there at the time of the bombing, was their probable target. But the reality of a South African conspiracy to assassinate Tambo – if that is what it was – is no proof whatever of a South African conspiracy to assassinate Palme.

Another possibility was that Kurds were behind the murder. The Stockholm police commissioner, Hans Holmér, arrested a number of Kurds living in Sweden, following allegations that one of their organizations was responsible for the murder. The lead led nowhere except to Holmér's removal from the investigation. Fifteen years later, in 2001, Swedish police officers interviewed the Kurdish rebel leader Abdullah Öcalan in a Turkish prison about his allegations that a dissident Kurdish group murdered Palme. But this lead also proved fruitless.

The Swedish police investigation was overall poorly organized, with bureaucrats and administrators making the key decisions rather than experienced police officers; meanwhile Sweden's most experienced murder investigators were left out or were brought into the investigation too late. Lisbeth Palme was only questioned by certain selected investigators and although she positively identified Pettersson at an identification parade she was apparently never called upon to identify Gunnarsson, the other prime suspect. Many police officers were shocked at the ineptitude with which the Palme case was handled. The investigation inspired a certain amount of black humour; 'The bad news is that the police are after us: the good news is that it's the Swedish police.'

Theories about Olof Palme's unsolved murder abound. Several of the theories link Palme's death to arms trading. One suggestion (from Bondeson) is that Palme built on his friendship with Rajiv Gandhi to secure Bofors, a Swedish armaments company a deal to supply the Indian Army with howitzers. However, Palme did not realise that Bofors had used a company based in England to influence Indian government officials in concluding the deal. Bondeson alleged that on the morning he was assassinated Palme had met the Iraqi ambassador to Sweden, Muhammad Saeed al-Sahhaf. They discussed Bofors, which Muhammed Saeed al-Sahhaf knew well because of its arms sales during the Iran-Iraq War. Bondeson suggested that the ambassador told Palme all about Bofors' activities behind the scenes and that Palme was furious. Palme's murder could have been triggered by this conversation, if either Bofors arms dealers or the middlemen had a prearranged plan to silence the prime minister if he should ever discover the truth and endanger the deal with India. Like many conspiracy theories, this is fascinating but ultimately unconvincing.

Another possibility is that the Red Army Faction of Germany assassinated Palme. Indeed it seems they claimed responsibility via an anonymous phone call to a London news agency. They supposedly assassinated him because he was the prime minister of Sweden during the 1975 occupation of the West German embassy in Stockholm which ended in failure for the Red Army Faction.

The mystery may never be solved. It remains a possibility that more than one of the leads we have looked at is true. Perhaps BOSS (for example) was behind the assassination, and perhaps one of the 'lone gunmen' was hired to do the job – and take all the blame. But so much disinformation has been spread about that it is very difficult to get at the truth of what happened that night on an ordinary street corner in Stockholm, when a prime minister was shot and no one, incredibly, was brought to justice for it.

PRESIDENT ZIA UL-HAQ

1988

ON THE AFTERNOON of 17 August, 1988, Pak One, an American-built Hercules transport plane, took off from the military air base at Bahawalpur in Pakistan. The VIP passengers included Mohammad Zia ul-Haq, army chief of staff and president of Pakistan, who was returning to Islamabad after seeing the demonstration of a new American tank.

General Zia had been reluctant to go to Bahawalpur that morning, but the commander of the armoured corp, his former military secretary, had been extraordinarily pressing, saying that the entire army command would be there and implying that Zia's absence might be taken as a slight. As it had happened, the much vaunted American tank missed its target every time. Zia went on from the fiasco to a good-humoured lunch with his top generals. Before re-boarding the plane, he embraced the generals who were not travelling back to the capital.

On the flight back to Islamabad his close friend, General Akhtar Abdur Rahman, sat next to him. He was chairman of the joint chiefs of staff and the second most powerful man in Pakistan. He had headed the ISI, Pakistan's equivalent of the CIA, for 10 years and in that role he had been Zia's architect for the war in Afghanistan against the Soviets. It was his ISI that organized, trained and equipped the Mujahedeen; and now the Mujahedeen was on the verge of defeating the Soviet Union.

Rahman had not wanted to attend the tank demonstration either. He decided to go only when a colleague told him that Zia was on the verge of making major changes in the army and intelligence high command: Zia needed his advice. Zia had already made one precipitate decision by firing his own prime minister and dissolving parliament on 29 May 1988. It was inevitable that Zia would make radical changes in the military.

Also in the VIP section were Zia's American guests: Ambassador Arnold L. Raphel, who had known Zia for 12 years, and General Herbert M. Wassom, the head of US military aid to Pakistan. Behind them, eight of Zia's generals filled two rows of seats.

Lieut-General Aslam Beg, the army's vice chief of staff, waved Zia off from the runway, intending to fly back in a smaller jet. A Cessna completed the final security check of the area; this was a routine precaution ever since an unsuccessful missile attack on Pak One eight years before.

Separated from the VIP capsule by a door and three steps, was the cockpit and its four man flight crew. The pilot, Wing Commander Mashood Hassan, had been personally selected by Zia. When Pak One was airborne, the control tower at Bahawalpur routinely asked Mashood his position: 'Pak One, stand by.' There was no response from Mashood. Repeated efforts were made to contact Mashood, to no avail. Only minutes after take-off, Pak One was missing.

Meanwhile, villagers beside a river approximately 18 miles from the airport saw Pak One lurching up and down in the sky. After its third loop, it plunged directly downwards, burying itself in the desert. Then it exploded in a ball of fire.

It was 3.51 pm. After a flight lasting only five minutes, the plane had crashed and all 31 people on board were dead.

General Beg's jet circled for a moment over the burning wreckage. Once Beg realised what had happened, he ordered his pilot to head straight for Islamabad. Beg reacted as if a coup was under way and, that evening, army units moved swiftly to cordon off all the strategic locations in the capital.

The crash altered the face of politics in Pakistan in a way in which no simple *coup d'état* could have done. Zia had taken advantage of the ideal of an Islamic Pakistan when he seized power in 1977. He had seen that the Shah was unable to control Iran because he had underestimated the power of Islam, so Zia pursued a policy of 'islamization', reinstalling the law of the Koran. Public flogging was to be the penalty for drinking alcohol.

Now, with Zia and his top generals dead and no civilian government to take their place, there was a void. There was still the Army, with Beg now in command; the Army had always been the dominant power in Pakistan. There was also the opposition party, the Pakistan People's Party, founded by Zulfikar Ali Bhutto, which could now back Zia's arch enemy, Benazir Bhutto, in the November elections. This made possible Benazir's election, which could never have happened if Zia had remained in power.

Who sabotaged Pak One? Prime Minister Benazir Bhutto offered one explanation: divine intervention. For her it must have seemed so. As far she was concerned, Zia was the incarnation of evil. She could not understand why her father, Zulfikar Ali Bhutto, when prime minister, had selected him as head of the Army. Zia had then deposed him and committed judicial murder by having him hanged on a trumped-up charge; he banned Zulfikar Ali Bhutto's party, the Pakistan People's Party; he imprisoned Benazir and her mother; he had her two brothers tried and convicted of high crimes in absentia. Zia had destroyed her family.

Some human agency for the assassination has to be sought, even so. Benazir Bhutto's 34-year-old brother, Mir Murtaza Bhutto, headed an anti-Zia guerrilla group, sharing offices for a time with the PLO in Kabul. Its stated mission was to destroy the Zia regime by any means possible. Mir Murtaza admitted that he had attempted to assassinate Zia on five previous occasions. One of these earlier assassination attempts involved firing a missile at Pak One; on that occasion the missile had missed. Now, with his sister in a position to win the elections if Zia could be eliminated, Mir Murtaza had an extra motive.

The Soviet Union was another suspect. Zia had offended Moscow by his actions in Afghanistan to such a degree that it declared publicly, only a week before the crash, that Zia's obstruction could not be tolerated. The Soviet Foreign Ministry then took the extraordinary step of summoning the American ambassador in Moscow, to say to him that it intended 'to teach Zia a lesson'. The Soviets had the means to carry out this threat; they could have used the Afghan intelligence service, which had carried out several covert bombings in Pakistan. Pak One might well have been one of its targets.

The Pentagon did not believe the Soviets were behind Zia's assassination, simply because the American ambassador was on the plane. The Soviets would not have jeopardized glasnost by assassinating an American of this rank. On the other hand, the Soviets may not have known that the

American ambassador would be on the plane; he was not supposed to be there.

Rajiv Gandhi, the prime minister of India, informed Pakistan on 15 August that it would 'regret its behaviour' in supplying weapons to Sikh terrorists in India. The Sikhs had assassinated his mother when she was prime minister and Zia had had meetings with Sikh leaders. That may have given Rajiv Gandhi a motive.

A lot of people had motives for assassinating Zia. Zia's eldest son, Ijaz ul-Haq, who now lives in Bahrain, is conscious that his father was persuaded to go to the tank demonstrations that day by his generals. General Rahman was similarly manipulated into going on the same plane. This implies that the assassination was an army conspiracy, though there could have been additional layers to the plot.

Zia's policies had also offended the United States. The CIA were concerned that Zia was diverting a large share of the weapons supplied by America to a fundamentalist Mujahedeen group that was anti-American. The Americans were also anxious about the progress Zia was making towards building the first Islamic nuclear bomb. The Americans could foresee a workable and acceptable alternative to Zia in the Harvard-educated Benazir Bhutto.

An investigation into the plane crash included only seven US air force accident investigators. It has been suggested that that limited input was a deliberate attempt not to discover the real cause of the crash. It would be extremely embarrassing if the culprit turned out to be one or other of the superpowers, or indeed the Pakistan military elite, and one of these options was likely. This was certainly not a lone crazed gunman killing. The US State Department worked to control media perception of what had caused the crash, even issuing formal 'press guidance'. This deflected press attention from the report's actual conclusion that the probable cause of the crash was sabotage. Initial reports therefore explained that the crash was an accident, and only later was sabotage mentioned.

Unfortunately the plane carried no black box flight recorder, but it was still possible to eliminate a number of possibilities. No evidence of a mechanical failure could be found, so sabotage was the only explanation. The plane had not been blown up in mid-air, as it was in one piece when it had hit the ground. Nor had there been a fire in the plane before the crash. A post-mortem on the American general showed no soot in his windpipe, so he was dead before the fire engulfed the plane. The engines had not failed, as the propellers were turning at full speed when they hit the ground. The electricity had not failed, as the electric clocks had stopped at the moment of impact with the ground. Pilot error was unlikely to have been the cause, as the plane had safely taken off; pilot error only becomes a major factor at take-off and landing. The weather was perfectly clear.

The only remaining explanation was a deliberate act of sabotage. Analysis of chemicals found in the wreckage found foreign traces of pentaerythritol tetranitrate (PNET), a high explosive often used by saboteurs as a detonator. There were also antimony and sulphur; the compound antimony sulphide is used in fuses to detonate devices. A small explosion could have been used to burst a flask the size of a drinks can which contained an odourless poison gas that incapacitated the pilots.

It is very unfortunate that autopsies were not carried out on the crew to test this hypothesis, but it seemed the only workable scenario. Criminal investigators and interrogators were needed to find the people responsible. By February the Pakistan government had taken responsibility for the investigation out of the hands of the ISI.

During the radio silence when the control tower was unable to raise any response from Mashood, the Pak One pilot, other planes in the area picked up snippets of conversation. After three or four minutes of silence, a faint voice in Pak One called out 'Mashood, Mashood!' It was Zia's military secretary, Brigadier Najib Ahmed who apparently, from the weakness of his voice, was calling the pilot from the door at the back of the flight deck, where Najib had entered from the VIP seats. The radio was therefore switched on and picking up background sounds. The only conceivable reason why Mashood and the other three members of the flight crew did not speak, to Najib Ahmed or the control tower, was that they were unconscious and unable to speak, perhaps already dead. Presumably Zia and the other VIP passengers had become aware that the plane was out of control. Planes characteristically go into a pattern known as a 'phugoid' when there is no pilot control. An unattended plane dives towards the ground, then the mechanism in the tail automatically over-corrects for this downward motion, causing it to head upwards; this would tally with what the villagers saw from the ground. A plane of Pak One's weight without any pilots in control would have made three roller-coaster dives before crashing, which is exactly what the villagers had reported seeing. The passengers became alarmed and Najib Ahmed rushed to the cockpit door to find out what the pilot was doing. By that stage, it could only have been a matter of seconds before the plane nose-dived into the ground.

Security at the Bahawalpur airport was not particularly tight. It would have been relatively easy for someone to plant a gas bomb in the plane's cockpit that day. A repair crew, including some civilians, had worked on adjusting the cargo door of Pak One for two hours that morning, and they had entered and left the plane without being searched. Any of them could dropped a gas bomb, perhaps of paralysing VX nerve gas, into the cockpit's air vent.

But few of these possibilities were ever followed up, and none of them was made the subject of a systematic and determined investigation. Autopsies were not carried out on the bodies of the flight crew. The explanation offered at the time was that Islamic law requires burial within 24 hours, though this could not been the real reason as the bodies were not returned to their families for burial until two days after the crash. In the Pakistan Air Force, autopsies were routinely carried out on pilots who died in cases of air crashes — regardless of Islamic custom.

The strangest aspect of the plane crash was the speed with which it was forgotten, in spite of the fact that it caused the death of the head of state who was the main ally of the US in the war against the Russians in Afghanistan. There were no repercussions, no cries for vengeance, no efforts to find the assassins. In the United States, the decision was made to block any FBI interest in investigating the death of its ambassador. The greatest casualty of all, as so often in political assassinations of this kind, was to be the truth.

YITZHAK RABIN

1995

BORN IN JERUSALEM in 1922, Yitzhak Rabin was the fifth prime minister of Israel, from 1974 until 1977 and again from 1992 until his death in 1995. He grew up in Tel Aviv, graduating with distinction from the Kadoori Agricultural High School. His ambition at that time was to become an irrigation engineer. Rabin married his wife Leah in 1948, the year of Israel's independence.

During the 1948 Arab-Israeli War, he directed Israeli operations in Jerusalem and fought against the Egyptian army in the Negev. One episode of the 1948 war that troubled him long afterwards was the forced expulsion by the Israel Defence Forces of fifty thousand Arab civilians from the towns of Lod-Ramle. He felt very guilty about it. When Rabin mentioned it in his 1970s memoirs, the censor removed the sensitive passage from his book. By 1964 he had become chief of staff in the Israel Defence Forces. Under Rabin's command, the Israel Defence Forces overwhelmingly defeated Egypt, Syria and Jordan in the Six-Day War of 1967. When the Defence Forces captured the Old City of Jerusalem, Rabin was among the first to visit it. In the run-up to the Six-Day War Rabin had had a nervous breakdown, caused by the stress of being unable to prevent it; he was not a natural aggressor.

Rabin retired from the Defence Forces and became a diplomat, serving as ambassador to the United States beginning in 1968. In 1973, he was elected to the Knesset and appointed minister of labour. Shortly after this he succeeded Golda Meir as prime minister of Israel. His term in office came to an end when it emerged that his wife had a US dollar bank account, then illegal in Israel; Rabin resigned, which was taken as a sign of high integrity.

Rabin held a number of offices under prime ministers Yitzhak Shamir and Shimon Peres. While in opposition, Rabin from 1990 to 1992 battled for the leadership of his party, which Shimon Peres had held since 1977. In 1992 Rabin became chairman of the Israeli Labour Party and in the elections that year he and his party won a clear victory over the incumbent prime minister Yitzhak Shamir.

Yitzhak Rabin went on to play a leading part in the signing of the Oslo Accords, which created the Palestinian Authority and granted it partial control over parts of the Gaza Strip and West Bank. In the run-up to the signing of the accords, the Palestine Liberation Organization leader Yasser Arafat wrote Rabin a letter renouncing violence and recognizing Israel; on the same day Rabin sent Arafat a letter officially recognizing the PLO. For his role in the Oslo Accords, Rabin was awarded the 1994 Nobel Peace Prize, which he shared with Yasser Arafat and Shimon Peres. Some Israelis saw him as a hero, some as a traitor for giving away land they saw as rightfully belonging to Israel – and here were sown the seeds of his assassination.

On 4 November, 1995, after attending a rally promoting the Oslo process at the *Kings of Israel Square* in Tel Aviv, Rabin was assassinated as he returned to his car parked in Ibn

Gevirol Street. The assassination was filmed from a rooftop by a Tel Aviv resident, Ronni Kempler, and it is possible on the Kempler videotape to make out the assassin loitering near the prime minister's car after the peace rally. The assassin moved forward out of the crowd, easily approaching Rabin from behind to shoot him twice in the back at point-blank range. The killer's outstretched left arm almost touched Rabin as the two shots suddenly flashed out. The 73-year-old prime minister fell to the ground and was immediately covered by his bodyguards. The assassin was Yigal Amir, a 25-year-old right-wing radical who had strenuously opposed Rabin's signing of the Oslo Accords. When Ronni Kempler was asked why he was filming the car park at the time, he said, 'The whole time I had the feeling that something bad would happen. There was anxiety in the air.'

Rabin was taken to the nearby Ichilov Hospital in Tel Aviv, where he died on the operating table as a result of massive blood loss and a punctured lung. Amir's trial was postponed for over a month to give defence lawyers time to review the evidence, though Amir freely confessed to being the assassin. Amir said he committed the assassination in an effort to prevent Israel from handing over holy land to Palestinians. He said Rabin wanted 'to give our country to the Arabs.'

The assassination of Yitzhak Rabin was a shock for most Israelis, and ceremonies were performed near the place of the assassination, his home, the Knesset and even the home of the assassin. Rabin's funeral was attended by many world leaders, among them President Clinton of the United States, King Hussein of Jordan and President Hosni Mubarak of Egypt. Clinton described Rabin as a 'martyr for peace' and 'a man completely without pretence'. Acting Israeli Prime Minister Shimon Peres was another of those who spoke at the funeral. He said that Rabin warned him that there was a threat of assassination as they stood together at the peace rally – on the very night that he was shot dead. The Israeli government assigned a huge force of ten thousand police, soldiers and security agents to protect the world leaders and dignitaries who travelled to Israel for the funeral. The PLO leader Yasser Arafat did not, even so, think it was safe for him to attend. He nevertheless said in a CNN interview given in Gaza that he mourned the loss of the man he called his partner in peace. He said, 'I am very sad for this awful event', and described Rabin as 'one of the most important, courageous men in Israel'.

The burial in a hillside cemetery in west Jerusalem followed a two-hour memorial service that ended with the chief rabbi of the Israeli army chanting kaddish, the traditional Jewish prayer for the dead.

A national memorial day was established to commemorate the day of Rabin's assassination. The *Kings of Israel Square* has been renamed in his honour. In spite of his military career Rabin is remembered by most as a great man of peace. After his death, he has become a national symbol, especially for the Israeli Left. Whether his untimely death and the ensuing halt to the peace process and rise of the Israeli Right were connected is hard to tell.

KING BIRENDRA
BIKRAM OF NEPAL

2001

BIRENDRA BIKRAM WAS born in Kathmandu in 1945, and reigned as King of Nepal for 29 years. He was educated at Eton, Tokyo University and Harvard, becoming the first Nepalese king to study abroad. Birendra succeeded to the throne when his father, King Mahendra, died in 1972. Though autocratic, he was a popular and enlightened ruler. He developed the tourist industry and managed to maintain Nepal's independence in spite of pressure from India, China and the Soviet Union. In foreign affairs, Birendra followed a neutral non-aligned policy, seeking to create a 'zone of peace' in Southern Asia between China and India.

Although Birendra himself was generally seen as affable and benevolent, he was also remote from his people, retreating behind the gates of the Narayanhiti Royal Palace, and standing back from any activities that could have made a positive difference to the lives of ordinary Nepalis. Some saw the intellectual stagnation of Nepal at that time as a characteristic fostered by a regime incapable of looking beyond its own security.

King Birendra ruled as an absolute monarch for 18 years before the mounting agitation for political reform led by Bishweshwar Prasad Koirala, who persuaded him to lift the ban on political parties. He held a referendum on the constitution. As a result of this, in November 1990 Birendra approved a new constitution which preserved his status as monarch, but also restored the multi-party Western-style democracy his father had abolished. In the succeeding 10 years King Birendra stuck closely to the letter and spirit of the constitution, which showed him to be a genuine convert to democracy.

It seems that it was a domestic quarrel, not a political coup, that led to Birendra's assassination. On June 1, the royal family of Nepal were at a family dinner at the Narayanhiti Royal Palace. According to the official news reports, the king's son, Crown Prince Dipendra, became furious with his mother because she refused to give her approval for his marriage. The prince is said to have left the dining room, changed into military fatigues and then returned to the family gathering with an Uzi sub-machine gun and an M-16 assault rifle. Then he sprayed the room with bullets. King Birendra and Queen Aishwarya, their son Prince Nirajan, their daughter Princess Shruti, two of the king's sisters, his brother-in-law and a cousin were all killed in a volley of gunfire. The massacre was carried out by Birendra's eldest son and heir, Crown Prince Dipendra Bir Bikram Shah Dev, who afterward turned the gun on himself and after lingering in a coma died three days later. For those three unconscious days he was King of Nepal.

There are some problems with this explanation of events. There had been few outward signs of rifts within the royal family, and no suggestion that there was any kind of disagreement between King Birendra and his son Dipendra, before the massacre. The prince had given no sign that he was capable of killing his mother and father. Born in 1971, he had been educated in Nepal and at Eton. The headmaster of Eton said Dipendra was a very popular boy and was also liked by his teachers. He was known to have an interest in guns and hunting and was a karate black belt, but those who knew him described him as an amiable and gentle man. The only blemish on his record was the allegation that he drank heavily while at Eton.

There was, at the time and subsequently, some suspicion that Dipendra was set up, that someone else was behind the massacre and that Dipendra was a victim of the assassin just like the rest of the family. There were riots in the street as angry crowds clashed with the police. Protesters demanded the truth about the massacre and a curfew was imposed.

Suspicion rested on the dead King Birendra's younger brother, Gyanendra. At the time of the assassination, Gyanendra was on his way back from a visit to Chitwan, a national park on the border with India. He was the only close member of the royal family who was absent from the fateful dinner, and he succeeded to the throne once Birendra and Dipendra were dead. The conspiracy theory had Gynanendra's son, Prince Paras, involved in a plot. According to one version, Gyanendra simply waited at Kathmandu airport until he heard the news that Prince Paras and his troops had carried out the assassinations. According to the same story, those who knew the truth about the assassination had to leave Nepal and still go in fear of their lives.

There is in fact very little to support the wild allegations that were made against Prince, now King, Gyanendra, and his son Prince Paras and it is impossible to believe that Gyanendra would have put his wife at such terrible risk by staging an indiscriminate mass shooting in her presence; his wife was at the fatal dinner party. It is a hypothesis that just defies credibility, even if some Nepalis at the time may have believed it. But there is one anomaly in the Dipendra suicide scenario that is worrying. Dipendra was right-handed, and it is virtually impossible for a right-handed person to shoot themselves in the left temple; it is certainly a very unnatural position in which to hold a gun. That one fact on its own suggests that Dipendra was perhaps not, after all, the assassin.

PIM FORTUYN

2002

PROFESSOR PIM FORTUYN was a rising star in Dutch politics who, some thought, had the potential to be a future prime minister. His unusually high media profile was generated by his unequivocal right-wing views on immigration. He was repeatedly attacked verbally in the media and political rivals freely referred to him as a fascist. Specifically, Fortuyn advised against unrestricted Muslim immigration, and because he was specific he was almost inevitably branded as a racist, as well as a xenophobe and a fascist. Fortuyn was regularly compared with the French right-winger Jean Le Pen, although apart from the immigration issue the two men had little in common.

Pim Fortuyn also attracted attention because he was not only openly but flamboyantly gay. One reason why he condemned further Muslim immigration was that those newcomers to Holland refused to become assimilated in a socially and sexually liberal Dutch society, in which gay sexuality is accepted. Fortuyn was particularly aware of the tension because he lived in Rotterdam, where it has been estimated that 45 percent of the population is Muslim. Fortuyn claimed that some of his gay friends had been beaten up by young Moroccans in Rotterdam. Really, his campaign was against the intolerance of incomers to his country.

Fortuyn's anti-immigration policy naturally found many supporters among Dutch people. Perhaps surprisingly, the second-in-command in Fortuyn's party, called 'Pim Fortuyn's List' was an Afro-Caribbean immigrant, Joao Varela. What Fortuyn identified as the root of the problem was not race but culture. Fortuyn commented, 'What we are witnessing now is a clash of civilizations, not just between states but within them.' The media nevertheless had difficulties in taking seriously an outspoken gay man professing concern over the loss of Western values; he broke across the journalists' stereotypes. One newspaper columnist, Professor Smalhout, reflected on the media role in demonizing the man in the months leading up to his murder: 'Pim Fortuyn was made an outcast by the politically correct Netherlands. He was depicted as a fake professor, a second Hitler . . . a neo-Nazi, a narcissistic homosexual and a political outcast. Practically all the media took part; it was the fashionable thing to do, to have a go at Professor Pim.'

Despite many threats to his life, Pim Fortuyn was given no police protection. In an interview shortly before his assassination, Fortuyn expressed fears that he might be attacked. He had received threats by phone, email and letter. A few weeks earlier, protesters had thrown cream pies laced with urine in his face. Most Dutch politicians travelled without any personal security, and often used public transport, but Fortuyn did occasionally use private bodyguards, though he could not afford to have them all the time.

At the age of 54, Pim Fortuyn was attacked as he left a radio studio in the central Dutch city of Hilversum, just nine days before a general election in which he was expected to do well. His anti-immigration ticket was predicted to pick up at least 15 percent of the vote. He was shot six times and suffered multiple wounds in the head, chest and neck, and died shortly afterwards. Huge crowds took to the streets of Rotterdam after his assassination in protest against the role of the media and the government in Pim's death. About three hundred people gathered outside the parliament building in The Hague to express their anger at the killing.

Acting Prime Minister Wim Kok, described the murder as 'deeply tragic first of all for him and for all his loved ones. It is also deeply tragic for our democracy.'

After an emergency session, the Dutch government called a halt to political campaigning, and a decision on whether the election itself would go ahead under such unsatisfactory conditions was deferred for a few days.

Eyewitnesses said that a single gunman shot Fortuyn as he was getting into a chauffeur-driven limousine in the media park where the radio station is located. It was unclear how the gunman gained access to the media park, which was a gated and enclosed area with its own security. How did the killer reach Fortuyn without going through tight identity and security checks?

Four people chased the gunman, who apparently fired in their direction. Minutes later, police arrested a 33-year-old white Dutch man, Volkert van der Graaf, with the gun in his pocket and charged him with murder. Van der Graaf was an animal rights activist, and there was speculation in the media suggesting that he may have been involved in another killing, the murder of Chris van de Werken, an environmental official, in 1996. Members of Pim Fortuyn's party asked the justice minister to reopen the investigation into van de Werken's death in the light of Fortuyn's murder. Van der Werken had been responsible for farm inspections and in this capacity had clashed with van der Graaf over the former's inspections. It was also significant that van der Werken was killed in a similar way to Fortuyn; he was shot at close range with a small-calibre handgun loaded with silver-tip hollow-point bullets. Van der Graaf had been interviewed by police after Van der Werken's murder, but had not been a suspect in the case.

The justice minister rejected the call to reopen the van der Werken investigation, saying that since the case had never been closed there was no need to reopen it. The minister also repeated that van der Graaf was not a suspect in the earlier murder case. Volkert van der Graaf was tried only for the Fortuyn assassination. In a statement to the panel of three judges, van der Graaf admitted shooting Fortuyn and said he would not do it again: he regretted 'the grief I have caused so many', but he also believed he had prevented suffering by halting Fortuyn's rise to power, which he compared to Hitler's. The prosecutor, Koos Plooy, said van der Graaf was a calculating killer who had lied about his motive and only regretted getting caught. Plooy said the true motive was fear that Fortuyn would lift a ban on the breeding of animals for fur – mink-farming in particular. In the period before the assassination, van der Graaf had been working 80 hours a week on a campaign against commercial farming and was described by other activists as a fanatic. He had also stock-piled ammunition in his home at Harderwijk.

Van der Graaf was sentenced to 18 years' imprisonment for perpetrating the Netherlands' first political assassination in more than 300 years. There had been speculation when he was first arrested that van der Graaf was acting on behalf of a militant environmentalist group called Milieu-offensief (or Environmental Offensive), but it emerged that he was acting entirely alone.

Pim Fortuyn's leaderless party went on to make huge gains in the elections and joined a conservative governing coalition. Infighting among Fortuyn's successors – they changed their leadership three times – led to the collapse of the government and new elections in January 2003. Journalists commented that the assassination of Pim Fortuyn would increase political tensions in many parts of Europe, where issues of immigration, race relations and nationalism were coming to the centre of the political debate.

ANNA LINDH

2003

ANNA MARIA LINDH, born in Stockholm in 1957, was a Swedish Social Democratic politician who served as minister for the environment from 1994 and then as minister for foreign affairs from 1998 until her assassination in 2003. She became involved in politics at the age of twelve, joining the local branch of the Swedish Social Democratic Youth League and protesting against the Vietnam War.

Lindh studied Law at Uppsala University. She graduated and was elected a member of parliament in 1982. In 1984 she became the first woman president of the Swedish Social Democratic Youth League. Her six years as president were marked by a strong commitment to international affairs, for Nicaragua, Vietnam, South Africa and the Palestinians, and against the arms race. In 1994, following a Social Democratic election victory, the new prime minister of Sweden Ingvar Carlsson made her minister for the environment.

Following the general election in 1998, Göran Persson appointed Lindh as minister for foreign affairs in the new government. Having made influential friends across the world during her time at the helm of the Swedish Social Democratic Youth League, Anna Lindh was an ardent supporter of international cooperation, both through the United Nations and in the European Union. Travelling with the EU foreign and security policy spokesman Javier Solana in Macedonia during the Kosovo/Macedonian crisis, she negotiated an agreement that averted a civil war in the country. Lindh criticized the invasion of Iraq in 2003; unsupported by the United Nations, it had to be a failure. She also advocated greater respect for international law and human rights in the Israeli-Palestinian conflict, criticizing the behaviour of both sides.

Anna Lindh seemed likely to be Göran Persson's successor as prime minister of Sweden. In the final weeks of her life, she was working hard in the pro-Euro campaign, running up to the Swedish referendum on the Euro, which was held just three days after her death. As one of the most popular pro-Euro politicians, the campaign organizers used her as a front person by the campaign, so her face was on billboards all over Sweden on the day she was murdered.

She was shopping with a friend at the NK department store in central Stockholm, when she was stabbed repeatedly by an unknown assassin late on the Wednesday afternoon. The assassin had apparently stolen a hunting knife from the Clas Ohlsson shop in the Galeria, and then followed Anna Lindh to the first floor of NK. She was taken to Stockholm's Karolinska Hospital, where she remained in a critical condition throughout the night and died of a haemorrhage from her stab wounds the following day. She was 46. Norway and Sweden are countries with open societies, where top officials from the prime minister down can be seen in restaurants, walking unescorted along the streets or shopping on their own. King Olav of Norway once remarked that he didn't need bodyguards when he went out for a walk, because he had four million Norwegians to protect him. But this attitude may change after the assassination of Anna

Lindh. It was the second, apparently random and apparently pointless, assassination of a high-profile Swedish politician in less than 20 years – and in a stable democratic country of nine million people. First Olof Palme, then Anna Lindh. In both cases there were no bodyguards. In both cases the Swedish security service was nowhere to be seen.

A week later, the Swedish police were still hunting for Anna Lindh's murderer. The manhunt naturally dominated the news in Sweden, as did speculation about the unknown killer's possible motives. As with the Palme case, theories multiplied, partly fired-up by newspaper editors' needs to fill their columns. Often material was made up, just as it was in the Palme case. The problem is that the fog of speculation and wrong information can make it very difficult to see the events for what they really are.

The unexplained murder of Olof Palme in 1986 led to two unsuccessful attempts to convict Christer Pettersson. The prosecutions were resorted to after all kinds of other suspects and leads had petered out. Enquiries regarding Victor Gunnarsson, the Kurdish Workers Party, South Africa's secret intelligence service, the Iranians and the Iraqis had led nowhere. These leads were generally supplied by the press, which had put itself under constant pressure to come up with an explanation of a great contemporary tragedy.

One highly controversial view is that the mystery of Palme's assassination has not been solved because the Swedish security service refused to acknowledge to investigators that it unwittingly exposed Palme to assassination by asking London to provide a secret review of his bodyguard protection. One theorist believes that this then gave hardliners in London, in collaboration with similar hardliners in

Washington, the opportunity to arrange Palme's assassination (London and Washington wanting to put the Cold War back on an East-West axis). Equally, one could go for cock-up rather than conspiracy – a well-intentioned request for a review resulting in an unintended window of opportunity for a madman to take a shot at the Swedish prime minister.

Anna Lindh's killer was eventually caught, arrested and put on trial. He was Mijailo Mijailovic, the 25-year-old son of Serbian immigrants. He admitted stabbing Anna Lindh, but blamed his action on voices in his head. Mijailovic was sentenced to life imprisonment for the murder. Then the Swedish Court of Appeal, a panel of five judges, unanimously overturned the life sentence, ruling that Mijailo Mijailovic was 'a traumatised person with significant psychiatric problems' and suffered from 'borderline personality disorders'. The killer's lawyer had argued that he had been under the influence of a cocktail of anti-depressants at the time of the murder and had had no intention of killing her. The court decided that what was needed was not imprisonment but psychiatric treatment. If that was really true, it calls into question why this allegedly random murder looked like the purposeful removal of Sweden's next prime minister. It is possible that the poster campaign was responsible, that Mijailovic suddenly saw a face that was unaccountably extremely familiar, a face seen on a thousand hoardings, and that he reacted to that. It could be that it was no more than Anna Lindh's celebrity that brought about her death and, unlike most of the other assassinations in this book, the political profile was nothing to do with it.

PART TWO

CONSPIRACIES: REAL AND IMAGINED

RELIGIOUS CONSPIRACIES

THE GREAT GODDESS

MANY PEOPLE HAVE come to accept, to take for granted, that in ancient times a Great Mother Goddess dominated people's religious beliefs. It is a 'given' that runs through both archaeological and anthropological literature, and in recent decades it has appeared in feminist literature too.

Middle Eastern religions of the Iron Age featured a mother goddess who was the great symbol of the earth's fertility. She was worshipped under various names. Scholars have seen versions and variants of her in virtually every part of the world, and this is quite natural as she is seen to represent the creative force in all nature, the mother of all things, the being responsible for the renewal of life. We would expect to find her everywhere. The later forms of the mother goddess cult in the Middle East introduced a less important male deity, who was sometimes seen as her son, sometimes as her lover, sometimes both. These later male divinities were known by different names in different places, as Adonis, Attis or Osiris. Unlike the Great Mother Goddess, who was thought of as living for ever, undying, the male consort died and was resurrected each year in an act that symbolized the seasonal power of the earth to regenerate.

The Great Mother was the dominant figure in ancient Middle Eastern religions, but she was also worshipped in Greece, Rome and Western Asia. In Phrygia and Lydia she was known as Cybele. The Babylonians and Assyrians knew her as Ishtar. In Syria and Palestine she was known as Astarte. The Egyptians called her Isis. In classical Greece she was worshipped under several names – Gaia, Hera, Rhea, Aphrodite and Demeter. In classical Rome she was known as Maia, Ops, Tellus and Ceres.

The Great Mother Goddess permeated the religions of the region, and was even present in Christianity, which was fundamentally a late Iron Age religion. Many aspects of the personality and iconography of the Virgin Mary show that she was a Christian transformation of the Great Mother. She was calm, sweet, neutral, dependable, enduring. She also had two aspects, as both mother and virgin. Her son Jesus was mysteriously both a god and yet had to undergo death and resurrection.

There is no doubting the reality or the power of the Great Mother Goddess in antiquity in the Middle East, but was she a universal figure and is there really evidence that she prevailed? Before considering that, it is worth switching to the present day, to see the 'Great Goddess' cult as it now manifests itself. Feminists of the late twentieth century latched onto the idea of a primeval Great Mother Goddess in order to validate women's claim to primacy. Arguing for the extreme antiquity of goddess-worship was a way of using history to reinforce a claim, rather like the old white South African claim that the white men arrived in South Africa either just before or at about the same time as the Zulus, giving the white men an equal or superior claim on the land.

The classical Greek Hera was seen as a late, and distorted and weakened, version of the Great Mother. By that stage, she had been transformed into the nagging and impotent wife of the all-powerful father god. Feminists who think in this 'revised history' way actively promote a return to goddess worship as a reaffirmation of creativity and birth, the female principle in men and women, the interconnectedness in life, and above all the primary importance of women.

The Goddess has taken on not just a socio-political role in the modern world but a geographical and ecological role. The Goddess is both the earth and the heavens and therefore is a personification of the global ecosystem. James Lovelock described to the novelist William Golding his view of all the processes of the Earth functioning and interacting with one another as if the Earth was a living organism; Golding suggested that he should name his theory Gaia, after one of the ancient manifestations of the Great Mother Goddess. Gaia is all that is living, and all that lives is part of her. To damage or pollute the earth is to damage the Goddess and oneself. This weird revival of the Great Mother cult has brought geography and religion together.

Above all, though, the revival is a prop for the empowerment of women. Men are reduced, just like Adonis and Attis, to the role of lesser beings who come to impregnate but then are dispensable. Clearly, the Great Mother Goddess is much more than mere archaeology, but a socio-political force and a weapon in environmental debate. With the Great Goddess reinforcing feminism, the characteristics of the 'female spirituality principle' become the most desirable characteristics. *Men* are required to display these desirable characteristics. *Men* have to be gentle, forbearing, biddable, submissive. Language too has to be reinvented and becomes highly sexualized. Any functionary title with the suffix 'man' in it has to be abolished. 'Chairman' becomes 'chairperson' or even 'chair'. 'History' becomes 'Herstory'. Subtler still is 're-member'.

The recent Great Goddess movement has led female pre-historians – or perhaps 'preherstorians' – to look to archaeology in the hope of finding validation for their theories of a golden age, a lost feminist utopia. This was a peace-loving, egalitarian society spread across the whole of Europe, with Mother Goddess worship at its centre. Neolithic European female fig-urines from five thousand or more years ago seemed to confirm this. The pioneer of the goddess movement is the archaeologist Marija Gimbutas, who spent 30 years studying cult objects and interpreting them, reconstructing ancient myths. Another female archaeologist, Ruth Tringham, criticized Gimbutas's methods, accusing her of bending the facts and interpreting artifacts to fit her feminist agenda; Gimbutas used the figurines to show 'to her own satisfaction the contrast between the peaceful character of . . . Old Europe and that of the [warlike] society which destroyed it'.

One example of Marija Gimbutas's approach to symbolism is her interpretation of the zigzag. This was a common symbol in art 5,000 years ago, and has even been found in artwork 40,000 years old. It clearly represents water, as Gimbutas said, but she went on to claim that it therefore represents the Mother Goddess as the Life-Giver. An even odder example is Gimbutas's interpretation of the bull's head – a masculine image if ever there was one – as a representation of the goddess because it is shaped like a uterus. This type of interpretation is clearly strongly influenced by personal agenda.

The ideas of Marija Gimbutas have been very influential, partly because half the population – the female half – wanted to believe in them, partly because it gave a belief system and therefore coherence, colour and vividness to a period that was otherwise little known and rather shadowy.

There was a general acceptance that throughout neolithic Europe people participated in this Great Mother Goddess religion, with women as spiritual leaders. One of the bonuses to this approach was that there was a ready-made set of interpretations for the enigmatic signs and symbols carved and painted in antiquity. The spirals that were found in megalithic monuments in north-west Europe from around 3,000 BC represented cyclical time, the unending stream of vital energy that keeps life going. The spiral is a representation of the snake, an archetype for the cyclical mode of life. Unfortunately, where some archaeological evidence for goddess worship was found, it was seen as support for the whole of the Great Mother Goddess hypothesis, which is untrue. At an early village called Catal Hoyuk in Turkey, an altar dating to the neolithic period was found with clay figurines of a goddess and wall paintings of a bull. The famous statue of a woman giving birth upon a throne with two leopards at her side was found there too. This was taken as proof of a Great Mother Goddess cult.

Undoubtedly there were cults of goddesses in antiquity, but there were also cults of gods. The reason why the archaeological evidence has been interpreted in such a biased way is simply that people with a contemporary, ie twentieth or twenty-first century, socio-political agenda frequently seek to project back into the past their modern-day concerns. There was a good example of this recently in a British TV documentary, where a UK politician tried to demonstrate that the Roman Empire was essentially an early form of the

EU. Even if it was, it would validate neither the EU nor the Roman Empire. Establishing that women were supremely important in antiquity is a preliminary to arguing that women are supremely important – or at least should be supremely important – today. But asserting the existence of a universal Great Mother Goddess cult in antiquity does no service to prehistory, as it is a distorted and exaggerated presentation of the past. Nor does it do any service to the present, as a revival of such a cult is clearly absurd. Nevertheless, there are those who seek to do just that in a misguided attempt to inflate the importance of women. Those who promote the idea have done so very effectively, by producing a stream of literature reinforcing it; endless repetition of the idea conditions people to accept it – like a number of other modern myths, as we shall see.

MARY MAGDALENE

THE STORY OF Mary Magdalene is intimately linked with the story of Jesus. She was a contemporary of Jesus, knew him well, supported him, and was one of the small number of female disciples named in the four canonical (ie officially approved) gospel accounts of the life of Jesus. Her relationship with Jesus and with the other disciples was evidently unusual, and there are inconsistencies in the way she is presented, inconsistencies that suggest something is being concealed. This may be because of misreporting, or patchy memory – the gospels were written down in the second half of the first century, some decades after the turbulent and emotional highly charged events they describe. Alternatively it may be because significant aspects of Mary Magdalene's character and role were deliberately suppressed.

When Jesus was crucified, Mary Magdalene was one of the small number of supporters who stayed to witness the appalling scene. She was also the one who visited the garden tomb early in the morning of Easter Day to anoint the body; it was she who discovered that the tomb was empty. As the star witness to the resurrection, Mary Magdalene had a central role in the Christian myth, yet it seems that the early church did everything possible to play down her importance. She was there at the beginning of a movement that was going to transform the West, yet she was systematically denigrated by church historians and that denigration was reinforced by centuries of religious artwork portraying her as an hysteric, a sinner, a fallen woman, a prostitute, an outcast repenting her sins in the wilderness.

The story of Mary as a prostitute, who is fallen and yet redeemed by Jesus's forgiveness, has been developed into a powerful mythic image of redemption. No matter how low you fall, you can be reformed and forgiven. It is powerful and vivid, but it is not what happened to Mary Magdalene. Mary Magdalene is mentioned in each of the New Testament gospels, but nowhere in those texts is it said that she was a prostitute. What appears to have happened is that at some stage Mary Magdalene became confused with two other women in the Bible. One of these was Mary the sister of Martha who lived at Bethany, a village just outside Jerusalem, and who provided Jesus with accommodation when he visited the city. The other was the unnamed sinner from the Gospel of Luke. Both of these women are described as washing the feet of Jesus with their hair. Today, this seems a very odd thing to do, a distinctive action that must have held some special meaning, but it may have been a ritual gesture that was made by many Jewish women in certain situations – perhaps as a special ceremonial mark of respect.

It was not until the end of the sixth century that Pope Gregory the Great made an official announcement that Mary Magdalene was the unnamed sinner. He declared in a sermon that the three characters were one and the same. So, from AD 591, the date of Pope Gregory's announcement, Mary Magdalene was officially labelled as a sinner. There followed many centuries when Mary Magdalene was marginalized because of her sinful past. Gradually, during the Middle Ages the label 'sinner' was hardened up into 'prostitute'. The Catholic Church did eventually declare that a mistake had been made, that Mary Magdalene was after all not the penitent sinner, but this declaration of rehabilitation did not come until as late as 1969.

So, if Mary Magdalene was not the hysterical repentant sinner, who was she? The surviving four gospels give very little away about her. There are no personal details of her age, status or family. The fact that she was a female disciple suggests that she was a woman of independent means, and it is clear from what is said about Martha and Mary, the sisters who lived at Bethany, that wealthy women were very important in providing Jesus with material support – certainly accommodation and food, probably even money. The women in the story are largely sidelined because that was the nature of society in the world where the story was being told and retold in the century or two after the death of Jesus. Men were the doers, the movers and shakers. It was unthinkable that a woman could have been a significant protagonist in the development of Christianity. Some scholars have suggested that Mary Magdalene was the otherwise nameless 'Beloved Disciple', who has usually been assumed to be John, but there is no reason why the Beloved Disciple should not have been a woman.

Her name provides a clue about her, suggesting that she came from a town called Magdala. There is a place today called Magdala, 120 miles north of Jerusalem on the shore of the Sea of Galilee. There was an ancient place of that name, which is mentioned both in the New Testament and in Jewish texts. Its full name was Magdala Tarichaea, which meant 'The Tower of Salted Fish'; it was a fishing village by the Sea of Galilee. Perhaps Mary Magdalene and her presumed wealth were connected with the fishing industry. Certainly other disciples of Jesus were involved in fishing. One Jewish text says that Magdala was judged by God and destroyed because of its fornication. Possibly this criticism of the place, for its fornication, somehow became a criticism of the woman who came from that place. If so, it is clearly a very unjust condemnation, and there is no reason whatever to assume from her place of origin that Mary became a prostitute.

Married women usually carried their husbands' names, and since Mary did not it is possible that she was unmarried. Or – equally possibly – she was married but the writers of the gospels did not want to draw attention to her married state.

Mary may have been set apart from the rest of the community by epilepsy. The Gospel of Luke tells us that Jesus cast seven demons out of Mary. Jesus was known as an exorcist. In each of the four canonical gospels, one of his main activities is the cleansing ritual of exorcism. The exorcisms and healings were probably intended to go together with the teaching that the kingdom of God was at hand. In the first century, illness, and mental illness especially, was put down to possession by demons. People believed that demons possessed people who had done something wrong. Whatever the cause of her possession, Mary's exorcism – her faith-healing cure from epilepsy, perhaps – was the catalyst that made her a follower of Jesus. From then on she travelled with Jesus. The four gospels emphasize the role of the male disciples, but it is evident from occasional references both there and in the Acts of the Apostles that there were many female disciples too.

The male disciples seem to have taken their wives with them. Mary Magdalene travelled with Jesus, whether as a single woman or as somebody's wife.

This brings us to one of the most sensational theories about Mary Magdalene, that Mary Magdalene and Jesus were married. This theory has been popularized in recent years by books like *The Holy Blood and the Holy Grail* (1982) and *The Da Vinci Code* (2003).

The wedding at Cana described in St John's Gospel was, some argue, the marriage of Jesus himself. Those supporting this view argue that the mother of Jesus is described as telling the servants to do what Jesus wishes; this reflects the role of the groom's mother, who according to Jewish tradition took charge of the servants at a wedding. The marriage of Jesus, to any woman, is an almost impossible proposition for the Catholic Church to accept, partly because such strenuous efforts were made in the first few centuries to reduce or eliminate the role of women in Jesus's mission, partly because the church has developed the compensating idea that Christ has an allegorical wife in the church itself. If Jesus was literally married, he could not be metaphysically married as well without being a bigamist. So the church has built such a massive 'post-Jesus' superstructure onto Christianity that it has become impossible or intolerable for Christians to believe that he was literally married.

Nowhere in the New Testament does it say that Jesus was married, but nowhere does it say that he was *not* married either, which makes it look like an open question. On the other hand, bachelorhood was very rare for Jewish men at the time when Jesus lived; it was generally regarded as a transgression of the first mitzvah, or divine commandment, to be fruitful and multiply. According to this reasoning, it would have been unthinkable for an adult unmarried Jew to travel about teaching as a rabbi. It would also therefore seem likely that Jesus, as a conscientious Jew, would have fathered children – even though these are not mentioned in the gospels. But we have to accept that the gospels are not biographies of Jesus in the modern sense. They make no pretence at completeness, but focus on the events and sayings that were regarded as important in the late first century for preaching and converting people to Christianity. That Jesus was married with children would have had no bearing on the matter and therefore the matter was left without comment.

There is, inevitably, a counter-argument to this. Judaism at the time of Jesus was very diverse and the role of the rabbi was not yet well defined. It was not until after the destruction of the Second Temple by the Romans in AD 70 that Rabbinic Judaism became dominant and the role of the rabbi became more uniform in Jewish communities. Before the time of Jesus, unmarried teachers were known in the communities of the Essenes; John the Baptist was also celibate. St Paul was a later example of an unmarried itinerant teacher. From his comments in Matthew, it seems that Jesus himself approved of voluntary celibacy for religious reasons. So, the marriage of Jesus really is an open question. He may have been celibate or he may have been married; if he was married, it is more than likely that he was married to Mary Magdalene.

But the Acts of the Apostles and the four gospels are not the only source of information about Mary Magdalene. In 1945, at Nag Hammadi in southern Egypt, two men came across a sealed ceramic jar. Inside, they discovered a hoard of ancient papyrus books. They were never given as much public attention as the Dead Sea Scrolls, but they turned out to be much more important in supplying new information about early Christianity. The Nag Hammadi texts were written in Coptic, the language of early Christian Egypt, and they tell us about the early Christians. They include the Gospel of Thomas, the Gospel of Philip and the Acts of Peter. These texts were deliberately excluded from the Bible because the content conflicted with current Christian doctrine, which makes them even more informative, even more interesting. They focus on events and issues that are ignored or skated over in the Bible. To take one example, the New Testament gospels say that after his resurrection Jesus spent some time talking with the disciples, but little is said about the content of these crucial last conversations. The 'apocryphal' or unofficial gospels found at Nag Hammadi tell us what Jesus said. Whether the apocryphal gospels are in any sense truer historically is difficult to tell, but they certainly contain genuine traditions about Jesus that for one reason or another were deliberately excluded from the New Testament.

Here for the first time in centuries was a new source of information about Mary Magdalene. She appears frequently as one of the leading disciples of Jesus. In certain texts where Jesus is in discussion with his disciples, Mary Magdalene asks many informed questions. Whereas the other disciples at times seem confused, she is the one who understands. And this may be why the texts were suppressed. In a misogynistic early church where men were regarded as the prime movers, it was unacceptable to have a Mary Magdalene putting the male disciples right.

Mary Magdalene is a key figure in the Gospel of Philip. It contains some information about Mary which has led to one of the most controversial claims made about her. This text was unfortunately damaged by ants, so certain words have been completely eaten away, leaving a text with crucial gaps. The damaged text reads:

> *And the companion of the . . . Mary Magdalene . . . loved her more than all the disciples, and used to kiss her often on her . . . The rest of the disciples . . . They said to him 'Why do you love her more than all of us?' The Saviour answered and said to them, 'Why do I not love you like her? When a blind man and one who sees are both together in darkness, they are no different from one another. When the light comes, then he who sees will see the light, and he who is blind will remain in darkness.'*

The gaps are extremely tantalizing. It is tempting to infer that the text when intact read as follows:

> *'And the companion of the Saviour, Mary Magdalene, spoke (or entered). Jesus loved her more than all the disciples, and used to kiss her often on her mouth. The rest of the disciples were angry (or jealous).'*

Of course it is possible that Jesus kissed Mary on the cheek or the forehead, but if so the text would be less likely to draw attention to it. Most scholars have assumed that the text seeks to emphasize a particularly intimate and special relationship and that a kiss on the mouth was intended. This opens the door to the possibility that Jesus and Mary were lovers, perhaps even husband and wife. While it may seem unlikely that Jesus's marriage could go unmentioned in the four gospels, it was the norm in those days for men to marry; it would have occasioned comment if he had not been married, and the New Testament makes no comment either way. So the Nag Hammadi text has opened the door to Jesus having a wife and Mary Magdalene being that wife.

Some scholars interpret the kiss, even if on the mouth, as a spiritual symbol. Mary accepts the kiss and she similarly accepts the teaching of the word of God. Jesus and Mary kissing mouth to mouth may not entail sexuality, but instead the transmission of divine knowledge. Certainly in the apocryphal text Mary Magdalene appears not only as the disciple he loved most but also as a symbolic figure of heavenly wisdom.

There is other evidence that Mary was the closest companion of Jesus, some of it in the Bible itself. The Bible says that Mary Magdalene was present at the two most important moments, the crucifixion and the resurrection. She was prominent at both events. She was one of the women who kept vigil at the tomb, as it was customary at that time for Jewish women to prepare bodies for burial. When Mary went to the tomb, she found that the body of Jesus had gone. The Gospel of John gives the fullest account. Mary ran in a state of shock to where the (male) disciples were gathered to tell them the news. They did not believe her. Peter and another (male) disciple went back to the tomb with her, to see for themselves. When they went into the tomb, Peter saw the discarded shroud and was upset and angry, assuming that the tomb had been robbed and desecrated. The two of them left without any reference to Mary.

Then, something even more extraordinary happened. Mary Magdalene was alone when someone asked her why she was crying. Thinking it was the gardener, she said, 'They have taken my Lord's body and I do not know where it is.' The gardener spoke her name. She recognized the voice, looked up and saw Jesus, risen from the dead. Overwhelmed, she moved towards him and reached out to him. He stopped her, perhaps because the blood shed during the crucifixion had made him unclean: 'Do not touch me!' Jesus sent her to tell the other disciples that he had risen from the dead.

It is matter of faith or a matter of mindset whether we say that Jesus *really* stood before her resurrected, or that Mary believed that she had seen him. Either way, it was that profoundly significant moment in Mary Magdalene's experience that took Christianity in an important new direction. The concept that Jesus did not die, or had been miraculously raised from the dead, meant that his mission had after all not been a failure. On the contrary, the mission was a great success, changing from a small movement to an entirely new religion, and the person who declared this was Mary Magdalene. The resurrection of Jesus was the turning point for Christianity, and it was Mary Magdalene who interpreted the scene at the empty tomb in this way.

On the strength of what we are told in the canonical gospels, Mary should have been recognized as an apostle – a key figure in the founding of Christianity. She seems to meet all the criteria set out in the Bible. One reason why she was not recognized in that way may lie in another long lost apocryphal text. In a Cairo bazaar in 1896, a German scholar discovered a leather-bound copy of a curious papyrus book, the Gospel of Mary.

The Gospel according to Mary Magdalene begins its account some time after the resurrection. The disciples had just had a vision of Jesus, in which he encouraged his disciples to go out and preach to the world, but they were afraid to do so because he was killed for it. If Jesus was killed, they would be killed too. Then Mary stepped forward and told them not to worry because Jesus would be there to protect them. She succeeded in changing their minds. So once again Mary Magdalene saved Christianity and made sure that it continued. After that, the disciples began to discuss the sayings of the Saviour, in other words starting the long process of recalling everything Jesus had said and interpreting it. It would not be long before some of them thought of writing down agreed versions of the sayings and events that were going to be useful in propagating the new religion.

In the Gospel of Philip, Mary Magdalene was presented as a symbol of wisdom. In the Gospel of Mary, she was presented as the one who was in charge, telling the disciples what they should do next and explaining Jesus's teachings.

Peter invited Mary to tell them some things that she might have heard from Jesus, but which the other disciples had missed. A special relationship between the two is implicit in this request. She agreed: 'Yes, I will tell you what has been hidden from you.' She described a vision of Jesus she had had and a conversation with him. Mary related the details of this conversation, to do with spiritual development and the soul's life-long battle with evil. But the men did not easily accept Mary's authority. Andrew interrupted with the comment that what she was saying seemed strange; what she was telling them were very different from the teachings they had from Jesus himself. Peter agreed: 'Are we all supposed to turn round now and listen to her? Would Jesus have spoken privately with a woman rather than openly to us? Did he prefer her to us?'

Matthew defended Mary and countered Peter's attack on her. Peter evidently resented the fact that Jesus chose Mary above the other disciples to interpret his teachings. Peter saw Mary as a rival for the leadership of Christianity itself. With the benefit of hindsight, we know that Peter need not have feared. Most people two thousand years on think of Peter as the rock upon which the church was established. He is seen as the main disciple and Mary Magdalene is seen as a kind of marginal figure in the story. But the Gospel of Mary makes it clear that it was by no means inevitable.

There was a great deal of fluidity in the early church. Many gospels were written, though in the end only four were selected by the church as a worthy basis for Christian teaching; the rest were consigned to oblivion, the Gospels of Peter, Thomas, Philip and Mary among them. Irenaeus (AD 130–200) was the person who made this momentous decision. He was a bishop and a disciple of Polycarp, who in turn was a disciple of Ignatius, disciple of the Apostle John. Irenaeus made his decision on a 'rule of faith', or consistency of text with what were then regarded as orthodox Christian beliefs. The gospels of Matthew, Mark, Luke and John were first century 'lives' of Jesus reflecting the apostolic tradition, whereas the slightly later 'rejected' gospels written apparently in the second century belonged to a different genre. The four gospels contain many elements of Jesus's Judaean culture and even original Aramaic figures of speech. At least Irenaeus selected four; his rival Marcion produced his own edited version of the Gospel of Luke, which he asserted was the *one and only* true gospel. Irenaeus was uncompromising and relentlessly rejected other opinions about the gospels, including those that favoured the then-fashionable Gnostic tradition. The gospels Irenaeus rejected belonged to that Gnostic tradition which claimed to hold a secret oral tradition from Jesus himself. Now that the long-suppressed Gnostic writings have been rediscovered, at least it can be seen that Irenaeus's description of them was accurate and honest.

Irenaeus insisted that there must be exactly *four* gospels, no less, no more. His arguments depended on number magic. Four covenants had been given by God to man: the rainbow, circumcision, the Ten Commandments and the teachings of Christ. There were four zones in the world, and four winds, so there had to be four pillars to form the foundation of the church. Even more bizarre was his number argument that the cherubim, the angels of the Old Testament, had four faces, of a lion, an ox, an eagle and a man. These four images were to become the symbols of the four gospels. However compelling such arguments may have seemed in the second century, today they seem very strange, inadequate, inappropriate and frankly dotty. But there was material in the rejected gospels that was a serious problem to people like Irenaeus.

The Gospel of Mary is very radical. It presents Mary as a teacher and spiritual guide to the other disciples, not just a disciple but a leader of the disciples – a guru in her own right. The early church could not accept that a woman could occupy that position. As early as the third century there are writings that refer to the Gospel of Mary and they reveal the degree to which that gospel was despised and dismissed by the early Church Fathers. The chief disciples, the apostles, had to be men. That after all was the fundamental justification for priests, bishops and popes being men. Behind the suppression of Mary Magdalene's true role in the founding of Christianity was a conspiracy to ensure that women were excluded from office in the church, to keep the jobs for the boys. That conspiracy entailed one of the nastiest smear campaigns of all time; an honest, virtuous disciple of Jesus who appears to have rescued Christianity in the days and weeks following the Crucifixion was vilified and turned into a personification of sin – even if it was sin repented. At least it looks as if the conspiracy is ending and the truth is emerging.

POLITICAL CONSPIRACIES

PERKIN WARBECK – OR KING RICHARD IV?

IN 1490 A YOUTH appeared in the streets of Cork in Ireland, claiming to be Richard Plantagenet, duke of York, second son of Edward IV, the late king of England. He was claiming to be the rightful heir to the throne of England currently occupied by Henry VII. It had been generally assumed that he was dead, murdered as a child, along with his elder brother, in the Tower of London. Was this youth really one of the Princes in the Tower, one of the two boys who had supposedly been killed at Richard III's orders in 1483? If he was, how had he survived? If he was not, who on earth was he? And, either way, what would Henry VII do about him?

In 1460, an earlier Richard duke of York claimed descent from Edward III and on the strength of this tried to proclaim himself king. He was rebuffed and killed. The next year, his son defeated Henry VI in battle and was crowned Edward IV. Edward was king in fact, though not by hereditary right. The Yorkist claim was not strong; their line had passed twice through women, Henry VI still lived and, as many people at the time knew full well, Edward was not really the son of Richard duke of York in any case. He was a bastard and a usurper. Edward was pushed out by Warwick the Kingmaker but in 1471 he recovered his crown.

In 1483 Edward IV died very unexpectedly at the age of 40 leaving dangerous heirs in the form of two children, Edward and Richard. Perkin Warbeck told the story how as a fatherless 9-year-old he and his 12-year-old brother had been imprisoned in the Tower by their uncle, Richard of Gloucester. Edward was supposed to be waiting for his coronation, but was murdered instead. He, Richard, had been spared and sent abroad, where he travelled from country to country for 8 years. During that time, Richard III had been king of England and killed at Bosworth, and the Lancastrian claimant Henry VII, also with a weak claim to the crown of England, had usurped the throne. Perkin was waiting for his moment to claim back the crown for the Yorkists.

This was how most of Europe saw Perkin Warbeck in 1493. But after Henry VII captured him in 1497, a 'revised' and very different history was released, one that suited the Tudor case far better. This was formally written and Perkin was forced to sign it. He was not a prince at all but the son of a customs-collector, John Osbeck, who worked on the River Scheldt at Tournai. The youth's name was established as Piers Osbeck. He was employed by John Strewe, a merchant, who was possibly English, and then by Lady Brampton as a page, which took him to Portugal in 1487. Tiring of this, Osbeck joined the service of a Breton merchant who took him to Ireland, where Yorkist sympathizers pressed him to be the Yorkist pretender. That was Henry VII's version of events.

Lady Brampton's husband, when questioned by Spanish investigators at Setubal in Portugal in 1496, gave a different version. Again the boy came from Tournai, where he had been born the son of a boatman called Bernal Uberque. He had not gone into a trade of any kind, but had learned to play the church organ. Then he had given this up at the age of 14 and become a servant boy to the Bramptons. Sir Edward Brampton thought the boy was called 'Piris'.

Sir Edward's story is significantly different from King Henry's official version. There is also something odd about Sir Edward's willingness to take the boy all the way to Portugal and then dispense with him on arrival. He just handed the boy on. It may be that Sir Edward was trying to ingratiate himself with the king by showing how insubstantial the boy was; Brampton was able to pass on a surprisingly large amount of information about the boy and his origins, given that he was not interested in keeping him and had not bothered to catch his name.

The plot thickens when we discover that Brampton's own origins were shadowy. His real name was not Brampton or Brandon, but Brandao. He had been a Portuguese Jew, and was taken into a house for converted Jews in Holborn in about 1468. At his baptism in 1472 he was sponsored by Edward IV; though this might seem startling, it was in fact the custom for the monarch to act as godfather to Jewish converts. He also took the king's christian name, Edward, as his own, along with a new surname, Brampton. Like his servant boy, Brampton was not at all what he seemed.

Brampton had changed sides several times and was, significantly, in the context of this story, consistently helpful to King Richard III. In July 1483, shortly after the two princes had been confined in the Tower, he was paid £350 for unspecified services. In 1484, after the princes had disappeared, he was awarded £100 a year in perpetuity 'in consideration for services to be rendered by him'. These were major rewards for unspecified secret assignments. The timing suggests they were something to do with one or both of the princes.

According to the notorious 'confession' wrung out of Piers by Henry VII's heavies, he had been Brampton's page at the time when Brampton was in service as an usher of Edward IV's bedchamber. In this position, Piers had been able to get very close indeed to the real Richard duke of York; he actually saw and possibly played games with the young duke he would one day impersonate. There were other sources he could draw on for information too, such as the memoirs of one of the king's heralds at Windsor, giving details of the royal family's domestic and court life in 1472.

Piers became attached to the retinue of Pero Vaz, a Portuguese knight, and then, though he was still only a page, he began to attract attention. Rui de Sousa was a most reliable witness, a prominent Portuguese courtier of impeccable reputation. He described the page as 'very pretty and the most beautiful creature I have ever seen'. He also confirmed that he had arrived in Portugal with Edward Brampton. He said little about the boy's identity except that Pero Vaz 'treated him like a page', which suggests that that was not appropriate, that de Sousa thought the boy was much more than a page. A herald added that the boy had *already* been identified as the duke of York.

The boy was attractive, then, but he also drew attention because of the extravagance of his dress. King Joao of Portugal had imposed strict sumptuary laws – no one was allowed to wear silk or brocade – yet this boy ignored them and was opulently dressed in the latest fashion.

In 1489, Henry VII sent Richmond Herald out to Portugal 'for certain causes' – perhaps to find out more about this boy who said he was the duke of York. In 1491, now aged 17 or 18, Richard suddenly set sail for Ireland, a place with strong Yorkist sympathies. His gorgeous costume, which included a long silk gown, convinced the Irish that he was of royal blood straight away; who else would wear such clothes? He acquired followers. Brampton's version substantiates this and confirms that the clothes were Richard's own. If the dressing up seems to us a little suspect, we must remember that it was the custom for Portuguese sailors to dress up when landing on an unfamiliar African shore. They routinely put on what they called their 'gala clothes', their Sunday-best. And that is probably what Richard duke of York was doing when he landed at Cork. The Irish were captivated by his astonishing clothes, his beauty, his graceful manners.

In 1493, King Joao sent Martin Behaim the globe-maker as an emissary to 'the King's son in Flanders', and at that date only Richard duke of York fitted that description. Behaim wrote a letter describing his secret mission and explicitly identified his subject as 'the young King of England, who is at present with the King of the Romans (ie Maximilian) so that he may live and keep his court there.' It is clear that by this stage there was no doubt in Behaim's or King Joao's minds about the boy's identity; he was one of the two sons of Edward IV. Behaim's expedition had been an ordeal. He had been intercepted en route by the English, taken to England and kept there for three months, in his own words 'on account of the young king'. Clearly, by 1493, Henry VII and his advisers were aware of the existence of Richard duke of York on the European mainland, and were worried about him. If he could convince enough people that he was who he said he was – Edward IV's son and therefore the rightful heir to the English throne – he could become a serious threat to Henry VII.

Ten years earlier, in 1483, Richard III had made a very public attempt to annihilate the young duke's claim, but probably few would remember that now, and Henry VII would have found it politically difficult to refer back to arguments advanced by his arch-enemy, Richard III. Richard tried to prove that the princes were illegitimate by showing that their father, Edward IV, had been contracted to marry Eleanor Butler before he married Elizabeth Woodville, making the Woodville marriage invalid. Richard III had this argument presented in public for him by a cleric, Dr Shaw, outside St Paul's Cathedral. Dr Shaw was also made to suggest that Edward IV had himself been a bastard son of Cecily of York by a common soldier called Blaybourne. It may have seemed absurd, but George, duke of Clarence, had put this same story about and it may have been one of the reasons Edward had him killed; if Edward was the son of an archer, while George was the legitimate elder son of Richard duke of York, it was George who should be on the throne, not his elder half-brother – and that was a very dangerous claim. Edward had his half-brother George put to death in the Tower. Now that Edward himself was dead, Richard had nothing to fear from him. He could take the risk and say openly that Edward IV was illegitimate. The idea that Edward IV was illegitimate was fairly well known. Charles the Bold of Burgundy often called him 'Blaybourne' when in a rage, long before Dr Shaw's public lecture on the Succession.

The upshot was clear. In the summer of 1483, after Edward IV's death, Richard III really *was* the rightful king. For a few weeks after that the two boys were seen playing in the gardens in the Tower, then never seen again. All sorts of stories circulated about their imagined deaths. They were forcibly bled to death, they had been poisoned with herbs, they had fallen into the then water-filled moat and been washed out to sea. It was also generally assumed in these conspiracy rumours that Richard III was behind the young princes' death. He was the one with most to gain by their death. The charge of murdering his nephews strengthened the Tudor cause against Richard III, so this became the official history in the sixteenth century. The discovery of two skeletons in the seventeenth century seemed to prove that the boys were indeed murdered, but modern forensic tests show that the bones do not match the royal brothers. So no proof has ever emerged.

The fact remains that the princes may have been spirited abroad and given new identities. Which is where Piers Osbeck, later known as Perkin Warbeck, comes into the story. Brampton received large rewards from Richard III, and appeared with one mysterious boy in his entourage in Portugal. In January 1485 James Tyrell, a royal officer, was given wool to the value of £3000 'for divers matters concerning greatly the king's weal.' It was an enormous fortune, so Tyrell must have done the king an enormous favour.

Side by side with rumours of the princes' murder there were rumours that they had gone to 'some secret land', and this is to some extent supported by the fact that in 1484 Elizabeth Woodville reached an understanding with the new king. It is hard to see how she could have done this if Richard had just killed her two sons. In the past little has been made of the fact that Richard and his brother George had been through precisely the same process themselves, as young princes of about the same age, back in 1461. They had been sent to Utrecht in the Low Countries for their safety, by their own mother. As a result of this experience, which he would undoubtedly have remembered vividly, Richard might well have seen spiriting his nephews away to the Low Countries in secret as the solution to the problem; it relieved him of a serious political problem and ensured their physical safety.

When the claimant turned up, it is slightly odd that there seems to have been little speculation about the events that led to his appearance in Tournai, but perhaps Richard had agreed, with Tyrell, Brampton and no doubt a number of other conspirators, that no one should discover that. Warbeck himself would at first only say that God had touched him and he had escaped. It was a miracle. Later he would add that he been handed over to 'a certain lord' to be killed after his brother had been killed, but that this unnamed lord had taken pity on him. In the darkness of some chamber in the Tower, he had been irrationally spared. But it was too traumatic for him to recall in detail. A Frisian chronicle written in 1500 mentions that Buckingham had killed one child and spared the other, that the surviving prince had been secretly abducted out of England, and that the survivor was Richard duke of York; this is consistent with the story that Richard himself told.

If Piers Osbeck or Perkin Warbeck was in reality not the surviving duke, how had he been trained and educated to become a credible impostor? Henry VII later laid the blame at the door of John Atwater, an Irish merchant who was twice mayor of Cork. Henry VII had him arrested in 1499 and described as 'the first mover and the half-inventor' of the fraud. Henry was careful not to lay all the blame at Atwater's door. There were others implicated in the conspiracy – or what he portrayed as a conspiracy. One was John Taylor, who had been a servant of George duke of Clarence, and who would have been in a strong position to teach Perkin Warbeck the ways of court life, and the particular mannerisms of the young duke. When Taylor was arrested in France in 1499, the Milanese ambassador reported (presumably Henry's view) that it was Taylor's idea to take the boy to Ireland.

King Henry VII's approach to the entire Warbeck episode was ambivalent. He wanted the false claim to be scotched, but he was reluctant to have people executed for it. He was very eager to get his hands on John Taylor, but he did not have him executed; he preferred to imprison him and pardon his son. He preferred to put more blame on Atwater than on Taylor, but he also thought that more blame still lay elsewhere. Atwater was a Yorkist, though not specially committed to the duke of York. Taylor was less interested in the duke of York than in helping the cause of Edward earl of Warwick, the son of George duke of Clarence; he had after all been Clarence's servant. Taylor had been involved in an earlier conspiracy for his master, to introduce a duplicate of the duke's son at Warwick Castle while the real son was spirited away to Ireland or Flanders, where he would be safe to raise rebellion later. Edward IV forgave Taylor for his part in this odd scheme, even giving him a job as forester and bailiff on Clarence lands in Worcestershire.

Edward earl of Warwick was a figure almost as shadowy as the duke of York. Born in 1475, he was a year and a half younger than the duke. In 1484, after losing his son, Richard III named Warwick as his heir, but this did not last long. There was said to be something wrong with Warwick, a mental deficiency of some kind. It was said he did not know a goose from a capon. He always needed to have things explained to him. Richard III quickly decided that he was unfit to be king and looked for an alternative heir. After

Richard's death, though, Warwick had no shortage of supporters. An impostor, a false Warwick, was taken to Ireland in 1486, and even crowned king in Dublin. This child-king was taken to England in 1487 in a kind of mercenary invasion organized by his minders, Lovell and Lincoln. This fiasco ended with Lincoln dead, Lovell fleeing to Flanders and the child-king sent off to work in the real king's kitchens to work as a scullion. Whoever he really was, he was named as Lambert Simnel. There was a bizarre moment when Henry VII displayed the real Warwick in public in London alongside Lambert Simnel, the fake Warwick. The idea of a young Yorkist prince, whether surviving or recreated, real or fabricated, was firmly rooted in everyone's mind.

After Richard's outing in Cork, he became the protégé of his aunt, Margaret of York, now Dowager Duchess of Burgundy. Their meeting at her palace in Malines was described by Margaret in emotional terms. 'I recognized him as easily as if I had last seen him yesterday or the day before (for I had seen him long ago in England).' She knew he was authentic because of his conversation and by his mannerisms. 'I indeed for my part, when I gazed on this only male Remnant of our family – who had come through so many perils and misfortunes – was deeply moved . . . I embraced him as my only nephew and my only son.' Richard might well have clung to his Aunt Margaret. His mother, Queen Elizabeth the Queen Mother, had just died, though he still had a grandmother living, Cecily the duchess of York, who was Margaret's mother and who would live until 1495.

The assumption made by those who believe that he was an impostor is that Margaret knew he was, and that she had in effect constructed him. The view of Margaret in Henry's court was not favourable. She in her turn hated and despised Henry. It was said that Margaret had sent agents out to find a suitable candidate for the imposture, and that after finding one in Tournai she had schooled him in the ways of court life, and taught him everything he needed to know about the House of York. Margaret's main helper in this was Stephen Frion, who had been French secretary to Edward IV, Richard III and Henry VII before transferring to Margaret's service. The scenario as far as the English court was concerned was that Frion and his men had found their candidate and brainwashed him until he really believed that he was Richard Plantagenet, duke of York, rightful heir to the English throne.

Charles VIII of France, himself not much more than a boy, saw sponsoring Richard Plantagenet as an opportunity to bring Henry VII down. In 1491 he promised Richard help against Henry VII, describing Henry as a 'criminal usurper', which is exactly how Henry VII saw Richard. King Charles invited Richard to his court, where he treated him as if his claim were perfectly true. Charles was evidently won over by Richard and commended him to the king of Scots, James IV, as Edward IV's son. Only nine months on from his debut in Cork – and Richard had the confidence of two European kings.

Maximilian, king of the Romans, was persuaded that Richard was the real thing by three hereditary marks on his body. It is not known for certain what these were, but Richard was ready to show them to anyone to prove that his claim was true. Richard Plantagenet's cause was strengthening. He had the support of the kings of France and Scotland, the Holy Roman Emperor and the sister of Edward IV of England. Maximilian was a man of poor judgement. Machiavelli wrote that he was very fickle; 'he takes counsel from nobody, yet believes everybody.' So maybe Maximilian's support means little. The other crowned heads of Europe found supporting Richard an excellent way to tease and disadvantage Henry VII; it didn't mean necessarily that they believed Richard was authentic.

It was said that he looked very like Edward IV, and the portrait sketch that survives shows a very similar nose and chin. His elegant courtly manner also marked him out as an aristocrat. The ultimate proof came when he wrote a dictated letter, signed 'Richard of England'. The phrasing was very similar to that used in his proclamation of a few weeks earlier, and so probably accurately represents his style, a very high-flown and musical style. It is in fact reminiscent of the style of Lord Rivers, who was the tutor to the two princes. The way Richard signs off gives a flavour of his elegance; 'And our lord Jesu preserve you in all honour joy and felicity, and send you the accomplishment of your noble heart's desire.'

Why should his cause be doubted? In my view the main flaw in his case is that only one prince came forward; only Perkin survived. If, as he claimed, he survived by chance when his brother was murdered, it suggests that Richard was an incredibly incompetent murderer. There would have been no point in Richard III having just one of the brothers killed. If he killed Edward and left Richard alive, he was still in danger. If on the other hand Richard III made provision for his nephews' safety abroad in the same way that his mother had ensured his own safety, both princes should have emerged. The story only makes sense if both princes were killed, or neither.

One possibility is that Buckingham really did lose his nerve when it came to killing the younger boy, though that seems unlikely. Another possibility is that Richard was lying about what happened in the Tower – and he was evidently reluctant to talk about that – because he knew that his brother Edward had survived too. Perhaps Edward had made the decision to remain in obscurity; perhaps he died a natural death.

When the news that Richard Plantagenet was alive swept across England in 1493, it created all kinds of uncertainties, hopes of profit for some, fear of loss for others, the prospect of a revived civil war. Some who followed the new cause were people who felt they had not done well enough out of King Henry's usurpation. Cells of plotters who wanted Richard to succeed developed all over England, all watched with interest by the king and his spies. The king was most disturbed when someone he looked on as loyal, Sir William Stanley, tuned out to be a supporter of Richard. If the various cells had been better co-ordinated, the planned coup might have been effective. Stanley had unfortunately waited for a signal to come from another plotter, and waited too long. Along with many others he was arrested for treason. Many were condemned without trial, then hanged or beheaded. Stanley was tried, condemned and beheaded, and never offered any explanation; he had been prepared to spend his 'great heaps of money' to put Richard on the throne, when only 10 years earlier he had dangerously changed sides in the middle of the Battle of Bosworth to put Henry on the throne. Maybe he thought Henry was not grateful enough for his throne.

Now it was serious. Henry VII would kill – kill anyone – to block Richard's progress. Abroad, plans for an invasion of England continued to develop. Margaret gave 8,000 crowns to provision the invasion force. A fleet sailed from Vlissingen in

July 1495 but was easily routed on landing at Deal. Although a few unfortunate Kentish labourers joined Richard's cause, they were hanged for it and generally there was no enthusiasm for this unknown prince. The invasion failed.

Richard now turned to the young king of Scots for refuge, support and power base, and the Scottish king was glad to oblige, mainly because possessing Richard meant that he had bargaining power with Henry and the rest of Europe. In November Richard reached Scotland, to be supplied at once with a beautiful young bride, Lady Katherine Gordon. Within the year a Scottish invasion of England was planned, and it was James's idea, not Richard's. It sealed Richard's fate. Once Henry had Richard in custody he would never be able to let him go.

The army marched in September. It turned out that Richard was too squeamish for war. At Berwick he and the Scottish king had an angry exchange, in which Richard tearfully begged James to stop savaging his people. He referred to the fallen English as 'mine'. James revealingly told him that he was interfering in another man's business, which gave away that James was just using Richard's cause as an excuse. Richard simply rode away. James sent men after him with a present and an apology. The invasion petered out. Henry even so prepared to mount a huge offensive against the Scots.

Richard stayed on in Scotland for almost a year. Support seemed to melt away. He tried to enlist the help of Spain. Meanwhile Henry conspired with the Spanish to deliver the trouble-maker into his hands, and pressed the Scots to end their association with him. In June 1497, Henry mobilized his huge army and navy to resolve the situation. As the English ships sailed north, Richard was diplomatically ejected by

James, sailing from Ayr to Ireland in a small unarmed ship aptly named the *Cuckoo*. From Ireland, Richard sailed to Cornwall, apparently still with the idea of claiming his throne. He captured St Michael's Mount, where he left his wife and son, then marched to Bodmin, gathering support as he went. At Bodmin, surrounded by three thousand followers, he was proclaimed king. He had similar success in Devon.

Henry was now offering a huge reward for his capture, but it was for the capture of Perkin Warbeck, a boatman's son, not for a royal prince. As Richard marched east, Henry became more confident of victory. Richard's hoped-for invasion from Scotland did not happen; the detour via Ireland, and Richard's earlier squeamish and unsoldierly behaviour ruled it out. He gathered supporters along the way, but they were the poor and uneducated, not the nobles and gentlemen. For under two weeks Richard IV was at the head of a kind of peasants' revolt. He laid siege to Exeter, gave up and then took his motley army towards Taunton. His nerve failed and suddenly in the middle of the night he fled towards Beaulieu on Southampton Water. There Henry VII had him dragged from sanctuary – he had done this to other men before – and taken back to Taunton. He wanted to meet the trouble-making boy face to face.

At their meeting, Henry claimed the boy admitted everything. He was not Richard but Piers Osbeck. It may rather be that Henry gave him no choice, that he told him who he was now. After that came public demonstrations of surrender and a humiliating confrontation by his wife, staged by Henry, in which the boy had to own up, again and again, to deceiving everyone. Katherine was heartbroken and could not stop sobbing. She must have known that Henry would demand this sort of spectacle if her husband was captured, but that made it no less painful.

Then came the formal confession document, which defined who the boy was for history, for posterity. He was Piers Osbeck, born in Tournai. To confuse matters a French version of the confession appeared which was slightly different. There the family name appears as 'Werbecque', which explains the form 'Warbeck' that had become Henry's followers' derisive nickname for the unfortunate impostor. It was well known in Europe that Henry was dissatisfied with the biography that had been assembled by his agents. When the French wanted Henry's friendship, they presented him with the information that the young man was a boatman's son; when they wanted to put some pressure on him, they referred to him as Richard duke of York. The truth, even if Henry had wanted it, was virtually unachievable.

His information led the young man's story back from Ireland via Portugal to Tournai, where there was a Jehan Werbecque whose son had gone missing. It was tenuous, un-convincing. People would soon speculate that the Werbecques had simply given shelter to a fugitive prince.

The captive was made to write to his mother, which at first seems loaded with authentic detail, but actually contains significant mistakes. He signs himself 'Wezbecq', when in Tournai his alleged family was known as 'Osbeck'. His mother's name was Caisine, not Catherine. The address was wrong. The only true note is in the writer's reference to Henry as pitiless. The author was trapped, having to own up to a false identity as a Flemish commoner out of fear for what Henry would do to him. What is emerging is that it is likelier that he was Richard than Perkin. Once we see him as the real duke of

York, certain key facts fall into place. For instance, the 'mother' in Tournai was startlingly uninterested in getting in touch with him for the simple reason that she was not his mother.

Henry let most of the West Country rebels off, after hanging the ringleaders at Exeter. He was in no hurry to kill Perkin, and may have intended to let him stay on at his court like Simnel. For the time being Perkin was allowed to walk about at court, apparently freely but always under guard. He might have survived in this way, as a court curiosity, for the rest of his natural life had he not tried to escape. But in June 1498 he slipped away, only to be caught four days later and sent to the Tower. He was brutally beaten up, then closely confined. Then he was set up by *agents provocateurs*. They placed him within speaking distance of Warwick, Clarence's son, and encouraged them to plot together. By November they had been sentenced to be hanged, drawn and quartered. Warwick's sentence was commuted to beheading. Perkin's was not.

On the scaffold, he confessed (again) that he was Peter from Tournai and that he had called himself the son of King Edward at the request of others. Recent historians have said that these last words must have been true. The man was about to die and to die speaking a lie would have endangered his soul. But Richard was a chancer, a gambler, and he may have hoped that by going along with Henry's demand he might get a last-minute reprieve – or a quicker death. He did not get his reprieve, but they cut him down from the gallows dead, which means that Henry showed him some mercy, possibly for agreeing to the lie.

In a bizarre epilogue, Richard's widow, Lady Katherine Gordon, was also the victim of an imposture. She was kept by Henry at his court – he became very friendly towards her –

and was rarely seen. In 1510, a beautiful woman appeared in Scotland claiming to be her.

Was the claimant Richard duke of York or Piers Osbeck? The evidence is evenly balanced. Certainly there is no definite evidence of any kind, documentary or archaeological, that the princes were murdered in 1483. James Tyrell was said to have confessed to their murder, but only by Sir Thomas More in his 1514 *The History of King Richard the Third*. No one else had asserted it, and if such a confession had been made in 1502, Henry VII would certainly have used it against the claimant. Those alleged by More to have committed the murders, Tyrell, Dighton and Forest, were never accused of the crime, and Dighton was still alive at the time when More said Tyrell confessed. The only evidence pointing to Tyrell as the murderer of the princes was the reward given to him by Richard III, but the unexplained 'services' Tyrell rendered to Richard III were very possibly the rescuing of one or both of the princes – not their assassination.

The Perkin Warbeck affair is really a multiple conspiracy, and because of its enormous complexity it is possible to assemble several different scenarios. The conventional post-Tudor view has always been the pro-Tudor view, mainly because the Tudor monarchs were such brilliant propagandists. The pro-Tudor view is that Perkin Warbeck was an impostor. But, once we recognize that the Tudors were dishonest, unscrupulous and ruthless, we can see that it is at least equally likely that he really was Richard duke of York, Richard IV of England, and that Henry VII was the usurper who conspired against him. If so, Henry VII was at least as villainous as Richard III, even assuming that Richard III had Edward V murdered; Henry too was a regicide. It may be significant that after Richard IV's execution, Henry's health went into a steep decline, perhaps connected with feelings of guilt or remorse. Within a few months of ordering Perkin Warbeck's hanging, Henry VII started work on his own tomb.

THE DEATH OF
PRINCESS DIANA

1997

ON 31 AUGUST, 1997, the world was saddened by the sudden, violent and completely unexpected death of Princess Diana, the ex-wife of Prince Charles. She died, as everybody knows, in a car crash in a tunnel in the centre of Paris. The Mercedes she was being driven in was travelling fast, perhaps too fast, and for some reason it hit one of the supporting pillars in the tunnel. In the crash, she sustained internal injuries from which she died a couple of hours later in hospital. Ever since, there has been speculation about the nature of the crash: whether it was a simple accident resulting from an error of judgement or impaired concentration on the driver's part, or a deliberately staged assassination.

Diana had been spending a great deal of time with her new boyfriend, Dodi Fayed, and the visit to Paris came immediately after a yachting holiday they had spent together in Sardinia. They returned to Paris in the afternoon of 30 August aboard Dodi's private jet and they were then taken in a Mercedes driven by Dodi's regular Ritz chauffeur, Philippe Journot, to Dodi's apartment on the rue Arsene-Houssaye. The Mercedes was followed by a Range Rover carrying the couple's luggage, driven by Henri Paul. The Fayed family said that during this short journey the couple's car was harassed by photographers on motorbikes and a dark car tried to cut in front and slow them down. Was this perhaps a failed attempt to cause the Mercedes to crash, or merely a way of enabling the paparazzi to get better quality pictures?

A senior British source said that at least six MI6 officers were stationed in the British Embassy in Paris on the weekend of the crash. At least one of these MI6 officers was on orders to follow Diana and Dodi after they arrived from their holiday. The US National Security Agency confirmed that Diana was the subject of monitoring at the time. A long-standing informant at the Ritz Hotel in Paris was being paid by MI6.

Diana and Dodi Fayed paid a brief visit to the Villa Windsor, the former home of the duke of Windsor, now owned by Dodi's father, Mohammed Al Fayed. At the time, the contents belonging to the dead duke and duchess were being auctioned. At 4.35 p.m. the couple arrived at the Ritz Hotel where they relaxed in the Imperial Suite. Diana telephoned Richard Kay, the *Daily Mail* columnist who was one of her closest friends among the press, to tell him she was planning to change her life radically by giving up her public role. Dodi phoned his cousin to say that he hoped to marry Diana by the end of the year.

By this time, a number of paparazzi had congregated outside the hotel. At 6.00 p.m., Dodi went out to collect a ring, perhaps an engagement ring, from a jewellers; Diana had previously chosen the ring from a sister shop in Monte Carlo. Some Ritz employees claimed that Henri Paul, the driver, drank several glasses of *Ricard pastis*, a powerful cocktail at one of the Ritz bars during the late afternoon, but others insist that Paul drank only pineapple juice. Whether

Henri Paul drank alcohol or not, it does not automatically mean that he caused the crash; nor does it rule out the possibility of a conspiracy.

At 7 p.m. Diana and Dodi left the Ritz by the back door to be taken back to Dodi's apartment in the Mercedes by Dodi's usual driver, Philippe Journot. They planned to go out to dinner at Benoit, a bistro off the rue de Rivoli. Dodi told his butler to have champagne on ice ready for their return, whispering, 'I'm going to propose to her tonight.' Thinking the couple had gone out for the evening and that his work was over for that day, security officer Henri Paul went home, after leaving instructions to call him immediately if Diana and Dodi returned to the hotel.

At about 8 p.m. the couple reached a perfume shop on the Champs Elysees, but it was in a busy area and photographers flocked around the car making it impossible for them to get out. They headed for the Benoit bistro, where once again they were pestered by a hoard of press photographers. They decided to return to the more secure surroundings of the Ritz. On this return journey they were pursued by about 30 photographers.

Closed-circuit TV images show the couple arriving back at the Ritz at 9.50 p.m. Diana appears in these images to be somewhat distressed, probably by her encounter with the paparazzi outside the hotel. The Princess's relationship with the press was equivocal to say the least. She ran away from journalists and photographers like a frightened rabbit on days like this, but she also courted them and deployed them with great adroitness when it suited her. The Ritz night security manager, M Tendil, summoned Henri Paul, who appeared 17 minutes later at 10.07 p.m. A CCTV camera recorded Henri Paul parking his Mini at the Ritz with no obvious signs of drunkenness. Another CCTV camera recorded him entering the Ritz, again showing no sign of drunkenness. It was said that Henri Paul was in a bar when he was called back to the Ritz, but the bar staff insisted that he drank no alcohol while he was there. It is true that no one knows precisely where Henri Paul was for much of the evening, but equally no one has produced any evidence to suggest that he drank any alcohol during this time. On the contrary, teams of British journalists who tried to track down leads provided by the French police (on the so-called wild drinking bout while he was off-duty) failed to find a single witness who saw Paul drink anything alcoholic at all. Diana's British bodyguard, Rees-Jones, also confirmed that Henri Paul had shown no signs of being intoxicated or unfit to drive; if he had, they would not have let him drive them.

At around 11.00 p.m. Dodi received a call on his mobile phone. After ringing off, he seemed agitated and asked to speed up the remainder of the meal. It is not known what this phone call was about. After the meal, the couple decided to return to Dodi's apartment. The decision was then made to use Dodi's Mercedes 600 and a Range Rover, the cars Diana and Dodi had been using all day, as decoy vehicles to draw off the paparazzi. Most of the paparazzi were already stationed by the Range Rover, which was parked at the main entrance of the hotel in the Place Vendôme.

Dodi did not use his usual driver for this particular journey. At 11.37 p.m., he decided to use Henri Paul to drive the car instead. Henri Paul was an advanced driver and fully qualified to drive the Mercedes; he had been to Germany twice to take the Daimler Benz special driving courses, in which he showed great proficiency. Henri Paul took his driving seriously. Together he and Dodi devised a plan to lure the paparazzi away by using Dodi's usual driver to drive one of the decoy vehicles. An alternative Mercedes was to be used for the journey back to Dodi's apartment. This Mercedes did not have tinted windows. Consequently, one of the photographers was able to photograph the couple in the car together as it drew away from the hotel.

Diana and her bodyguard, Trevor Rees-Jones, appeared at the back door of the Ritz at 10 minutes past midnight. There they met Henri Paul, who had driven the Mercedes without any difficulty and parked it close to the back door. At 12.19 p.m., Dodi and Diana listened to Henri Paul outlining the departure plan for them; Paul seemed to be in charge. Still photos and CCTV film of this scene show all three of them behaving normally. Paul does not appear drunk, and Dodi and Diana are not responding in a way that suggests that they think he is drunk. Henri Paul then went out to start the Mercedes.

At 12.20 a.m., Diana and Rees-Jones left the Ritz by the back door. There were photographers outside, and Diana immediately covered her face. Rees-Jones escorted Diana to the car. She sat on the passenger side of the back seat and Dodi joined her seconds later on the driver's side. Some photographers spotted the Mercedes on the rue Cambon as it left the hotel, and gave chase. Eventually, there were a dozen motorcycles and cars following the Mercedes, but mostly several hundred metres behind the Mercedes. *The Times* reported that earlier in the evening Henri Paul was laughing a lot and taunting photographers who claimed that, as Henri Paul pulled away from the hotel on the rue Cambon, he said,

'Catch me if you can.' But it is clear from other evidence that Henri Paul had no contact with the paparazzi. The photographers who gave the statements did so when they were under arrest, and may well have wanted to make it look as if Paul was out of control and behaving provocatively, as if he was to blame for the accident, not them.

At 12.21 a.m., the Mercedes headed towards the tunnel where Diana and Dodi were to die. Then peculiar things began to happen. At midnight, the 17 traffic cameras located inside the Place d'Alma tunnel all stopped recording images when the electricity supply in the tunnel mysteriously failed. Not one of the 10 traffic cameras on the route from the Ritz to the Place d'Alma tunnel was working at the time of the crash. A motorist was fined for speeding 15 minutes before, based on evidence from a speed camera near the tunnel entrance. There has never been any other sudden power failure at the tunnel at any other time before or after the crash. This becomes highly significant once it is realized that those video cameras could have supplied crucial evidence about the identity and behaviour of other vehicles entering the tunnel at about the same time as the Mercedes.

Another peculiar event was the fact that all the police radios in Paris went off-air just before Diana's Mercedes entered the tunnel, making a quick emergency response in the event of any road accident virtually impossible. Many conspiracy theorists see this as clear evidence of foul play.

The first reports of the crash suggested that the Mercedes was travelling at 120 mph in order to shake off the paparazzi. In fact, the evidence suggests that Paul was driving at between 60 mph and 70 mph – which is relatively normal for that type of road at that time of night.

A cab driver was overtaken by the Mercedes on the Place de la Concorde: 'There was a limousine, a Mercedes, with several motorcycles behind and near it. I thought it was an escort, but there were too many [motorcycles] for one car.' But the cab driver did not think the Mercedes was speeding.

There is evidence that the Mercedes was closely followed by two cars and a motorcycle. The quickest and most direct route from the Place de la Concorde to Dodi's apartment on the rue Arsene-Housaye, would have been to go north-west along the Champs-Elysées toward the Arc de Triomphe, but instead Henri Paul used a much longer route by turning onto the rue de Rivoli, which runs south-west toward the Place d'Alma tunnel, in the opposite direction to Dodi's apartment. It is worth asking why Henri Paul chose this longer route.

One possibility is that Henri Paul wanted to avoid the many traffic lights on the shorter route, so as to prevent the pursuing photographers catching up – and taking pictures of Dodi and Diana while they were stationary at the red lights. A second and more sinister possibility is that the Mercedes could not use the preferred shorter route because it was prevented by a car deliberately blocking the way along the Champs Elysées; some witnesses gave evidence of this. Henri Paul was therefore *forced* to take the only other available route – the route that led to the fatal tunnel. It is also significant that the two cars and the motorbike closely pursuing the Mercedes were not driven by paparazzi. The drivers and rider still remain a mystery.

A third possibility is that Henri Paul was not just working for Dodi Fayed but was in addition being paid by MI6 to give them information on Diana's intentions and whereabouts. If this is true then Paul may have informed MI6 that he was driving the couple home. MI6 then gave him instructions to take the alternative route on this journey, the route to the tunnel. Perhaps the reason was the relatively innocent one of prolonging the journey to enable Paul to listen to more of the couple's conversations; MI6 may have been keen to find out more about the proposed marriage. But there is no positive evidence of this – only speculation. All we can know for certain is that something significant stopped Henri Paul from taking the obvious, shorter, route to the apartment.

Moments before the Mercedes went into the tunnel, Dodi Fayed was seen holding his mobile phone. It is not known who he called, but it would seem likely that it was his butler, to let him know that they were on their way to the apartment. At this point, Diana's bodyguard belatedly decided to put his seat belt on. Why did he do that? Did he know something the others didn't? Bodyguards usually avoid using seat belts so that they have maximum freedom of movement.

A British secretary who was living and working in Paris, Brenda Wells, said she was driving back from a party when she saw a dark-coloured car following Diana's Mercedes. Brenda Wells was driving towards the tunnel when she was forced off the road by two motorbikes chasing a large car, and then she was overtaken by a black car. This important witness vacated her flat in Paris after giving her statement to the police and has subsequently disappeared without trace.

Apparently one motorcycle preceded the Mercedes into the tunnel. Two people who were approaching the tunnel from the west, Mark Butt and Dr Mailliez, saw a man on a motorcycle emerge from the east (ie travelling in the same direction as the Mercedes). The motorbike stopped, did a U-turn and drove the wrong way back into the tunnel.

Some witnesses reported seeing a helicopter hovering over the tunnel just before the crash. Presumably the helicopter was monitoring events on the ground. The police often monitor traffic by helicopter, but the French police disclaim all knowledge of it so its presence there is a complete mystery. Even more sinister is the evidence of eyewitnesses who reported seeing at least one sniper within the tunnel at the time of the crash.

As the Mercedes approached the tunnel, it was being chased by a motorcycle and two vehicles. One of the vehicles, a white Fiat Uno, may have rammed the Mercedes just before the crash and this caused it to spin out of control. As the Mercedes got close to the tunnel entrance, at 12.23 a.m., at least one motorcycle stopped Brenda Wells's car from going into the tunnel. Just moments before the crash, several witnesses saw a bright flash of light, then heard a loud bang coming from the tunnel.

Two witnesses said that a car driving in front of the Mercedes forced Henri Paul to start braking and veer into the left-hand lane just as it entered the tunnel. The tunnel was completely dark, because the lights had been turned off a few minutes earlier. Franck Levi said that his car was two cars ahead of the Mercedes; he saw a motorcycle with two riders cut in front of Diana's car, then he saw a bright flash. After he saw the flash, he saw the Mercedes' headlights veer left, right and then left. He lost sight of the Mercedes as he left the tunnel. He pulled over to the kerb, as his first impulse was to go back to see what had happened, but his wife intervened, saying, 'Let's get out of here, it's a terrorist attack.'

Another witness, Brian Anderson, saw a powerful motorbike swerve in front of the Mercedes seconds before it crashed. He also noted that the driver of the Mercedes appeared to be in command of the situation, and showed no signs of being drunk. Anderson saw a damaged motorcycle on the ground, in the tunnel, as he and his taxi driver passed the scene of the crash. The only other known mention of this damaged motorcycle was in a CNN report on the day of the crash. Anderson's statements confirmed the existence of this motorcycle. He offered to give a formal statement, but the police never took one from him.

Gary Hunter, a British lawyer, was staying in a third-floor hotel room next to the tunnel at the time of the crash. He heard the crash, then 'a car speeding from that direction . . . I saw a small car drive up the street with another car practically stuck to its back bumper . . . The first car looked like a Fiat Uno or a Renault Clio. The other car was a Mercedes . . . They both spun round together and sped off down the street at a suicidal pace, more than 100 miles per hour . . . I thought it was very strange that they were travelling so dangerously close to each other . . . Their behaviour made me wonder exactly what they had been up to in the tunnel when the crash happened.' He added that it 'looked quite sinister'; he had the impression that the cars were escaping from the scene.

Mr Hunter volunteered to give the French authorities a statement, but they refused to see him. It was only after the Fiat Uno story was corroborated, and his remarks had been picked up by the media, that the French authorities finally asked Scotland Yard to take a statement from him – two months later.

Two pedestrians told police that the Mercedes had to avoid a black Peugeot moments before it crashed. This car, like the motorcycle and the white Fiat Uno, has never been traced.

The Fiat probably collided with the Mercedes, leaving fragments of its rear lights. There were also traces of paint from a white Mercedes. However, even though it is virtually certain that these two cars were indeed involved in or at least witnessed the crash, neither the specific vehicles nor their drivers have been identified.

Two Americans were walking outside the tunnel when the crash occurred. They saw a bright flash of light come from the tunnel, then they heard a loud explosion, then they heard the crash of the impact. They rushed to the tunnel to find out what was going on. An unknown person ran towards them, from the direction of the crash and told them to go back because the car was going to explode, which it did 20 seconds later. They saw someone jump out of the crashed car. Another person was seen lifting the driver's head from the Mercedes' steering wheel to stop the car horn from sounding.

Here were three crucial witnesses, who must have seen the crash and therefore also the cause of the crash, yet – almost incredibly – at the time of writing they have still not been traced. Given the nature of the incident and the saturation media coverage given to it, the three people involved can be in no doubt as to the importance of the testimony they could give, of the questions they could answer. Yet it appears that they have not come forward. It is not surprising that many commentators on the death of Diana have suspicions that they were directly involved in orchestrating the crash and determining how it would be interpreted. The person who lifted Henri Paul's head from the steering wheel could just as easily have injected him with alcohol in order to make it look as though he had been drunk while driving. Who were these people?

As well as the three people seen by the American walkers, there were at least another four key witnesses – the rider of the motorcycle and the drivers of the white Fiat, the white Mercedes and the black Peugeot – and so far none of these people have been traced either. When the police arrived at the crash scene, some 'paparazzi' obstructed them, making it difficult to reach the Mercedes. But perhaps these people were not paparazzi at all. They could instead have been the team of assassins ensuring that vital evidence was removed from the crash scene, and also ensuring that misinformation was in place.

No explanation has been given for the power cut in the tunnel, which prevented the traffic cameras from working. This remarkable coincidence means that there is no video evidence of the Mercedes' final approach to the tunnel, and even more critically no video evidence of the vehicles that went into the tunnel with it.

Something significant caused Henri Paul to drive straight into the thirteenth of the line of concrete pillars separating the two opposite flows of traffic inside the tunnel. Henri Paul and Dodi Fayed died instantly. Diana was injured and died later. The bodyguard was injured and eventually recovered. The very bright flash of light inside the tunnel just before the crash may hold the key to it. Some have interpreted this as a camera flashlight, which would be consistent with a paparazzi chase. Others say it was too bright for that. The attorney for the Ritz Hotel was shown copies of two photographs that had been confiscated by French police, showing Henri Paul dazzled by a bright flash of light. Beside him was the bodyguard, immediately pulling down a visor to protect himself from the flash. Also visible was the yellow headlight of a motorcycle. Rees-Jones appeared to realize that the light was from a strobe gun, and that he needed to protect his eyes from it. He would certainly have had experience of strobe lights in his army career. It is a distinct possibility that the motorcyclist (or rather his passenger) who overtook the Mercedes in the tunnel deliberately blinded Henri Paul with a strobe light in order to make him crash.

At 12.27 a.m., two minutes after the crash, the paparazzi arrived to discover the wreck of the Mercedes. A few minutes later, Frederick Mailliez, an emergency doctor employed by a private firm, arrived at the scene. He said that he held Diana's hand, spoke to her, took her pulse, put the resuscitation mask on her, told her she was safe. Astonishingly, he did not see her condition as catastrophic, though he did call for help. Within five minutes of the accident, two ambulances arrived, each with a doctor on board. Yet, Diana was not moved from the scene of the crash and the medics present appeared to behave as if there was no particular urgency to rush her to the hospital. One interpretation, the most natural one, is that her condition was not considered to be life-threatening. Mailliez said that the back of the Mercedes had not been seriously damaged in the crash, and there was no difficulty in reaching Diana.

There are problems with Dr Mailliez's testimony, in that he seems to have changed his story. Initially he was quoted as saying that Diana told him that she was six weeks pregnant. Those who see a conspiracy at work here suggest that Dr Mailliez was ordered by some authority, perhaps the French Police, to withdraw his earlier comments which revealed too much. His assessment of Diana's non-terminal condition is also peculiar. Did he really make that assessment, or was he pressed to say so by others? He was at Diana's side for 45 minutes, which gave him plenty of time to observe all her injuries, and any changes in her condition. Interestingly, the initial BBC and ITN news reports, released immediately after the crash, said that Diana had only suffered concussion, a broken arm, and some cuts to her thigh. Six weeks after the crash, Dr Mailliez changed his story completely and said that Diana was seriously injured, and that he felt that she would not survive. Something happened in the meantime to make him change his story. Was it just hindsight – that at the time he had underestimated the extent of Diana's internal injuries, and that he revised his 'diagnosis' after her death, simply to save professional face?

An ambulance arrived within 15 minutes of the crash, but it was at least another 38 minutes before the paramedics got Diana into the ambulance, ie an incredible 53 minutes after the crash. It was said that this was because Diana had to be cut free from the Mercedes, but this was totally untrue, because the back half of the car was very little damaged and Diana could have been lifted out easily through the door. In fact, according to one of the ambulance crew, Diana was removed from the car almost immediately when the paramedics arrived, so it is very hard to understand why she was not lifted into the ambulance straight away and taken to hospital.

At that stage, Diana was not only very much alive, she was conscious and talking to people. According to one of them Diana said, 'Help, they are trying to kill us!' Another said Diana was semi-conscious, agitated, and saying to photographers, 'Leave me alone.'

The ambulance took at least another 45 minutes to carry Diana to the Pitié Salpêtrière Hospital – 45 minutes to travel less than 4 miles! The city streets were very quiet, yet the ambulance apparently travelled at walking speed. This is unaccountable in view of the fact that a large team of medics including 10 surgeons was waiting to treat Diana at the hospital. Also hard to understand is the fact that the ambulance passed two other hospitals where she could have been treated. A French doctor specializing in emergency response said that Diana should have been taken to the Val de Grace military hospital; in his opinion Diana could have been taken there by helicopter and she could have been operated on within a few minutes.

One explanation is that the ambulance drove slowly in order to prevent any aggravation of Diana's injuries. Within sight of the hospital, the ambulance driver pulled off the road for 10 minutes, allegedly so that Diana could be given an injection of adrenaline. However, senior hospital doctors deny that this took place. Diana suffered a serious injury to her left pulmonary vein, which should have been attended to as quickly as possible in hospital. So far, no convincing explanations have been given for what happened on that fatally slow journey.

Diana's injury led to sustained slow blood loss, which could have been stopped by surgery. The slow bleeding would not have killed her if she had been delivered to hospital within 15 minutes of the accident. We must remember that Dr Mailliez thought Diana's condition was 'not catastrophic'. The celebrated heart surgeon Christian Barnard also wrote that Diana could have been saved if she had reached the hospital in time. The critical question must be asked: why was Diana not rushed to hospital?

The ambulance arrived at the hospital at 2.05 a.m., an hour and 42 minutes after the accident. By this time, Diana was in a very serious state; she had lost a lot of blood and was in shock; she went into cardiac arrest. She was resuscitated and kept alive for another two hours. At 4.05 a.m. Princess Diana died. Conspiracy theorists have suggested that the delay in getting Diana to hospital was deliberate, that it was part of the conspiracy to ensure that she did not survive; this is a very serious accusation to bring against the French emergency services, and no evidence has so far been brought forward to substantiate it. Nevertheless the long delay has yet to be adequately explained.

Her body was embalmed immediately after her death, apparently at the insistence of the British government and the royal family. A decision was made, in London, to fly the body back to Britain as soon as possible and the order was passed to the French authorities by the British Ambassador Sir Michael Jay. Without that order, a full autopsy would have been conducted in Paris. Embalming the body before a post-mortem goes against normal UK practice. Because the procedure made it impossible for UK pathologists to tell whether she was pregnant or not, it was suggested that this was the reason; as it is, no reason was given.

The news of the fatal crash was broadcast at about 9.00 a.m. The first reports suggested that Diana had only minor injuries. This has been interpreted as reinforcing the initial assessment of the doctor at the scene of the crash, but it may be no more than the normal turbulence that surrounds a major story as it breaks. The Queen's first thought seems to have been to retrieve any jewels that may have belonged to the royal family; people often focus on the relatively trivial in such situations as a displacement activity, a kind of psychological self-defence. The royal family came in for a lot of criticism in the popular press for appearing to be unmoved by Diana's death. The *Daily Express* ran the headline 'Show Us You Care'. The truth is that the royal family behaved as they normally do, and as many British families do in bereavement, which is to hide their feelings in public and grieve in private; it was rather the British public that behaved abnormally on this occasion, with a huge and near-hysterical public outpouring of grief.

The French inquiry (October 1997 to January 2002) concluded that the deaths of Diana and Dodi Fayed were caused by Henri Paul's high-speed drunk driving. His blood carried more than three times the legal alcohol limit. Henri Paul's parents insist that the blood sample taken after the crash did not belong to their son. British police also doubted the authenticity of the blood sample; they are suspicious because the blood sample contains such a high level of carbon monoxide that Henri Paul would barely have been able to walk to the car, let alone drive it. It may be that an innocent mix-up in the laboratory or morgue may have led to the wrong sample being tested. Perhaps the sample came from the body of someone who had committed suicide by inhaling car exhaust fumes. Identifying the blood specimen is crucial.

By January 2002, increasing numbers of people wondered whether Diana had been murdered, because she had clearly become an embarrassment to the British establishment and because so many questions about her death remained unresolved. Some even went so far as to suggest that the royal family was somehow involved in Diana's death. Prince Philip showed enormous restraint over the repeated accusations levelled at him by Dodi Fayed's father. But the proposition that one or more members of the royal family conspired to have Princess Diana killed is preposterous. Other candidates suggested by conspiracy theorists include French Intelligence, the British Intelligence services, the CIA, Mossad, the Freemasons and the IRA.

On the day the long-delayed inquest began, it was reported that 10 months before her death Diana had written a letter to her former butler, Paul Burrell. In that letter she said that she suspected Prince Charles of trying to kill her. According to extracts leaked to the press, she wrote, 'My husband is planning "an accident" in my car.' Royal commentators said the letter raised questions about Diana's state of mind, that it revealed her mental instability and in fact *reduced* the credibility of her allegations about Prince Charles's behaviour. By the end of 2004 it was announced that the former head of London's Metropolitan Police, Sir John Stevens, would head an inquiry into Diana's death. He said, 'We have new witnesses. We have new forensic evidence.' Whether the Stevens Report will really get to the bottom of the mystery remains to be seen; there are certainly a great many questions to answer. But none of this story is straight-forward. Before the inquiry was complete, in July 2006, the coroner, Michael Burgess, resigned from the case; and it was Michael Burgess who invited Sir John Stevens to examine the allegations that Diana's death was not accidental.

THE TWIN TOWERS

2001

ON 11 SEPTEMBER, 2001, a coordinated series of terrorist attacks was launched at the United States, and mainly against its civilian population. On that day 19 men working for the Al Qaeda organization commandeered four commercial passenger jet airliners, abducting their passengers and in effect turning the aircraft into powerful guided missiles. Each group of hijackers included one trained pilot. Two of the pilots succeeded in crashing their planes into the World Trade Center towers in New York City, one plane into each tower. American Airlines Flight 11 crashed into the north side of the North Tower at 8.46 a.m. local time. United Airlines Flight 175 crashed into the South Tower at 9.03 a.m. local time, an event which was captured on live television by reporters from around the world who had their cameras trained on the buildings after the first crash. The crash damage was structurally crippling, causing both towers to collapse completely within two hours.

The pilot of the third team successfully (ie according to the terrorists' plan) crashed a plane into the Pentagon Building in Virginia. American Airlines Flight 77 crashed into the Pentagon at 9.37 a.m. local time.

Half an hour later, the passengers and crew members on the fourth hijacked aircraft, United Airlines Flight 93, tried to wrest control of their plane from the hijackers. The hijackers lost control of it as they fought with the passengers and it crashed in a field just outside Shanksville in southwest Pennsylvania, at 10.03 a.m. local time. Debris from the plane was found up to eight miles away. No one survived in any of the hijacked aircraft and altogether nearly 3,000 people died in these attacks. The loss of life was enormous, but the fatalities were nevertheless fewer than at first thought. At the time of the attacks about 16,000 people were below the levels where the planes hit the World Trade Center complex. Of these, nearly everyone escaped by evacuating the towers before they collapsed.

Even so, most of the deaths were in and round the World Trade Center, where 2605 civilians and firefighters were killed. For a long time there was great uncertainty about the number of dead, partly because the collapsing buildings tore and shredded the victims' bodies into tiny and often unrecognizable fragments. Bone fragments were still being found as late as 2006 when the Deutsche Bank Building was demolished.

As well as the 110-floor Twin Towers, five other buildings at the World Trade Center site and four subway stations were either destroyed or severely damaged. All seven buildings in the World Trade Center Complex had to be demolished. The Deutsche Bank Building across the street from the World Trade Center eventually had to be demolished as well, due to the toxic conditions inside it which rendered it unusable. Part of the Pentagon was severely damaged by fire and collapsed.

Passengers and crew members were able to use their mobile phones to make calls from the stricken planes. They reported that several hijackers were on board, and the FBI later confirmed that there were four or five on each plane. It seems that to gain control in each plane they used box-cutte knives to kill stewards and at least one passenger. They also used bomb threats and tear gas to keep passengers at bay.

In the fourth plane, the passengers discovered on their phones that other planes had been hijacked and deliberately crashed into buildings and realized that that was the fate intended for them too. They knew the only way to prevent the hijackers from crashing into another building was to regain control of the plane, or force it down prematurely in a rural area where as little damage would be done as possible. One of the passengers, Todd Beamer, rallied the passengers in an onslaught on the hijackers, with the phrase, 'Let's roll.' Later it would become the war cry for American soldiers fighting Al Qaeda in Afghanistan. Shortly afterwards, the aircraft crashed into a field, killing everyone on board.

Conditions inside the World Trade Center were appalling, as floors filled with flames and smoke. More than two hundred desperate people jumped to their death from the burning towers onto the streets and rooftops of adjacent buildings far below – just to escape a worse death inside the building. Those on the levels above the point of the plane's impact were trapped; some made their way up towards the roof in the hope that they would be rescued there by helicopter, but no such rescue could be attempted as the towers were like huge chimneys belching out great plumes of thick billowing smoke, making it impossible for helicopters to land. The occupants in any case found that they were unable to get out because the doors to the roof were locked. Much would be said later in the 9/11 inquiry about the unsatisfactory emergency exit routes within the buildings.

It must have seemed as if the only worse thing that could happen next was that the fire and smoke would gradually spread upwards through both towers, engulfing the whole of the top of each building. But far worse than that was to follow. The impact of the planes flying into them had seriously weakened the structure and the buildings totally collapsed. The South Tower (WTC 2) fell at about 10.05 a.m., after burning for almost an hour. The north tower (WTC 1) fell at 10.28 a.m., after burning for an hour and 43 minutes. A third building, 7 World Trade Center (WTC 7) also collapsed, but later in the day at 5.30 p.m., after being heavily damaged by debris from the collapse of the Twin Towers a short distance away. The fires had weakened the trusses supporting the floors, so the floors sagged. The sagging floors pulled on the exterior steel columns to the point where the columns bowed inwards. With the core columns damaged, the buckling exterior columns could no longer support the buildings, so the towers collapsed, floor upon floor, folding up like a telescope.

The explosive and spectacular collapse of the Twin Towers released thousands of tons of toxic debris, including asbestos, lead, mercury and very high levels of dioxin from the fires. The fires went on burning for three months in a scene of appalling and unearthly desolation that became known as Ground Zero. The discharge of toxins led to debilitating illnesses among rescue workers and the residents, students and office workers of Lower Manhattan and Chinatown.

Virtually every country in Europe has experienced invasions, sometimes repeated invasions, but the United States has had no experience of invasion or coordinated terrorist attacks. As a result, the attacks created large-scale confusion and disbelief. It was a major culture shock, a national rite of passage far more momentous than Pearl Harbor.

The 9/11 attacks were the result of a well-organized conspiracy. According to the 9/11 Commission Report, Khalid

Sheikh Mohammed was the mastermind behind the attacks, though apparently in some matters he was guided or overruled by Osama bin Laden, who therefore must take his share of responsibility for the events. Originally, 27 members of Al Qaeda were supposed to enter the United States to take part, but in the end only 19 participated. Ramzi Binalshibh and Mohamed al-Kahtani, who were both thought to have been intending to join the team, were denied entry into the US. Al-Kahtani was later captured in Afghanistan and imprisoned at Guantanamo Bay.

It was alleged that Zacarias Moussaoui was considered as a replacement for Ziad Jarrah, one of the conspirators who at one point threatened to drop out because of tensions amongst the plotters. The plan to draft Moussaoui onto the team was not in the end put into effect, allegedly because the Al Qaeda hierarchy doubted his reliability. Moussaoui was arrested in America on 16 August 2001, four weeks *before* the attacks, on a token charge of violating immigration laws, but the real reason was that FBI agents suspected him, after he had taken flying lessons earlier that year, of having plans to commit an act of terrorism. In April 2005, Moussaoui pleaded guilty to conspiring to hijack planes, and to involvement with Al Qaeda. He nevertheless denied that he knew beforehand about the 9/11 attacks. At his sentencing hearing in March 2006, Moussaoui claimed that, on Osama bin Laden's instructions, he and Richard Reid were due to hijack a fifth plane and fly it into the White House. Moussaoui's own defence lawyers did not believe this; they dismissed it as fantasy, saying that he was only peripheral to Al Qaeda, a 'hanger-on'. On 3 May 2006, Moussaoui was sentenced to six consecutive life terms in prison without parole. At least two FBI agents suspected beforehand that they 'knew' what it was Moussaoui was involved in, but failed to get permission from their superiors, even after repeated requests, to obtain a warrant to search Moussaoui's computer.

Moussaoui's claim that at one stage the plan was larger in scale and included flying a plane into the White House seems to have some truth in it. According to another 'insider', there was even a plan to mount a simultaneous attack on London; the Palace of Westminster and Tower Bridge were the targets. The attack on London was allegedly aborted at the last minute when the would-be hijackers, who were actually waiting to board the planes they were going to hijack and destroy, saw the colossal scale of the damage that had been done in America, which was far greater than they had expected. They panicked and fled. Presumably, the hijackers had no idea that the Twin Towers were going to collapse completely.

In February 2006, President Bush revealed that Al Qaeda had also initially planned to crash a plane into the tallest building in the western United States, the Library Tower in Los Angeles, on the same day. This attack was postponed by Osama bin Laden, and subsequently foiled as security intensified. The American government also claimed early on that the White House and Air Force One (the president's plane) had been targets, although the source of these threats was not disclosed.

The 9/11 attacks, as carried out, were incredibly ambitious. If the additional attacks had also been carried out the effect on the West would have been paralysing. They might be thought of as major military attacks, the equivalent to an invasion without a prior declaration of war. They might be thought of as war crimes, except that no state of war existed. They are referred to as terrorist attacks, in spite of their huge scale. Because they were attacks on unprepared and innocent civilians, they might also be regarded as crimes against humanity.

The American government came to the conclusion that Osama bin Laden and Al Qaeda were responsible for the attacks. Five days after the attacks Osama bin Laden denied responsibility; 'I stress that I have not carried out this act, which appears to have been carried out by individuals with their own motivation.' Later he admitted responsibility. In November 2001, American soldiers found a videotape in the ruins of a house in Jalalabad in Afghanistan, and on the tape Osama bin Laden admits to Khaled al-Harbi that he knew beforehand about the attacks. The following month bin Laden released another video praising the act of terrorism against America; 'It was a response to injustice, aimed at forcing America to stop its support for Israel, which kills our people.' Then in 2004 bin Laden publicly acknowledged his organization's responsibility for the 9/11 attacks and admitted his own involvement. His justification for the carnage was that 'we are a free people who do not accept injustice, and we want to regain the freedom of our nation'. The motives underlying the Al Qaeda campaign were listed in a 1998 fatwa issued by Osama bin Laden and others; America's support of Israel, its occupation of the Arabian Peninsula and its aggression against the Iraqi people. America stands condemned because it plunders the resources of the Middle East, dictates policy to the governments of those countries, has military bases in the Middle East in order to threaten Muslim states and seeks to divide and politically weaken Muslim states. It was exactly as might have been predicted with the improving education and the rise of nationalism in the Middle

East – that the West's expectation that it could continue to exert imperialist control over the area was unrealistic; it could only provoke increasing resentment and frustration.

Finally, in a sound tape that was broadcast by Al Jazeera in May 2006, bin Laden owned up; he personally had given the 19 hijackers their orders. It appears, according to some commentators, that he wanted to provoke a very strong anti-Muslim response in America in the hope that this would ensure that Muslims in the Middle East would react as violently as possible to any stepping-up of American involvement in their region. And the reaction was indeed strong and provocative. Following the attacks, eighty thousand Arab and Muslim immigrants were fingerprinted and registered under the US Alien Registration Act of 1940. There were some hate crimes in America directed against people who were Middle Eastern in appearance. At least nine people were murdered within the United States as part of the retaliation. Balbir Singh Sodhi, one of the first victims of this demonization phenomenon, was shot dead on 15 September, 2001. The poor man was a *Sikh*, not a Muslim; an unenlightened American shot him for wearing a turban.

Most governments and newspapers round the world condemned the terrorist attacks. Only a month after the attacks, America was able to lead a broad coalition of international forces into Afghanistan in pursuit of Al Qaeda forces. The intention was to topple the Taliban government for harbouring a terrorist organization, and there was the faint hope that they might find and capture or kill bin Laden himself. Pakistan decisively aligned itself with the United States in the war against Osama bin Laden and Al Qaeda. Many countries introduced anti-terrorism legislation, freezing bank accounts of businesses and individuals suspected of having Al Qaeda links. Civil rights protections were also circumvented. The American military set up its highly controversial detention centre at Guantanamo Bay in Cuba, and the legality of these protracted detentions without trial has been questioned by member states of the European Union, the Organization of American States and Amnesty International.

Several conspiracy theories have emerged, including the speculation that the US government knew of the impending attacks and failed to act on that knowledge, or even planned the attacks. Some people question the accepted account of 9/11, speculating that the collapse of the World Trade Center was caused by explosives. The idea of involving the American establishment in setting up the catastrophe is that it would have been a way of justifying invading Afghanistan and any other countries of the American administration's choice. Some argue that a commercial airliner did not crash into the Pentagon, and that United Airlines Flight 93 was shot down by the US military to prevent it from reaching its target. Doubtless new conspiracy theories will appear in future years.

The attacks prompted the Bush administration to declare a 'war on terrorism', to bring Osama bin Laden and Al Qaeda to justice and stop new terrorist networks emerging. It launched an invasion of Afghanistan which was the main refuge of Al Qaeda. Other countries, such as the Philippines and Indonesia, also increased their military readiness to deal with conflicts with Islamic extremist terrorism. Bush also had his sights on Iraq, which he portrayed as a hotbed of terror, so the origin of the later invasion of Iraq is clearly and explicitly traceable back to 9/11. There was no evidence that the Iraqi dictator, Saddam Hussein, was involved in any way in the 9/11 atrocity, but polls showed that enough Americans thought he might be to justify an invasion. The conspiracy that led to the 9/11 attacks was very effective. It was a spectacular blow to American national pride and complacency, and it produced vivid images – notably the photographs of the Twin Towers with flames and smoke pouring from their upper floors – that have become iconic. The ramifications and implications of the 9/11 attacks have been enormous, prompting the West into invasions which have been very costly to America and its allies and which it may well come to regret.

GLOBAL WARMING

GLOBAL WARMING IS the biggest single media issue and the biggest international political issue in the world today, outstripping even terrorism, simply because nowhere in the world is safe from its effects. In spite of its high profile, global warming has never been fully explained in terms that ordinary people can understand. It frequently comes up in political discussions and interviews, as an aside, a given, a presumption, and often as the justification for some questionable political decision – yet the underlying complexities are never adequately explained, let alone questioned. Global warming is the upward trend of temperatures in the lower atmosphere over the last hundred years, and graphs of temperature measurements show this warming as an overall increase of half a degree Celsius. An integral part of the global warming scare story is that more (and faster) warming is predicted for the future. The predictions of increases of 1.5 or even 5 degrees over the next 100 years are clearly not simple projections into the future of what is happening now.

A lot of the predictions as well as the message that man-made carbon dioxide is causing the temperature increase have come from a single organization, the Inter-Governmental Panel for Climate Change, the IPCC.

The Earth's climate has certainly warmed up measurably and noticeably, and the effects will be serious if the warming continues. It has been predicted that 80 percent of South

Africa's unique collection of wild flowers will disappear, 97 percent of coral reefs will be killed, and polar bears will be wiped out. It has also been predicted that sea level will rise and low-lying areas will have to be evacuated. Sea level has risen by 10–25cm over the last 100 years and may rise by another 31–47cm in the next 100 years. A 40cm sea level rise by 2080 will put another 75 million people living on low ground at risk from annual flooding.

The world's climatic regions will change too. Noticeable seasonal changes that have happened already include the very mild UK autumn of 2005, when temperatures were 2.5 degrees above the 30-year average and sunshine was 50 percent above the average; as a result it was an unusually green autumn and early winter. Oak leaves now regularly fall at the end of October, a week later than 30 years ago. South-east England will suffer permanent water shortages. Much more serious is the possible shutdown of the Atlantic Conveyor, the huge figure-of-eight circulation of water round the North and South Atlantic Oceans, and the diversion of the Gulf Stream, which at the moment bathes the British Isles in warm tropical water and keeps British winters mild. The diversion of this water away from Britain (towards Portugal) could have catastrophic effects on the climate of Northern Europe, even launching an Ice Age in Britain. Ironically global warming could lead to a sudden regional cooling on a grand scale.

But some of the predictions that are commonly published in the media are based on completely false assumptions. More extreme weather has often been predicted. It is often said that there are more storms these days and that global warming will bring even more. Yet even the IPCC confirmed in 1996 that there is no evidence of any increase in extreme weather events in the twentieth century. In 2001, the IPCC modified this slightly by saying that there has been an increase in precipitation and in high-intensity rainstorms. Analyses of hurricanes and cyclones from the second half of the twentieth century actually show an overall slight decrease in sustained wind speeds, from 41 m/sec in 1945 to 38 m/sec in 1995.

There is overwhelming observational evidence that the weather conditions round the world have NOT become more severe, and yet the popular myth continues. One way the case for severer weather conditions has been argued up has been to cite the growing cost of storm damage. Global damage related to weather increased from around 2–5 billion US dollars in the 1960s to 30–100 billion in the 1990s. On the face of it this could be interpreted as showing that the weather became 20 times worse during that period. But the increase can be explained in other ways: by population increase, the great increase in settlement on low ground, and inflation. Bigger financial losses reflect greater wealth almost everywhere. When hurricane damage cost is adjusted for inflation, there is no overall pattern, apart from a decrease during the period 1960–2000, with the single exception of the high cost of one storm, Hurricane Andrew.

But does this mean that the case for global warming and its predicted intensification been exaggerated? The statistics are powerfully influential. One newspaper reported in February 2006 that 'a top climatologist', Michael Coughlan of the Australian Bureau of Meteorology, commented on NASA figures for 2005: *the world is now hotter than at any stage since prehistoric times*. The problem with this type of comment is that, although there may be general indications of prevailing temperatures on a century or millennium scale in the prehistoric past, there are no temperature measurements as such – there is no fine detail in the archaeological record on the scale that we as human beings experience or measure. Further on in the same newspaper report it emerged that this was based on CO_2 readings, which are 27 percent higher than the highest level recorded (in the rocks) for the last 650,000 years – but that presupposes that CO_2 controls temperature, so there is a catch in the reasoning. The case for CO_2 controlling temperature has not been proved, and therefore the argument that people (who are blamed for the current 'excessive' output of CO_2) are to blame for climate change has not been proved either. The reasoning is flawed.

Another part of the global warming story is the feedback effect. In other words, as it gets warmer, the world warms itself up. As it gets warmer, more water is evaporated into the atmosphere and water vapour is a greenhouse gas, a gas that traps heat. Another feedback effect is related to the area of the world under permanent snow and ice. Ice caps and glaciers reflect the sun's heat back into space, helping to keep the Earth cool. The warmer the atmosphere gets, the smaller the area of snow and ice becomes, and less heat is reflected back into space, so the Earth gets warmer – and so on. It is thought that the opposite feedback effect explains why the onset of ice ages is quite sudden. It may also explain why the ending of the last cold stage 10,000 years ago, which we must remember was an entirely natural event, was very abrupt.

The feedback effect is a very important part of the story, as it becomes, in itself, a warming factor, obscuring the effects of other factors. In February 2006, newspapers were running a major story that the planet had reached a point of no return, the 'tipping point'; climate change was unstoppable, irreversible. The *Independent* ran a front page declaring that a 'special investigation reveals that critical rise in world temperatures is now unavoidable.' This included some alarming statistics, including the idea that a 2 degree rise in global temperature (not above the present temperature but above the temperature in the pre-industrial era, before the Industrial Revolution of the eighteenth century) was unavoidable and that this would produce a wide range of serious environmental effects, including the extinction of polar bears, the loss of over half the Arctic tundra, and the killing of 97 percent of the coral reefs. The news story was fuelled in part by the publication of a new book by James Lovelock, in which he stated that it was too late to reverse global warming. The *Independent* commissioned some climatologists to check some of the data.

One problem is that the 2 degrees increase is being added to the pre-eighteenth century level, in other words 2 degrees warmer than the unusually cold period of the Little Ice Age. Once again, the statistics have been improved in order to make a more frightening scenario. The *Independent* story, by Michael McCarthy, the newspaper's Environment Editor, said that it is already 0.6 degrees warmer than the pre-eighteenth century reference point; in fact it is more like 1.0 degree warmer, which means only 1 more degree of warming, not the 2 implied on the front page.

Behind all this is the well-known greenhouse effect. It is the increasing amount of carbon dioxide and the other greenhouse gases in the atmosphere that is causing the warming, we are told. Man-made emissions of carbon dioxide started in a small way when people started making fires for cooking and heating, but took off in a big way with the start of the Industrial Revolution in about 1750 and has now reached a high level; 7 gigatonnes of carbon from carbon dioxide are released into the atmosphere every year. The additional carbon dioxide going into the atmosphere comes from power stations burning coal, oil and gas, from factories burning fossil fuels and from vehicles powered by fossil fuel. It must therefore be economic development starting with the Industrial Revolution that is to blame.

The Toronto Conference of 1980 led to the creation of the Intergovernmental Panel on Climate Change (IPCC), which was set up jointly by the World Meteorological Organization and the United Nations Environmental Programme. At the Rio Earth Summit in 1992 the IPCC made a devastating report to world's political leaders. Since then the IPCC has repeatedly developed the case for a man-made greenhouse effect underlying the increase in temperature during the twentieth century, each time with more frightening prognoses for the future. Other causes than greenhouse gas emissions have scarcely been mentioned in the press releases issued by the IPCC.

Although represented in the press as a scientific think tank, the IPCC has a very particular remit that is often overlooked. Its role is specifically 'to assess the scientific basis of the risk of human-induced climate change'. That is in reality a fairly narrow remit. It is not interested in exploring or highlighting any natural changes in climate. The IPCC has in effect been commissioned to make the case for the prosecution, and like any good lawyer it has downplayed any evidence that might benefit the defence. The result has been a stream of imposing-looking reports that mention what are called 'natural forcings' of the climate but give far more space to the dangers of man-made effects. The IPCC's major publication, *Climate Change 2001*, is representative in that it contains chapters on solar variations but gives huge emphasis to man-made greenhouse effect. It uses language that is dense with scientific terms and therefore unsuitable reading for journalists or the general public; what the journalists are given is a summary, which zooms straight in on man-made greenhouse effect.

The IPCC has become an evangelical organization, a think-tank with a mission to persuade governments to change their energy policies to something greener and entire populations to change their way of life. In fact some sceptics have likened the IPCC to an international political party, a kind of Global Green Party, intent on getting us all out of our cars and going to work on bicycles, and returning us to the world of windmills, sailing ships and ploughs drawn by teams of shire horses. But how far is a conspiracy involved? If carbon dioxide is increasing and cars and power stations are producing increasing amounts of carbon dioxide, then surely government strategies regarding power production need to change and so do the lifestyles of people in the More Economically Developed Countries (MEDCs)?

The most alarming aspect of all of this is that there is no evidence whatever that the steadily increasing amounts of carbon dioxide in the atmosphere have had anything at all to do with the temperature changes. It is true that temperature has increased during the twentieth century, but only overall, not consistently and not in every decade. In fact, something very interesting emerges when the temperature graph is extended back to around 1870. It can then be seen that there have been several temperature troughs, around 1885, 1905 and 1965, when it was significantly cooler, while carbon dioxide levels were rising either slowly or rapidly. There is, in short, no connection.

There is, on the other hand, a very close connection between the Earth's temperature and the heat received at ground level from the sun. This is referred to as total solar irradiance (TSI) and it is controlled by two things: the amount of energy arriving at the edge of the atmosphere from the sun and the amount of dust put into the atmosphere by volcanic eruptions. All the major temperature changes, on the decade scale, over the last 400 years are exactly paralleled by the TSI graph. This was discovered back in the 1970s, and more recent research has confirmed it. There are even graphs which show it in the IPCC report *Climate Change 2001*, but the text does not draw attention to them.

The sun itself seems to be the major factor; the dust veil index is a less important factor. Very big volcanic eruptions can produce enough dust to blot out the sun and reduce temperature. A model of temperature change using a combination of sunspots and volcanic activity is all that is needed to 'predict' the climate changes of the last 400 years, including the cold phase of the seventeenth century and the global warming of the twentieth century. A number of scientists have explored this theory, and been convinced by it, though their views do not see the light of day in the IPCC reports. In the IPCC's 1990 report it was actually admitted that the views of a minority of its writers 'could not be accommodated'.

It may all sound very academic, the dry and dusty stuff of university textbooks. But the issue matters a great deal, impacting as it does on nearly every aspect of our lives. If the warming is part of a natural process or complex of processes, we almost certainly cannot do anything about it, and there is little point in worrying about it. It also matters that the IPCC and the politicians who are riding on the IPCC's predictions are shaping policies round the belief that carbon dioxide is to blame.

The IPCC produces well-publicized reports at regular intervals, and the summary of each one is designed to scare the pants off everybody. In early 2006, it produced another report which headlined the news that a temperature rise of 1 degree C. could reduce the Greenland ice cap, a rise of 2 degrees could destroy the West Antarctic ice sheet, and a rise of 3 degrees could shut down the Gulf Stream. The warming currently predicted would raise sea level by 7 metres globally, inundating cities round the world (Sydney, Helsinki, Lagos, Bombay, Los Angeles, Rio de Janeiro and Norwich were specifically listed); what was not emphasized was that this would be the result of the whole of the Greenland ice sheet melting, yet that is not expected to happen within the next few centuries. So the newspaper headlines were once again cleverly captured by the IPCC, but by sleight of hand. If the Greenland ice sheet were to melt away completely, it would probably take 1000 years to happen, and only then would the low-lying cities be flooded.

This information was also presented as if it was the result of new research, whereas the same examples were published in earlier reports. The latest volume of doom prediction was graced with a foreword by the British prime minister, who declared that the risks were greater than ever thought. The prime minister has no known expert knowledge of this area, so presumably he was prompted by his Chief Scientific

Advisor, Sir David King, a chemist who advocates the building of a new generation of nuclear power stations.

The IPCC has quoted a figure of $5–6 billion as the total cost of defending property in the US as a result of a one metre rise in sea level. While the sum of money quoted may be true, the one metre of sea level rise is more than twice the sea level rise that is actually expected by 2100. Feeding the media exaggerated and misleading pseudo-information of this kind is little short of mischievous.

One scientist argued that atmospheric CO_2 needs to be set at 400ppm rather than the current UK government target of 550ppm, while another argued that fixed targets are pointless because it is really not known what a safe CO_2 level is. The UK government's conference on *Avoiding Dangerous Climate Change* held at the UK Met Office in 2005, and chaired by Dennis Tirpak (Head of the Climate Change Unit of the OECD in Paris), set the maximum of 400ppm for all the greenhouse gases combined as a safe upper limit if a further rise in temperature is to be averted. That 400ppm limit was based on a paper presented by Malte Meinhausen of the Swiss Federal Institute of Technology. The *Independent* newspaper interviewed an unnamed 'very senior scientist', who said 'I would think it's definitely over 400, probably about 420.' That prompted The *Independent* to ask Professor Keith Shine, Head of the Department of Meteorology at Reading University to calculate it precisely. Using the latest available figures (for 2004) he calculated greenhouse concentration had reached 425ppm. Of that 379ppm are CO_2 itself, 40ppm are methane, measured in CO_2 equivalent, and nitrous oxide another 6ppm. So, the tipping point the UK government warned us about has already been passed.

Some climatologists are reluctant to lump together the effects of all the greenhouse gases, because there is a further consideration to be taken into account – the effect of aerosols reducing the temperature. Dealing with CO_2 concentrations alone is simpler. Lumping together all the greenhouse gases may appear to give a fuller picture, but it may be misleading. Professor Shine admitted to being uncertain about the aerosol effect at the moment.

In 1992 the IPCC formulated 6 scenarios, which it gave the inscrutable names 'IS92a–f'. Scenario IS92a is the one most often quoted, the business-as-usual scenario, which is what the IPCC thinks will happen to the world if nothing is done to reduce greenhouse gas emissions. It is treated as a kind of benchmark, but some of its components have been wrongly calculated. One is the rate of population growth. If population seems irrelevant, it has to be remembered that people are supposed to be the generators of atmospheric warming by being burners of fossil fuel; the more people there are the more CO_2 will be produced – or so the simple logic of the IPCC goes. Their 'a' scenario assumes a world population of 8.4 billion in 2025, but the UN forecast suggests that it will be 8.0 billion. Scenario 'a' expects methane to go on increasing, which is odd as the growth rate for methane has been declining for some time and is currently zero. This miscalculation alone leads to an overestimation of warming by the year 2100 – an overestimation by over five percent. More worrying still is the fact that scenario IS92a assumes that CO_2 concentrations will go up at a rate of 0.64 percent per year from 1990 until 2100, but that is above the observed rate. In the 1980s atmospheric CO_2 increased by 0.47 percent per year. In the 1990s that rate actually fell to 0.43 percent per year, so there is no justification for setting the high growth rate of 0.64 percent. This may sound like nit-picking and playing with numbers in order to win an argument, but what sound like small discrepancies become greatly magnified by the compound interest effect across several decades. The higher growth rate pitched into the equation by the IPCC in scenario 'a' leads to a projected doubling of CO_2 in 109 years. By contrast, if we use the actual growth rates of the 1980s and 1990s, the CO_2 would not double for 154 years. This would obviously lead to a much slower rate of warming.

The rate of CO_2 growth has always been below 0.5 percent per year, yet none of the standard computer simulations use that as a ceiling figure; most use 1 percent, perhaps just for the sake of simplicity and convenience. Yet even the IPCC admits that 1 percent per year is 'on the high side'. It is in fact much worse than an oversimplification; it is a crude doubling of the measured rates of carbon dioxide growth, and it means that all the calculations that are based on it are going to lead to exaggerated scenarios. It leads to the doubling of atmospheric CO_2 in less than 70 years, whereas the observed rates suggest that it will take almost twice as long, actually doubling in 120 years. It is odd that modellers using sophisticated models and sophisticated computers appear to have settled for a simple round number to make the calculation easier, when their computers could as easily handle the true figure of 0.6 percent (for CO_2 and all the other greenhouse gases together). The IPCC has more recently developed forty different scenarios. The IPCC has explicitly abandoned the idea of predicting the future, and now speaks instead of 'possible futures'. One group of scientists within the IPCC has admitted that the scenarios are no more than attempts at computer-aided story-telling.

If industrialization is to blame, there should be a steady and uninterrupted increase in the carbon dioxide level in the atmosphere and a steady uninterrupted increase in global temperature. In fact, there have been episodes of cooling since the Industrial Revolution started. In fact, looking at the last 400 years, we can see that there have been several episodes of cooling: in the seventeenth century, around 1815, around 1885, around 1905 and around 1965. There was no de-industrialization at these times so there must be other processes in play. Something else must be causing global warming.

The long-term changes in temperature have been due to astronomical variations: the changing tilt of the Earth's axis, the circular movement of the Earth's poles of rotation, and changes in the shape of the Earth's orbit. These cyclical changes explain the pattern of glaciations and warm stages of the Ice Age. It is the short-term changes within the last 500 years that are of more concern to us, and they must be caused by some other variable.

Volcanic activity is one important variable. The large-scale nineteenth century eruptions of Tambora (1815) and Krakatoa (1883) produced huge amounts of ash and large-scale cooling. The Pinatubo eruption of 1990 was big by twentieth century standards, but not by long-term standards, and by no means as big as the Krakatoa eruption. The lack of big ash eruptions in the twentieth century has allowed the atmosphere to warm up. More important still are the variations in the sun, as we saw earlier. We think of the sun as having constant heat, but its radiation varies measurably. Records of sunspot numbers exist from the seventeenth century to the present day. The number of sunspots increases and decreases in an 11-year cycle. There are also 80-year and

180-year cycles. Each peak in the sunspot cycle is associated with warmer and wetter weather. In the twentieth century the peaks got gradually higher. In other words, the sun has become more active, drenching the Earth with more radiation, and could easily be the main cause of the warming.

The temperature trough lasting from 1885 into the 1890s was not due to any human effect – there was no de-industrialization. Instead it could have been caused by the ash veil from the Krakatoa eruption of 1883, or a shutdown of sunspot activity. Both happened and most likely the Earth cooled as a result of these two factors acting together. A model of global temperatures from 1600–2000 can be constructed, 'predicting' temperature from a combination of sunspot numbers and dust veil index. Excitingly, and bewilderingly, it replicates the actual global temperatures remarkably closely – including the otherwise very hard to explain temperature troughs of 1815, 1885, 1905 and 1965.

Many climate scientists, swept along by the carbon dioxide craze, and misled by the underlying (and apparently forgotten) remit of the IPCC, have dismissed solar weather as a cause because they do not see how there could be a cause and effect relationship between sunspots and Earth weather. But clearly there is! One recent study group admitted that 57 percent of the temperature variations were due to solar variations and that therefore less than half were due to greenhouse gases; on that basis it predicted a temperature increase of only 1.5 degrees C over the next 100 years, as compared to the IPCC's far more frightening 2–5 degrees. The greenhouse gases play a much smaller part than we have been led to believe.

The IPCC is manned by scientists who are quite capable of arriving at this conclusion, but because of the way the organization was set up they choose to emphasize carbon dioxide. When challenged about the other factors, they airily wave them aside as natural variables. But it is precisely these natural variables that lie behind the temperature variations of most of the last 400 years.

Is there some reason other than the organization's remit to explain why the IPCC seeks to play up the role of carbon dioxide? It may be partly explained by the growth of the green movement and the politicization of the environment. Before about 1980, both politicians and journalists in the West were fairly heedless of environmental destruction. Now there is something approaching a witch hunt. Michael Palin was recently heavily criticized in *The Times* for his air travel, which allegedly produced over 35 tonnes of carbon dioxide in the space of two years, 2003–5; making the TV series *Around the World in 80 Days* generated 24 tonnes, it was said, 12 times as much as the average car emits in a whole year.

Suddenly everything that happens has become our fault. A recent front page in a UK national newspaper ran the headline, *How Europe is choking itself – and the world*. A long list of serious problems followed, problems that need to be addressed, but they were all tagged to the concept of man-made global warming. Many of the problems can be tackled and ameliorated individually, regardless of what is causing them. Flooding has become a more and more serious problem in European river floodplains, but it can be addressed by identifying the areas most at risk from flooding and ensuring that they are not developed for housing. Some of the areas are lower-risk – likely to be covered by a shallow sheet of water once in 5 or 10 years – and planning authorities could easily insist that any residential or commercial properties built on them must be raised 1m from the ground, either on piers or on under-storeys used for utilities such as stores or garages. One of the reasons why river floods have become so serious in Europe is the process of urban expansion. Many towns began, historically, as small settlements on valley sides; they have expanded sideways and down onto neighbouring floodplains.

The IPCC has made it its business to emphasize that people are to blame for such problems by warming up the atmosphere. An initial report draft in early 2000 read 'the balance of evidence suggests that there is a discernible human influence on global climate'. In April 2000, after discussion among IPCC members, the text was altered to 'there has been a discernible human influence on global climate'. This is a very significant firming-up compared with the initial rather cautious comment. By October 2000, it had been changed again, to 'It is likely that increasing concentrations of anthro-pological greenhouse gases have contributed substantially to the observed warming over the last 50 years.' In the official summary, that statement was further toughened up: 'most of the observed warming over the last 50 years is likely to have been due to the increase in greenhouse gas concentration.' And that is a far cry from the initial 'finding', if indeed it could ever have been called that. The spokesman for the UN Environment Project, Tim Higham, said 'There is no new science, but the scientists wanted to present a clear and strong message to policy makers.'

So, it has been admitted that the IPCC has political intentions. It seeks to make politicians make particular decisions. It does this by producing periodic reports that appear to contain scientific findings, and indeed do contain an impressive mixture of old and new observational data, and then adding very carefully worded polemical epilogues that are designed to push policy-makers in a particular direction. The IPCC is not, as the newspapers like to present it, a panel of objective scientists, but a band of eco-warriors committed to the cause of saving the world, bent on forcing world-wide political change. The IPCC wants to change individual lifestyles everywhere, restraining consumption, and steering people towards more sustainable lifestyles and it has so far been clever at manipulating the media to publish its views very effectively.

Some might argue that it doesn't really matter what is causing global warming; that we need to concentrate on learning how to live with it. But it does matter. If global warming is caused by people (in particular, by power stations, factories and vehicles), then industrialization in countries currently undergoing rapid economic development is almost certain to produce further warming. Political debates and disagreements then revolve round the ethics of unrestrained growth, and the right of states to make their own decisions about the way they choose to develop. How ethical is it for countries that have already undergone development, like Britain, to try to put restraints on the way other countries, like China, develop? Moreover, if the greenhouse effect is man-made, if we are causing global warming, we could change our behaviour to rectify the situation, as many environmentalists and politicians want – and obviously it would be sensible for us to change our behaviour rather than risk destroying the planet. But if we are not causing global warming, then we should resist the political and social measures that are being pressed on us. If the temperature is rising for some reason other than carbon dioxide emissions, then stringent and expensive measures to reduce them are intrusive and irrelevant and we should certainly question the need for them – and we should oppose them.

If people are *not* causing global warming *none* of the following are necessary:

- the EU targets for cutting greenhouse gas emissions set for member countries
- the Kyoto Protocol
- the hugely expensive series of summit meetings about carbon emissions
- the movements to penalize car users with heavy fuel tax
- congestion charges in cities
- prohibitive parking charges in towns and cities
- moves to penalize air travellers with airport taxes
- the campaign for a new generation of nuclear power stations.

If global warming is not the great environmental conspiracy of our time, then it looks very much like it. The way scientific evidence and arguments are crafted to produce a particular outcome has all the hallmarks of a conspiracy, one that has conditioned the great majority of people to accept that man-made increases in carbon dioxide are warming the planet. The conspiracy is successfully preoccupying politicians and ordinary people across the world in much the same way that the Cold War and the fear of a nuclear war gripped them in the 1960s. The Cold War turned out to be based on a delusion, and it may be that atmospheric carbon dioxide will in time be seen to be as harmless as the Russian Bear.

Why are the IPCC and its supporters so determined to promote a simple 'we are to blame' explanation? Why is the role of solar weather constantly downplayed? And why are politicians in nearly every country going along with the International Panel for Climate Change's doctrine? It is partly the organizational remit. It may be accentuated by a simple bandwagon effect, like the witch-hunts of the seventeenth century. Some of those leading the witch-hunt are eco-warriors who were themselves educated and conditioned back in the 1970s and 1980s, during the campaigns to save the rain forests and the whales. And the politicians who fall in with them are of two persuasions. Some are simply moral weaklings, people who see what looks like being a great crusade as a fast track to personal advancement. Others are unscrupulously using the carbon dioxide ticket to justify tax, transport and energy policies. One thing is certain: we do not have to live in the climate of fear that has been whipped up.

FAILED ASSASSINATIONS

THE GUNPOWDER PLOT

1605

IN 1603 ELIZABETH I, queen of England, died and was
succeeded by James I, the Scottish king. Since he was tolerant
towards Catholics in his own kingdom and the son of the
Catholic Mary Queen of Scots, it was hoped that he would be
more tolerant of English Catholics, who had suffered a
significant level of persecution under his predecessor.
Unfortunately he was not more tolerant, and several young
Catholics, led by Robert Catesby (son of Sir William Catesby,
a prominent leader in the Catholic community), decided that
violent and extreme action was the only solution. They
devised a very ambitious plan to blow up the Houses of
Parliament killing the king and possibly the prince of Wales,
as well as most of the members of parliament, in the belief
that they would be replaced by an entirely new political elite
who would be more sympathetic to the Catholic cause – and
if possible a new, and Catholic, monarch. The plan was also
to kidnap the surviving royal children, to stop any of them
being installed as a replacement Stuart monarch, and launch
an insurrection in the Midlands. This incredible, doomed,
scheme was hatched in 1605.

One of the core conspirators was Thomas Percy, the man
who is believed to have thought of the idea of murdering
King James. It was Percy who hired the house next door to
parliament, where the barrels of gunpowder were planted.

Thomas Percy was the brother-in-law of another conspirator, Jack Wright, and the father-in-law of Robert Catesby, the leader of the conspirators. The conspirators first hired lodgings which were adjacent to Parliament House, and began digging a tunnel that they hoped would take them directly under their target. Some modern theorists claim that the authenticity of the tunnel story is dubious, and the brief mention of it in the plotters' confessions throws little light on the issue. It was said at the time that the uncompleted tunnel became unusable due to the high water table; it simply filled with water leaking in from the Thames. It was also said that the massively thick walls of the parliament house blocked progress. The tunnel was abandoned. Instead, a cellar was soon acquired by Thomas Percy within the parliament buildings, just under the House of Lords. In this cellar the conspirators placed 36 barrels (almost 2 tons) of gunpowder which were carefully hidden by billets of wood and pieces of iron.

On 26 October William Parker, 4th baron Monteagle, received an anonymous letter warning him not to attend the Opening of Parliament on 5 November. Many believe that this letter was written by Francis Tresham, who was one of the 13 conspirators – a late joiner – and also Lord Monteagle's brother-in-law, but it has never been proved that he was the author. The conspirators were at first alarmed that their plot had been discovered but the information received by them over the following days convinced Catesby that it was safe to continue with their plans; Fawkes had revisited the cellar and found that nothing had been touched.

In the early hours of 5 November the authorities, in the shape of a troop of armed men led by Thomas Knyvet, a Justice of the Peace, stormed the cellar and found Guido

Fawkes there, lantern in hand, with the 36 barrels of gunpowder. Fawkes had been caught red-handed. He initially gave his name as John Johnson, was immediately arrested and subsequently held prisoner in the Tower of London, where he was tortured to reveal the names of his co-conspirators. When the remaining conspirators heard about Guido (or Guy) Fawkes's capture they fled London for the Midlands, with the exception of Francis Tresham who for some reason chose to stay in the capital.

In spite of the late hour, Fawkes was taken straight to the king to explain himself; it was one o'clock in the morning and the king was in his bedchamber. Fawkes was incredibly bold and defiant, admitting openly that his intention was to kill the king. He looked at the Scottish courtiers surrounding James and added that he wanted to blow the Scots back into Scotland. After that, Fawkes was taken away for the first of a series of interrogations. Torture was illegal in England at that time, but still permissible at the express orders of the king. The king, not unnaturally in the circumstances, was content to see Fawkes suffer, and he was keen to know the extent of the conspiracy. The king wrote his instructions accordingly: 'The gentler tortours are to be first used unto him, *et sic per gradus ad maiora tenditur* [and from there by stages to the greatest], and so God speed your goode worke.' By 9 November, after enduring long hours of torture, Fawkes revealed the names of the other conspirators and the full extent of the conspiracy.

At Holbeche, the conspirators did what they could to prepare the house, which was unmoated and not fortified in any way, for a siege. They told those not willing to make a stand that they should escape as best they could. During the flight from Warwick Castle by way of Hewell Grange (the home of Lord Windsor), where apparently they stole weapons and munitions, their store of gunpowder got wet in the pouring rain. In desperation the conspirators laid the powder out on the hearth in front of a fireplace to dry. A stray spark landing in the gunpowder caused a sudden explosion that blinded John Grant and slightly injured Robert Catesby, Ambrose Rookwood and Henry Morgan. It was an accident that was full of irony, and it demoralized them completely. When Thomas Wintour asked his co-conspirators what they intended to do, they said simply, 'We mean here to die.'

Stephen Littleton and Thomas Wintour went off to Pepperhill, the Shropshire home of Sir John Talbot, 10 miles away, in the hope of rallying more support. Sir John sent them away with a flea in their ear, saying that it was more than his life was worth to help them, which confirmed the low expectations of Robert Wintour who had said that it was utterly pointless to go for help to Sir John.

By eleven o'clock the following morning, Walsh's men had surrounded the house. Thomas Wintour, Jack Wright, Kit Wright and Ambrose Rookwood were shot in the courtyard outside Holbeche, perhaps while attempting to put out a fire that Walsh and his men had started in an attempt to flush the conspirators out into the open. The two Wrights were wounded and dying, but Thomas Wintour managed to make it back to the house, where he found that Robert Catesby and Thomas Percy were the only defenders left who were not incapacitated by their injuries.

Catesby said, 'Stand by me, Mr Tom, and we will die together.'

The three men stood close inside the front door of the

house, before going outside to face their death. Catesby and Percy, standing side by side, were shot down simultaneously. Robert Catesby managed to crawl back inside the house; he found a picture of the Virgin Mary and clutched it to him until he died. The soldiers rushed into the house and captured Wintour. Those present at the siege said later that the soldiers' behaviour was unconducive to the survival of those who lay dying; with medical help, they might have survived.

The front of Holbeche House is still exactly as it was at the time of the siege. The front door from which the conspirators made their last, suicidal dash into the musket fire is still there. The front wall of the house is still pitted with the musket holes from the bullets fired in the Gunpowder Plot siege. Some of the musket holes are beside upstairs windows, showing that those defending the house were trying to gain a height advantage over their attackers.

A tunnel leads from the dining room. Surprisingly no mention was ever made of this possible escape route at the time, though it must have existed in 1605. The tunnel has yet to be explored, and it is not known where it leads, but presumably to a neighbouring property. Perhaps this was the route that many of the associates of the conspirators used to escape. Those who stayed for the shoot-out must have made a conscious decision to stay and die quickly, rather than escape, be captured and then die slowly and terribly.

Most of the conspirators were either killed or arrested at Holbeche House on 8 November; Francis Tresham was arrested on 12 November; Robert Wintour was captured two months later. All the survivors ended up in the Tower of London. They were tried for high treason in Westminster Hall on 27 January, 1606 and all were convicted and sentenced to death. The executions took place in the Old Palace Yard at Westminster, symbolically in front of the building the conspirators had hoped to destroy, on 30 and 31 January, Fawkes being executed on the second day. All the conspirators were hanged, drawn and quartered, the customary method of execution for traitors. Their heads and other body parts were displayed at various places round London and Westminster.

The actual cellar where the gunpowder was stored was destroyed in the great fire of 1834, but parts of its fabric are on display at Sir John Soane's Museum in Westminster. The lantern Guy Fawkes was carrying when he was arrested is in the Ashmolean Museum in Oxford.

That summarizes the widely accepted traditional version of the Gunpowder Plot. An alternative possibility, which was claimed by many Catholics at the time, is that the conspirators were framed by Robert Cecil, the earl of Salisbury. Cecil deeply distrusted Catholics and wanted to prove that they were working against the good of the country. Cecil is quoted as saying, 'We cannot hope to have good government while large numbers of people [ie Catholics] go around obeying foreign rulers [ie the Pope].' He believed that their split loyalty made them unreliable subjects.

Francis Tresham was an agent working for Cecil. Tresham was the cousin of Lord Monteagle, and it was Tresham who sent Monteagle the note warning him of the imminent attack. Lord Monteagle received the warning letter at night. This in itself might not seem significant, but it seems that the night in question was the *only* night that year when he stayed at home. This suggests that he was expecting the letter. Some researchers have suggested that he was to some extent involved in the plot and that he himself wrote the letter, in effect turning king's evidence.

Whoever wrote the Monteagle letter, Monteagle certainly showed it to Cecil and this formal exposure resulted in the arrest of Guy Fawkes, who had been assigned to guard the gunpowder and who became history's scapegoat for the Gunpowder Plot. The cellar where the gunpowder was stored was rented to the conspirators by a close friend of Robert Cecil, which suggests, though does not prove, that Cecil and his associates were colluding with the conspirators. Perhaps Cecil was concerned when he heard from his spies that the Plot was grinding to a halt because of difficulties with the tunnel, and he decided to egg the plotters on by making the cellar available to them.

Although the other conspirators were either killed on arrest or imprisoned and executed, Francis Tresham fell sick and died shortly after arrest. Did he sense that his spymaster, Cecil, was going to betray him and perhaps take poison to escape the pain and ignominy of hanging, drawing and quartering? Or was he perhaps 'removed' at Cecil's orders, so that he could never reveal to anyone that the great plot to kill the king was really Cecil's?

It seems likely to me that the Catholic plot to kill the king was real, but that when Cecil found out about it, probably fairly early on, he allowed it come very close to fruition in order to extract the maximum propaganda value out of it. The capture of Guy Fawkes was a piece of theatre, Cecil's last-minute 'rescue' of king and parliament to prove how dangerous the Catholics were – and how indispensable he was.

In fact, the store of gunpowder was no small matter. Recent research has shown that if it had been ignited, it would have caused enormous damage. If the 1605 Gunpowder Plot to destroy the English parliament and kill the king had succeeded, it would have not only have destroyed the parliament chamber but taken a large part of central London with it. Fawkes was a gunpowder expert, having used explosives while serving in the Spanish army during their occupation of the Netherlands; he was much more than a nightwatchman. The explosion would have destroyed Westminster Abbey and undermined buildings as far away as Whitehall, the site of Downing Street today. Severe structural damage would have been sustained by buildings up to half a kilometre away. Because the cellar walls were solid masonry, and the gunpowder was packed into barrels, the full force of the blast would have been directed upwards, as Fawkes intended – into the chamber where the king and parliament were to assemble. There is no doubt that everybody in the chamber would have died.

If the letter to Monteagle was a genuine tip-off not to attend the State Opening of Parliament, and the gunpowder had been ignited as planned, then the personal warning would indeed have saved his life. The effect on the power structure in Britain would have been far-reaching and profoundly changed the course of British history. With the king, the prince of Wales and most of the English aristocracy dead, a very differently-composed elite would have taken its place and the history of the seventeenth century would have unfolded in a different way. As it was, the failed Gunpowder Plot had a spectacularly adverse effect on English Catholics. They were seen as dangerous subversives, and the cause of Catholic emancipation was set back by many decades.

POPE JOHN PAUL II

1981

IN MAY 1981 Pope John Paul II was shot at while being driven in a white open-topped jeep through a crowd of 20,000 people after his weekly public audience in St Peter's Square. The Pope was hit by four bullets, two of which lodged in his intestines. He was hit in the abdomen, left hand and right arm, but the bullets missed any vital organs and doctors were able to save his life.

He was incredibly lucky to survive this violent and murderous attack, which was clearly intended to kill him.

At first the gunman, Mehmet Ali Ağca, claimed to be a member of the Marxist Popular Front for the Liberation of Palestine but that cover story was quickly blown apart when that organization denied any knowledge of him. Later he said that in Sofia, he was once approached by the Bulgarian Secret Service and Turkish mafiosi, who offered him three million German Marks to assassinate the Pope. The Bulgarian Secret Service was allegedly instructed by the KGB to assassinate the Pope because of his support of Poland's Solidarity movement. That seemed more credible, but Ağca gave many conflicting statements on the assassination. Attorney Antonio Marini said: 'Ağca has manipulated all of us, telling hundreds of lies, continually changing versions, forcing us to open tens of different investigations.'

Ağca described himself as a mercenary with no political orientation, although he is known to have been a member of the Turkish ultra-nationalist Grey Wolves organization. As a youth, he was a petty criminal and a member of street gangs in his home town, later becoming a smuggler between Turkey and Bulgaria. He is believed to have gone to Syria for a two-month course in weaponry and terrorist tactics. He claims this was undertaken as a member of the Popular Front for the Liberation of Palestine and paid for by the Bulgarian government, although it is not known if this is true.

After the terrorist training he worked for the far-right Turkish Grey Wolves, who were at the time destabilizing Turkey; this led to a military coup in 1980. It is not known whether the ultra-nationalist Grey Wolves were being used by the Bulgarian Secret Service or the CIA. On 1 February 1979 in Istanbul, acting under orders from the Grey Wolves, he murdered Abdi Ipekci, the editor of the moderate left-wing newspaper *Milliyet*. He was caught thanks to the evidence of an informer, tried, convicted and sentenced to life imprisonment. After serving only six months of this sentence, he escaped from an Istanbul military prison and fled to Bulgaria.

According to investigating journalists, Mehmet Ali Ağca collaborated with Abdullah Catli, second-in-command in the Grey Wolves, on the 1979 assassination of Abdi Ipekci in Istanbul, and it was Catli who then helped to organize Ağca's escape from prison. Some think that Abdullah Catli may have been implicated in the attempt on the Pope's life too. According to Reuters, Ağca 'escaped with suspected help from sympathizers in the security services'. Journalists noted that at the scene of the Mercedes crash in which Abdullah Catli died, his body was found with a passport under the name of 'Mehmet Özbay', which was an alias that was also used by Mehmet Ali Ağca. It looks very much as if the two men were working closely together on assignments, possibly even swapping identities with each other.

Starting in August 1980, Ağca began to zig-zag across southern Europe, swapping passports and identities as he travelled. His motive seems to have been to conceal the fact that he had come from Bulgaria. He entered Rome on 10 May 1981, arriving by train from Milan. Ağca says that he met three accomplices in Rome, two Bulgarians and a Turk; the operation was to be commanded by Zilo Vassilev, the Bulgarian military attaché in Italy. Writers contributing to *Le Monde diplomatique* allege that the assassination attempt was organized by Abdullah Catli, for the sum of three million marks, which was paid to the Grey Wolves.

The plan was for Ağca and a second gunman called Oral Çelik to shoot the Pope in St Peter's Square. A small explosion would generate general panic and confusion in the crowd gathered in the square to see the Pope, enabling them to escape to the Bulgarian embassy. When the day arrived, 13 May, they sat in the square, harmlessly writing postcards as they waited for the Pope to appear. As the Pope slowly passed close to him, Ağca managed to fire three shots before he was then grabbed by surrounding spectators and stopped from firing any more, which could well have proved fatal. They also prevented him from escaping. Çelik seems to have lost his nerve; he panicked and left the square without firing at the Pope or setting off his bomb.

All of that emerged much later, but even at the time it seemed likely that Ağca was a hitman hired by Bulgarians. In his boarding house close to the Vatican Ağca left a letter, in which he wrote that he wanted 'to demonstrate to the world the imperialistic crimes of the Soviet Union and the United States'. Whatever view one takes of Pope John Paul and his enormous influence on people and events, it is hard to see how he could have been held responsible for any crimes perpetrated by the Great Powers. It was a very peculiar reason to give for killing him and some other motive must really have lain behind Ağca's assassination attempt.

The Turkish authorities had warned Interpol about Ağca, but he had slipped into Italy disguised as a student after escaping from a Turkish prison where he was being held on murder charges. Ağca was captured immediately after the shooting in St Peter's Square. A photograph taken by a spectator clearly showed Ağca holding the gun above his head and pointing it at the Pope, perhaps a fraction of a second before he fired. There was never any doubt that he was the assassin.

After he recovered from the shooting, Pope John Paul II asked people to 'pray for my brother (Ağca), whom I have sincerely forgiven'. In 1983, the Pope asked to meet Ağca; the two men met and spoke in private in the prison where Ağca was being held. The Pope also got in touch with Ağca's family, meeting his mother and brother. In February 2005, during the Pope's final illness, Ağca sent the Pope a letter to wish him well but also warning him that the world would end soon. When the Pope died, about a month later, Ağca's brother gave an interview, saying that Mehmet Ali Ağca and his family were saddened by the Pope's death. Apparently Ağca requested leave to attend the Pope's funeral, but the Turkish authorities rejected his request.

Almost immediately after the attack in St Peter's Square Vatican officials quietly advanced the theory that it was the Soviet Union who had authorized the assassination attempt. There was speculation that Bulgarian secret service agents had hired Ağca's services on behalf of the Soviet Union. The motive was assumed to be the growing democratic movement that was gaining momentum in Pope John Paul's native Poland at the time and was openly and strongly supported by the Pope himself. That development in Poland was rightly seen as a serious threat to the stability of Communism in Eastern Europe, and would in due course lead to the dramatic fall of Communism in Eastern Europe and even more spectacularly to the collapse of the Soviet Union. Seen in this way, even though he was primarily a spiritual leader, Pope John Paul was a natural target for a political assassination. His political influence was enormous.

At the time of the shooting, there was no evidence whatever that Ağca had not acted alone. Italian investigators nevertheless uncovered evidence of ties between Ağca and Bulgarian agents. Some observers felt that Ağca's story about a Bulgarian connection was doubtful, pointing out that Ağca did not mention it until he had been kept in solitary confinement and visited by Italian Military Intelligence agents.

Not long after the shooting, Sergei Antonov, a Bulgarian working in Rome, was arrested on the strength of what Ağca had said; he was accused of being the Bulgarian agent who masterminded the plot. In 1986, after a protracted trial, he was found not guilty. The evidence Ağca gave was often contradictory and included the wild claim that he was Jesus Christ; under these conditions a conviction was unlikely. The Bulgarian connection had begun to fall apart by September 1991, when a former CIA analyst revealed that his colleagues, following orders from above, had falsified their analysis in order to support the accusation of a Bulgarian connection. He declared that the CIA after all had no proof concerning the alleged Bulgarian connection.

The Pope's contribution to the investigation was quite extra-ordinary. In addition to befriending his would-be assassin, he issued, or rather half-issued, a remarkable utterance about the event in St Peter's Square. It was on 26 June 2000 that Pope John Paul II released the 'Third Secret of Fatima'; he claimed that Ağca's assassination attempt was the fulfilment of this Third Secret of Fatima. The church did not fully disclose the contents of this Secret, believing that it was too momentous, that it actually predicted the end of the world. While in prison on remand, Ağca was widely reported to have developed an obsession with Fatima; during the trial he claimed that he was the second Messiah, a new Jesus Christ, and called on the Vatican to release the details of the Third Secret. This was a very long way from the Bulgarian connection.

Then, out of the blue in March 2005, it was reported in two Italian newspapers, *Corriere della Sera* and *il Giornale*, that files belonging to the old East German secret service had been found. It was said that they contained documents confirming that the Soviet Union had ordered the attempt on the life of Pope John Paul II. The files from the Stasi, the East German spy agency, confirmed the suspicions long held by Vatican officials. Documents in the newly opened files showed that the KGB ordered the assassination attempt which was as suspected at the time carried out by the Bulgarian secret service. Dimitar Tzonev, a spokesman for the Bulgarian government, said that officials in Sofia were prepared to hand over their secret service archives to the Italian commission charged with the task of investigating the attempted assassination of the Pope. An Italian parliamentary commission was also to carry out an investigation of KGB recruitment in Italy.

Corriere della Sera reported that the KGB gave the order to assassinate John Paul II, and Bulgarian agents recruited Ağca to carry it out. It was a classic three-layered conspiracy, with a small team of assassins, a Bulgarian organization behind them and, carefully distancing itself from the operation, the Soviet KGB who commissioned the murder. The report confirmed a theory unusually advanced by the victim, the Pope himself, in his book *Memory and Identity*. John Paul wrote that he was convinced Ağca was not acting on his own initiative: 'someone else planned and commanded it.' But until 2005 there was no conclusive proof of Soviet involvement.

Mehmet Ali Ağca served 19 years of a life sentence in Italian prisons for his brutal, near-fatal attack on the Pope. In June 2000 he was pardoned by the Italian President Carlo Azeglio Ciampi and handed over to prison officials in his native Turkey, where he resumed the sentence he had received for the murder of Abdi Ipekci and two bank raids carried out in the 1970s. Before escaping to attack the Pope, Ağca had served only 6 months of his 'life' sentence, which under Turkish law is reckoned to be 36 years. He made a plea for early release in November 2004, on the grounds that he had spent nearly 20 years in an Italian prison, but a Turkish court announced that he would not be eligible for release until 2010. However, he was released on parole based on good behaviour on 12 January, 2006, only to have his parole revoked shortly afterwards. The Turkish Supreme Court ruled that his time served in Italy could not be deducted from his Turkish sentence and he was returned to jail. The former Minister of Justice, Hikmet Sami Turk, who was in post at the time of Ağca's extradition, said that in his view setting Ağca free was at best a 'serious mistake', and that he should not be freed before 2012.

An unexpected additional Turkish connection appeared

when the Kurdish separatist leader, Abdullah Ocalan, said while under house arrest in Italy that he was prepared to testify about the attempt to kill the Pope in 1981. He also had things to say about the unresolved murder of the Swedish Prime Minister, Olof Palme. In an interview Ocalan accused the then Turkish military government of colluding in the assassinations. He said he had no proof who carried out the attacks but wanted to talk to the investigators about the situation in Turkey after the 1980 military coup. He claimed that many dangerous people were released from prison to carry out 'special tasks'. They included Mehmet Ali Ağca. It is difficult to evaluate Abdullah Ocalan's intervention in the case, but it may not be unconnected with the growing diplomatic crisis between Italy and Turkey as Turkey tried to get Ocalan extradited to Turkey on terrorism charges. The German authorities also issued warrants for Ocalan's arrest. Under Italian law Ocalan could not be extradited to Turkey because the death penalty was in force there, and the German government decided not to press for his extradition for fear of upsetting the large Turkish and Kurdish population in Germany.

It now seems unlikely that the full extent of the conspiracy behind the attempted assassination of Pope John Paul will ever be known. It is sobering to see a near-assassination that, at first, looked very much like a classic lone gunman assassination. Subsequent events show that it was nothing of the kind, but Mehmet Ali Ağca, the lone gunman who was photographed shooting the Pope, worked hard and effectively to confuse his interrogators, and the full extent of the web of conspirators is now very hard to trace.

MARGARET THATCHER

1984

IF APRIL IS the cruellest month, October is the conference month – in the world of British party politics. The week of 8–12 October in 1984 was booked for the Conservative Party Conference in Brighton. The prime minister, her cabinet ministers and many of her political staff stayed at the Grand Hotel on the seafront. In the customary way, the final, climactic day of the conference was to be dominated by a speech from the party leader and Prime Minister, Mrs Margaret Thatcher. In the middle of the night of 11–12 October, she was working late in her hotel room putting the finishing touches to her speech.

Not long after 2.35 a.m., she was called on by her Principal Private Secretary, Sir Robin Butler, who wanted her to cast her eye over another paper. A few moments later, at 2.40 a.m., as Mrs Thatcher sat down in an armchair with her back to the window, a bomb exploded with devastating effect in another room in the hotel.

Eyewitnesses who saw the explosion saw a piercing flash lighting up the seafront. That initial flash triggered a chain of destruction. Masonry was flung out into the road, tearing the heads off parking meters and shattering a seafront shelter on the promenade. Seriously weakened by the explosion, a whole column of the Grand Hotel's structure collapsed together with a tall strip of the facade. A huge chimney stack on the hotel roof fell, crashing down through ceilings and floors, taking with it sleeping politicians and their partners and plunging them down, floor after floor, towards the foyer and basement. In the vertical section of the building that was affected, the devastation was almost total. Many people were trapped in a mountain of wreckage, while others, lucky to escape, staggered bewildered out into the street.

The prime minister's bathroom was extensively damaged barely two minutes after she had left it, but she and her husband Denis miraculously escaped completely unhurt. Thatcher changed her clothes and was then escorted by the security guards to Brighton police station. She and Denis were taken to Lewes, where they stayed for the rest of the night. As she left the hotel she was composed enough to give a brief informal statement to John Cole of the BBC. Margaret Thatcher had been the principal target in the bombing, yet she had escaped uninjured. Many others were less lucky. The Conservative Chief Whip, John Wakeham, found himself trapped in the darkness under tons of rubble. He asked his rescuers, 'Keep talking to me. Keep me alive.' His wife was dead. The Trade and Industry Secretary, Norman Tebbit, was also trapped in the rubble for a time. Eventually he was pulled out with only minor injuries. His wife Margaret was left permanently disabled.

In total, five people lost their lives in the explosion and over 30 were left injured. The bombs failed to kill Margaret Thatcher or any of her ministers. They did however kill Conservative MP Sir Anthony Berry and John Wakeham's first wife Roberta. Sir Donald Maclean was in his room with his wife, Muriel, when the bomb exploded; she was killed in the explosion and Sir Donald seriously injured. The other victims killed by the blast were Eric Taylor and Jeanne Shattock. Given the scale of the explosion and the extent and severity of the damage it was surprising that more people had not died.

The following day at 9.30 a.m. as scheduled, and in characteristically combative form, Mrs Thatcher made her conference speech undeterred, without knowing the number of dead and wounded. She understandably omitted most of the planned attacks on the Labour Party from her speech, as a far greater adversary had made itself felt. She said the bombing was 'an attempt to cripple Her Majesty's democratically elected Government. That is the scale of the outrage in which we have all shared, and the fact that we are gathered here now – shocked, but composed and determined – is a sign not only that this attack has failed, but that all attempts to destroy democracy by terrorism will fail . . . This government will not weaken; this nation will meet the challenge; democracy will prevail.'

It was assumed immediately and by everyone that the IRA had planted the bomb as part of its terror campaign to get the British out of Ireland. It did indeed turn out to be an IRA attack. The IRA claimed responsibility the following day and said that they would try again. Their statement included the words, 'Today we were unlucky, but remember we only have to be lucky once. You will have to be lucky always.'

The plot to bomb the Grand Hotel had been designed some three years before as an act of revenge for the hard-line stance Mrs Thatcher had taken over the death of Bobby Sands and other IRA hunger strikers who were fighting for political status in prison. The man who was assigned to carry out this particular crime, which was no less than an attempt to assassinate the British prime minister and as many of her cabinet colleagues as possible, was Patrick Magee.

Patrick Magee was born in Belfast but spent his boyhood in England. At the age of 18 he returned to Belfast, lured there by the conflict and by the chance to fight. He soon became involved with the Provisional IRA and bombing became his speciality. He made the unlikely claim that he was a pacifist before he joined the IRA. Despite his commitment to the IRA cause he has, he now says, always struggled with the consequences of his violent actions; 'I have to grapple with the fact that that I've hurt human beings.' Nevertheless, his early taste for violence was soon noticed in the IRA and by the height of the troubles in the 1970s, he had become the IRA's Chief Explosives Officer.

In 1973, he was sentenced to two years imprisonment after admitting to being a member of the IRA. He served his time at the Maze Prison. Another prisoner who was in the Maze at the same time as Magee recalled: 'His whole aim in life was to get the Brits out of Ireland.' Magee carried out successful bombings in Northern Ireland. After that, it is believed that he was sent to London where he was to form an IRA splinter cell. With his English upbringing, technical skill and loyalty to the IRA cause, he made a good undercover agent for the IRA on the mainland of Britain. Before long he was making his mark in England.

There were attempts to blow up a tank of aviation fuel at Canvey Island and a gas holder at Greenwich. Both of these crimes were linked to Magee. But somehow he avoided being captured by the police, escaping to Amsterdam and Dublin, and then returning to south-east England to plan the IRA's most outrageous attack: the attempted assassination of the entire British cabinet. It was, in its way, as wild an idea as the Gunpowder Plot, except that this time the gunpowder went off.

After they had sifted through tons of rubble from the Grand Hotel, police forensic experts were able to identify exactly which type of bomb had been used and which type of timing device too. It was possible to determine the date when the bomb had been primed and placed behind the bath panel in one of the bedrooms – room 629. As a piece of police forensic work, it was a masterpiece. Within just two months from the explosion, the police had identified Magee as their main suspect.

Undercover work by the police confirmed that Magee had gone back to Holland. They were also able to build up a detailed picture of Magee's friends and associates. The investigations were nevertheless slowed down by the use of a lot of false names and documents which muddied the trail.

It was above all the skill of the forensic scientists at Scotland Yard's laboratory in Lambeth that led to the conviction of Magee as the man who bombed the Grand Hotel in Brighton. David Tadd, a fingerprint expert with 18 years' experience, managed to identify a palm print and a fingerprint extracted from a registration card for room 629. They belonged to a man going under the name 'Roy Walsh'. The same prints were found at the Rubens Hotel in London, where another bomb was discovered and successfully defused. These prints from the Rubens Hotel and the registration card for room 629 at the Grand matched those that had been taken from Magee when he had been stopped for a driving offence as a teenager many years before. Magee had stayed in the hotel under the false name of Roy Walsh three weeks prior to the conference and planted the bomb, with a long-delay timer, in his room, number 629.

Magee was arrested on his return to the UK. A team of armed police descended on the flat in Glasgow that he was using as the headquarters of his terrorist operation. The police found a stockpile of bombs, weapons and timers nearby.

Magee was tried and the forensic evidence was strong enough to secure a conviction. He was the mastermind behind the IRA's most daring attack on the British establishment. It was really only by chance that Margaret and Denis Thatcher and Norman Tebbit and a lot of other people had not been killed in the blast. In September 1986 Magee was given eight life sentences at the Old Bailey and should therefore have spent the rest of his life in prison. The judge, Justice Boreham, called Magee a man of exceptional cruelty and inhumanity and said that he must serve at least 35 years behind bars. In response to this, Magee, now with nothing to lose, lifted his clenched fist and shouted in Gaelic the Irish Republican slogan 'Tiochfaidh ar La' – *our day will come*.

And he was right. Magee was to serve only 14 years of his 35-year sentence, because he was granted early release under the terms of the 1998 Good Friday Peace Accord. During his prison term he married an American woman and completed a doctoral thesis on fiction related to the conflict. The early release of Magee caused widespread revulsion across the UK. A spokesman for Number 10 referred to Magee's release as 'very hard to stomach'; early prisoner releases like this one were 'certainly the most unpalatable and awkward part' of the Northern Ireland peace process. The move was criticized by Unionists and Conservative MPs, who urged Mr Tony Blair to stop the paramilitary prisoner releases until the terrorists had handed in their weapons. The policy looked to some very much like appeasement, with convicted terrorists allowed back onto the streets, and no weapons handed in whatsoever. The former Home Secretary and future Conservative leader Michael Howard said that Magee's release was a disgrace. He had himself increased Magee's tariff to mean his 'whole life'. David Trimble, the First Minister designate of Northern Ireland, said: 'It now seems that the victims are the only people who are serving a life sentence.'

But not everyone was against Patrick Magee's release. Harvey Thomas, the former Conservative Director of Presentation, who was himself caught in the Brighton blast, said that people must be prepared to forgive. 'I take the view now that if the law says he has served his time, then, in a sense, that should be an end of it, unless he commits some other crime.' Richard Baker, the manager of the Grand Hotel, said he would be prepared to forgive and forget, even going so far as to say he would be prepared to have Magee stay as a paying guest.

Magee has subsequently reflected on his actions. 'It does cause a re-appraisal of the past but my bottom line still is that my involvement in the Irish Republican Army and the whole armed struggle was necessary simply because we had no other course. But I have to regret the fact that people were hurt.' He sees the Grand Hotel attack as paving the way for peace: 'The awareness that it could have been worse actually gave the IRA more leverage than if they had actually killed Mrs Thatcher. In fact, if half of the British Government had been killed it might have been impossible for a generation in the British establishment to come to terms with us.' He regrets the killings but sees them as necessary; 'After Brighton, anything was possible, and the British for the first time began to look very differently at us.'

The Grand Hotel bombing permanently changed the face of party political conferences. Now very tight, near-military-style police security is the norm at such events. It was a shock to discover how vulnerable Britain was to acts of terrorism. It seems that no amount of security can stop a determined terrorist.

CELEBRITY-STALKERS

JOHN LENNON

1980

ON 8 DECEMBER, 1980 at 10.49 p.m., the limousine belonging to John Lennon and Yoko Ono drew up outside the Dakota apartment block in New York. Lennon was returning home with his wife from a recording session. The doorman, José Perdomo, opened the car doors for them, Yoko getting out first. She was closely followed by John, who was carrying a tape recorder and some cassettes. The killer had been waiting for them and he said 'Hello' to Yoko as she passed him. Lennon gave the man a long, hard look. He had seen him before that day and signed an autograph for him; he may have wondered why he had reappeared. As John walked past him, the man stepped back, pulled out a .38-calibre revolver, and dropped into combat stance, with his knees bent, arms stretched out and one hand supporting the other at the wrist.

Redundantly, the killer asked, 'Mr Lennon?' He fired two shots, hitting John in the back, spinning him round. Blood poured from the wounds as the killer took aim again and fired three more shots. One missed, but the other two bullets hit John's shoulder. Mortally wounded, John staggered up the steps into the Dakota's front lobby, instinctively trying to reach safety.

Inside, Lennon fell down, moaning, 'I'm shot, I'm shot!' Jay Hastings, the security man, summoned the police and then rushed to John's side to take off his shattered glasses. He took his own jacket off to cover John. He thought of using his tie as a tourniquet, but could not see where he could tie it; blood was pouring from John's chest and mouth. He was clearly dying.

New York Police Officers Tony Palma and Herb Frauenberger ran into the lobby to see John lying face down with Yoko standing over him crying. Palma turned the body over. He saw that the victim was badly injured and shouted at his partner, 'Grab his legs and let's get him out of here!' They lifted him into the back of the squad car and drove him at high speed to Roosevelt Hospital, where the major trauma team was already alerted. The two bullets that hit him on the back had both pierced a lung and passed right through his chest. A third had shattered his left shoulder blade. A fourth had hit the same area and ricocheted inside his chest, where it severed his aorta and windpipe. Cardiac massage was unsuccessful. John Lennon was dead. The cause of death was shock produced by massive haemorrhaging; he had lost 80% of his blood.

There were those who wanted to turn the incident into a conspiracy, and turn the murderer into a scapegoat, but the inescapable conclusion is that John Lennon was murdered by a crazed lone gunman, a deranged celebrity-stalker. Mark Chapman, who was convicted of the murder and is serving a life sentence in Attica Prison, had planned to kill Lennon but, just in case he failed, he had drawn up a back-up hit list as well. Chapman spoke about this when he applied for parole in 2000. The three other celebrities named on the list were not officially released, but Jack Jones, the author who has researched the Mark Chapman case for many years, said that the others were Jackie Onassis, George C. Scott and Johnny Carson.

Chapman said his desire to kill Lennon began after seeing photos of the pop singer standing in front of the Dakota apartment building. He spoke of an obsession on the night he killed Lennon, and claimed he heard a small voice – 'probably something very evil' – telling him 'just do it'. He gave vanity, jealousy, anger and stupidity as his 'reasons' for wanting to kill Lennon and other celebrities. He tried to persuade the Parole Board that he posed no threat to Lennon's family or other celebrities if paroled; he said he was now free from any mental illness. He nevertheless believed that he belonged in prison. Yoko Ono wrote to the Parole Board asking it not to release Chapman, on the grounds that he had said that John Lennon would forgive him and want to see him go free. When challenged with this, Chapman admitted that he had no right to put words into his victim's mouth.

In 2000 the Parole Board denied Chapman parole, reminding him that the murder was calculated, unprovoked and had been planned over a protracted period of time; he had been obsessed with killing John Lennon. The Board also gave him his motive – the need to be acknowledged. Chapman was a classic needy case, an attention-seeker.

Mark David Chapman is still in prison, in a cell 6 ft by 10 ft at Attica Correctional Institution near Buffalo. He appears to be a model prisoner, apparently freed of the demons that in 1980 told him to kill his one-time hero, yet he has little chance of ever winning parole. Mark David Chapman has appeared to be a paragon before, during his boyhood and the years leading up to the killing: appearances are deceptive.

He has little to do except read, watch television and think about the murder he committed in 1980. He has in effect been encouraged in this introspection by the hundreds of hours of interviewing by psychiatrists following his arrest. As many as *nine* psychiatrists were prepared to testify at his trial. For the first six years in Attica, he refused all requests for media interviews. He did not, he said, want to fuel the perception that he had killed Lennon to become a celebrity himself, which shows an astute mind at work. He nevertheless eventually gave in to temptation and gave several long interviews – which he admitted enjoying. It is very clear that celebrity is what he was after, in both senses; he stalked and killed a celebrity – in order to become a celebrity himself. That is the simple truth.

Mark Chapman is full of contradictions. In his first two years at high school, he was a drug user who ran away from school for two weeks. In his last two years, he was a born-again Christian distributing Bible tracts. He was short-tempered and vengeful. He was sacked from several jobs.

But some described a very different person. As a teenage YMCA summer camp worker, he was idolized by other children. He was made assistant director of the summer camp because of the leadership qualities he was believed to show. The executive director of the YMCA branch said, 'If there ever was a person who had the potential for doing good, it was Mark.' He was similarly successful working with Vietnamese refugees at a resettlement camp. A colleague recalled his success, 'Especially with the children – he was like the Pied Piper.' He became the director's right hand man.

Against this, there was a suicide attempt, which shows his dark side. As he recovered, the light side returned. He cheered up other patients and on his release the hospital hired him. His supervisor said, 'All the patients just loved that boy, and I can't say enough good about him.'

Chapman told his psychiatrists that he was unhappy as a child. He was picked on by other boys for being a poor athlete. They called him 'Pussy'. Isolation made him invent imaginary friends. 'I used to fantasize that I was a king, and I had all these Little People around me and that they lived in the walls. And that I was their hero and was in the paper every day and I was on TV every day, their TV, and that I was important. They all kind of worshipped me, you know. It was like I could do no wrong.' When he wanted to entertain his subjects, he would give concerts for them, playing them records, especially the Beatles. 'And sometimes when I'd get mad I'd blow some of them up. I'd have this push-button thing, part of the [sofa], and I'd like get mad and blow out part of the wall and a lot of them would die. But the people would still forgive me for that, and, you know, everything got back to normal.' Well, relatively normal.

He lived in dread of his father, who he said beat his mother. 'I'd wake up hearing my mother screaming my name, and it just scared the fire out of me, and I'd run in there and make him go away. Sometimes I think I actually pushed him away.' He fantasized about getting hold of a gun and shooting his father. He claimed his father never gave him emotional support. 'I don't think I ever hugged my father. He never told me he loved me. And he never said he was sorry.'

But many adults did not see this interior world, the dark side of Mark Chapman. They considered him to be a normal American boy, who appeared to share the interests of other boys of his age: rockets, UFOs and the Beatles, whose records he played endlessly. They saw a Boy Scout leader who taught guitar at the YMCA. The YMCA director who worked with Chapman said, 'It was a very happy family, and Mark was a happy, well-adjusted boy.' Appearances can be very deceptive, and the Parole Board has not been taken in by Chapman's switch back to the light side. He was turned down for parole for the third time in October 2004, despite what the Parole Board called his exemplary discipline record. One reason for turning him down was the many threats to kill him if he was released. Even in prison, he is kept in solitary confinement for his own protection; Lennon may well have been a hero to some of his fellow inmates. Because his release would probably be a death sentence, Chapman seems fated to spend the rest of his life in his tiny cell.

JILL DANDO

1999

IN 1999, THE 37-year-old Jill Dando was a very popular British TV presenter at the peak of a successful career, fronting programmes such as the *Six O'Clock News*, the *Holiday* programme and *Crimewatch*. Apart from this professional success, she was happy in her private life and looking forward to marrying her fiancé, gynaecologist Alan Farthing. Then, on 26 April 1999, she was murdered at the front door of her home in Gowan Avenue, Fulham, west London. Her killer accosted her on the doorstep, pointed a 9mm semi-automatic pistol at her head, fired a single shot and disappeared. She was given emergency treatment at Charing Cross Hospital, but she was declared dead just after 1 p.m.

It was a complete mystery. Jill Dando had no known enemies and the police had no initial leads to go on. Although the murder had taken place in a suburban street in broad daylight, it had happened without preamble and so quickly that no one really saw anything. Detectives pinned their hopes on a smartly dressed man carrying a mobile telephone who was reported as being seen walking calmly but briskly away from the scene of the murder. Over the next few days there were several reported sightings of the suspect, who seemed to have disguised himself with heavy black-framed spectacles. On 30 April the police released an E-fit image of the prime suspect. Detective Chief Inspector Hamish

Campbell, who was leading the murder inquiry, also released closed-circuit TV footage showing a metallic blue Range Rover that travelled south along Fulham Palace Road shortly after the killing. On 5 May the inquest was opened, and DCI Campbell disclosed that the prime suspect made his getaway on a number 74 bus; he also used his mobile telephone before getting off at Putney Bridge.

By 10 May there were signs that Scotland Yard was dissatisfied with the lack of progress. There was an announcement that senior detectives would be appointed to review the murder inquiry. A week later *Crimewatch*, the TV programme that Jill Dando herself had hosted together with Nick Ross, featured a reconstruction of her murder and an appeal from Mr Farthing. The programme generated 500 calls from the public. Then detectives arrested a man and released him again.

The months passed and still there was no arrest, in spite of a reward being offered. On the hundredth day after her death a newspaper offered an additional large cash reward to anyone who could help catch the killer. Jill Dando's agent for 10 years, Jon Roseman, said he was optimistic that Miss Dando's brutal killing would be solved, and he urged people to rack their brains for new leads; like everyone else who had known Jill Dando, he was struggling to come to terms with the murder.

DCI Hamish Campbell revealed that the bullet that had killed Jill Dando was very unusual. It carried distinctive marks that made it different from any bullet seen in Britain before. It raised hopes that the bullet might help to identify the killer. The marks were the result of hammer blows, apparently delivered in order to hold the bullet in place by 'crimping' the cartridge case. This might have been a trademark, a habit or just an idiosyncrasy on the part of the killer. It was unclear whether this finding took Campbell any closer to deciding whether the killer was an obsessive fan or a contract killer: those two possible scenarios were emerging. The crimping might have been done after the bullet was removed from its case to make some alteration to it, perhaps to turn it into a dum-dum (expanding on impact) or to remove powder to make the report quieter.

A 41-year-old local man called Barry George was eventually arrested, tried and convicted of the murder, though many people believe he is innocent of the crime, and even more people believe that his conviction was unsafe. Barry George was an obsessive by nature, and he was certainly interested in celebrities, so it was understandable that the police would think that he was the celebrity-stalker who killed Jill Dando.

Barry George denied the killing, but a jury of six women and five men convicted him by a 10-1 majority after an Old Bailey trial lasting nearly two months. His solicitor, Marilyn Etienne, said afterwards that Barry George was 'devastated' by the conviction and that preparations were being made for an appeal. Passing a life sentence, Mr Justice Gage told George: 'You have deprived Miss Dando's fiancé, family and friends of a much loved and popular personality.' The evidence used to achieve this conviction was threefold. There was a small amount of forensic evidence: a fibre from his trousers found at the scene of the crime and a speck of gunfire residue in his coat pocket. There were eyewitnesses who believed they saw him in the area. There was also his personality profile: he was obsessed with guns and with media celebrities. The evidence was very slight and circumstantial, and many people at the time believed that it was inadequate to justify a conviction. Indeed, many of the lawyers and reporters who attended the trial sensed this and had anticipated an acquittal; they were taken by surprise when the jurors convicted Barry George on a 10-1 majority.

Doctors reporting on Barry George said that he had 'psychiatric personality characteristics' and hated women. He had a conviction for a sex offence too; when he was 22 he had been convicted of attempting to rape a language student. Celebrity-stalking was also one of his traits. He had been arrested in combat gear outside the London home of Princess Diana. He had used several different names including Barry Bulsara, the original surname of the Queen singer Freddy Mercury. When police searched his flat, they found copies of the BBC's in-house newspaper, *Ariel*, published after Jill Dando's murder, and featuring her picture on the front page. This was, in police eyes, very incriminating evidence.

Barry George denied knowing of Jill Dando. This is hard to believe, though the denial can be explained as a distortion produced by the stress of police interrogation. Feeling threatened by the situation he found himself in, Barry George may instinctively have fallen back on denying *everything* the police put to him. Similarly, the detectives thought it highly significant that he had tried to create a false alibi by telling staff at a charity and a local taxi firm about his movements on the day in question and what he was wearing. The reality was that Barry George was a loner, literally on his own a great deal of the time, had no alibi that he could remember and therefore knew that he was vulnerable.

Once Barry George had been convicted of killing Jill Dando, all other possible theories were discounted. But one of them at least deserves attention. A year after George started his prison sentence, The *Guardian* carried a reflection on his trial. Barry George, it said, was a man with many problems. He had suffered learning difficulties, he had as many as six identifiable personality disorders, he had been unemployed for over 20 years and was probably unemployable. Far from being a character assassination, this newspaper piece was designed to show that Barry George was completely incapable of planning and carrying out the crime that had 'successfully' taken Jill Dando and her neighbours totally by surprise, killing Jill with a single shot, removing himself from the crime scene so quickly that only two people saw him (briefly), and eluding arrest for several months.

The murder, by contrast, bore the hallmarks of a ruthless and well planned operation. In addition, it happened only three days after British and US planes had bombed the Radio-Television Serbia building in Belgrade, killing 16 employees in an attack provocatively described by Tony Blair as 'entirely justified'. Earlier that month, Jill Dando had made a high-profile BBC appeal on behalf of Kosovan Albanian refugees. There was speculation that there was a clear link between the events, and that Dando had been killed in retaliation for the Nato bombing of Serbian journalists. This theory was one of the main planks of Barry George's defence. His defence counsel Michael Mansfield QC told the jury, 'The television station was owned and run by the Milosevic family and was deliberately targeted by NATO, using a cruise missile, because it was seen as the main purveyor of Serbian state propaganda. Jill Dando by this stage had become . . . the personification and embodiment of the BBC.'

The police eventually ruled out Serbian responsibility, partly on the grounds that the three-day gap between the bombing and the murder was not long enough to plan and carry out a revenge killing. The murder certainly could not have been planned and carried out in just three days. The police did not seriously consider that it might have been planned weeks in advance. The method of killing was itself a vital clue to the kind of crime this was. As Jill Dando was about to unlock the front door of her home, she was grabbed from behind; there was a recent bruise to her right forearm. With his right arm, the attacker held her, forced her down onto the ground, so that her face was almost touching the tiled step. Then, with his left hand, he fired a single shot at her left temple, killing her instantly. The bullet entered her head just above her ear, parallel to the ground, and came out the right side of her head and into the door, leaving a mark 22cm above the doorstep. This clinically executed one-shot murder was silent. The gases escaping as the gun was discharged, which normally cause the report, instead exploded inside her head, so there was virtually no sound. Jill Dando's neighbour, Richard Hughes, was working at the front of the house and heard no gunshot, only a brief, sudden cry.

Another highly significant aspect of the murder was its speed. Richard Hughes estimated that only 30 seconds passed between the sound of Jill Dando getting out of her car as she arrived home and the sound of the murderer closing the gate as he left; the police estimate an even shorter time than that. Major Freddy Mead, a ballistics expert, told Mansfield at the trial that it was 'difficult to imagine how [the killing] could have been bettered'. Everything pointed to a professional hitman, not to Barry George.

Forensic examination of the bullet and cartridge case showed that there were no rifling marks on the bullet. Rifling marks inside the gun barrel spin the bullet, making it more accurate at long ranges. This can be interpreted in two ways. As the prosecution argued, Barry George may have used a deactivated weapon. The gun laws in Britain had been tightened up following the serious incidents at Hungerford and Dunblane, and many guns had been deactivated by having the barrel rifling and other mechanisms removed. But there is another interpretation – that a custom-made, smooth-bore, short-range weapon had been deliberately selected for the task. The killer had planned all along to place the weapon against his victim's head, and had had practice in killing in this way, so there was no need for rifling in the barrel.

There were other unusual features of the crime. By the time of the murder, Dando was spending a great deal of time with her boyfriend at his home in Chiswick. Her house was up for sale, and she returned there infrequently. Her attacker must have spent a long time waiting outside her house, as he would have had no idea when she would be returning.

Two of Jill Dando's neighbours saw the gunman leaving the scene, and he slowed down noticeably when he realized that one of them had spotted him hurrying. The gunman was a white, well-dressed man with dark hair and a solid build; he wore a dark, Barbour-style jacket; he also appeared to be carrying a mobile phone. After committing the murder, the gunman turned left, apparently to walk the length of Gowan Avenue, when the more obvious escape route would have been to turn right. Even so, nobody definitely saw the gunman before the attack, and only these two witnesses definitely saw him after it.

One solution to this mystery is that the killer had an accomplice, who drove him to and from Dando's home in a car. If the killer waited inside a car for Dando to return, it would explain why he went unnoticed before the murder; he was just an inconspicuous occupant of a parked car. When she arrived at the house, the gunman got out and the accomplice drove the car some distance to a pre-arranged rendezvous down the road. The gunman joined him there after the shooting. In that way, there would be no visible connection between the vehicle and the crime. At 10.15 a.m., a traffic warden was about to issue a ticket to a blue Range Rover illegally parked on Gowan Avenue, but she stopped when the driver waved her away. This encounter was dismissed by police, but it may have been significant.

Josip Broz Tito's Yugoslav secret service UDBA carried out assassinations in foreign countries, and got used to the idea of acting with impunity. Nikola Stedul, who was living in exile in Scotland, became a target for Yugoslav agents after becoming president of the Croatian Movement for Statehood. In spite of being shot five times outside his home in October 1988, Stedul survived, and a neighbour was able to take the registration number of the gunman's hire car. The gunman was arrested later that day at Heathrow airport. He proved to be a Yugoslav master assassin responsible for 10 political murders in various countries. In May 1989, a British court found him guilty of attempted murder and sentenced to 15 years in prison.

Tito's heir, Slobodan Milosevic, the President of Serbia from 1989, developed his own Serbian-controlled security services, with an assassination department, the JSO. The favoured method of operation in foreign countries was an experienced lone assassin delivering one silent shot at very close range. Milosevic utilized the sinister talents of Zeljko Raznatovic, the warlord known as Arkan. By 1990, there were warrants for Arkan's arrest in several western European countries. Enjoying the full patronage of Milosevic, Arkan may have come to believe himself above the law, but in September 1997 Arkan was indicted for war crimes by the international tribunal in the Hague; Milosevic himself was to follow.

US and UK planes bombed the Radio-Television Serbia building, killing 16 employees. Serbia had little hope of a revenge strike at the US, but there were several British targets to choose from: Tony Blair; Defence Secretary George Robertson; Jamie Shea, the NATO press spokesman; and the BBC, for which Milosevic nursed a particular hatred. As government ministers with bodyguards and other security, Blair and Robertson would have been near-impossible targets. The director-general of the BBC, John Birt, presented similar difficulties. Having just espoused the cause of the Kosovan Albanians, Jill Dando was an obvious and easy target. The timing of the Dando shooting is significant. On 11 April, Milosevic began his strike back at his media enemies. Slavko Curuvija, the owner and editor of the independent newspaper *Dnevni Telegraf*, which was critical of Milosevic, was shot dead outside his home in central Belgrade. Jill Dando was killed just over a fortnight later. The day after the shooting, a caller to the BBC said: 'Because your government, and in particular your prime minister Blair, murdered, butchered 17 innocent young people. He butchered, we butcher back. The first one you had yesterday [Dando], the next one will be Tony Hall [chief executive for BBC News].'

On 12 May, there was a security scare at the home of Jamie Shea in Brussels. Shea had no security. He and his family were moved to safety and given protection by NATO security and the Belgian police. It looked as if an assassination attempt on Shea had been foiled. This was 16 days after Dando's murder, which in turn had happened 15 days after the murder of Curuvija. A pattern of sorts begins to emerge.

The National Criminal Intelligence Service received a report, which may or may not have been true, that Arkan himself was behind Dando's murder. If so, it may be impossible to find out exactly what happened. Almost inevitably, Arkan himself became the target of an assassination. On 15 January 2000, four men in running gear approached him and his bodyguards outside the Intercontinental Hotel in Belgrade. They opened fire on Arkan at close quarters with submachine guns, hitting him three times in the face, and he died on the way to hospital. Maybe he knew too much about the involvement of Milosevic in war crimes. Maybe he had begun a secret plea bargaining negotiation with the Hague, offering to give evidence against Milosevic, Mladic and Karadzic.

Like the police, the prosecution in the Barry George trial dismissed the Serbian theory because there was too short a time interval between the Radio-Television Serbia bombing and the murder. But if the murder was planned following Jill Dando's television appeal rather than the bombing, the murderers would have had three weeks to prepare. A second reason for discounting a Serbian connection was that Milosevic had not claimed responsibility, but that is a misreading of the way east European politics work. Although the IRA might have made a claim of responsibility in such a situation, and frequently did, East European secret services never did. So, neither of the reasons given at the trial for dismissing the Serbian involvement was valid.

Barry George still languishes in prison, perhaps persuaded that he did kill Jill Dando – and perhaps he did. But Barry George had no expertise in weapons, nor the capability to modify them. He had no car. He had no money. No incriminating forensic evidence was found in his flat. The 'gunfire residue' found in his coat pocket might have been a trace of a firework from several years earlier, or the coat could have become contaminated while in police custody; it was photographed and therefore handled before analysis, so contamination was possible. He was under police surveillance for three weeks before his arrest, yet gave no reason to indicate his guilt. Jill Dando's two neighbours, who were the only eyewitnesses, did not identify Barry George as the gunman in an identification parade. And, most disturbing of all, Barry George turns out to have had an alibi. Staff at Hammersmith & Fulham Action for Disability alerted the police because of George's strange behaviour and mental state when he arrived at their centre soon after the murder. Although they did not realize it, the timing they gave for his arrival, about 11.50 a.m., gave him an alibi. George would have needed at least 30 minutes to get home, change his clothes and then walk to the centre, but he was seen there only 20 minutes after the shooting.

Barry George's conviction joins an ever-lengthening list of cases in which poor forensic evidence has been given far too much weight in court. Was Jill Dando killed by a celebrity-stalker? Or was she killed by a Serbian hitman – perhaps even Arkan himself – on the orders of Slobodan Milosevic?

MILITARY CONSPIRACIES

UFOs AND THE
ROSWELL INCIDENT

OVER THE LAST 50 years thousands of people have reported seeing objects they could not account for in the sky. When these sightings have been analysed, most of them have been explained in terms of meteorites, planets, stars, weather balloons, marsh gas or clouds. A small percentage of sightings remain impossible to explain.

The Unidentified Flying Object, or UFO, is commonly a disc or cigar shape, and early on it was realized that the cigar might be a foreshortened view of a disc. Sightings have in some cases been backed up by still or movie photography, or by radar. Any idea that they might be ordinary aircraft or experimental aircraft of some kind has been rightly set aside on the grounds that the UFOs move in an entirely different way. They accelerate and decelerate much more rapidly than planes and are capable of far more advanced aerobatics. The can hover, motionless, like a helicopter. They can move straight up and down. They can dart off at remarkably high speeds, like a jet plane. They can also change direction and speed in a far more agile way than any aircraft.

The main reason why people are so interested in UFOs that they represent a possible point of contact with civilization outside the solar system. A recurring idea is th they might be visiting spacecraft from outside the solar system, from some planet orbiting a distant star. They therefore offer the tantalizing possibility of meeting intelligent creatures from another world. They also offer a possible threat to the future of mankind, because there is no way of knowing what the intentions of these visitors might be.

Most of the sightings belong, probably significantly, to the period of the Cold War, when fears of conquest by an alien civilization gripped both East and West. If UFO sightings only began in 1948, it would be tempting to interpret them as paranoid delusions, projections brought on by panic. But there were occasional sightings long before that. An ancient Egyptian papyrus describes a mysterious disembodied 'circle of fire' that appeared in about 1500 BC. Then there was the prophet Ezekiel's vision of a strange wheeled vehicle arriving from the sky and landing in what is now Iraq in 592 BC. This had celestial occupants, each of which had four faces and four wings. The four faces were those of a man, a lion, an ox and an eagle, and these were to become the four symbolic identities later allocated to the writers of the four canonical gospels. In the Iron Age world inhabited by the prophet Ezekiel, these heavenly visitors were naturally interpreted as cherubim or seraphim – angels. If the same creatures had visited the Earth in the late twentieth century, there is no doubt that they would have been viewed as extra-terrestrials, as aliens. What we see is conditioned by what we are.

The Roman writer Julius Obsequens in the fourth century D compiled a Book of Prodigies. One of these prodigies was a sighting in 216 BC of 'things like ships' in the sky; at Arpi, east of Rome, a round shield was seen floating in the sky. Again in 99 BC 'a round object like a globe or round shield travelled across the sky from west to east'. The round shields of those times were, significantly, saucer-shaped.

In AD 393 a bright globe suddenly became visible in the night sky near Venus. A peculiarity of this sighting was the clustering of other globes round the initial globe. They jostled one another into different formations, including one resembling a long sword-like flame. A similar set of moving lights was seen for several hours by an entire Japanese army in 1235. General Yoritsume ordered a full investigation into the event. The report has a familiar, modern ring to it. The general was told that the whole incident could be explained entirely in terms of natural processes; 'it is only the wind making the stars sway'. From this we can see how right we are to be sceptical of all official reports!

The reported sightings continued through the Middle Ages and on into the Age of Reason. In 1733, Mr Cracker of Fleet in Dorset saw a UFO on a bright sunny day. This object looked startlingly like a modern aircraft, from Mr Cracker's description, though of course he had never seen one. He described 'something in the sky . . . darting . . . the colour like burnished or new washed silver'. In one respect it outperformed a modern aircraft – in its speed. It shot off at high speed, 'like a star falling in the night'; in other words it moved as fast as a meteorite, and this capacity for amazing speeds is something that crops up again and again in UFO reports. Mr Cracker noted that his sighting was corroborated by at least two other people watching from another vantage point.

In 1878 a Texan farmer saw a dark disc-shaped object travelling high in the sky 'at a wonderful speed'; he described it (for the first time) as a 'saucer'.

It was the 1947 sighting by Kenneth Arnold, a civilian

pilot, that introduced the modern wave of UFOs and ufology. Arnold was flying near Mount Rainier when he was aware of two flashes of light. When he looked to see where the flashes had come from he saw nine shining objects coming from the direction of Mount Baker, swerving round the mountains. From their positions in relation to the mountains, Arnold estimated their speed at 1600mph, which was three times faster than any plane could fly at that time. Arnold described the objects as 'flat like a pie pan and so shiny they reflected the sun like a mirror'. They moved oddly, 'like speedboats on rough water ... like a saucer would if you skipped it across the water'. Just 10 days later another pilot, Captain E. J. Smith of United Airlines, saw a formation of five similar objects just after taking off from Boise in Idaho. He and his co-pilot Ralph Stevens watched the saucers until, after a minute or so, they whizzed off at an astounding speed and were replaced by another four unidentified objects. Possibly this was the same group of objects that Arnold had seen just over a week earlier.

The Arnold sighting turned out to be the start of the modern age of flying saucers. It was reported globally and it prompted the US Air Force to launch a formal investigation. Dr Allen Hyneck, an astronomer, divided the sightings into categories. There were sightings over 500 ft away, comprising 'nocturnal lights', 'daylight discs' and 'radar visuals'. Then there were sightings at shorter distances, comprising 'close encounters of the first kind', in which there was no interaction between the UFO and the environment, and 'close encounters of the second kind', in which there some interaction, such as burns on the ground, interference with car ignition systems, physical effects on people or animals. The most sensational reports were categorized as 'close encounters of the third kind', in which the occupants of the UFO were seen. As the enquiry proceeded, there were even claims that people had contact with the occupants of the UFO or were temporarily detained by them in their spacecraft; these came to be known as 'close encounters of the fourth kind'.

The best example of the nocturnal lights sightings appeared at Lubbock, Texas in August and September 1951, when a huge wing-shaped UFO with blue lights on the rear edge was seen by hundreds of people. Observers thought it was much larger than a B-36 aircraft. One man, Carl Hart, photographed the wing and his photograph clearly showed the regular pattern of tail-lights. The air force investigators were unable to explain the phenomenon, but confirmed the genuineness of Hart's photograph. Although some lights can be explained away as due to natural atmospheric conditions, this distinctive V-formation can only have been artificial. The reports came in thick and fast, and independently, from widely spaced locations; they cannot have been made with any knowledge of the other reports coming in at the same time. There is no possibility that these sightings were a hoax.

Another sighting, fascinating for an entirely different reason, was at Leary in Georgia in January 1969. The witness this time was President Jimmy Carter, who was outdoors waiting to address a meeting. President Carter later said, 'I am convinced that UFOs exist because I've seen one. It was a very peculiar aberration, but about 20 people saw it . . . It was the darnedest thing I've ever seen. It was big; it was very bright; it changed colours; and it was about the size of the moon. We watched it for 10 minutes, but none of us could figure out what it was.'

Many of the photograph-supported sightings turned out

to be hoaxes. Scores of amateur photographers rigged up dustbin lids or saucepan lids on wires. Other sightings are more sinister. Towards the end of 1978 Frederick Valentich was flying a small plane across the Bass Strait between Australia and Tasmania. He used his radio to ask Melbourne to check for confirmation of a large aircraft with four bright lights, but he was told that there were no reported aircraft in the area. Over the radio he reported the approach of the unidentified object. 'It's approaching from due east of me. It seems to be playing some sort of game, flying at a speed I cannot estimate . . . It is flying past. It has a long shape . . . coming for me right now . . . It has a green light and sort of metallic look on the outside. The thing is orbiting on top of me.'

At this point, Valentich's engine began to falter and cough. He called, 'Proceeding King Island. Unknown aircraft now hovering on top of me.' A loud metallic sound lasting 17 seconds was heard over the radio, and then communications went dead. No trace of Valentich or his plane was ever found. It is possible that he simply developed engine trouble, ditched in the sea and did not survive the crash, but because of the strange craft hovering over his plane his father believed he had been abducted by aliens.

There have been other reports of UFOs 'buzzing' aircraft. In 1975, over Mexico City, Carlos Antonio de los Santos Montiel was approaching the city in a light aircraft, a Piper A-24, when he found his plane vibrating for no reason. Beyond the right wing tip he saw a black disc about 10–12 ft in diameter, then to the left he saw another. Most alarming of all, de los Santos Montiel, saw a third disc coming at him from dead ahead. This third disc scraped the underside of the plane. Then he found that the plane's controls had stopped working, yet the plane carried on flying smoothly at 120mph. When the discs let him go, the plane's controls resumed and he was able to radio to the tower at Mexico City airport. By this stage he was in tears. His story was believed, because the airport controllers had been tracking the three objects on their radar screens throughout the incident. One of the controllers described the objects' bizarre behaviour. 'The objects made a 270-degree turn at 518mph in an arc of only 3 miles. In my 17 years as an air traffic controller I've never seen anything like that.'

One of the earliest reports of a close encounter of the first kind was in July 1948. At 2.45 a.m. near Montgomery, Alabama, two airline pilots, Clarence Chiles and John Whitted saw what they thought was a jet fighter streaking towards them 'with terrific speed'. It was about 100ft long, cigar-shaped with no protruding fins. An intense dark blue glow came from the side of the object and ran the entire length of its fuselage; the exhaust was a red-orange flame. There was no doubt in the two pilots' minds that this was a spaceship. They even saw rows of portholes along the side of it. When the UFO disappeared into some cloud, Chiles visited the cabin to see what the passengers had made of the experience. Only one of them was awake: Clarence McKelvie. He had seen a brilliant light flashing past the window. 'It looked like a cigar with a cherry flame going out the back. There was a row of windows. It disappeared very quickly.'

Scientists have been quick to offer everyday rational explanations for flying saucers, and a great many of the sightings can indeed be explained in terms of unusual atmospheric conditions, weather balloons and aircraft. It seems very likely that some of them are psychic in origin. The psychologist Carl Gustav Jung wrote a very perceptive essay on the subject and he noticed that a great many of the sightings are reported by people whose testimony we would think was irreproachable, such as pilots and law enforcement officers. Jung's explanation is that these people are trained to function totally in the world of the everyday, and large areas of their minds are left under-exercised. Every so often the unconscious mind asserts itself, projecting an archetype into the conscious mind. What people are 'seeing' is therefore a projection of the unconscious mind. This, and the fact that the images fall within a fairly narrow range of shapes and behaviour patterns, fits well with both the range of reports and with Jung's view of modern man's neglect of the unconscious mind.

The same idea has been developed by Jacques Vallee, who has shown that sightings of UFOs seem to permeate ancient as well as modern writings, playing a significant role in the creation of myths. The strange otherworldly experiences that accompany UFO sightings certainly accord well with the idea of a 'paranormal' element.

Jung pointed out that it is no accident that what people very often see is a disc. The circular shape symbolizes the universal, the whole, and is a powerful archetype. Why would there be a surge of UFO sightings in the 1940s and 1950s? Jung suggested that the idea of a visitation by a superior civilization, whether benign or not was significant in a world that had been wrecked by two world wars; the shining disc was a symbol of human hopes and fears in an uncertain world. The psychic approach has been fruitful. Those who reported being abducted by aliens were hypnotized, and their stories contained large numbers of common elements. The 'victim' sees a shining light, is guided to the spacecraft in a semi-conscious or 'out-of-body' state, and has an experience outside time in which he or she is examined by aliens. The really significant thing is that the same sequence of events is described by hypnosis subjects who have not witnessed a close encounter but are asked to imagine one. It is as if we are all programmed to project the same images of extra-terrestrials in much the same way, when prompted to imagine them.

The extra-terrestrials seen at Flatwoods, West Virginia, in 1952 were unusually repellent. A group of children saw what looked like a meteorite land on a hilltop one night in September and went to look at it together with some adults, one of whom was a soldier. They saw a ball as big as a house, making a hissing, throbbing sound. One of the group shone a torch at what looked like animal eyes up in a tree and they all saw a huge figure perhaps 15 ft tall. It had a blood-red face and glowing greenish-orange eyes. The monster – there is no other way to describe it – floated slowly towards them, and they ran down the hill, terrified. Afterwards, two parallel skid-marks and a large circle of flattened grass were found on the site, and an unusual smell.

A more typical sighting of extra-terrestrials was the one by Jennie Roestenberg and her two children at Ranton near Shrewsbury in October 1954. They saw a disc-shaped aluminium-coloured saucer hovering over their house. Mrs Roestenberg saw two aliens through transparent windows in the side of the saucer. The aliens were very pale, with shoulder-length hair (which was very unusual in the 1950s) and very high foreheads. All of their features were concentrated in the lower half of their faces. They were wearing turquoise ski suits and transparent helmets. As the saucer hovered, the humanoid aliens looked down 'sternly, not in an unkindly fashion, but almost sadly, compassionately'.

The details of this encounter are telling. It is, in all but name, a visitation by angels. Encounters of this type suggest that the witnesses are projecting a need to believe that there is 'something out there watching over them'. The accounts are a cry for faith. No wonder there was a surge of such encounters in the twentieth century, a century of faithlessness.

In September 1961, Barney and Betty Hill had a close encounter of the fourth kind when returning home in Portsmouth, New Hampshire after a holiday in Canada. As they drove along, they became aware of a bright moving light following them erratically. After a time it appeared in front of them, so Barney stopped the car and got out to observe the object through binoculars. He could see up to about 10 figures in shiny black uniforms moving about inside the spacecraft behind a double row of windows. Betty could not see the figures; she only heard her husband repeat, 'I don't believe it!' The UFO was by this time only 100 ft away and 70 ft up. Barney shouted, 'They are going to capture us!' and jumped back into the car. He drove off and, though they could no longer see the UFO they guessed it was right above them. They heard a sound like a tuning fork, felt drowsy, and then realised they had lost two hours.

The Hills reported their experience, or what they could remember of it, to the nearest air base. About 10 days later, Betty began to have nightmares in which she recalled some of the things that happened in the missing two hours. She saw a group of up to 11 men dressed in uniforms and military caps standing in the road, barring their way. The men assured them they would not be harmed and led them into the flying saucer. There the aliens took samples of Betty's hair, fingernails and scrapings of skin cells. Although they were released unharmed, the Hills experienced intense anxiety feelings, for which they needed psychiatric help. The psychiatrist, Dr Benjamin Simon, used a time-regression therapy technique, and under hypnosis a remarkable story emerged. The Hills' stories matched very closely, corroborating each other. One remarkable detail was the star map the leader of the aliens showed Betty when she asked where he came from. Betty was able to redraw this map under hypnosis. It was only some years afterwards that new astronomical information revealed that there was a cluster of stars close to a binary star called Zeta Reticuli; it closely matched the star map drawn by Betty Hill. Zeta Reticuli is not visible in the night sky north of the tropics, and so Betty could not have seen it for herself.

It all sounds like a genuine enough story, but Dr Simon remained convinced that the Hills were suffering from a fantasy. The reason why Barney's account corroborated Betty's was simply that Betty had already described to Barney in detail everything she had experienced in her dreams or hallucinations; he knew her 'experiences' as well as she did. The couple convinced themselves and each other that the had been abducted by aliens.

Many of the close encounter stories suffer from fundamental lack of credibility. It is not at all unlikely that highly intelligent life forms and advanced civilizations exist on planets revolving round other stars in this and other galaxies. Carl Sagan gave an optimistic estimate that within the Milky Way, our own local galaxy, there might be as many as a million civilizations. But they would need to have developed a very remarkable technology in order to travel close to the speed of light in order to get here. And that raises a crucial question. Why on earth would members of a sophisticated advanced civilization developing many light-years away invest hundreds of years of their time, and large quantities of whatever they use for money, to travel to the Earth to get a few samples of hair and nail-clippings from Mrs Betty Hill of Portsmouth, New Hampshire? It seems like a very unlikely project. Another reason for being sceptical is that as Carl Sagan has said the accounts of the spaceships and their occupants are 'stodgy in their unimaginativeness'. The aliens are a bit too much like human beings, and their spaceships are a bit too much like the ones drawn in children's comics – a probably source of the material for some of the fantasizing. Some of the encounters utterly defy belief, yet they are fascinating even so.

In April 1961 a plumber called Joe Simonton in Wisconsin heard a noise in his yard. When he looked out he saw a silvery globe floating a few inches off the ground. When he approached, the hatch opened and he saw three individuals inside. They were young, five ft tall with dark hair. One gave Simonton a silver-coloured jug, indicating that he wanted it filled, so Simonton filled it with water. He watched one of the aliens cooking and used sign language to indicate that he wanted some; he was given two biscuits. He ate one. When analysed, the other was found to contain flour, sugar and fat. After the picnic, the UFO took off at a 45 degree angle. This story has much of the flavour of old English folk tales of encounters with fairies.

So, then, are UFO stories explained away as weather phenomena or fantasies? Is there no hard proof that UFOs really exist, that they really are alien craft from outer space?

There are some alleged UFO crashes and it has been alleged that the authorities have deliberately concealed these events from the public to avoid spreading alarm and hysteria. This is where the conspiracy comes in.

The first and most famous UFO crash was the Roswell incident. Perhaps by coincidence, this occurred on 2 July 1947, only a matter of days after the highly publicized Arnold UFO sighting. At 9.50 p.m., Mr and Mrs Wilmot were sitting on their front porch when a large glowing object travelled at high speed across the sky from the south-east, and headed towards Corona, to the north-west. They only saw it for 40–50 seconds, but it was long enough for the Wilmots to identify its shape as oval. From what happened later it would appear that the craft changed direction during its descent, flying north-west over Roswell, then turning to fly west after about 50 miles, taking it over Socorro to crash in the Plains of San Agustin 50 miles west of Socorro.

The next morning, Barney Barnett, a civil engineer, was working in the desert 250 miles west of Roswell when he saw the sun glinting on some metal. He thought it was a crashed aircraft, and went to have a look. What he found was a metallic disc about 30 ft in diameter. 'I tried to get close to see what the bodies were like. They were all dead as far as I could see and there were bodies inside and outside the vehicle. The ones outside had been tossed out by impact. They were like humans but they were not humans. The heads were round, the eyes were small, and they had no hair. The eyes were oddly spaced. They were quite small by our standards and their heads were larger in proportion to their bodies than ours. Their clothing seemed to be one-piece and grey in color. You couldn't see any zippers, belts, or buttons.'

While he was examining it, a small group of people arrived, claiming to be an archaeological research team from the University of Pennsylvania. Barnett later told his friends, 'I noticed that they were standing around looking at some dead bodies that had fallen to the ground . . . the machine was kind of a metallic disc. It was not all that big. It seemed to be made of a metal that looked like stainless steel. The machine had been split open by explosion or impact.' The apparent discovery of bodies of humanoid aliens was sensational.

Shortly afterwards, an army jeep arrived and all the civilians were ordered to leave the site. Barnett said, 'We were told to leave the area and not talk to anyone whatever about what we had seen . . . that it was our patriotic duty to remain silent.' This was the first indication that the Roswell Incident was going to be covered up. Even so, when the officers returned to the Roswell base, an official press statement authorized by Colonel William Blanchard was released, confirming that wreckage of a flying disc had been recovered. Strangely, no one was ever able to trace any member of the team of archaeologists who visited the scene; their testimony has never been heard. Were they perhaps not archaeologists at all?

At his ranch 75 miles north-west of Roswell, about halfway between Roswell and the crash site, Mack Brazel found widely scattered wreckage including pieces of metallic foil the morning after hearing an explosion in the night. The unidentified wreckage, scattered over an area three-quarters of a mile long by several hundred feet wide, consisted of various types of debris. Brazel wondered whether this material had something to do with the flying saucers people had seen in the neighbourhood recently, told the sheriff and the sheriff referred him to the army air force base just outside

Roswell. Troops converged on Brazel's ranch, cordoned it off and searched it. Major Jesse Marcel, a staff intelligence officer of the 509th Bomb Group Intelligence Office at the Army Air Forces base at Roswell Field, said he had seen nothing like it before. 'There was all kinds of stuff: small beams [with an I-shaped cross section] about three eighths or a half inch square with some sort of hieroglyphics on them that nobody could decipher. These looked something like balsa wood and were of about the same weight, except that they were not wood at all. They were very hard, although flexible, and would not burn. There was a great deal of unusual parchment-like substance which was brown in color and extremely strong, and a great number of small pieces of a metal like tinfoil, except that it wasn't tinfoil.'

Shortly after that, Major Marcel was ordered to load the debris of the disc onto a B-29 and fly it to Wright Field (now Wright-Patterson Air Forces Base) at Dayton, Ohio, for examination. On arrival at an intermediate stop at Carswell Army Air Forces Base, Fort Worth, Texas (headquarters of the Eighth Air Force), General Roger Ramey took over and ordered Marcel and others on the plane not to talk to reporters. A second press statement was issued, stating that the wreckage was the remains of a weather balloon and its attached tinfoil radar target, and this was prominently displayed at the press conference. Meanwhile, the wreckage of the metal disc arrived at Wright Field under armed guard; Marcel returned to Roswell and Brazel was held incommunicado for nearly a week while the crash site was stripped of every scrap of debris.

By 7 July, local radio stations were picking up the story, which only grew when the authorities attempted to stifle it.

A news broadcast from Albuquerque describing this fantastic story was interrupted and the radio station in question was warned not to continue the broadcast: 'Attention Albuquerque: cease transmission. Repeat: cease transmission. National security item. Do not transmit. Stand by.'

Then General Ramey, from Fort Worth in the neighbouring state of Texas, went on the radio to explain that the Roswell incident was a case of mistaken identification and that the army knew of no flying saucers. The army held a press conference at which they claimed the wreckage was from a weather balloon. Mack Brazel was convinced that what he found was not from a weather balloon. Marcel too was convinced that the material had nothing to do with a weather balloon or radar target. His testimony should not be dismissed, owing to his background in aviation: he had served as bombardier, waist-gunner and pilot and been awarded five medals for shooting down enemy aircraft in the Second World War. Perhaps significantly, following the Roswell incident he was promoted to Lieutenant Colonel and assigned to a Special Weapons Programme. He was certain that no bodies were found among the debris at the Brazel ranch, and that whatever the object was it must have exploded above ground level. Brazel's son collected some fragments, but when two years later he mentioned in a bar that he had them he had a visit from the military, who demanded that he hand the pieces over. If the remains really were those a weather balloon, it seems unlikely that the army would have been so concerned to remove all trace of it.

The wreckage of the saucer was taken in strict secrecy from Wright Field to Muroc Air Force base in California, where it was inspected by President Eisenhower. As for the bodies of the aliens – a now-notorious film was made of what is supposed to be an autopsy of one of the alien corpses. Opinions differ as to the authenticity of the film, but there is a growing presumption that it was a hoax.

It is not certain that the wreckage found at the two sites belonged to the same craft that had somehow managed to remain airborne for over 100 miles before crashing on the Plains. It is possible that two entirely separate accidents happened on the same night within 150 miles of each other. It has also been suggested that there was a collision between two craft, perhaps two flying saucers, one of them crashing at Roswell, the other making it to the Plains of San Agustin before crashing. The quality of evidence varies between the two crash sites. The material gathered at the Brazel ranch was real enough, as it was displayed at a press conference and photographed there. There is far less evidence to substantiate Barnett's story, and as already mentioned even the archaeologists are untraceable. The Barnett story should nevertheless not be entirely dismissed.

How much of the entire incident at Roswell was a hoax? It is possible that the metal disc part was a hoax, but was there a genuine UFO crash, which the US military tried very hard to keep secret? Or was this a crash of something else, an unstable experimental craft that was being developed by the US Air Force, which they did not want the general public – or the Russians – to know about? Experiments certainly were being carried out on planes of different shapes and designs, and it is now known that some were circular. This might explain some of the sightings of flying saucers.

If a genuine UFO crashed on the Plain, it may be that the military planted the debris at the Brazel ranch in order to distract media attention from the real crash site away to the west. The display of hardware from the Brazel ranch at a press conference and the weather balloon explanation would have been enough to satisfy public curiosity, while the military spirited away the debris from the San Agustin site for secret investigation at a military air base. It was a carefully stage-managed piece of counter-intelligence.

But what of the dead aliens? It is just possible that they were the human crew of an all-too-terrestrial craft. One of the photographs of a badly incinerated corpse inside the Roswell saucer has a pair of wire-frame spectacles, half-concealed behind the corpse's shoulder. This seems to suggest that the victims were not aliens at all. What then of the bizarre fake autopsy? It is just possible that this film was an elaborately staged hoax commissioned by the military in order to put people off the scent – another piece of counter-intelligence. In a way, it would matter little whether people believed that the film proved the existence of flying saucers and aliens, or that it was an elaborate hoax; the purpose of diverting them from the military reality behind Roswell, the harsh reality of the Cold War, would be achieved. But nagging doubts remain. Of the original witnesses involved in the discovery or subsequent cover-up 10 out of 30 identified the object as extra-terrestrial.

THE WAR AGAINST IRAQ 2003

THE DEATH OF DAVID KELLY

THE MILITARY INTERVENTION by the West in the Middle East from 1990 onwards has generated not only controversy but multiple accusations of conspiracy. What lay behind the American decision to intervene when Iraqi troops crossed the (disputed) frontier between Iraq and Kuwait? Why did the American administration decide after the terrorist attacks on the World Trade Center and the Pentagon that Iraq must be involved? What were the real reasons for the American-inspired invasion of Iraq in 2003? Did Saddam Hussein have weapons of mass destruction or not? If not, why did both the American and British governments go on insisting that he did? Did the British weapons expert David Kelly commit suicide, was he killed as a reprisal for misleading Iraqi officials, or was he killed by European security services to silence him?

Dr David Kelly was a government expert in Iraqi weapons programmes. Suspicions grew that the US and UK governments' intelligence on Iraqi weapons – the justification offered for the invasion of Iraq – was not only untrue but had been deliberately falsified. David Kelly was named as the source of a controversial BBC report alleging that the British government had 'sexed up' a dossier supplied by the intelligence services on Iraq's weapons capability. The government denied the allegations, named Kelly to the press, and it was clear that Kelly was in an untenable situation.

Dr Kelly went missing from his home in Oxfordshire on 17 July, 2003 and his body was found in a copse nearby the next day. In the days leading up to his death, Kelly had testified before Parliament's Foreign Affairs Select Committee that he was not the source of a BBC story making the very serious accusation that the British government had made false claims about Iraq's alleged weapons of mass destruction. The press were quick to announce that Dr Kelly had committed suicide by cutting his wrist, a verdict confirmed at a 15-minute hearing after the Hutton Inquiry, but several analysts had their doubts; significant information about the death was withheld. The early press reports declared that the death had been 'confirmed as suicide', when legally neither the police nor the media had the authority to make such an announcement.

One problem was the method of suicide Dr Kelly was alleged to have used: a self-inflicted knife wound to the wrist. It is a method of suicide that men use very rarely, and more significantly it is a method that is seldom successful as it takes such a long time to die. Why would Dr Kelly try to commit suicide using the slowest and least reliable method possible, out in the open, where he might easily be seen and stopped. He was said to have cut the ulnar artery in his wrist, which is an inaccessible minor artery that would have been difficult and painful to sever. The knife he was said to have used was a blunt gardening tool. Nothing about the wrist-cutting scenario seems to have any credibility at all. On top of that, too little blood was found at the scene for Dr Kelly to have bled to death.

Oxfordshire coroner Nicholas Gardiner tried hard to extinguish the controversy, but his attempt at 'fire-fighting' was less than successful, as Mr Gardiner himself admitted. 'This hearing will do little to put an end to the controversy relating to the death of Dr Kelly,' he said. That was inevitable, partly because the establishment had decided that the inquest was not to be re-opened, partly because the outcome of the hearing had already been published in the press: it was a foregone conclusion. Having reviewed the evidence that had not been presented to the Hutton Inquiry, Mr Gardiner said he was satisfied there was no need for further investigation; the lord chancellor believed there were no exceptional reasons why the inquest into the death of Dr Kelly should be re-convened and neither did he. The Hutton Inquiry's findings, that Dr Kelly had killed himself, would stand.

Out in the car park, after the Oxford hearing, the Kelly Inquiry Group were handing out press releases. The Kelly Inquiry Group was a loose affiliation of barristers, doctors and other interested parties who were concerned about Dr Kelly's death. They were fundamentally dissidents who did not believe that the full story had been told, and they wanted answers to some key questions. They wanted to know why Dr Kelly's body had apparently been moved after his death. They wanted to know the identities of the 'three individuals in black or dark clothing' who were 'seen acting suspiciously' at the scene of Dr Kelly's death on the morning his body was found. They wanted to know why a police tactical support operation – code-named 'Mason' – had begun nine hours before Dr Kelly had been reported missing. They wanted to know why the forensic report could not confirm that Dr Kelly had swallowed 29 Co-Proxamol tablets. The reason for that question was that the police had said that 29 Co-Proxamol tablets were missing from Dr Kelly's home, yet all that was found in Dr Kelly's stomach was the equivalent of one-fifth of a tablet. If that was true, Dr Kelly had not consumed enough drugs to kill him, or have any effect on him at all. If Dr Kelly had not bled to death and he had not taken too many tablets – what was the cause of death?

One member of the Kelly Inquiry Group, a national security lawyer, claimed that he spoke for a variety of people working in intelligence when he said that Dr Kelly had been murdered by a team of assassins and the charade of an apparent suicide was then played out to cover the murder up. The lawyer was Michael Shrimpton. His source within the intelligence community was someone who knew David Kelly personally, and who did not believe that he had committed suicide but had been assassinated.

It was said that it was known in advance in Whitehall that Kelly was going to die, but the murder was most likely organized by the French external security service, DGSE; nobody in MI5 or MI6 had been involved. Shrimpton suggested that the hit squad itself consisted of Iraqis from the former regime's Mukhabarat intelligence organization, and recruited in Damascus with the help of Syrian intelligence. The assassins were apparently flown into Corsica seven days before the murder, and it is thought unlikely any members of the hit squad are still alive today. It is not clear where this information came from, still less whether any of it is true.

The official version of events said that Kelly's body was found in a copse, but the forensic tents were set up in the adjacent field, which suggested to Shrimpton that the body was actually found in the field. This apparent discrepancy has not been explained, and in itself suggests that something is being hidden. The official version had Kelly cutting his wrist and bleeding to death, but there was too little blood at the scene for Kelly to have bled to death – at least where he was found. Shrimpton suggested that the incision in Kelly's wrist was made to conceal the needle marks where Kelly was injected with Dextroprypoxythene, the active ingredient in Co-Proxamol, and Succinylcholine, a muscle relaxant; the incision could not be taken as evidence of his bleeding to death, as highlighted by a group of six doctors in letters published in the British press.

Michael Shrimpton said that Kelly was murdered because he had been talking to the press and there was a fear that he might go on to discuss other matters with journalists. Dr Kelly was also due to return to Iraq, where he could have picked up fresh information, and Whitehall could not afford to trust him with any more information.

The Kelly Inquiry Group's story circulated in America, but it was given negligible coverage in Britain. Perhaps behind the scenes attempts were made to block the accusation that a department within the Blair government had sanctioned the murder of one of its own operatives.

The evidence of David Kelly's final hours does not point to a suicidal or psychologically tortured end for a scientist taking to his grave the truth about his relationship with the prime minister's office and the alleged 'sexing up' of intelligence regarding Iraqi weapons of mass destruction. In February, five months before his death, Dr David Kelly made a significant remark to a diplomat, David Broucher, the UK's permanent representative on the disarmament conference in Geneva. Kelly told Broucher that he, Kelly, would probably be 'found dead in the woods' if the UK invaded Iraq. Broucher thought at the time that it was a throwaway remark, but when he heard that Dr Kelly had indeed been found dead in the woods he naturally attached far greater significance to it. Mr Broucher said the remark was made after Dr Kelly explained to him that he had given assurances to senior Iraqi officials that if they co-operated with United Nations weapons inspections they would have nothing to fear. The implication was that if the US-UK invasion of Iraq went ahead, that would make him a liar. He would have betrayed his contacts, some of whom might be killed as a direct result of his actions. It was when Broucher asked him what would happen then that Kelly replied that he would probably be found dead in the woods. Broucher assumed that David Kelly was talking about a possible Iraqi reprisal, but after Kelly's death he thought Kelly 'might have been thinking on rather different lines'.

The Hutton Inquiry was a judicial inquiry chaired by Lord Hutton, set up by the British government to investigate the circumstances surrounding the death of Dr David Kelly. The inquiry opened in August 2003. Lord Hutton called an impressive array of heavyweight witnesses, including the Prime Minister Tony Blair, Defence Secretary Geoff Hoon, Joint Intelligence Committee chairman John Scarlett and Cabinet Office intelligence co-ordinator Sir David Omand. Kelly had been the source for reports made by three BBC journalists that the government, particularly the press office of the prime minister, had knowingly embellished the dossier with misleading exaggerations of Iraq's military capabilities. These were reported by the BBC journalist Andrew Gilligan on BBC Radio 4's *Today* programme on 29 May 2003, by

Gavin Hewitt on the *Ten O'Clock News* the same day and by Susan Watts on BBC2's *Newsnight* on 2 June. On 1 June Andrew Gilligan repeated his allegations in an article he wrote for the *Mail on Sunday,* where he named the government press secretary Alastair Campbell as the driving force behind the alteration of the dossier.

The government angrily denounced the reports and accused the BBC of poor journalism. In subsequent weeks the BBC stood by Gilligan's report, saying that it was based on a reliable source. The inquiry heard that Dr Kelly was shocked to hear newspapers were about to name him as the suspected source for BBC journalist Andrew Gilligan, because his superiors had told him it would be kept confidential. Following intense media speculation, on 9 July Kelly was finally named in the press as the source for Gilligan's story. Kelly apparently committed suicide in a field close to his home on July 17 (although this was not supposed to be officially confirmed until a coroner's report was released).

Lord Hutton concluded that the BBC's allegations that the government had knowingly 'sexed up' a report into Iraq' weapons of mass destruction – the so-called September Dossier – were unfounded. The dossier, according to Lord Hutton, was in line with the available intelligence, though the Joint Intelligence Committee, chaired by John Scarlet may have been subconsciously influenced by the government in other words the intelligence service told the government what it wanted to hear. The Ministry of Defence was at fault for not informing Kelly of their strategy which would involve naming him. Gilligan's original accusation was unfounded, Hutton said, and the BBC's editorial and management processes were defective.

The inquiry's findings prompted the immediate resignation of the BBC's chairman, Gavyn Davies, its Director-General Greg Dyke, and the journalist at the centre of the allegations, Andrew Gilligan – though they did not accept the report's findings. Lord Hutton retired as a Law Lord following the report's publication.

The Hutton Report exonerated the government more completely than had been expected by many observers before its publication. This was surprising in view of some of the accepted facts; that Tony Blair himself had chaired the meeting where the decision was taken to release David Kelly's name to the public; that the wording of the dossier had been altered to present the strongest possible case for war within the bounds of available intelligence; that some of these alterations had been suggested by Alastair Campbell; that experts within the Intelligence Community had expressed reservations about the wording of the dossier. In spite of this evidence the government was largely cleared of wrong-doing by Hutton. In large measure this was because evidence to the inquiry indicated that the government had not known of the reservations in the intelligence community: it seemed they had been discounted by senior intelligence assessors (the Joint Intelligence Committee), so Gilligan's claim that the government 'probably knew' that the intelligence was flawed was itself unfounded. Meanwhile, Hutton decided that any failure of intelligence assessment fell outside his remit, so even the Intelligence Services escaped censure.

Instead the report put heavy (and many believed unfair) emphasis on the failings of Andrew Gilligan and the BBC. Gilligan disagreed with the overall thrust of the report, but was ready to admit that he had attributed inferences to Kelly which were in fact his own. Lord Hutton also criticized the chain of management at the BBC, which had defended its story. The BBC management, the report said, had accepted Gilligan's word that his story was accurate, instead of checking Gilligan's records more thoroughly. This too seemed unfair to many people, as Andrew Gilligan was a very experienced and respected journalist, and therefore quite sensibly and rightly trusted by the BBC management.

There was considerable speculation in the media that the report had been deliberately written to clear the government. Although Lord Hutton disputed this claim at a later press conference, many people remain convinced that this was the case. Andrew Gilligan said, on resigning, 'This report casts a chill over all journalism, not just the BBC's. It seeks to hold reporters, with all the difficulties they face, to a standard that it does not appear to demand of, for instance, government dossiers.' Blair used the report to demand a retraction from those who had accused him of lying to the House of Commons, particularly Michael Howard, the Leader of the Opposition. The Butler Report in 2004 concluded that 'the fact that the reference to the 45-minute claim in the classified assessment was repeated in the dossier later led to suspicions that it had been included because of its eye-catching character'. The 45 minutes referred to the dossier's frightening revelation that Iraq not only had an arsenal of weapons of mass destruction but could launch them within 45 minutes. Andrew Gilligan claims that the Butler Report vindicated his original accusation that the dossier had indeed been 'sexed up'.

Several national British newspapers accused Hutton of participating in an establishment whitewash. The *Daily Mail* wrote in its editorial 'We're faced with the wretched spectacle of the BBC chairman resigning while Alastair Campbell crows from the summit of his dunghill. Does this verdict, my lord, serve the real interest of truth?' BBC workers paid for a full-page advertisement in The *Daily Telegraph* on 31 January to publish a message of support for Dyke:

> *Greg Dyke stood for brave, independent BBC journalism that was fearless in its search for the truth. We are resolute that the BBC should not step back from its determination to investigate the facts in pursuit of the truth. Through his passion and integrity Greg Dyke inspired us to make programmes of the highest quality and creativity. We are dismayed by Greg's departure, but we are determined to maintain his achievements and his vision for an independent organization that serves the public above all else.*

In some countries the reputation of the BBC improved as a result of its attacks on the British government during the Dr David Kelly affair. The BBC is sometimes viewed, especially outside the UK, as a puppet of the government. The BBC's willingness, in this case, to accuse the prime minister and the Ministry of Defence so publicly, unequivocally and fearlessly of wrong-doing enhanced its credentials as an impartial source of news.

Dr Kelly's revelation that the weak evidence for Iraq's possession of weapons of mass destruction had been 'sexed up' touched a nerve with the British government for a very particular reason. Those in power knew that they had taken Britain to war on a wild goose chase, on just this sexed-up evidence. The same suspicion inevitably fell on the American administration, which also claimed that it had evidence for

Iraq's possession of an arsenal of weapons of mass destruction – evidence which simply cannot exist because the weapons themselves never existed. This now looks like a much larger conspiracy. The Dr David Kelly mystery is unlikely to go away, as the authorities may have hoped. A member of parliament has, in 2006, produced his own dossier of evidence, showing that David Kelly did not kill himself, and challenging the findings of the Hutton Inquiry.

THE INVASION OF IRAQ

The Pentagon had wanted for some time to wage war against Iraq. Iraq was no threat to the United States. Iraq had not attacked the United States. Many observers believe that the purpose of this carefully planned double attack in 1990 and 2003 was commercial; its purpose was an imperialist one, to redistribute the markets and resources of the Middle East. The administrations of the two Presidents Bush, father and son, on behalf of the banks and oil corporations, wanted to dominate and control this strategic region. It was natural for the USA to do this in league with the former colonial powers of the region, Britain and France. The interests and wishes of the Iraqi people came nowhere.

It has been customary in such wars for the aggressor to mask the truth about its motive. This war was no exception, and a reason or pretext for the war that would find favour with the people of Britain in particular had to be found. There is evidence that the US was planning the Iraq War even before the Iraqi invasion of Kuwait in August 1990. It alleged that there is some evidence that the United States interfered in the Iraq-Kuwait dispute, and aggravated knowing that an Iraqi invasion of Kuwait was likely to result. Then America exploited the Iraqi invasion of Kuwait to carry out its own long-planned military intervention in the Middle East. Thus, at any rate, runs the conspiracy-theory version of events.

In a similar way, the British Prime Minister Tony Blair explained that the goal of the invasion of Iraq (the second Iraq war) was 'regime change'. Plainly that was not true, as there were plenty of other unsavoury regimes around the world under which human rights were being abused, and which Blair was not proposing to topple by force. Blair did not in any case think up regime change in Iraq on his own. Six months after the 9/11 attacks, Condoleezza Rice, who was at that time America's National Security Adviser, had a meeting with Tony Blair's chief foreign policy adviser, David Manning. According to David Manning, Rice did not want to talk about Osama bin Laden or Al Qaeda, as he had expected; she wanted to press for regime change in Iraq. Iraq was by then already the target, even though there was no known connection between Iraq and the attack on the Twin Towers. It was mystifying.

The so-called 'Downing Street memo' is another incriminating piece of evidence about the same issue. This memo is a transcript of the minutes of a meeting on 23 July 2002 between Tony Blair, his advisers and Sir Richard Dearlove, the then head of MI6. At that meeting, which was eight months before the invasion of Iraq, Sir Richard Dearlove explained that Washington officials had made clear at a recent meeting that 'Bush wanted to remove Saddam through military action, justified by the conjunction of terrorism and WMD [weapons of mass destruction]. *But the intelligence and facts were being fixed around the policy.'* In other words President George W. Bush, the son of the President Bush who had ordered the 1990 attack on Iraq for invading Kuwait, had made the pre-emptive decision 12 years later to remove Saddam Hussein from power; pretexts, reasons, justifications – and even facts – could be found later.

This raises the other reason given for invading Iraq, by both Blair and Bush: that Iraq possessed caches of weapons of mass destruction with which it was about to attack the West. A pre-emptive strike against the mad and dangerous dictator was necessary. But Saddam Hussein did not have stores of such weapons, and Dr David Kelly was one of the people who knew this. A British Foreign Office official wrote a memo to Foreign Secretary Jack Straw about the importance of winning popular and parliamentary support for a war against Iraq. 'We have to be convincing that: the threat is so serious/imminent that it is worth sending our troops to die for.' The Blair government then released an intelligence report which made the rash and unsubstantiated claim that the Iraqi government could launch a chemical or biological weapons attack (by implication on Britain) at 45 minutes' notice.

On 11 September 1990, President Bush Senior told a joint session of Congress that 'following negotiations and promises by Iraqi dictator Saddam Hussein not to use force, a powerful army invaded its trusting and much weaker neighbor, Kuwait. Within three days, 120,000 troops with 850 tanks had poured into Kuwait and moved south to threaten Saudi Arabia. It was then I decided to act to check that aggression.'

But satellite photographs taken by the Soviet Union that very day do not show any evidence of Iraqi troops in Kuwait or massing along the Kuwait-Saudi Arabian border. The

Pentagon claimed there were as many as 250,000 Iraqi troops in Kuwait, but refused to provide any evidence that would contradict the Soviet satellite photos. US forces, encampments, aircraft, tracks across the desert and so on can easily be seen, but no Iraqi troop concentrations, no tent cities, no clusters of tanks.

On 18 September, 1991, only a week after the Soviet photos were taken, the Pentagon was telling the American public that Iraqi forces in Kuwait had swelled to 360,000 men and 2,800 tanks. But the satellite photos do not show any tank tracks in southern Kuwait. They clearly show tracks left by vehicles servicing a large oil field, but no tank tracks. The Pentagon appears not to have provided Congress – or the press – with any proof of a build-up of Iraqi troops in southern Kuwait that would suggest an imminent invasion of Saudi Arabia. The Pentagon had in effect invited Americans to trust that what it said was true.

What actually happened was that Iraqi troops were eventually deployed along the Kuwait-Saudi Arabian border, but they were sent there as a response to the US military build up. The Pentagon version was critically misleading, by saying that the Iraqi invasion force was gathering – and this was used as an argument for deploying the US forces.

The George W. Bush administration steadfastly refused to negotiate with Iraq to find a diplomatic solution, evidently preferring military intervention. In August 1990, Iraq put forward a negotiation proposal, showing a willingness to make significant concessions in return for a comprehensive discussion of other unresolved Middle East conflicts. That offer was rejected by the Bush administration. The Iraqis made another offer in December; that too was rejected.

President Bush even refused to send Secretary of State Baker to meet Saddam Hussein before the deadline date of 15 January 1991, as he had promised to do two months earlier. Iraq offered to withdraw on 15 February 1991, two days after American planes had incinerated hundreds of women and children sleeping in a bomb shelter; Bush rejected that offer to withdraw. On 18 February 1991 the Soviet Union made a proposal requiring Iraq to abide by all UN resolutions. Iraq immediately agreed to this, yet four days later America launched the so-called ground war.

The US ground war against Iraqi positions resulted in huge casualties. It is thought that up to 100,000 Iraqi soldiers may have died after the Iraqi government had fully capitulated to all the US and UN demands. The US government therefore did not fight the war to get the Iraqis out of Kuwait; instead it went ahead with what amounts to a massacre, and this must have been in pursuit of some other foreign policy objective.

This objective is often given the generalized and attractive-sounding title, 'the New World Order'. The Bush administration assumed a willingness on the part of the Soviet Union to support American foreign policy in the Third World. The American government assumed that, if the Soviet Union was ready to abandon Iraq and other allies in the Third World then America and other western capitalist countries could return to their former dominant positions in the Third World. This amounts to a reinstatement of the old imperialist or quasi-imperialist order. The conduct of the first Iraq War alone shows that that the permanent weakening of Iraq is a key part of the New World Order.

The goals of US imperialism in the oil-rich Middle East

have remained fundamentally the same over the decades; the US works to eliminate or disable any nationalist regime challenging its dominance. The two wars against Iraq are part of a US strategy to return to the golden age when the US and a handful of west European countries were free to exploit the resources of the Middle East. The US economy has depended on this principle for a long time. Between 1948 and 1960 US oil companies received a total of $13 billion in profit from their Persian Gulf holdings, which amounted to half the return on all overseas investment by all US companies in that period.

The big American oil companies have fruitful partnerships with the ruling elites of Saudi Arabia and the United Arab Emirates, but they do not enjoy similar relationships in Iraq, Iran, Libya, Yemen or Algeria. It looks as if one aim of the US attack on Iraq is to throw into reverse the revolutionary movements that have swept the Middle East since the 1940s.

The New World Order is, after all, not so new. It is an attempt to go back to the 1920s and 1930s era of colonial domination, but imposed by Stealth aircraft, guided missiles and smart bombs. It is alarming, not least because it ignores the pure hatred of foreign domination by the broad mass of the people who live in the Middle East. The conspiracy to recreate a past era is dangerous for a number of reasons. One, it is clearly impracticable to impose foreign domination on a people increasingly empowered by education, nationalism and religious zeal. Two, lies will out, and the timed and dated satellite images tell their own story about what happened. The same is true for the whole weapons of mass destruction fairy tale; sooner or later it was bound to emerge that Iraq did not possess this sophisticated arsenal of weapons. Three, as warned by some legal experts, the attacks on Iraq could be construed as violations of international law; governments – especially nominally democratic governments – need to be seen to be behaving lawfully. Four, the occupation of Iraq could lead to a long drawn out and costly exercise in nation-building and it does not look as if either America or Britain had or has plans for this. Five, there is not sufficient cultural or political consensus within the multi-cultural West to carry through this kind of foreign policy; the general shift towards pacifism and non-intervention among the electorates in the West is enough, probably on its own, to make the strategy fail. The lesson of Vietnam has still not been learned. There have been open denunciations of the behaviour of the American military at Abu Ghraib and Guantanamo, and even mutterings about possible trials for war crimes.

Should we be surprised that the British and American governments have apparently conspired to launch this dangerous destabilization of the Middle East? Probably not. Those who govern us are by their very nature conspirators, manipulating situations, concealing their true intentions from one another and from electorates, offering us false noble-sounding motives for what they do in order to conceal their true ignoble motives. That is the nature of the world we live in now. One theme underlying many of the events described in this book is that *that* is the nature of the world as it has *always* been.